International Responses
to Mass Atrocities in Africa

PENNSYLVANIA STUDIES IN HUMAN RIGHTS

Bert B. Lockwood, Jr., Series Editor

A complete list of books in the series
is available from the publisher.

INTERNATIONAL RESPONSES
TO MASS ATROCITIES IN AFRICA

Responsibility to Protect, Prosecute, and Palliate

Kurt Mills

PENN

UNIVERSITY OF PENNSYLVANIA PRESS

PHILADELPHIA

Published by
University of Pennsylvania Press
Philadelphia, Pennsylvania 19104-4112
www.upenn.edu/pennpress

Printed in the United States of America
on acid-free paper

1 3 5 7 9 10 8 6 4 2

Library of Congress Cataloging-in-Publication Data
Mills, Kurt, author.
International responses to mass atrocities in Africa :
responsibility to protect, prosecute, and palliate / Kurt Mills.
    pages cm. (Pennsylvania studies in human rights)
    Includes bibliographical references and index
    ISBN 978-0-8122-4737-4 (alk. paper)
    1. Humanitarian intervention—Africa, Sub-Saharan—
International cooperation—Case studies.   2. Conflict
management—Africa, Sub-Saharan—International cooperation—
Case studies.   3. Genocide intervention—Africa, Sub-Saharan—
International cooperation—Case studies.   4. Intervention
(International law)—Case studies.   I. Mills, Kurt.
II. Title.   III. Series: Pennsylvania studies in human rights.
JZ6369 .M55   2015   2015009521

For Habibi

It's not too late
For making a new world
It's not too late
For making a better world
                    —Zap Mama, "A New World"

CONTENTS

ABBREVIATIONS

ADFL	Alliance of Democratic Forces for the Liberation of Congo-Zaire
ADF-NALU	Allied Democratic Forces-National Army for the Liberation of Uganda
AFRICOM	United States Africa Command
AMIS	African Union Mission in Sudan
AMISOM	African Union Mission in Somalia
APC	armored personnel carrier
APSA	African Peace and Security Architecture
ASF	African Standby Force
ASP	Assembly of States Parties
AU	African Union
CAR	Central African Republic
CNDP	Congrès National pour la Défense du Peuple
CONOPS	concept of operations
DPKO	Department of Peacekeeping Operations
DRC	Democratic Republic of the Congo
ECOWAS	Economic Community of West African States
FAC	Forces Armées Conglaises
FAR	Forces Armées Rwandaises
FARDC	Forces Armées de la République Démocratique du Congo
FDD	Forces pour la Défense de la Démocratie
FDLR	Forces Démocratiques pour la Libération du Rwanda
FDLR-FCA	Forces Démocratiques pour la Libération du Rwanda-Forces Combattantes Abacunguzi
FNI	Front de Nationalistes et Intégrationnistes
FNL	Forces Nationales de Libération
FPLC	Forces Patriotiques pour la libération du Congo
FRPI	Force de Résistance Patriotique en Ituri

GoS	Government of Sudan
GoSS	Government of South Sudan
HRW	Human Rights Watch
HSM	Holy Spirit Movement
IASC	Inter-Agency Standing Committee
ICC	International Criminal Court
ICG	International Crisis Group
ICGLR	International Conference on the Great Lakes Region
ICISS	International Commission on Intervention and State Sovereignty
ICRC	International Committee of the Red Cross
ICTR	International Criminal Tribunal for Rwanda
ICTY	International Criminal Tribunal for the Former Yugoslavia
IDP	internally displaced person
IEMF	Interim Emergency Multinational Force
IHL	international humanitarian law
IHO	international humanitarian organization
IRC	International Rescue Committee
JEM	Justice and Equality Movement
LDU	local defense unit
LJM	Liberation and Justice Movement
LRA	Lord's Resistance Army
M23	Mouvement du 23 Mars
MLC	Mouvement de Libération du Congo
MONUC	UN Organization Mission in the Democratic Republic of the Congo
MONUSCO	UN Organization Stabilization Mission in the Democratic Republic of the Congo
MSF	Médecins sans Frontières
NATO	North Atlantic Treaty Organization
NGO	nongovernmental organization
NMRD	National Movement for Reform and Development
NRA	National Resistance Army
NRM	National Resistance Movement
OAU	Organization of African Unity
OCHA	Office for the Coordination of Humanitarian Assistance
OTP	Office of the Prosecutor
P5	permanent members of UN Security Council

PoC	protection of civilians
PSC	Peace and Security Council
R2P	Responsibility to Protect
R2P^3	responsibility to protect, prosecute and palliate
RCD	Rassemblement Congolais pour la Démocratie
RCD-G	Rassemblement Congolais pour la Démocratie-Goma
RPA	Rwandan Patriotic Army
RPF	Rwandan Patriotic Front
SADC	Southern African Development Community
SLA	Sudan Liberation Army
SPLA	Sudan People's Liberation Army
STAREC	Stabilization and Reconstruction Plan for Eastern DRC
UDHR	Universal Declaration of Human Rights
UNAMID	UN Mission in Darfur
UNAMIR	UN Mission in Rwanda
UNAMSIL	UN Mission in Sierra Leone
UNGA	UN General Assembly
UNHCHR	UN High Commissioner for Human Rights
UNHCR	UN High Commissioner for Refugees
UNHRC	UN Human Rights Council
UNLA	Ugandan National Liberation Army
UNMIS	UN Mission in Sudan
UNPROFOR	UN Protection Force
UNSC	UN Security Council
UPC	Union des Patriotes Congolais
UPDA	Ugandan People's Democratic Army
UPDF	Ugandan People's Defence Force
URF	United Resistance Front
USAID	United States Agency for International Development
WFP	World Food Program
ZCSC	Zairian Camp Security Contingent

Introduction

Responding to Mass Atrocities

The core concern of this book is how have, can, and should mass atrocities be addressed? It is thus historical, analytical, and normative. It is historical because it examines how the international community responded to four cases of mass atrocities, although three of these situations are, in one way or another, still ongoing. It is analytical in that it provides a typology of the different types of responses and how these responses interact. It is normative because it begins with the underlying assumption that the international community should "do something" about mass atrocity situations, and that the "somethings"—military intervention to stop atrocities, holding individuals criminally responsible for atrocities, and providing basic assistance to help people survive the broader effects of mass atrocities—are all important developments and may all be appropriate, although perhaps appropriate in different ways and circumstances.

The first response—the use of military force to protect civilians and stop atrocities—is a core part of what has come to be known as the responsibility to protect (R2P). It follows from previous debates over humanitarian intervention, but is a reflection of a radical shift in the perceived balance between sovereignty and human rights. The second response I call the responsibility to prosecute, since it stems from an expanding recognition that those who commit atrocities should be punished. The third response I call the responsibility to palliate, because although there are significant humanitarian urges to help people in the middle of conflict, this particular response usually can do little more than treat the symptoms of a much more complicated situation. Taken together, these three sets of norms and practices are identified as R2P³—responsibility to protect, prosecute, and palliate. These responses, even though they are all rooted in an urge to stop human suffering, are very different types of actions. They accomplish very different things, over different timescales, and on different orders of magnitude, and are accomplished by very different types of actors. But the big question is whether they accomplish these different things in a mutually supporting way, where all the elements of the broad human rights edifice work seamlessly together to underpin this edifice. It will be obvious that the answer to this question is that there may be very significant trade-offs in using these responses—political trade-offs, practical trade-offs, normative trade-offs—and that they may not always be mutually supporting.

Policymakers are thus faced with a series of conundrums as they try to figure out how to protect people and keep them alive in the midst of conflict, while also preventing and ending conflicts and bringing perpetrators to justice. Military intervention might facilitate the delivery of humanitarian assistance—or it might endanger it. Issuing an arrest warrant might bring combatants to the negotiating table—or it might undermine a peace process. Providing humanitarian assistance might keep people alive in the midst of conflict—or it might contribute to the continuation of the conflict. Yet the international community has agreed that it has a responsibility to do each of these things to protect people and end suffering. So how does one prioritize responsibilities? This book provides no easy formula—the dynamics are fiendishly complex. However, by clearly delineating these manifold conundrums, and exploring how they play out in a variety of circumstances, the job of implementing these international responsibilities and stopping mass atrocities becomes a little clearer.

Defining Atrocities

The term mass atrocities is not unproblematic, given that language is employed to support action, prevent action, or cover up inaction in the face of widespread grave human rights abuses. I use the term "mass atrocity" here to include genocide, crimes against humanity, some war crimes, and ethnic cleansing. Genocide appears to have the most straightforward definition— "acts committed with intent to destroy, in whole or in part, a national, ethnical, racial or religious group,"[1] although the devil is in the detail, and in particular the assertion of the intent. Crimes against humanity are defined in the Rome Statute of the International Criminal Court (ICC) as including murder, extermination, forcible transfer of populations, torture, rape and a number of other acts undertaken in attacks against civilian populations (Article 7).

War crimes may be understood as

> serious violations of international humanitarian law directed at civilians or enemy combatants during an international or internal armed conflict, for which the perpetrators may be held criminally liable on an individual basis.[2]

Ethnic cleansing has been defined as "a purposeful policy designed by one ethnic or religious group to remove by violent and terror-inspiring means the civilian population of another ethnic or religious group from certain geographic areas."[3] Although there is no recognized crime of ethnic cleansing, it is against international law and would involve grave breaches of international humanitarian law, as well as potentially genocide and crimes against humanity.[4]

The term mass atrocity is preferred for its simplicity in avoiding having to write out "genocide, crimes against humanity, war crimes, and ethnic cleansing," although there will be instances where one must be specific about the crimes being discussed to communicate the magnitude of the crimes and the interests of humanity in responding.[5] As to a formal definition, I draw on the definition used by the Mass Atrocity Response Operations project: "widespread and systematic use of violence by state or non-state armed groups against non-combatants."[6] On the one hand, it elides the use of the emotive term "genocide," which cries out "never again" and demands action—that "somebody" should do "something"—and thus will be controversial. It appears to undermine gravity and immediacy. Yet all too often scholars, journalists, and diplomats get caught up in language that obfuscates rather than illuminates a situation. In Rwanda, western leaders fell over themselves with awkward linguistic constructions to avoid calling what was happening genocide—referring instead to "acts of genocide"—while in Darfur, there was much discussion about whether to call what was happening genocide or crimes against humanity. But in the end it did not matter whether President Bashir of Sudan or the Hutu leadership in Rwanda could be positively identified as having the intent to wipe out a specific group of people. The same people were dying—even though such language may be strategically deployed at times, I doubt that the victims or their families cared what those on the

UN Security Council called it. Thus, mass atrocities[7] will be used as an analytic category to indicate situations where large numbers of people are dying or otherwise being widely affected as a result of genocide, crimes against humanity, widespread war crimes, or ethnic cleansing. "Mass atrocities and associated humanitarian crises" may also be used to signal a recognition that most humanitarian crises are political in nature and tied into larger patterns of human rights abuse.

Conflict in Africa

The international responsibilities in mass atrocity situations discussed above are embedded within evolving political, geostrategic and normative realities. Globally, human rights norms and machinery are expanding and spreading, although ambiguously. The UN Security Council has become increasingly involved in human rights issues even as there is increasing tension between the traditional powers on the Security Council and a restive developing world, with emerging powers demanding more representation at the apex of global power, bolstered, again, by charges of neocolonialism. The responsibility to protect has been affected by the same charges, but there is hardly unanimity. Other global developments, such as the ICC, further underpin an expanding institutionalization of human rights, even as there is pushback against its focus to date on Africa and its problematic relationship to the Security Council. But Africa also serves as a stage for the post-9/11 global war on terror and the belief "that 'failed states' are ideal staging and breeding grounds for international terrorists."[8]

Africa has seen both advances and retreats in normative and practical human rights developments. The African Union (AU) Constitutive Act recognized an even more robust responsibility to protect three years before the UN did, although it has failed to implement this in any significant way. The responsibility to protect has found its voice in the norm of "non-indifference" in Africa, but exactly how such a double negative normative construction will be implemented is unclear. Thirty-four African countries are members of the ICC, yet the AU has repeatedly accused the ICC of being biased against Africa and called for it to suspend ongoing cases against Africans. Africa has high hopes for an African Peace and Security Architecture (APSA) and the development of an African Standby Force (ASF), but implementation has lagged far behind the hopes. And although the AU can present a public united front, there are still divisions among African countries and, at times, a reversion to Westphalian notions of sovereignty and anticolonialism that serve to prevent criticism of human rights abuses. Africa wants a larger say in global politics, demanding, for example, more seats on the Security Council, and a more even partnership between the AU and UN.

Africa was chosen as the focus of this book for a number of reasons. From a continental perspective, Africa has been the crucible for much normative development and practical application of norms. The genocide in Rwanda was one of the driving forces for the development of the responsibility to protect, but was also the site of one of the precursors to the development of the ICC. All the prosecutions by the ICC to date have taken place in Africa. The practice of humanitarianism has been significantly affected by experiences in not only Rwanda, but also Ethiopia, Sudan, Somalia and elsewhere. Furthermore, except for Europe, Africa has been the region that has developed most substantially in the area of peacekeeping activities, although even those developments have fallen significantly short at times. Somalia and the Democratic Republic of Congo (DRC), among others, have been the site of significant innovations and failures in the practical application of peacekeeping.

As to why these four countries—Rwanda, DRC, Uganda, and Sudan (Darfur)—the answer is many-faceted. Geographically, they are contiguous, with the DRC and Uganda bordering all three other countries, and Rwanda and Sudan having common borders with two of the others. They all have colonial histories that have significantly affected their modern development, although the experiences and legacies are different, with Sudan and Uganda having experienced British colonialism and the DRC and Rwanda having a Belgian legacy (with resulting French influence). Central and East Africa have been the focus of widespread gross violations of human rights since the end of the Cold War. Burundi, the Central African Republic (CAR), DRC/Zaire, Eritrea, Ethiopia, Rwanda, Somalia, Sudan, and Uganda have all seen a mixture of significant civil conflict, genocide, crimes against humanity, and war crimes, as well as significant humanitarian catastrophes. The conflicts have spread across borders and in many instances become interrelated, affecting neighboring countries like the CAR, Chad, and Tanzania. The conflict focused on the Rwanda-Congo-broader Great Lakes nexus has witnessed untold human suffering and devastation and has pulled in an even wider array of participants. The northeastern corner of the DRC, which borders Rwanda, Uganda, and Sudan, perhaps exemplifies the multinational, multi-actor, interrelated nature of conflict in Africa today. These four countries have each had their own internal conflicts, which have become internationalized as refugees and combatants flow unimpeded across borders, bringing their fighting and suffering to new countries and populations.

Kevin Dunn argues that Uganda's Lord's Resistance Army (LRA) has created a cross-border "insecurity complex.... transform[ing] a microregional conflict into a macroregional zone of insecurity."[9] One could expand this further to say that multiple dynamics have contributed to a regional insecurity complex that involves a dizzying array of state and nonstate actors and transcends sovereign boundaries even as those boundaries play a significant role in structuring multiple conflicts and widespread political and human insecurity. As will be seen, the Rwandan genocide and lack of international response led directly and inexorably to two decades of war in eastern DRC, millions dead, and the intervention of around a dozen countries, even as internal Zairean/Congolese dynamics proved fertile breeding ground for conflict. The spread of the LRA beyond Uganda pulled Uganda into the DRC and southern Sudan, as well as the CAR. Uganda was also the staging ground for the Tutsi invasion of Rwanda that ended the genocide. Sudan endured civil war for two decades—and used the LRA as part of its war against the south—before a relative peace was established and a new country was born in South Sudan. But it was the conflict in Darfur—in the western part of the country—that brought issues related to the responsibility to protect and international criminal justice to the fore, posing some of the first real tests for both R2P and the ICC—and the AU.

The conflicts are directly related, but they have all served, in a sense, as part of an African proving ground for the global responsibilities and responses at the core of this book. The international community has dealt with these conflicts in varying ways, which perhaps reflects partly the particular internal and regional dynamics of the conflicts, but also the broader geopolitical perspectives and interests of the main global powers. The response has ranged from apathy to a range of innovative, but not necessarily completely satisfying, actions. Rwanda highlights the dangers of ignoring genocidal situations and trying to use nonstate actors—humanitarian organizations—for activities that states and state-based organizations like the UN should be undertaking. It illustrates the vast unintended consequences humanitarians can have as they carry out their humanitarian imperative. And it was a testing ground for newly resurgent international criminal justice norms. The DRC was a reflection of those unintended consequences, but also of the inability of the international community to adequately respond to a fiendishly complex set of conflicts that spread across vast ungoverned spaces and borders. The UN slowly ratcheted up its response, declaring the protection of civilians its highest priority, and, in a very uneven, punctuated fashion, it tried to put this determination into effect. Even with millions dead, there was nary a whisper of the highly politicized responsibility to protect, even as the UN undertook proto-R2P activities. The DRC also puts in high relief the politicized nature of the ICC, as cases were chosen and narrowed to fit the specifications of the state. Uganda highlights the dangers, yet again, of the unintended consequences of unreflective humanitarian imperatives. But, most prominently, the very conundrums of inserting a global judicial body into the middle of an on-going conflict became apparent, with an asserted—if not always easily locatable—stark trade-off between peace and justice, as well as between local, traditional justice mechanisms and global, supposedly universal judicial authorities. Darfur also demonstrates this peace versus justice dynamic, although on a more global, geopolitical stage. Darfur was also the first post-R2P conflict, although the eventual international reaction would not have been recognizable to the original authors of R2P, given its tepid implementation and refusal to stand up to the government in Khartoum. Darfur also illustrates how humanitarians could become pawns in larger conflict dynamics.

R2P³

Each of these conflicts will be analyzed through a matrix which examines how the three sets of human rights related norms and practices identified above—protection, prosecution, and palliation (R2P³)—are understood, are implemented and may interact with each other. Chapter 1, which outlines and critiques the responsibilities and the actors who have taken on the responsibilities, develops the matrix, highlighting the major conundrums and tensions inherent in each of the responsibilities and their interactions. At the end of each of the subsequent case studies, the matrix for that case is presented, providing a summary of the main issues identified in the case.

While all four cases have elements of the R2P³ triumvirate, each case has a different focus and illustrates a somewhat different set of concerns and dynamics. Rwanda illustrates quite starkly the complex nature of humanitarian action, the trade-offs humanitarians are faced with, and the very difficult situation they can find themselves in when states and the UN refuse to act. It also demonstrates the potential for disaster when an adequate response to mass atrocities is not forthcoming. The DRC was this disaster. The particular focus here is the very slow development of military responses to widespread atrocities via peacekeeping and the protection of civilians concept. In only very rare instances did action that resembled R2P take place. Rather, most activities began with, and developed from, more classical understandings and practices of peacekeeping evolving into what Gareth Evans calls "peacekeeping plus."[10] The conundrums facing the ICC as it finds its feet and tries to gain state cooperation also feature. In Uganda, the story starts with the very ambiguous role of humanitarians in ultimately supporting state-sponsored forced displacement, but soon moves into a discussion of the proper role of the ICC in on-going conflicts. Central is the ongoing debate about whether there is a trade-off between peace and justice. Darfur, too, features the role of the ICC in ongoing conflict and its place in the increasingly complex arena of international security. We see tensions mount between the ICC and an increasingly assertive AU. Darfur also served as the first real test for R2P—a test it failed. In each of these cases, we further see conundrums and trade-offs as multiple responses are deployed simultaneously, illustrating, for example, the potential conflict between humanitarian action and civilian protection, or how the presence of the ICC may endanger humanitarian action.

A significant focus and element of the story of each of the cases will be the role of major Western states and the UN Security Council. This is because it is these states that have been pushing to a significant extent the responsibilities agenda and, indeed, are its political and financial patrons. They fund humanitarian action and peacekeeping, and, as in the case of Libya, have the requisite capabilities to engage in the most robust action to protect civilians—even if they have been reluctant to actually use those capabilities or provide necessary resources. Indeed, while the rich states provide the money, developing countries provide the majority of troops for peacekeeping operations. And the Security Council serves as a global legitimator or delegitimator of states and actions to address mass atrocities. African states and the AU are also central, since these African situations have been the crucible for the difficult work undertaken to create more capable African institutions and provide an African version of developing norms as part of Africa's attempt to provide "African solutions to African problems." The ICC also plays a star-ring role as a state-created semi-independent global justice actor with significant agency, but which is also under significant political and practical constraints. Humanitarian actors are also crucial to our story. Although at times identified with the broad brush moniker international humanitarian organizations (IHOs), there are significant differences. Some are affiliated with the UN and thus enjoy resources and official mandates even as they are constrained politically. Nongovernmental organizations (NGOs), on the other hand, do not suffer the same political constraints and are sometimes more able to be vocal about realities on the ground, but do experience significant situational constraints and are frequently used as political footballs.

Whose Responsibility?

This discussion of the main actors involved in responding to mass atrocities raises other questions about which responsibilities accrue to which agents, and furthermore, what exactly is the status of these responsibilities—are they legal, moral, ethical? These questions are far beyond the scope of this book, which is more concerned with the practical implementation and interpretation of international norms. Many of these questions are addressed elsewhere,[11] and Chapter 1 briefly touches on the origins and outlines of the three responsibilities, but some brief observations are in order.

First, the status and nature of these responsibilities varies significantly. The responsibility to protect is not a legal norm. It is a statement of intent, although the exact nature and seriousness of that intent is under question. There is no international law that absolutely requires any entity to militarily intervene to protect human rights, although a vague expectation can be found in the Genocide Convention and numerous statements by state officials over the decades, as embodied in the oft-repeated assertion "never again." And it is directly tied into more formal international human rights law, which outlaws many of the practices that may demand such intervention. It is thus a moral and political expectation based on decades of human rights development and diplomatic assertions. The responsibility to prosecute is more firmly established as a legal norm, particularly with the creation of the ICC, as well as the practice of universal jurisdiction, which, while it does not have the same firmly institutionalized legal status of the ICC, is a reflection of the expectation found in international human rights and humanitarian law that those who violate the law should be punished. The responsibility to palliate is a mixture of legal and moral norms. The Geneva Conventions talk about the right to offer humanitarian assistance, and the expectation that states will accept such offers. Furthermore, UN Security Council Resolution 2165 (2014) asserts the right of the international community to provide such assistance even in the absence of state consent. And states, through statements and practice, have recognized the necessity of providing such assistance. But, again, there is no international law which decrees that states or other entities must provide such assistance. It is thus a moral norm embedded in evolving international humanitarian law and practice. The expectation that states accept humanitarian assistance appears to be more formalized than the expectation that states provide such assistance in the first place.

Second, as to upon whom such responsibilities fall, the answer is equally ambiguous and multifaceted. The responsibility to protect can, in the end, be carried out only by states and state-based organizations like the UN. Indeed, the UN Security Council is formally identified as the repository of this responsibility (although the AU also claims the right to intervene in Africa). The question becomes what happens if the Security Council does not act. Do other entities have a responsibility? Periodically, regional organizations have taken it on themselves to intervene, as have individual states or groups of states. As the agents that have the capabilities to militarily intervene to stop atrocities, the responsibility may thus fall on states, but the legal and moral considerations in such situations are extremely murky. The responsibility to prosecute accrues to states, which have agreed to criminalize a wide range of human rights abuses and state-based entities created to prosecute such crimes. No other entities have the legal or moral standing to implement this responsibility. This is not so with regard to the responsibility to palliate. While certain moral and legal expectations may fall upon states, and state-based actors, such as the UN High Commissioner for Refugees, have been given a specific mandate—and thus a responsibility—to provide humanitarian assistance, nonstate actors have taken such responsibilities upon themselves, feeling a moral compunction to help those in need—the humanitarian imperative. At times, they have carried out responsibilities that fall upon states—either the target state, which has responsibilities to help its people, or other states and the UN, which have responsibilities to provide such help.

The responsibilities discussed in this book are thus a mixture of legal and moral expectations that fall upon a variety of actors—state, state-based, non-state. When discussing the "international community" to which such responsibilities accrue, I will refer primarily to states and state-based organizations like the UN, although with a recognition that non-state actors are increasingly important in carrying out such responsibilities.

CHAPTER 1

Interrogating International Responsibilities

[E]mergency humanitarian aid is a new duty encumbent upon the international community. . . . It obeys the principle that it is a moral duty to help civilians in distress wherever they may be.

The Security Council emphasizes the responsibility of States to comply with their obligations to end impunity and to prosecute those responsible for genocide, crimes against humanity and serious violations of international humanitarian law.

Each individual state has the responsibility to protect its populations from genocide, war crimes, ethnic cleansing and crimes against humanity. . . . The international community, through the United Nations, also has the responsibility . . . to help protect populations from genocide, war crimes, ethnic cleansing and crimes against humanity.

This book analyzes how the international community responds to mass atrocities, in particular in sub-Saharan Africa. I argue that as human rights have acquired increasing normative force globally, the international community has incorporated human rights into its responses to violent conflict. In fact, human rights are used to label some conflicts as more heinous and worthy of response than others. Genocide has become the main signifier for worthiness. It is the über crime, the "'super crime,'"[1] the worst imaginable violation of human rights—attempting to wipe out an entire group of people. Its invocation automatically brings about much anguish and angst and hand-wringing—if less actual response—among global political elites and newspaper editorial writers. Genocide invokes cries of "never again" and leads to calls to "do something." As we shall see, "something" can mean many things, or nothing at all, and might lead to whispers of "yes, again" because those with the means to "do something" may not see it as in their interest to act. They may do "something," but not necessarily what is required.

The international community has developed three types of responses that respond in some manner to the human rights issues raised by genocide, the "lesser" crimes of crimes against humanity and war crimes, and the vast humanitarian crises that accompany almost all contemporary conflict. These correspond to three responsibilities the international community has acquired over the last decades. The most famous and discussed responsibility—and indeed the one that provides the "responsibility" framework—is the responsibility to protect (R2P). While it incorporates a wide variety of actions, taking forceful military action to stop mass atrocities is the one that most concerns us. It is, in some situations, potentially the most effective response. However, while it has become the most talked about responsibility, it is also the least used. While there may frequently be good prudential reasons for this, it cannot be denied that in some situations the international community has utterly failed to follow through with this responsibility—which of course raises questions about how seriously the responsibility is taken.

While the responsibility to protect aims to physically stop the most heinous of human rights abuses, international criminal justice—what I call the responsibility to prosecute—holds people to account after the fact for these same abuses. While in one sense this is post facto punishment, the International Criminal Tribunal for the Former Yugoslavia (ICTY) was created while the war in the former Yugoslavia was still raging, and most of the cases being prosecuted by the International Criminal Court (ICC) are occurring in the midst of ongoing conflicts. So an additional motive for these activities is to affect the behavior of people who are engaging, or may engage, in these human rights violations—by arresting them, by creating inducements for them to stop, or by deterring such individuals from carrying out these violations in the first place. While this prosecution impulse ties into well-developed human rights norms, it may take rhetorical invocation of R2P to activate this responsibility. Indeed, it may be used in place of R2P action—or in conjunction with it.

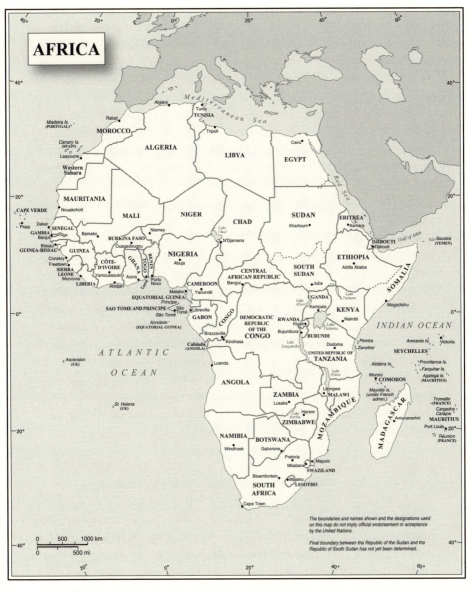

Map 1. Africa, Map No. 4045 Rev. 7, November 2011. United Nations.

The final responsibility to provide humanitarian aid to people affected by conflict created by the crimes mentioned above—what I call the responsibility to palliate—does not seek to stop the conflict, nor does it seek to punish people driving the conflict. Rather, it seeks to provide the displaced and other victims of conflict with food, water, shelter, and medical assistance so that they can continue to live at the most basic level. It takes conflict for granted and tries to ameliorate—palliate—the effects of conflict. In theory it has no grand political project like the other two responsibilities, although this is a convenient—and not always convincing—fiction. It may also be used when R2P is invoked, although many times the actors involved—in particular nongovernmental organizations (NGOs)—may be on the ground carrying out this responsibility before the invocation of "never again." Yet it, too, is intimately tied up with the other two responsibilities.

All three of these responsibilities come from the same human urge to stop suffering, and they are all heavily embedded in the twentieth-century human rights project, although there are also connections to the nineteenth-century development of international humanitarian law (IHL). Yet, the relationships between them are complex. This book seeks to disentangle and make clear these complexities. The core part of the book examines four case studies from central/east Africa to make concrete how the international community has—or has not—engaged with these responsibilities. First, however, these responsibilities require further explication. In the next sections I look more deeply at each of the responsibilities and associated norms and practices, briefly tracing their development and interrogating the concrete meanings of these responsibilities. I then turn to developing a framework for understanding how these responsibilities interact and the main conundrums faced by those deciding which of these responses to implement.

Humanitarianism: The Responsibility to Palliate

As Michael Barnett observes, "We live in a world of humanitarianisms, not humanitarianism."[2] Indeed, while I will briefly track the evolution of the idea and practice of *humanitarianism*, one must recognize that there are, in fact, multiple ideas about what humanitarianism is and how to practice it.

While some use the term "humanitarianism" to denote a wide variety of human-rights-supporting activities,[3] humanitarianism is distinct from human rights, even if they have overlapping ideational bases. Human rights are about making sure that all humans have access to the same protections from human-induced suffering and discrimination and have what they need to live in dignity. It is a political project that aims to order polities in such a way that individuals have access to the political process and their other rights are protected. Humanitarianism, while it may have broader social goals, is, in the end, about making sure that people can continue to live on a day to day basis in the most horrible and extreme circumstances. While we frequently use the term "humanitarian" to describe an individual who is attempting to do good in the world, the ambit and practice of humanitarianism as an "ism" is much more circumscribed. Humanitarian organizations—as opposed to development organizations, which focus on longer term economic and social progress throughout society—are focused on providing assistance—food, water, medical care, shelter—to individuals caught in the midst of conflict. They help refugees, internally displaced persons, asylum seekers, and other war-affected individuals gain access to what they need to survive on a daily basis—a "bed for the night."[4] This so-called classical humanitarianism does not deal with the broader political context in which it operates. It is all about saving lives. It is apolitical. However, this "pure" humanitarianism is under many pressures to go beyond this remit and become embedded in politics. As this occurs, life becomes much more complicated for humanitarians, and the choices faced by them—and the international community more generally—more difficult.

Michael Barnett and Jack Snyder[5] identify four types of humanitarianism, characterized by where humanitarians stand on two issues—whether or not they accept that they are political and whether or not they accept constraints on what they can accomplish. These are "bed for the night," "do no harm," "back a decent winner," and "peacebuilding." The first is the approach of the Red Cross Movement, and has been expounded by David Rieff in a book of the same name.[6] It is only emergency relief. It does not claim any goals or import beyond saving lives from one day to the next. Do no harm is essentially bed for the night with more reflection. While adhering to the previous goals, humanitarians will consider the consequences of their actions and whether or not their actions are doing more good than harm.[7] Such issues came to the fore in 1990s, as questions were raised about whether aid actually prolonged conflicts by providing resources or safe spaces for combatants in the form of refugee camps. Until then, there was an uncontested assumption that good intentions resulted in good outcomes.[8] Rwanda was one such situation where, as we will see, some organizations decided to withdraw because they felt they were doing more harm than good. This perspective still claims to be nonpolitical, but once one starts deciding who should or should not receive aid, one is making political as well as ethical judgments. Back a decent winner recognizes the constraints of humanitarian action while having a willingness to engage politically. It essentially looks for a "better" partner who can create a better peace even if this does not mean a broad-based liberal peace. When engaging with comprehensive peacebuilding, humanitarians look to the root causes of a conflict, including human rights abuses, and advocate the creation of a more just society that provides a basis for peace. It is avowedly political and it rejects the limited mission for humanitarianism advocated in the first strategy.

Advocating one version of humanitarianism over another will lead to different trade-offs and conundrums for humanitarians. The more you advocate political solutions, the less able you are to claim the classical humanitarian label which, theoretically, protects you in the field. Further, you may end up supporting activities and outcomes that are at odds with your intended goals as a humanitarian. These four categories are archetypes, and it may be possible to move between categories or occupy more than one category simultaneously, which creates even more tensions and complications.

An Abridged History of Humanitarianism

We can look to the mid-nineteenth century for the origins of humanitarianism. There were a number of efforts at this time to regulate warfare, which resulted in the creation of national Red Cross societies that would assist war wounded and the International Committee of the Red Cross (ICRC), as well as the first Geneva Convention for the Amelioration of the Condition of the Wounded in Armies in the Field in 1864, which established the principle of neutrality of those assisting the wounded. There followed many more conventions that provided protection for war wounded and those assisting them, as well as restrictions on the methods of warfare. These culminated in the 1949 Geneva Conventions, which comprehensively laid out the rights and duties of combatants and noncombatants in war. The 1977 Additional Protocols further extended the coverage (if not as comprehensively) in noninternational (i.e., internal) armed conflict. Thus, two important legal strands developed in IHL. First, states are constrained in how they fight—who they can target and what weapons and methods they can use are not unlimited.

Second, states have responsibilities toward those affected by war, including providing or allowing the delivery of humanitarian assistance, such as medical and food aid. Unlike war abolitionists, IHL takes war as a given and attempts to ameliorate the effects of war. It does not have the broad societal-changing goals of human rights. It is focused on the moment, the situation on the ground, and people in immediate need.

Over the decades, the ICRC has developed a set of principles to which most humanitarians aspire.[9] Of the seven core principles, four are the most important—humanity, neutrality, impartiality, and independence.[10] Humanity is of obvious importance—it is the core impetus, the reason behind the actions. Neutrality, impartiality, and independence form the superstructure of classical humanitarian action. Neutrality means not taking sides in a conflict. Impartiality requires the provision of assistance to all in need. Independence entails acting without any state guiding your actions. The ICRC strictly adheres to these principles, and most other nonstate humanitarian organizations also take them as core principles, although this has become harder to do. UN and other state-based humanitarian organizations, while professing adherence to these principles, have obvious problems with independence, since they are acting on behalf of states. Further, neutrality can be difficult to achieve if the UN has taken sides in a conflict. International humanitarian organizations (IHOs) use these principles as a protective cloak, hoping that combatants will perceive them as not involved with one side or another and not threatening them in any way, and thus having no reason to fear or harm them. While this may work to a certain extent, it is by no means a sure path to security for humanitarian workers and access to those in need.

The developments in 1949 coincided with other developments in the UN and elsewhere. In particular, the UN created the Office of the UN High Commissioner for Refugees (UNHCR)[11] in 1950, and the Refugee Convention followed in 1951. The latter created a framework to provide for the rights of a significant population of those affected by war—refugees. It outlined the responsibilities of states toward refugees, including the principle of *nonrefoulement*—no forcible repatriation. UNHCR had an initial budget of $300,000 and a three-year lifespan. In the ensuing decades, it dramatically expanded its remit and global presence.[12]

The 1990s saw UNHCR expand its presence substantially while changing the nature and scope of the organization. The number of refugees globally reached its peak in 1993 in the context of war in the Balkans and Somalia. Its experience in Bosnia changed the organization as it became involved in the midst of a conflict rather than on the edges.[13] Its personnel were put in harm's way and it was much more difficult for it to operate—it now had to negotiate with combatants to gain access to affected populations in the middle of fighting, and frequently the combatants were not willing to accommodate UNHCR. The UN also had a peacekeeping mission in Bosnia, but it had a weak mandate, and although it included protecting humanitarian aid efforts, it routinely failed in its mission.[14] Thus, humanitarianism became the perfect vehicle for the international community, which was under pressure to respond but which did not want to commit troops. At the same time, UNHCR began acquiring a wider remit as it began assisting internally displaced persons (IDPs). While undoubtedly helping many people inside Bosnia, UNHCR's actions also helped European states, which wanted to keep IDPs from becoming refugees and making their way to Germany and other western European countries. The right to seek asylum thus became the "right to remain"[15] and "preventive protection,"[16] and humanitarians became involved in "'containment through charity.'"[17] High Commissioner Sadako Ogata suspended UNHCR operations in Bosnia until it received better cooperation from all the combatants and peacekeepers. However, because Ogata was going to remove "the international community's symbol of concern,"[18] UN Secretary-General Boutros Boutros-Ghali ordered UNHCR to stay. Although they were myth before, Bosnia fundamentally exposed the mismatch between lofty humanitarian principles—in particular independence—and the reality of state-based humanitarian action.

Rwanda proved another turning point for UNHCR and other IHOs as genocide and complete and utter failure on the part of the international community to stop the genocide or address the aftermath created untenable situations and dilemmas for all IHOs. The North Atlantic Treaty Organization (NATO) intervention in Kosovo[19] brought humanitarianism further into the political fold. This process was complete by the early years of the new century as humanitarians became "force multipliers"[20] in Afghanistan and Iraq, and humanitarianism became just one more tool in the "War on Terror." The "War on Terror" has also eliminated the distinction between combatant and noncombatant, on which the principle of neutral and impartial assistance is based. As the United States and its allies pursue those they deem terrorists around the world, its adversaries become "evil," thus losing the protection (in the eyes of the United States) of the Geneva Conventions—and fundamental human rights norms more generally, such as the prohibition on torture—

and the notion of the battlefield has disappeared as the entire world becomes a battlefield.[21] This creates problems for humanitarians.[22]

From Classical to Rights-Based Humanitarianism

Indeed, humanitarians frequently end up in the middle of the most violent conflicts around the world, with little political or other support. They must negotiate access to populations affected by war and may find that they become part of the conflict, targeted by various actors in the conflict or manipulated as pawns.[23] Further, fundamental understandings of what the practice of humanitarianism entails have changed. Through the 1970s, humanitarianism, for the most part, was conceptualized and practiced along the lines of classical, bed for the night humanitarianism—delivering food and medical aid in the midst of conflict—although Conor Foley notes how even during the Biafra crisis in 1967 humanitarians acted in very political ways.[24] The move to rights-based humanitarianism—along the lines of the peacebuilding version identified above—has led to a situation where humanitarians frequently look at the root causes of conflicts—including human rights abuses—and the broader rights of those displaced or otherwise affected by war. IHOs will more frequently engage in advocacy for the protection of human rights, including calling for the use of the military to protect human rights. And, instead of international humanitarian law, international refugee law, and international human rights law being viewed as separate realms, they are now seen as interrelated, providing broader, more robust legal analysis.[25] At the same time, particularly as a result of the experience in Rwanda, the "do no harm"[26] model is being embraced, as IHOs become more reflective about the broader implications of their work.[27]

From Palliation to Power

In its most basic sense, humanitarianism is palliation. According to the World Health Organization, "Palliative care is an approach that improves the quality of life of patients and their families facing the problems associated with life-threatening illness, through the prevention and relief of suffering by means of early identification and impeccable assessment and treatment of pain and other problems, physical, psychosocial and spiritual."[28] In the medical sense, palliative care "intends neither to hasten or postpone death." It "provides relief from pain and other distressing symptoms" and "offers a support system to help patients live as actively as possible until death." The "illness," the symptoms of which humanitarians treat, is not the malnutrition and diseases from which those affected suffer. Rather, it is war and violent conflict itself. Thus, whereas palliative care "affirms life and regards dying as a normal process," humanitarianism as palliation affirms life but also regards war as a normal process. It takes the world and its illness—war—as it is and helps those affected by the illness—refugees, IDPs, and others—to stay alive, hopefully until the war ends and localized illness is cured, or until the illness—war—ultimately kills them. It treats the symptoms rather than effecting a cure. While many millions of people have been saved by humanitarianism, it must seem for some caught in the midst of conflict that the refugee camp is akin to a hospice, with humanitarians keeping refugees alive and comfortable until the war—either directly through an attack by armed forces or indirectly through malnutrition and war-associated disease—kills them. They thus become what has been described as the "well-fed dead."[29]

This description is in no way meant to devalue the work of humanitarians. Indeed, most people helped by humanitarians live to see the end of the war in which they are caught, and even those in hospices will appreciate the efforts undertaken to ease their pain and make them comfortable as the inevitable happens. Yet taking war as inevitable imposes rather severe limits on the goals of humanitarians. At the same time, some humanitarians do not take the inevitable as such, and attempt to go beyond palliation.

Humanitarianism as palliation engages with many different interests and perspectives. The ICRC may see palliation as the ultimate expression of humanity—you are keeping people alive for this one day, and hopefully the next, and the one after that, and so on.[30] And many other IHOs also see this as their humane goal, while others want to go beyond palliation and find a cure—that is, address the root causes that are leading to the disease of war, which is killing so many people. This creates operational problems. It also brings them into conflict with others who may prefer palliation as state policy. That is, while states—especially rich Western states with the resources to put toward stopping conflict—may want to see a particular conflict stop and prevent people from being killed—they do not necessarily want to invest the resources (troops) to do so. Palliation thus becomes the preferred course of action, and a substitute for more robust action. Thus, to bring the medical analogy to a close, instead of bringing in surgeons (troops) to excise the tumor of war and genocide, states bring in hospice workers (humanitarians) to keep people alive until the war ultimately kills them.

This recourse to the humanitarian international,[31] or the Land Cruiser Brigade,[32] appears to give IHOs significant power in the midst of conflict. Yet it also brings with it many problems as humanitarians become politicized, wedded to one side in a conflict, and perceived, according to Michael Hardt and Antonio Negri, as the "mendicant orders of Empire," "some of the most power pacific weapons of the new world order."[33] The white Toyota Land Cruisers of the IHO become a representation of the international community's response to conflict—more evocative than the armored tank—taking humanitarians into a realm of high politics, which conflicts with their humane palliation. As Michael Barnett and Thomas G. Weiss argue, "Humanitarianism has become institutionalized, internationalized, and prominent on the global agenda. It is an orienting feature of global social life that is used to justify, legitimate, and galvanize action."[34] As a result of the changing nature of conflict,[35] humanitarianism has become embedded within contemporary conflict. Of the three responsibilities that are at the core of this book, humanitarianism (palliation) has the most well-defined set of principles and the longest practice. Although it may have different interpretations and meanings, it is recognized and accepted as a good thing, an expression of our ultimate humanity. It is, in fact, recognized as a duty or responsibility of the international community.[36] This makes it a very powerful tool, not only for humanitarians themselves but for other actors who may want to use it for purposes other than what its supporters and practitioners may wish.

International Criminal Justice: The Responsibility to Prosecute

The modern international criminal justice regime, too, has its roots in the attempts from the mid-nineteenth century onward to regulate how war is fought. While perhaps only successful at the margins in limiting the death and destruction of war, international humanitarian law laid the groundwork for the criminalization of certain practices of war. The introduction into international law of crimes for which individuals can be punished theoretically changes the calculus of decision makers—both those waging war and those attempting to stop a war. However, its broader positive effects—including deterring individuals from undertaking certain outlawed activities—will likely be a long time coming. But, of the three responsibilities laid out here, it is the most legalized[37] and embedded in international law.

While there were previous instances of individuals being prosecuted for committing atrocities in war and violating the norms of the day,[38] we must look to the aftermath of World War II for the true roots of the international criminal justice regime and the evolving "responsibility to prosecute." In 1943, the Allied powers, in the Moscow Declaration, decreed that Germans who committed war crimes would be tried in the countries where the atrocities occurred, although the worst crimes would be tried by the Allies themselves. Soon after, the Allies created a UN Commission for the Investigation of War Crimes, which created a draft treaty for an international war crimes court. After the war ended, the Allies created the International Military Tribunal at Nuremburg to try those most responsible for atrocities during the war. A second tribunal was set up in Tokyo to try Japanese war criminals. The four crimes prosecuted at Nuremburg were crimes against peace, aggression, war crimes, and crimes against humanity, the latter of which had appeared after the massacres of Armenians during World War I.[39] The latter three would appear in the Rome Statute of the International Criminal Court more than forty years later.

The Convention on the Prevention and Punishment of the Crime of Genocide was adopted in 1948. Although the term genocide was not used until 1944,[40] and was not accepted by the judges in the Nuremberg trials,[41] some of the elements of the crime of genocide did appear under the general heading of crimes against humanity, and genocide has become the über crime— the worst of all imaginable things one can do in war. As will be seen, this status leads to sometimes strange results as all other crimes are compared to it in international discourse. The crime of genocide is defined, in part, as engaging in certain actions "with intent to destroy, in whole or in part, a national, ethnical, racial, or religious group." The actions include killing members of the groups and other elements of harm. While similar to crimes against humanity, it includes the element of intent to wipe out a group, and it is this intent which, in some way, makes it worse than the same actions without the mens rea[42]—the intent to wipe out the group.

The 1949 Geneva Conventions represented a significant point in the history of the attempt to "humanize" war. In addition to providing a basis for humanitarian action, it also further elaborated what states and individuals could and could not do during war and created a legal basis for individual responsibility for violations of the laws of war—war crimes. However, while the International Law Commission investigated the creation of a court to try individuals for international crimes,[43] and other international conventions were created to outlaw associated human rights abuses, such as the UN Convention against Torture and Other Cruel, Inhuman or Degrading Treatment or Punishment, the Cold War prevented any significant development. This changed in the 1990s when, in the aftermath of the Cold War, the international community was faced with a number of conflicts that seemed to defy adequate UN involvement to properly address and stop the conflict.

International Criminal Justice During and After Conflict

In 1991 war broke out in Yugoslavia as, in the aftermath of the end of the Cold War, parts of the country attempted to break away and create their own, independent countries. One significant element of the war was the ethnic dimension, as people were targeted because of who they were. Thus Bosniaks— Muslim Bosnians—were killed or pushed out of areas to create ethnically "pure" areas for Serbs and Croats. This became known as "ethnic cleansing." This term was used instead of genocide—even though many of the activities fit the definition of genocide—to reduce pressure on the international community to intervene.[44] The Genocide Convention and the "never again" norm would conspire to put pressure on the UN, and especially Western states, to intervene militarily to stop the killing and protect those being targeted. European states had an interest in the conflict in the form of the refugees flooding into Western Europe, although, rather than intervention initially, this led to the aforementioned "right to remain," and the safe havens that turned out not to be very safe.[45]

While the UN put in place a peacekeeping force, the UN Protection Force (UNPROFOR), it was relatively weak, without a robust mandate for civilian protection or the resources to carry out such a mandate. And the humanitarian response was hampered by parties to the conflict. Eventually, three years into the conflict, NATO took robust military action, which eventually led to an end to the fighting.[46] Before that, however, the UN Security Council created the International Criminal Tribunal for the Former Yugoslavia (ICTY) to try individuals from all sides in the conflict. It was the first time since the end of World War II that an international court had been set up to hold individuals accountable for crimes during war. While, in one sense, this represented an effort to divert attention from the fact that the Security Council had done essentially nothing to stop the fighting and ethnic cleansing (toothless peacekeepers and vast quantities of humanitarian aid notwithstanding), it served to resurrect the principles of Nuremberg. It was also important because it was the Security Council, the main body with a mandate to deal with the biggest issues of international security, that created the court. It firmly put international criminal justice on the international agenda. Given that the court was set up to prosecute individuals who were involved in an ongoing conflict, the ICTY created problems for those attempting to bring the fighting to an end. Indeed, it created incentives to continue fighting rather than come to an accommodation to end the war. If the war ended, those with outstanding arrest warrants might be arrested. The fact that it took sixteen years to arrest the last suspect on the ICTY docket, Ratko Mladic, and thirteen years to arrest his co-defendant Radovan Karadzic might hearten those who are facing such situations. Yet, they are, in the end, facing justice, as did former Serbian president Slobodan Milosevic, who was indicted in 1999 during the war in Kosovo and sent to The Hague in 2001—although he eventually died in jail before the trial was over.

The next phase in the reinvigoration of the international criminal justice regime came in 1994, when the UN Security Council created the International Criminal Tribunal for Rwanda (ICTR) in the wake of a genocide that killed 800,000 people. As will be seen in the next chapter, the UN utterly failed to prevent or stop the genocide. Nor did it adequately address the humanitarian crisis following the genocide when more than two million refugees fled to neighboring countries, setting the stage for an even bigger conflict in Zaire. However, the ICTR did allow some small measure of attention to be diverted from the failure of the international community to act. International courts thus became a substitute, yet again, for robust action to stop mass atrocities. Yet, the very fact that there was a felt need to cover up the failure to respond illustrated the effect of the "never again" norm, which would culminate in the responsibility to protect. Why try to cover up inaction unless there was an expectation that the UN, the Security Council, states—somebody—should respond?

Universal Jurisdiction

In the 1990s, another innovation in international criminal justice came to the fore with the expansion of the practice of universal jurisdiction. According to the Princeton Principles on Universal Jurisdiction, "Universal jurisdiction is criminal jurisdiction based solely on the nature of the crime, without regard to where the crime was committed, the nationality of the alleged or convicted perpetrator, the nationality of the victim, or any other connection to the state exercising such jurisdiction."[47]

Thus, according to this principle, one state may arrest or try somebody from another state who committed a crime—in this case, genocide, crimes against humanity, and war crimes—even though the crimes were not committed on the territory of the first state, the crimes were not committed by a national of the first state, and there is not necessarily any direct connection to the first state. The argument is that the crimes have transcended nationality and become international crimes, and thus all states have an interest in seeing that individuals who commit these crimes are punished and thus can claim jurisdiction over such individuals "as a trustee or agent of the international community."[48]

Although universal jurisdiction is still a highly contested concept, it gained currency in the 1990s as Western states started to initiate proceedings against numerous individuals. Perhaps the most famous was the case initiated by Spain against former Chilean president Augusto Pinochet.[49] However, a number of other countries have also begun proceedings against, or tried individuals for, the aforementioned crimes, including eight EU countries. Some of these have been against non-Africans—including U.S., Israeli, and Chinese leaders (prosecutions of which have foundered on the shoals of global power politics)—but many have been against Africans, involving cases from at least twelve African countries. Of the twenty-seven universal jurisdiction cases being pursued by EU states in 2009, ten were against Africans.[50] This focus on Africa has contributed to tensions between the African Union and supporters of international criminal justice mechanisms[51]—as will be seen in particular in the chapter on Darfur. There has been movement away from universal jurisdiction in some Western European countries, particularly as a backlash against attempts to indict Israeli and U.S. officials,[52] but it remains a significant element of the international criminal justice regime.

The International Criminal Court: Institutionalizing the Responsibility to Prosecute

In 1998 the pinnacle of the modern international criminal justice regime was created with the passing of the Rome Statute of the International Criminal

Court. More than 160 states were gathered in Rome, of which 120 voted in favor, 21 abstained, and 7 voted against, including only one African country—Libya.[53] It came into existence in 2002 when the required number of states had ratified the statute, which coincided with the creation of the Special Court for Sierra Leone—a domestic-international hybrid court created by the UN—and the development of another hybrid court in Cambodia. The creation of the ICC was a culmination of post-Cold War democratization, expansion of global governance and global institutions, and widespread recognition, and implementation, of human rights standards. It was a partial implementation of the "never again" norm, which, until Bosnia and Rwanda, had lain dormant since the Holocaust.[54]

The Rome Statute enshrines in international law individual criminal responsibility for genocide, crimes against humanity, war crimes, and aggression.[55] Furthermore, it created responsibilities for states parties. They accept the jurisdiction of the Court (Article 12), are required to arrest and surrender to the Court individuals for whom an arrest warrant has been issued (Article 89), and must provide other cooperation the Court may request (Article 93). As we shall see, it is precisely on the issue of cooperation, including arrest and surrender, on which there has been much conflict in Africa. And while the ICC is an independent entity, accountable to the states parties, it also has a relationship with the UN Security Council. There are three ways a case may come before the Court. According to Article 13, a state party may refer a case over which the Court would have jurisdiction to the Prosecutor, the Prosecutor may initiate an investigation, or the Security Council may refer a situation to the Court acting under Chapter VII of the UN Charter. Under Article 16, the Security Council may also defer an investigation or prosecution for up to a renewable twelve-month period.

The ICC has had a somewhat rocky early history. None of the major global powers—the United States, Russia, or China—are members. The United States was one of its early supporters, but for a variety of reasons voted against the Rome Statute in 1998, joining China, Iraq, Israel, Libya, Qatar, and Yemen. President Clinton did sign the Statute on 31 December 2000—the last day to sign without having to directly accede to the statute. A year and a half later President Bush "de-signed" the statute, declaring that the United States would not be bound by it. For the next few years the United States actively tried to impede the functioning of the ICC. Congress passed the American Service-Members' Protection Act in 2002, which prevented the United States from providing military assistance to any country that had ratified the Rome

Statute, and forced aid recipients to sign so-called Article 98 agreements in which they declared that they would not send any U.S. citizen to the ICC in The Hague. The U.S. softened its stance in 2005 when it allowed the UN Security Council to refer the situation in Darfur to the ICC, and has gradually further engaged with the court in the ensuing years, particularly after the Obama administration came to power. U.S. wariness and opposition to the ICC has both domestic ideational and international realpolitik roots,[56] which have not been resolved, although the U.S. has become more open to the ICC during the Obama administration.[57] Core issues have to do with the fact of the independent prosecutor and that the ICC is only loosely tied to the UN Security Council. The U.S. expresses concern about "political" prosecutions of U.S. citizens. Further, while the Security Council is able to refer situations to the ICC for investigation, and can temporarily suspend proceedings in a particular case, it is not beholden to the Security Council, where the U.S. exerts much power and has a veto. The ICC is thus more independent than the U.S. (and China and Russia) would like.

Although an expression of global support for human rights—which are frequently seen as in opposition to, or free from, politics—the ICC is intimately bound up in global politics. It was created through a global political process, it has ties to the most power global political body—the UN Security Council—and it touches on the most sensitive global political issues. It threatens presidents and prime ministers, as evidenced by the arrest warrants for President Omar al Bashir of Sudan and Moammar Qaddafi of Libya. It is embedded within contemporary conflict, as those who are engaging in violent conflict and carrying out some of the world's worst atrocities are subject to being arrested and sent to The Hague, and it has been invoked as a conflict management tool. One hope of its supporters is that it will deter leaders and individuals from initiating conflict and engaging in atrocities in the first place, although that hope seems far off. Although it is impossible to prove the negative, there is only minimal evidence that it has deterred anybody from doing unspeakable things. It will likely require a concerted record of numerous successful prosecutions before that hope might be realized. And, it is at the core of accusations of neocolonialism[58] since all of the investigations and active cases are in the developing world while the most powerful countries in the world are exempted from its reach.

Indeed, all of the active cases the ICC is prosecuting are in Africa.[59] Prosecutions are ongoing in cases related to Uganda, the Democratic Republic of the Congo (DRC), the Central African Republic (CAR), Darfur, Kenya, and

Côte d'Ivoire. The Prosecutor is also investigating the situation in Mali. Other potential situations for investigation include Afghanistan, Georgia, Colombia, Guinea, Honduras, Korea, and Nigeria, although they are only at the preliminary stages. The ICC also considered the situation in Palestine, deciding that it lacked jurisdiction, since it was unclear whether or not Palestine constituted a state[60]—although this might change now that Palestine has been admitted to the UN as a nonmember observer state.

The International Criminal Justice Problematique

The world thus has a functioning, if still under development, institution to try individuals accused of committing the worst atrocities. Criminal justice is, by its very nature, *retrospective*, but the ICC is embedded within contemporary global political realities and has been called to perform a *prospective* function—deterrence. It has also been deployed in the midst of conflict to perform a conflict *management* role—induce leaders to stop their atrocities or force them to step down. All three of these functions are highly problematic. It cannot deter until there is enough evidence to convince potential war criminals that there is a high likelihood that they will eventually get caught and be taken to The Hague to stand trial. We are not anywhere near there yet; indeed, the sixteen years it took to capture Ratko Mladic is unlikely to give an Omar al Bashir or a Moammar Qaddafi pause. It also assumes that such individuals are able to make rational calculations with regard to the possible consequences of their actions, which in many cases is in serious doubt.

The conflict management role is problematic at least partially because issuing an arrest warrant for a president or general in the midst of an ongoing conflict is just as likely to create an incentive to continue fighting as it is to induce them to stop. If one sees only the possibility of being arrested once a conflict ends, it is not likely that a president or general would just give up and end the conflict. The Security Council might use an ICC arrest warrant as a bargaining chip—as Radovan Karadzic argued U.S. envoy Richard Holbrooke did[61]—but even if this was done in good faith by the Security Council, it does not control the ICC. It can temporarily suspend proceedings for up to a year—indefinitely renewable—but it cannot permanently end an investigation or withdraw an arrest warrant—only the ICC can do that. And given the varying global political agendas of members of the Security Council, there is no guarantee that it would vote to suspend proceedings—a leader would do well not to base his or her future on the vagaries of global political will and expediency. Further, declaring an individual a war criminal and then withdrawing an arrest warrant does little to further the global human rights project embodied in the ICC. It would undermine the potential deterrent aspect of the ICC and signal that the ICC was nothing more than a global political tool of the great powers with little to do with protecting human rights.

Finally, its retrospective nature, while laudable and a significant incarnation of the global human rights project, is rendered problematic as it may interfere with domestic peace efforts. Such concerns arose in Uganda where the government instituted an amnesty law to induce members of the Lord's Resistance Army (LRA) to leave the LRA and be reintegrated into society.

International criminal justice, as embodied in the ICC and other institutions, is the most legalized and legally recognized of the three responsibilities, which makes it in some ways the safest legally—and morally—to invoke. Yet, since international law itself is a highly political realm, it should come as no surprise that the ICC can become highly embedded within global and domestic political processes, raising questions about how and when the ICC is—and should be—invoked. The failure of the UN Security Council to refer the situation in Syria to the ICC, even in the face of clear and ongoing atrocities, puts these questions in high relief.

The Responsibility to Protect

The most recently recognized responsibility, but the one that also provides the conceptual justification for the prior responsibilities qua responsibilities, is firmly embedded within, but also challenges, the contemporary state system. By labeling it a responsibility, the international community recognizes changes in the relationship between state sovereignty and human rights while also accepting the necessity of international action at times. However, R2P comes with many caveats, and its status as international law is less than certain. It is frequently equated with humanitarian intervention,[62] a concept with uncertain legal qualities frequently deployed by critics to imply neocolonialism. The concept as originally put forth under its current name goes far beyond humanitarian intervention. Yet, when discussing the types of situations of concern in this book, it is precisely the interventionist aspects that are most salient and most unique from a normative perspective. To understand the current conception(s) of R2P, however, a very brief overview of the practice of humanitarian intervention is in order to illustrate the changing debates and status within international relations.

The Practice of Humanitarian Intervention

Most histories of the practice of humanitarian intervention begin in the nineteenth century.[63] During this period there were a number of military interventions in Europe, justifications for which included "proto-humanitarian" arguments. The defining features of the discourse and practice of humanitarian intervention during this period were twofold. First, as today, not all situations that might have demanded a robust response actually received one. Second, the class of people deemed worthy of being rescued was significantly circumscribed. While the European powers intervened to save noncitizens, they were noncitizens of a particular type. One needed to be Christian—and indeed the right kind of Christian—to be worthy of saving. This contrasts markedly with today's universalistic conceptions of human rights and humanity, and arguments and actions to protect noncitizens around the world, although an expanded conception of humanity is no guarantee of action.

Although this expanded humanity and human rights concern was evident from the end of World War II, the Cold War and decolonization prevented any type of intervention on humanitarian grounds—or certainly the use of humanitarian arguments to justify intervention. The Cold War paralyzed the newly created United Nations and created concerns that military adventures might lead to superpower confrontation. Decolonization entrenched notions of absolute sovereignty and revitalized the doctrine of nonintervention. There were three interventions in the 1970s that many point to as possible humanitarian interventions, even though humanitarian justifications were not ultimately deployed in any of these situations. India intervened in East Pakistan in 1971 in response to massacres by the Pakistani military; Tanzania intervened in Uganda in 1979 to overthrow Idi Amin; and Vietnam pushed the Khmer Rouge from power in Cambodia in 1979. All three cases were relatively limited ventures (certainly from the perspective of the interventions that were to come) and were justified with nonhumanitarian arguments—and indeed in all three cases there were traditional regional strategic interests involved. They all also had the effect of saving lives—and getting rid of regimes that engaged in widespread gross human rights violations.[64] Yet the international community was not ready to accept humanitarian arguments. The doctrine of nonintervention would have prevented such arguments from succeeding. This highlights a significant change in global outlook as humanitarian arguments are given much more consideration today, such that states attempt to use humanitarian arguments for very unhumanitarian reasons—as well as for more evidently humanitarian purposes.

The post-Cold War world of the 1990s brought about conceptual and practical challenges to understandings of sovereignty and nonintervention. A raft of "new wars"[65] erupted in the aftermath of the Cold War as the Soviet Union fell apart and developing states lost their patrons. The first post-Cold War (or perhaps end of Cold War) intervention took place in Liberia as the Economic Community of West African States (ECOWAS) intervened in the civil war, which featured mass human rights violations and threatened regional stability. It did not have the initial approval of the UN Security Council, although it did receive the general approval of the international community afterwards. More important, however, was a declaration by the secretary-general of the Organization of African Unity (OAU), Salim A. Salim, who said that African governments who engaged in human rights abuses could no longer hide behind sovereignty.[66] This was a radical suggestion in 1990, and while still controversial, would attract much more support in Africa today. The 1991 creation of "no-fly zones" by the United States, UK and France in Iraq was intended to protect populations that were being persecuted by the Saddam Hussein regime. Operation Provide Comfort reflected a partial normative change as France argued that widespread human rights violations could legitimate UN Security Council action even if not identified as a threat to international peace and security, the traditional justification for forceful UN action.[67] Other interventions did see human rights and humanitarian concerns cited as threats to international peace and security, thus initiating an ideational change in Security Council practice.[68] In 1992–93 the United States undertook Operation Restore Hope in Somalia, taking over from a failed UN mission. The Security Council justification made the direct connection between humanitarian crises and international peace and security. However, the actual level of commitment to humanitarian objectives was demonstrated when the United States pulled out after only a few months when its forces suffered more—and particularly humiliating—casualties than expected.

I have already mentioned the international failures in Bosnia and Rwanda. Although the intervention in Bosnia began as a rather lackluster affair, the massacre of 8,000 people in Srebrenica spurred NATO to action. It engaged in a bombing campaign that eventually led to an end to the war. But, overall, the UN experience in Bosnia was rather ignominious. This should not have been surprising, however, given that a year before the UN allowed 8,000 people to be killed in Srebrenica, it allowed 800,000 to be killed in Rwanda. The issue in Rwanda was not sovereignty. Rather, it was that no country (except for France, late in the day, and very ambiguously) had any interest in sending in troops to stop the slaughter. European states found the interest five years later in Kosovo when NATO intervened to protect Armenian Kosovars from Serbia. This, too, was an ambiguous intervention, given that the larger Serbian human rights abuses seemed to come *after* the intervention started.[69] And, the intervention occurred in the absence of UN Security Council approval, since any Security Council resolution would have been vetoed by Russia, given its ties to Serbia. As with Bosnia, there were traditional state interests involved—the general stability of the region, as well as the prospect of yet more refugees flowing into Western Europe. However, Kosovo also represented an assertion of a new doctrine on the part of some states that justified (unilateral) military intervention on humanitarian grounds.

Recognizing Responsibilities

During the 1990s, and in the context of changing ideas about human rights and the above mentioned interventions (or noninterventions), a number of authors addressed the balance between sovereignty and human rights.[70] They argued that rather than being in opposition, human rights were constitutive of state sovereignty. If a government abused its people, it could lose legitimacy and the state might lose its immunity to nonintervention. Further, there was discussion about whether there was a right or a duty to intervene, and under what conditions. The developing norm of a right and, indeed, a duty to intervene to protect gross violations of human rights was given voice in 2001 by the Canadian-sponsored International Commission on Intervention and State Sovereignty (ICISS) in a report entitled *The Responsibility to Protect*.[71] It recognized a shift in the human rights versus state sovereignty discourse by arguing that claims to sovereignty entailed responsibilities. It also moved the debate away from discussing a right to intervene to a responsibility to protect those who might be threatened by gross violations of human rights or humanitarian crises. The ICISS noted three main responsibilities: to prevent genocide and other humanitarian catastrophes, to react when such situations occur, and to rebuild after a complex humanitarian emergency has ended.

This norm was endorsed by the UN Secretary-General's High-level Panel on Threats, Challenges and Change,[72] and UN Secretary-General Kofi Annan highlighted and affirmed this developing norm intended to set the agenda for the 2005 World Summit.[73] He also called on the Security Council to develop principles for the use of force. The 2005 World Summit Outcome document stated that the international community has a responsibility to address widespread gross violations of human rights, even if it means using force. However, the World Summit endorsed a somewhat different and watered down version of the ICISS proposal.[74] The norm has been more forcefully recognized by the African Union in its Constitutive Act. Article 4h states the following principle: "the right of the Union to intervene in a Member State pursuant to a decision of the Assembly in respect of grave circumstances, namely: war crimes, genocide and crimes against humanity." While there is ongoing rhetoric in Africa regarding the neocolonial character of humanitarian intervention, and much debate about the proper balance between human rights and sovereignty, this was still a stunning reversal—three years before the World Summit—of the unflinching support for absolute sovereignty and nonintervention, and indicates continuing global normative development, even if it has yet to be invoked.

Prevention

The ICISS identified prevention as one of the three main elements of R2P. The World Summit recognized the responsibility of the international community to prevent genocide, war crimes, ethnic cleansing, and crimes against humanity. However, of the twenty mentions of prevention in the outcome document, more than half were focused on preventing conflict. There is a significant connection between conflict and human rights abuses, since the crimes listed above generally occur within the context of war. Yet this is not a new responsibility for the international community. Indeed, the UN was founded to prevent war. That it has failed spectacularly many times in its more than six decades does not negate that this is a well-established responsibility on the part of states. Further, such prevention can include a wide variety of activities, such as development, which, while plausibly related to preventing the conditions under which genocide might occur, are also conceptually distinct from the core idea of protecting people from the most heinous of mass crimes.[75]

Alex Bellamy argues that there are four main tasks that the international community can engage in to prevent such atrocities: early warning, preventive diplomacy, ending impunity, and preventive deployments.[76] While these are all worthwhile activities, the first two are already well-used, if not always effective, tools. Ending impunity has already been recognized through the creation of the International Tribunals for the Former Yugoslavia and Rwanda, and the creation of the International Criminal Court. However, the *protective* value of such measures is still in doubt. While indicting a head of state or rebel leader might serve as pressure or an inducement to stop fighting, it may also create conditions where the reverse inducements are created. Such leaders and others may have an incentive to continue fighting because otherwise they might be vulnerable to capture and transfer to the Hague. We have a very small sample of such actions taking place before or during a conflict from which to generalize. And, so far, the latter dynamic seems more prevalent. Lord's Resistance Army leader Joseph Kony was reluctant to sign a peace agreement in Uganda as long as there was an ICC arrest warrant for him, and Omar al Bashir of the Sudan has, so far, been defiant of the ICC since an arrest warrant was issued for him. Similarly, Qaddafi demonstrated little interest in ending his human rights abuses and stepping down before he was forcibly removed from power. Thus, such international criminal justice measures do not, at present anyway, properly fall under the heading of prevention. The fact that the Rwandan genocide might have been prevented if the UN peacekeeping mission on the ground had been listened to when its commander presented evidence of the impending genocide, calls into question the willingness of the international community to engage in the necessary preventive activities.

Thus, prevention may include activities only tangentially related to heading off such mass atrocities, and it includes activities that have long been in the international community's toolbox but have not been implemented to the extent necessary. As such, they are not necessarily the most important part of the newly recognized responsibility to protect. Further, in a rather fundamental sense they do not (with the possible exception of preventive deployment) *protect* in the sense of defending or shielding from harm. Preventive activities are obviously extremely important, but in the context of an ongoing genocide not as relevant as other activities.

Reaction

Paragraph 139 of the Outcome Document, which lays out the international community's commitment to react to genocide and similar situations, begins by mentioning peaceful means of response, including humanitarian means. And paragraphs 132 and 133 (although not under the heading of R2P) discuss protecting IDPs and refugees, two of the most vulnerable groups in such situations. The question becomes, however, to what extent are humanitarian activities actually *protective*. As we shall see below, while many claims are made by humanitarians about protection, the actual protection they can provide is quite modest.

Paragraph 139 then continues to commit the UN, on a case by case basis, to taking collective action under Chapter VII of the UN Charter—that is, using force against the wishes of a state. Such military protection (as opposed to the humanitarian protection discussed above) involves what is frequently called humanitarian intervention—the use of military force to compel a government to stop human rights abuses or to otherwise stop such abuses. The force may overthrow a government committing human rights abuses, apply other military pressure (such as the NATO bombing in Kosovo), serve as an interpositional force between warring parties committing human rights abuses, physically protect vulnerable populations, provide relief aid and ensure that food, medical supplies, and so forth can be delivered. This last activity may not have the same protective value as physically shielding people from harm, at least not in the long term. Since humanitarian military action can have many goals and outcomes, it is important to be clear about what one is advocating or pointing to as a responsibility in a particular situation. Bellamy argues that the term humanitarian intervention was avoided because many developing countries especially were wary of such terminology, seeing it as little more than a cover for neocolonial interventions.[77] Yet this is what the UN recognized, and it represents perhaps the most important element of the R2P as elaborated by the World Summit. In fact, while the ICISS, Bellamy, and others make valid arguments that all the other activities mentioned by the ICISS and the Outcome Document are necessary in the context of mass atrocities, they pale in comparison to the potential effects—both on the ground and in the international legal and normative realm—of military intervention.

Rebuilding

The third element of R2P identified by the ICISS entails a commitment to rebuilding a society after a conflict. This includes economic development, institution building, and developing the rule of law, among other activities. Such a commitment, identified under the heading of peacebuilding rather than responsibility to protect in the Outcome Document, is relatively uncontroversial—although it raises questions of neocolonialism for some developing countries and the extent of the international community's presence in postconflict societies. Such activities, to the extent that they contribute to the strengthening of a viable, peaceful state, may aid in preventing recurrence of conflict. However, with regard to the issue at hand, how the international community responds to an extant genocide or complex humanitarian emergency is of secondary importance. It may contribute to the protection of people after a conflict ends, but it does not *protect* people in the midst of conflict.

Thus, while the original conception of R2P as put forth by the ICISS, and partly endorsed by the World Summit, was very wide-ranging, if one is interested in effective, long-term protection of people caught in mass atrocity situations, the potentially most important element is the commitment to use Chapter VII enforcement mechanisms. This is because in some situations this may be the only way to protect people from being slaughtered. Further, it is a significant, if still somewhat ambiguous, affirmation of evolving normative and practical developments away from strict adherence to sovereignty. This is not to say that such actions may be appropriate in all instances, or that there may not be genuine disagreement about the relevant course of action. And it certainly does not mean that such tools will be used in all, or even many, situations where large numbers of people are being killed. Indeed, as we have seen, there are two other main responses the international community uses, which are conceptually distinct from military intervention, are possibly less effective, and may actually impede the use of more effective measures.

Protection

From the previous discussion, we have seen the development of three broad areas of human rights norms and practices that have been recognized in some manner or another as *responsibilities* of the international community: (1) palliate—ensure that people caught in the midst of conflict are fed and sheltered and provided with medical attention; (2) prosecute—eliminate impunity for those who commit genocide, crimes against humanity, and war crimes; and (3) protect—ensure that those at risk of genocide and other mass atrocities are not killed. All of these have *humanitarian* and *human rights* characteristics, but to the extent a division can be created between the two, they all have a different balance. *Palliation*, while part of the broad concern with the other that characterizes human rights, does not have the same connotations with regard to *changing* society. Rather, it *responds* to the situation in the most minimal way possible, although those who practice or advocate rights-based humanitarianism alter the balance in favor of advocating for change while also offering the *humanitarian* response. *Prosecution* is the enforcement element of the development of international humanitarian law that was created to provide minimal levels of protection for particular classes of people in the midst of conflict. Yet it is also part of the broader human rights project that attempts to remove impunity for those who engage in the worst human rights violations. *Protection* is the most far reaching. It has a broad agenda that aims to prevent large-scale human rights abuses, stop ongoing abuses, and rebuild societies after the abuses end. Yet the most important element of this new norm, principle, or whatever one calls it, is the stopping or reacting element. This responsibility to react is what used to be called humanitarian intervention. But it is the formal recognition of the *intervention*—that is using military force[78]—element for the *humanitarian* purpose of keeping people alive that is new and also the part of R2P that actually protects in the context of mass atrocities. Yet, as we have seen, all three practices make claims about *protection*. We thus need to further investigate the meaning of protection.

Humanitarian Protection

Humanitarian organizations like UNHCR or the ICRC see several protective elements to their work. Providing food, shelter, medical aid, and other resources to refugees and others affected by war and genocide have direct protective benefits for the individuals affected—it can literally save their lives. However, beyond this direct effect, other types of protection can be noted. UNHCR, for example, argues that merely having a presence on the ground in a conflict situation can be a form of protection. Their presence is an indication that the international community is watching, and can thus serve as a deterrent. However, sometimes that is not enough and it becomes clear that all the international community is doing is watching—and hoping that humanitarianism will suffice. UNHCR also talks about legal protection—which is its core mandate. This involves ensuring that refugees' and asylum seekers' rights are protected—making sure that states live up to their legal obligations under international refugee law, including the prohibition on *nonrefoulement*, obligations to examine asylum claims, and requirements for providing access to resources for refugees.[79]

The ICRC has a similar mandate, and although it frequently talks about relief and protection, David Forsythe argues that "the ICRC's humanitarian protection in the field encompasses primarily traditional protection and relief protection."[80] Traditional protection is essentially identical to UNHCR's legal protection. Thus, as with UNHCR, the ICRC works to protect individuals by ensuring that states live up to their international human rights responsibilities. Its prison visits seek to accomplish similar goals, Forsythe points out, while "In relief protection there can be an element of supervision and representation, along with the central effort to provide the goods and services necessary for minimal human dignity in conflict situations."

Oxfam, an NGO that frequently works in the midst of conflict situations, recognizes the limits of its protection capabilities: "Oxfam . . . is not a specialist protection organisation. . . . For us, protection means improving the safety of civilians in our humanitarian programming. In practice, it means trying to reduce the threats of violence, coercion and deliberate deprivation to civilians, and reducing their vulnerability to these threats."[81]As an NGO, while it wants to contribute to the protection of civilians under its care, it is constrained in what it can actually accomplish. It further constrains itself by significantly restricting its interactions with peacekeeping and other military forces that may sometimes be needed to deliver assistance—and thus protection.[82]

Thus, humanitarian action can include both traditional (legal) protection and relief (material) protection. Both are necessary for maintaining human dignity and both are responsibilities of the international community. Yet the international community frequently chooses to emphasize humanitarian protection, which, while immediate, only provides partial protection and does not address longer term protection issues, at the expense of root cause, longer term options. Further, while the terminology of protection may be used, such organizations do not have the mandate or capabilities to actually physically *protect* people. They are not armed and, if an army or group of rebels decides to enter an IDP camp, there is little they can do to stop them. Indeed, as noted above, such activities might more properly be described as *palliation* rather than *protection* in that in the context of genocide or ethnic cleansing they may mitigate suffering but do little to provide robust, and long-term, action to stop the killing. Such activities are frequently undertaken by nonstate entities that do not have the capabilities or mandate to do anything other than deliver food and water and medical care—obviously worthwhile endeavors, but not backed up by the full authority and force of the UN or individual states. And, even when the *authority* of the UN is present, if it is not backed up by the *power* of the UN, that authority may be meaningless.

Prosecution Protection

Does the increasingly elaborate international criminal justice regime, with its courts in The Hague and practices of universal jurisdiction, *protect* people? We consider the rule of law to be a cornerstone of a peaceful and just society. We have domestic courts and legal proceedings designed to punish wrongdoers. This legal edifice is also assumed to deter people from committing crimes in the first place. Thus, through deterrence it protects people from harm, and by putting criminals behind bars it keeps criminals from harming anybody else. The deterrent effect of domestic legal systems is difficult to measure.[83] Further, the legal system relies on police officers to arrest wrongdoers, as well as be a presence on the street to deter wrongdoing and physically protect people. It is far from perfect, but domestic criminal justice systems do provide protection, if by no means total. The international criminal justice regime works very differently. It was conceived of as a retrospective system that would deal with people after they had committed their atrocities, which is of little comfort to the thousands or millions of civilians who might die in a conflict. Further, compared to the crimes committed and lives lost, extraordinarily few people have been tried before international courts or domestic universal jurisdiction proceedings. And it can be no other way. Indeed, the first Prosecutor of the ICC stated that his aim was to go after maybe a half dozen of those most responsible in a particular conflict.[84] This will leave hundreds and thousands of people who have committed serious crimes in a conflict to go free. The ICC has no resources to extend beyond that small number of people. Nor does it have the ability to get its hands on any more. It is completely reliant on states and the UN to deliver suspects to its door in The Hague, and unlike domestic contexts where there is a police force whose job is to do exactly that, the Prosecutor does not have his or her own police force to go out and arrest people. They are completely reliant on a very ad hoc process that only functions when states or other actors decide it is in their interest to arrest somebody,[85] and even if it is in their interest, they may not have the means. The fact that it took sixteen years to arrest Ratko Mladic indicates that justice is far from automatic. The protective effect of deterrence, unsure as it is in domestic contexts, is, at the present time, close to nonexistent, and will only have a chance of having any significant value after a long record of successful prosecutions in The Hague is assembled, with alleged perpetrators coming to trial in much less than sixteen years.

Although international criminal justice is retrospective in nature, there are now attempts to use it to affect the course of conflicts in which the crimes are being carried out. The involvement of the ICC is sought by parties or observers to the conflict as a conflict management strategy.[86] Initial experience in places such as Darfur and Libya indicate the extreme limits of the ability to use threats of being sent to The Hague to alter perpetrators' behavior. And without stopping the killing, it is difficult to make the case for the *protective* effect of international criminal justice. At the same time, invoking the ICC can make the protection of people even more difficult. Yet it is difficult to fault the advocates of the ICC and similar mechanisms, for certainly we do want the purveyors of atrocity to be held accountable. But, again, we must be modest in our expectations.

Military Protection

R2P includes many activities, but if we are interested in keeping people from being killed in an atrocity situation, it is the reactive, or *active*, element that is crucial. While the term humanitarian intervention has fallen out of favor, this is the type of activity that could—possibly—protect people. While humanitarians can keep people alive—at least those to which they have access— if a group is intending to kill people in a refugee or IDP camp, for example, there is little they can do. Food will not stop the *janjaweed* in Darfur. Nor will all the international legal principles advocated by the committed people at the ICRC or UNHCR or, for that matter, the legal machinations and pronouncements emanating from The Hague. No, what is sometimes needed is a soldier (or a brigade) with a gun standing at the entrance to a refugee camp with a mandate and a will to use it against those who want to rape or kill the people in the refugee camp. And they must be there night after night, and at times they must go after the people intent on massacres and either bring them to justice or—and let's be clear about what is required— kill them. We have seen instances where the international community has the will to countenance and support such activity. However, the overall record is dominated by abject failure, the Srebrenica massacre and the Rwandan genocide being only two of countless examples where those with the ability to intervene forcefully have not recognized and acted on their responsibilities.

Further, the "hard edge" of R2P is hardly without problems. There are legal issues, although these are becoming less important, especially with regard to UN action. There are practical issues. You need to find the right people and the right equipment and get them to the right place at the right time. The people—and those commanding them—have to be willing to use that equipment. The resources deployed must be appropriate for the job at hand. And you need to make sure you do not make the situation worse, by inflaming the situation, killing the wrong people, or affecting, for example, the delivery of humanitarian assistance. These are not easy things to address, and there are constant prudential debates about the appropriateness of a particular response in a particular situation. And there may be situations where you just cannot do what is needed—or at least all of it. You need to recognize that not every situation can be addressed. In other words, there are limits. Too often, however, the international community has not demonstrated a willingness to explore those limits.

Protection of Civilians

R2P is an inherently political construct. It gets to the heart of core issues of sovereignty and war and peace and global power politics. And while it has been superficially accepted by the World Summit, the UN Security Council, and in other fora, it is still highly controversial. It attracts suspicion in parts of the world that have experienced colonialism and military intervention for less than humanitarian reasons—even if the notional balance in the relationship between sovereignty and human rights has changed. The use of humanitarian arguments to justify the war in Iraq in 2003 certainly does not help the depoliticization of R2P and does little to quell the suspicion. However, parallel with, and indeed prior to, the R2P debate has been another relevant discourse having to do with the protection of civilians (PoC). PoC partially, but not completely, overlaps with R2P. It aims to protect people in the midst of conflict, and has been included in Security Council resolutions mandating peacekeeping operations since 1999. It is separate from debates over military intervention and builds upon a growing consensus about the need to protect civilians from the effects of conflict. While it may contain a military element in the form of peacekeeping, it is very different from R2P since peacekeeping is (generally) more consensual, and PoC has a much wider array of (softer) tools at its disposal.

PoC is understood as a conceptual and operational construct and has a complex relationship with R2P. Like R2P, it has its roots in the failures of the 1990s, but while its evolution has paralleled R2P, it has come to mean something somewhat distinct and more palatable for many countries than R2P.[87] In 1999, Secretary-General Annan stated in his Report of the Secretary-General to the Security Council on the Protection of Civilians in Armed Conflict that PoC "is fundamental to the central mandate of the Organization."[88] In 2004, the Secretary-General, noting that PoC had already been included in a number of peacekeeping operations, called for "the rapid deployment of a force to protect civilians."[89] The connection to peacekeeping is key since it is the context of peacekeeping that makes PoC more palatable than R2P for many UN member states.

The Security Council first engaged with the protection of civilians debate in 1999 when it passed Resolution 1265. It followed this up with Resolutions 1674 in 2006 and 1894 in 2009, which were much stronger in both their condemnation of violence against civilians and the stated willingness to act. The UN General Assembly's Special Committee on Peacekeeping, known as the C-34, agreed to include a PoC subsection in its annual report.[90]

The debate over, and application of, PoC has been particularly prominent in the DRC. However, we must start with the multiple interpretations of PoC. The standard starting point is the definition of protection used by the ICRC, which has been adopted by the UN Inter-Agency Standing Committee (IASC), the body created by the General Assembly to coordinate UN and non-UN humanitarian actors: "Protection is defined as all activities aimed at obtaining full respect for the rights of the individual in accordance with the letter and spirit of the relevant bodies of law, namely human rights law, international humanitarian law and refugee law."[91] This is very broad and encompasses a wide variety of activities, which, according to the ICRC, include responsive activities—those which directly respond to an abuse; remedial action—restoring dignity and living conditions; and environment-building—creating an environment where individuals can enjoy their full panoply of rights. This is so broad as to be meaningless. It is, in one sense, coterminus with the global human rights project. How it is interpreted and implemented is key. The definition from the Office for the Coordination of Humanitarian Assistance (OCHA) adapts this broad understanding:

A concept that encompasses all activities aimed at obtaining full respect for the rights of the individual in accordance with the letter and spirit of human rights, refugee and international humanitarian law. Protection involves creating an environment conducive to respect for human beings, preventing and/or alleviating the immediate effects of a specific pattern of abuse, and restoring dignified conditions of life through reparation, restitution and rehabilitation.[92]

This definition was accepted by the UN Mission in Sudan (UNMIS) in the draft UNMIS POC Strategy-Security Concept.[93] The understanding of what this means for UNMIS is narrowed a bit in the Concept:

> The full gamut of POC is very wide. UNMIS is taking a layered approach to developing an UNMIS-specific POC strategy. Three layers of protection will be covered in the strategy: protection of civilians under imminent threat of physical violence; protection of civilians with regard to securing access to humanitarian and relief activities; and the longer-term aspect of protection in the context of Human Rights (HR) and Conflict Prevention and Management. *This concept covers the inner layer of POC within the UNMIS POC Strategy—the protection of civilians under imminent threat of violence.* . . . Sexual, gender or child violence will not be treated separately in this Concept as they are all forms of "physical violence."

Thus, while still broad, it focuses more on physical protection, but also on protecting humanitarian activities. It is also tied into broader political goals of conflict management and protection. At the end it also points to a key issue in the context of the development of PoC, namely that particular groups have also been singled out for protection treatment in various UN resolutions—for example, women[94] and children.[95]

PoC language was included in the mandate of ten[96] UN peacekeeping operations between 1999 and 2009, and an additional six[97] UN-sanctioned operations led by regional organizations or individual states.[98] This language frequently includes admonitions for peacekeepers "to protect civilians under imminent threat of physical violence" and to provide a "safe and secure environment."[99] The mandate frequently also includes the caveat "without prejudice to the responsibility of the host state."[100] This indicates the relationship of PoC to the core of UN peacekeeping and in particular that peacekeeping relies on the consent of the host state to operate. When the state does not facilitate the creation of a secure environment for its citizens by protecting them, or when it carries out violence itself against its citizens, PoC can be severely undermined. This highlights a key difference between R2P and PoC. While R2P is about protecting civilians, the tools available to decision makers under the heading of R2P are potentially more robust than with PoC. Under R2P, the UN can authorize the use of force against the wishes of a state, as was done in Libya. PoC relies on the consent and cooperation of the host state. There is frequently confusion about the status of PoC in the peacekeeping mandate. Even when robust Chapter VII language is included that allows the use of force—"all necessary means"—the intent of Security Council is not always clear, and frequently commanders in the field see the Chapter VII language as an add-on that fits uncomfortably with a Chapter VI core. The fact that peacekeepers have to maintain relationships with multiple partners, including the state, makes using robust force problematic. This has been a particular issue in Darfur, where the government has placed severe restrictions on peacekeepers that interfere with the PoC mandate. This is not surprising, given that it is the government that is either carrying out or supporting a large part of the violence, but it highlights the problematic nature of PoC in the context of peacekeeping. Further, peacekeepers are frequently not given the tools they need to carry out such robust action. Nor is it frequently clear to those commanders on the ground exactly *how* they are supposed to carry out their PoC mandate, since there is no operational guidance from the Security Council for what PoC actually means.[101]

Yet, as noted, there is a consensus within the UN regarding PoC. Because of this consensus, and the fact that it has a somewhat independent lineage from, and different connotations than, R2P, it is easier to talk about in the Security Council and other diplomatic exchanges. UN humanitarian agencies, such as UNHCR and OCHA, use the terminology of PoC rather than R2P because it describes better what they do and also seems to take politics out of the equation. Likewise, humanitarian NGOs will frequently also engage more with the PoC terminology, even when talking about R2P situations, because it makes conversation with states easier and less threatening. Humanitarian organizations may also not see the value added of R2P over PoC or the relevance of R2P to their activities. As many humanitarians will point out, PoC has been around for a while, and the protection activities they engage in do not fall under R2P. They perceive PoC as nonpolitical,[102] or at least argue that PoC can be deployed nonpolitically, whereas R2P cuts to the core of issues related to sovereignty—issues they do not want to point to, even if their work raises significant issues of sovereignty. R2P is seen as not useful, and there is significant wariness about the equation of PoC and R2P, even as many PoC activities are being repackaged as R2P.[103] R2P is perceived as a Security Council concern, or something that happens in New York, whereas the more Geneva-centric humanitarian community sees PoC as much more relevant.[104] Some humanitarians can also be cynical and note that many concepts and developments do not actually result in much, and so they try to stay out of the entire debate.[105]

Even though PoC may be portrayed as apolitical, it is still political since it deals with highly charged political situations, but it appears to *depoliticize* situations. In some situations, this may be positive since it allows states to talk about concrete measures to protect people without getting caught in the high politics of sovereignty. On the other hand, these situations *are* political and require political response at the highest levels, and thus PoC might undermine the debates that need to happen within the R2P framework. Further, to the extent PoC is seen as something that happens in the context of peacekeeping, it can be an impediment to genuine *protection* in the sense of physically protecting people under imminent threat of harm. If a peace-keeping commander needs to get the permission of the host state to fly helicopters—assuming he or she has been given helicopters and other requi-site tools in the first place—his or her ability to deploy troops when and where needed to respond to that imminent threat is severely compromised. While R2P is less accepted as a political, legal, and operational concept, it does bring an element of robustness that is lacking in most peacekeeping PoC mandates and, more important, practice.

Complementary or Conflicting Responsibilities?

I have outlined above the main human rights and humanitarian tools and concepts the international community has to respond to mass atrocities and associated humanitarian crises. In one sense, they all derive from the concep-tual and practical developments in the human rights and international human-itarian law regimes over perhaps the last 150 years, but in particular the last seventy years. They all have the same goal—to protect lives. One might assume, then, that they are mutually supporting. That is, the implementation of one would support the implementation of another. As we will see, however, this is not necessarily the case. Indeed, applying one or more of these responses may, in fact, get in the way of, or undermine, other responses. Further, having re-course to one may provide an excuse to diplomats and policymakers not to implement another response that may be more effective. In this section, I will briefly outline some of the conundrums faced by practitioners (see Table 1.1).

Humanitarianism, even in its most basic palliative form, can save lives. Yet, it cannot end the conflicts that lead to atrocities. This requires political action. Nor can humanitarianism save lives in all circumstances—particularly when parties to a conflict have as their goal, or significant tactic, to kill civil-ians or drive them out of their territory. Yet, as we shall see, the presence of humanitarians on the ground can give the illusion of adequate response when, in fact, the response is far from adequate. More robust action may be required, but the mere presence of humanitarians may reduce pressure on states to act.

Thus, palliation reduces the prospects for protection. However, with rights-based humanitarianism, humanitarian actors themselves may be highlighting human rights abuses and calling for further action. This can put pressure on states to take further action, but it can also make their positions as humanitarian actors more precarious. They may either be targeted by parties to the conflict or kicked out of the country by the government, thus reducing or eliminating their ability to provide food and other resources to victims of conflict. As a result, people may die from malnutrition or lack of medical care. So the question becomes whether the greater good of a possible (if unlikely) humanitarian intervention to stop a conflict or more robustly protect civilians from attack is outweighed by the almost certain death of more people because of a lack of humanitarian assistance. This is a rather difficult decision to make. Most NGOs, because of their innate humanitarian ethos and mission, will choose to stay, although on occasion they have decided that they are doing more harm than good, thus violating the "do no harm" principle. There may thus be a negative symbiotic relationship between palliation and protection (notwithstanding humanitarian claims to protection). Palliation saves lives, but it is also significantly limited in what it can actually achieve in protecting people from violence.[106] It can also, at times, contribute to the continuation of a conflict, and it also provides a smokescreen for states who do not want to intervene. Calling for intervention might bring further long-term protection, although that is far from certain; it is more likely to reduce the humanitarian assistance available to victims of conflict.

Prosecution can punish people for their crimes. However, inserting prosecution into the middle of a conflict can have unforeseen consequences and require difficult trade-offs. The most obvious is that potential prosecution can have an impact on peace negotiations, with the very unhumanitarian impact of prolonging the conflict. Combatants with arrest warrants against them may be less likely to come to an accommodation, knowing what possible fate might await them. Such international action might also interfere with domestic efforts to institute amnesty laws that might contribute to peace processes and postconflict reconciliation. States that have become a party to the ICC[107] no longer have complete autonomy in domestic criminal affairs. At the same time, they may try to use the ICC for their own domestic purposes as a weapon in the conflict.

Furthermore, the ICC poses difficult questions and danger for both palliators and protectors. For palliators, who may have significant information that could be of use to prosecutors,[108] they are posed with the same question vis-à-vis intervention. Do they release the information, exposing the crimes, or pass it on to the prosecutors, thus helping to ensure that perpetrators face justice—an outcome which pretty much all palliators would support[109]—or do they keep silent? Eric Dachy puts it starkly: "either we compromise our ability to aid victims by testifying, or we protect criminals in order to continue to provide assistance."[110] The former action might further one *human rights* goal, but it could also imperil their activities, as they are branded as informers and targeted or kicked out of the country, thus undermining their *humanitarian* mission. Most IHOs will follow the latter course of action for this reason, although they may quietly pass information to human rights organizations, which can thus use it for their advocacy activities. This creates a division of labor, which could have positive outcomes—the information gets out, while humanitarian organizations are not recognized as the source of the information.

In addition, ICC action might negatively affect humanitarians, even when they have no connection to the action. They can be tarred with the same brush as *human rights* actors. Some parties to a conflict might see them as all part of the group of *internationals*, and blame *humanitarians* for the actions of their *human rights* brethren, thus imperiling their actions. More generally, with the development of individual criminal responsibility, combatants have an interest in ensuring that there are no witnesses to their atrocities, including humanitarians, and thus may want to deny them access to protect themselves.[111] The ICRC has been granted a specific exemption in the Rome Statute from being called to testify,[112] although NGOs have not. During the Rome Statute preparatory meetings, Médecins sans Frontières (MSF) specifically did not request such an exemption, seeing such action as part of its *témoignage* (witnessing). At the same time, it did not want to be one of the "informal auxiliaries to the justice process" where it participated in a formal evidence gathering function (leaving that, instead, to human rights NGOs).[113] Or, as will be seen, they can be used as pawns in other ways.

Also, as with palliation, prosecution can create an excuse not to intervene and protect. It is one more action that can demonstrate that states are doing "something" while not necessarily taking the action required to protect people and stop the fighting. While this should certainly not deter the prosecutors from doing their jobs, the mere fact of the existence of the ICC and other international criminal justice mechanisms can contribute to a more complicated and complex global geopolitical context in which decisions on how to respond to mass atrocities are taken. Although, in some cases, such as Syria, which lies at the heart of extremely complicated global geopolitical dynamics and which engages directly with conflicting great power interests, there is no appetite for even the ICC.

Finally, to come full circle, R2P and related PoC protection activities can have multiple possible outcomes, which may have positive or negative consequences for humanitarianism and human rights. A military intervention might just succeed and end the fighting, which in turn creates space for a political settlement. We have seen precious few of these cases. It might provide a presence, for a time, that has a significant protective effect. These situations are slightly more numerous, but the issue always becomes the will to continue the action, particularly if the interveners take increasing numbers of casualties.[114] The intervention might also provide space for the humanitarians to do their job and deliver humanitarian assistance—although the issue of the staying power of the intervention forces will become an issue. These are all possible positive effects. But an intervention might have negative consequences. It might imperil the humanitarian mission. It might create incentives for certain parties, in particular rebel groups, to become more intransigent or otherwise encourage them, thus prolonging a conflict.[115] It can also lead to civilian casualties. It must be recognized from the start of any R2P action that civilian casualties are inevitable. There are ways to mitigate this and reduce the potential for dead civilians. Yet, all too often, the interveners do not want to take such actions, at least partly because it may imperil their own troops. This was illustrated all too clearly in Kosovo, where NATO restricted itself to high-altitude bombing of Serb positions, rather than exposing their airplanes to antiaircraft fire or the dangers of putting troops on the ground, which would inevitably have led to NATO casualties. As a result, more civilians were killed than might have been the case otherwise. Humanitarians thus need to keep this in mind when advocating for intervention.

We thus have a very complicated relationship between these three sets of responsibilities and associated practices. The choices made by decision makers and actors on the ground are difficult and complex. While the three responsibilities—protection, prosecution, and palliation—all come from the same broad human rights and humanitarian project, their efficacy and eventual impacts are such that they are not necessarily mutually reinforcing. Rather, they may at times undermine each other—either intentionally or unintentionally.

Furthermore, the question of how best to protect those affected by mass atrocity situations and associated humanitarian crises is difficult to answer. Palliation saves lives; yet, in the most extreme circumstances, it cannot

Table 1.1. Responsibility Conundrums

	Protectors	*Prosecutors*	*Palliators*
Protection	+protect people +end fighting −civilian casualties −incentives to prolong conflict	+deter abuses −reduce prospects of intervention	+work with protectors to deliver assistance +highlight abuses and need for protection −create illusion of protection −reduce prospects of intervention −contribute to continuation of conflict
Prosecution	+increase pressure to surrender/arrest −undermine efforts to apprehend	+punish perpetrators +uphold human rights/rule of law −undermine peace processes −prolong conflict −used as weapon	+support human rights −focused on assistance rather than prosecution
Palliation	+support humanitarian assistance −endanger humanitarian assistance	+protect humanitarians −endanger humanitarian assistance	+keep people alive −well-fed dead −open to manipulation −contribute to continuation of conflict

protect individuals from government troops, warlords, paramilitaries, or rebel forces. Prosecution punishes criminals; yet it might also make peace negotiations more difficult. And, in the absence of evidence of a significant deterrent effect, it cannot be claimed to protect people in harm's way. Robust R2P activities can physically protect people, but it can also endanger them. There is also little appetite on the part of those who could protect to actually do so in most situations. It is thus a very unsure route to protection. All three of these responsibilities have a role to play in assistance and protecting those affected by widespread violent conflict and human rights abuses. The issue, as always, comes down to political will to choose and implement the most appropriate response(s), although this will is in little evidence in too many situations.

CHAPTER 2

Rwanda: The Failure of "Never Again"

We in the United States and the world community did
not do as much as we could have and should have done
to try to limit what occurred in Rwanda in 1994. . . . We
must have global vigilance. And never again must we
be shy in the face of evidence.

We will not deny that, in their greatest hour of need, the
world failed the people of Rwanda.

The genocide in Rwanda in 1994, which claimed around 800,000 lives, illustrated the failures of the international community in the post-Cold War
world. Yet, as much as anything, it was the response that did occur—and in
particular the role of humanitarian action—combined with this failure and
the resulting conflict in neighboring Zaire, which was an even more significant
legacy. As will be clear, it is difficult to address the first two conflicts that are
the subject of the present and following chapters—Rwanda and DRC/Zaire—
separately. To a significant extent, one begat the other. Rwanda, which was
ignored by the international community, became the watchword for "never
again!" while DRC/Zaire exists below the global radar, even though the death
and devastation eclipses the Rwandan genocide.

This chapter will briefly discuss the origins of the genocide in Rwanda
and the global context in which the genocide occurred. It will examine how
the failure of the international community to respond to the genocide and
adequately deal with the humanitarian and security aftermath led directly
to the conflict in the DRC/Zaire. It will look at how the emerging responsibilities played out. It was failure in Rwanda that helped set the scene for the

development of R2P. Yet before R2P there was the "never again" norm, which structured how the international community talked about the genocide, even if it had little effect on the response. The creation of the International Criminal Tribunal for Rwanda helped set the scene for the eventual establishment of the ICC, but in Rwanda demonstrated the problematic nature of international justice mechanisms. But it was the humanitarian response that led to much soul-searching on the part of humanitarians and raised significant questions about the role of humanitarianism in the midst of conflict.

Heading Toward Genocide

The early 1990s were a period of hope internationally. The Cold War had ended, the UN was no longer deadlocked, conflicts such as those in Namibia and Mozambique were being settled, and the UN began to flex its muscles a bit more as it expanded peacekeeping operations around the world. Yet this optimism was soon dashed as the UN failed for three years to adequately address the spreading conflict in the former Yugoslavia and also failed to bring to an end the fighting in Somalia, which began in 1991 and continues to this day. The Rwandan genocide has been covered in exhaustive detail elsewhere.[1] Rather than going over old ground, the discussion below will highlight details that are salient for the ensuing analysis of competing responsibilities and pinpoint how the international community's failure to deal with the genocide and its aftermath led directly to a much bigger crisis.

In the late nineteenth and early twentieth centuries Rwanda was controlled by Germany. After World War II, control of Rwanda was transferred to Belgium. As part of their strategy to control the population, the Belgians manipulated and reified previously fluid identities, resulting in two major groups—the minority Tutsi who ruled over the majority Hutu (as well as a much smaller group of Twa). Rwanda has experienced multiple instances of genocide and other conflict since it became independent of Belgium in 1962. Many Tutsi fled the country, in fear of the Hutu majority regime that took power at independence. Genocide occurred in 1963, and more Tutsi fled to neighboring countries—in particular Uganda—with more fleeing in 1972. In 1973, Juvénal Habyarimana, a Hutu, took power in a coup.[2]

In 1990, Tutsi militants in the Rwandan Patriotic Front (RPF)—many of whom had been trained and incorporated into the Ugandan military—invaded Rwanda. This failed, at least partly because France and Zaire sent

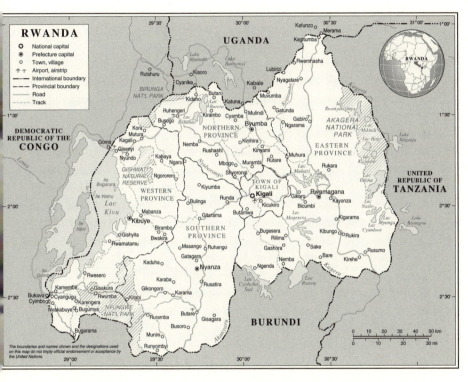

Map 2. Rwanda, Map No. 3717 Rev. 10, June 2008. United Nations.

forces to protect the government. Killing of Tutsi followed, as did further in-cursions from Uganda.[3] An RPF attack in February 1993 led to renewed ne-gotiations in Arusha, Tanzania, eventually resulting in a peace agreement (the Arusha Accords) and the creation, later in 1993, of a UN peacekeeping mission—the UN Mission in Rwanda (UNAMIR), led by Canadian general Roméo Dallaire.[4] General Dallaire had originally planned for 8,000 troops, although the eventual number agreed on was 2,548. This was due to reluc-tance on the part of the United States and UK to fund yet another mission, with 80,000 troops in 17 UN peacekeeping missions already deployed, and with the U.S. responsible for one-third of the peacekeeping bill. Furthermore, the failure of the U.S. in Somalia made the U.S.—and the UN—more skit-tish about robust peace operations. They were worried about crossing the "Mogadishu Line" from peacekeeping to peace enforcement. Both UN and U.S. reviews of peacekeeping led to criteria that would constrain the use of force in UN operations, and thus delimited the possible boundaries of UN peacekeeping operations, including Rwanda.[5] The U.S. initially wanted a to-ken force of 500 troops, but eventually relented to a certain extent, allowing a large, but still inadequate, force to be created.[6] The mandate of the mission was to support the transition to democratic governance. However, UNAMIR was severely underequipped and undersupported from the start, lacking a full complement of troops, key equipment such as helicopters and armored personnel carriers, desks, and chairs, and money to pay the troops.[7]

On 11 January 1994, Gen. Dallaire sent a cable to the Secretary-General's military adviser in New York, informing him that the Hutu leadership was planning to engage in mass killings against the Tutsi population,[8] and indi-cating that he intended to seize weapons being stockpiled for the genocide.[9] He was told not to undertake this activity, and the cable disappeared into the ether.[10] UNAMIR's second in command, Luc Marchal, said the "Mogadishu Syndrome"—the reluctance to engage in robust peacekeeping activities in the wake of the disastrous U.S. mission in Somalia in 1993 (also known as the "Somalia Syndrome")—explained this inaction.[11] On 3 February, Dallaire was told that he could *monitor* action by the police to investigate reports of, and seize, arms caches. He would have to inform the government, and since mem-bers of the government were complicit in the planned genocide, they were given plenty of warning of any operations, and the arms caches were never found.[12] He also informed U.S., French, and Belgian diplomats. The first two countries dismissed the threat, while Belgium argued for more robust pre-ventive measures, which came to nought.[13]

Three months later, on 6 April 1994, President Habyarimana's plane was shot down. There is great speculation as to who was responsible; most point to Hutu militants,[14] although Tutsi leader Paul Kagame has also been accused.[15] Kagame was cleared in a 2012 French report.[16] This event provided the shock that started the genocide. The killing of Tutsi by Hutu extremists—the *interahamwe*—started immediately. On 7 April ten Belgian peacekeepers, who had been sent to protect the prime minster, were killed. Belgium decided to pull out its peacekeepers on 12 April.[17] There were calls in the Security Council to pull UNAMIR out entirely,[18] even though Dallaire had asked for more troops to reinforce his dwindling force. At one point he estimated that 4,000 troops would have been sufficient to stop the killing and protect hundreds of thousands of lives.[19] On 10 April he requested 5,000 troops and a more robust mandate. By this time, while not using the word genocide, he realized that widespread crimes against humanity were being carried out, with 50,000 people killed in four days.[20] An independent report looking back at the events argued that 5,000 troops could have saved 500,000 lives, more than half the estimated 800,000 killed in the ensuing three months.[21] Indeed, nineteen years later, President Clinton admitted that the United States could have saved at least 300,000 people if it had intervened.[22] The president of the Security Council that month, Colin Keating from New Zealand, appealed for a robust response.[23] Reports were sent by Gen. Dallaire and others detailing the killing.[24]

The pleas fell on deaf ears. Iqbal Riza, deputy to Department of Peacekeeping Operations (DPKO) head Kofi Annan, questioned whether peacekeepers should be involved in protecting civilians.[25] The U.S. had little interest in Rwanda, which was strategically unimportant. It did not want to send in its own troops, and it did not want to fund yet another expanded peacekeeping operation with a much more robust enforcement mandate. Not wanting to commit to anything, it indicated from the beginning that the UN was the best place to address the situation. At the UN, it argued for pulling out of UNAMIR.[26] The UK, too, was little interested.[27] The French, who were deeply implicated in supporting the Habyarimana regime and had strategic and culture interests in Rwanda, did not want to support any action that might in the end support the English-speaking RPF, which had immediately entered the country to stop the genocide of its co-ethnics.[28] Western countries did, however, send in forces to evacuate foreigners, a task with which UNAMIR had been authorized to assist.[29] On 13 April, the RPF sent a message to the president of the Security Council describing the situation as genocide,[30] invoking the Holocaust.[31] Nigeria, which sat on the Security Council, wanted UNAMIR to be able to act more robustly, a suggestion that went nowhere.[32]

The Security Council took its first action on 21 April. It did not withdraw UNAMIR. Neither did it reinforce it. Rather, it decided to draw UNAMIR down to a force of 250 troops to negotiate a cease-fire, assist humanitarian operations, and "monitor and report on developments in Rwanda."[33] Observe is what it mostly did. With so few troops and a weak mandate, its hands were tied. The members of the Security Council were well aware of the implications of their (in)action.[34]

After the genocide, there were denials from U.S. and other officials that they knew what was going on at the time—a denial repeated by President Clinton four years later during his apology to Rwanda[35]—although it was revealed in 2004 that the Clinton administration was aware of a " 'final solution to eliminate all Tutsis' " significantly before the genocide began.[36] Alan Kuperman argues that the earliest President Clinton could have known that genocide was occurring was 20 April.[37] While this may or may not be true, what is true, first, is that diplomats and policymakers in a number of important countries and the UN knew there was widespread killing happening that beyond "mere" political killings—crimes against humanity. Second, President Clinton—and other leaders—did not ask the questions necessary to determine exactly what was going on. President Clinton never convened senior advisers to discuss the situation.[38] Third, there was a concerted effort to avoid the term genocide.[39] When asked whether genocide was happening in Rwanda, a U.S. State Department spokesperson indicated (weeks later, on 10 June) that "acts of genocide" had occurred,[40] even though the U.S. National Intelligence Daily for 23 April, a classified document that would have been distributed to several hundred government officials—and thus contained information which Clinton would have had access to—noted an " 'effort to stop the genocide, which relief workers say is spreading south.' "[41] Oxfam used the word genocide on 28 April in a public statement,[42] and by the end of April, Dallaire was using the term.[43] The ICRC issued a statement indicating that " 'whole families are exterminated . . . the cruelty knows no limits,' "[44] claiming that 100,000, and as many as 300,000, people had been killed.[45] Amazingly, Rwanda was allowed to keep its seat on the Security Council and participate in discussions. On 29 April, Ambassador Keating, along with ambassadors from Argentina, Spain, and the Czech Republic, tried to get the Security Council to release a statement indicating that genocide was occurring.[46] On 17 May the Security Council passed Resolution 918, which used the language of the Genocide Convention but did not use the term genocide itself.

This is a clear indication of the force of the word. If one uses awkward verbal constructions such as "acts of genocide" or refuses to use the "G word" altogether, one is obviously trying to avoid the implications of using the word. To use the word would be to acknowledge responsibility—which would bring one under pressure to act. Indeed, as a paper prepared by the Office of the U.S. Secretary of Defense stated on 1 May: "*Be careful. Legal at State was worried about this* [using the term genocide] *yesterday—Genocide finding could commit* [the U.S. government] *to actually 'do something'.*"[47] Although a State Department spokesperson indicated that the Genocide Convention did not have an "'absolute requirement'" to intervene, there was worry that this was the expectation. Here we see the clear working of the "never again" norm, the precursor to R2P. U.S. policy-makers felt there would be an expectation on the part of the public that the U.S. would live up to this perceived requirement. This was the last thing they wanted to do. So they manipulated and twisted words. The norm put pressure on policy-makers to act, but the action they took was perverse. The situation was denied, obfuscatory language was used, responsibilities were avoided. The "never again" norm was so powerful that when this norm collided with perceived state interests, policy-makers denied reality. There was recognition that people were being killed in Rwanda, but it was put down to civil war, tribalism, political killings, deep-seated ethnic hatred—in other words, the usual story from Africa.[48] But instead of making the case to stop the killing, the Genocide Convention was used to prevent such action. As long as the situation was not called genocide, there was no political downside to not reacting. Such is the status of genocide as the über crime that all other crimes can be made to pale in comparison. The Genocide Convention provides a shield against having to take action against "lesser" crimes. On June 10, the same day as the infamous "acts of genocide" briefing by a State Department spokesperson, Secretary of State Warren Christopher finally said that "If there is any particular magic in calling it genocide, I have no hesitancy in saying that."[49] Indeed, there is magic in the term, and it can be stripped of its power by the simple act of avoiding the term.

The media did little to put pressure on the Security Council to act. It was portrayed as tribalism—age-old ethnic hatreds which flared up periodically and which the international community could do little about.[50] Even when the *New York Times* identified it as genocide on 23 April, it concluded that little could be done.[51] The *Guardian* agreed.[52] Other newspapers had little interest in covering the story as a result of "compassion fatigue."[53] As Edward Girardet argues, "it took the concept of genocide"—again that magical incantation—"the deliberate destruction of human life based on ethnic, racial, or religious discrimination—to convince most editors finally to cover the story."[54] Even this less than helpful coverage was short-lived. The momentous elections in South Africa, which signaled the end of apartheid, took place and the world's press corps moved en masse to South Africa to cover the elections and the inauguration of Nelson Mandela.[55]

At the same time, the Pentagon discussed the possibility of blocking the the broadcasts of Radio Mille Collines, which had been advocating and facilitating the genocide. This would not have stopped the genocide, but it might have slowed it down. But even this was too much; instead, one senior Pentagon official advocated for contributing to food relief.[56] On 4 May UN Secretary-General Boutros Boutros-Ghali called Rwanda a genocide, calling for intervention.[57] On 11 May the ICRC delegate in Rwanda, Philippe Gaillard, told the UN High Commissioner for Human Rights that 250,000 people had been killed.[58] On 13 May, Gen. Dallaire submitted a report to the Security Council asking for an additional 5,500 troops.[59] This was authorized four days later, with a mandate to protect civilians.[60] This was just authorization; deployment depended upon a further report by the Secretary-General. Ambassador Keating called the resolution a "sham."[61] Indeed, UNAMIR II would not be deployed until after the genocide had ended and the RPF had taken control.[62]

On 24 May, the French minister for human rights, Lucette Michaux-Chevry, used the term genocide.[63] On the same day Warren Christopher finally authorized use of the term genocide—if in an incoherent, muddled way.[64] A report by the Secretary-General to the Security Council finally recognized Rwanda as genocide.[65] This, however, did not lead to any swifter response. Dallaire wanted to create safe areas in Rwanda to protect civilians. The United States wanted to engage in "outside-in" protection—creating safe areas on the borders with Rwanda, thus obviating the need for military intervention in an ongoing genocide.[66] The U.S. offered fifty armored personnel carriers (APCs) stored in Turkey. However, they arrived after the genocide ended without guns, radios, manuals, and spare parts. The UK offered old trucks in return for a significant amount of money (the demand for money was eventually rescinded).[67]

The one even somewhat robust military response came, eventually, from the French. Through its Opération Turquoise it deployed in excess of 2,500 highly trained troops from the French Foreign Legion. This was completely separate from UNAMIR—indeed, there was little consultation with Gen. Dallaire.[68] France got the go-ahead from the Security Council on 22 June—after the vast majority of people had been killed. The week before, Foreign Minister Alain Juppé said, "We have a real duty to intervene in Rwanda. . . . France is ready, with its main European and African partners, to prepare an intervention on the ground to put an end to the massacres and protect the populations threatened with extermination. . . . France will live up to its responsibilities."[69]

The question was which responsibilities he was talking about—those found in the Genocide Convention and the "never again" norm, or France's ties to its Hutu clients? This was not made any clearer by Prime Minister Édouard Balladur when he stated, just days before the RPF took power, that "France has sent its soldiers out of a moral duty to act without delay in order to stop the genocide and provide immediate assistance to the threatened populations."[70] It went in with lots of firepower—firepower Dallaire could have used earlier to protect people. Rather than going to areas where Tutsi were being slaughtered, the French went to areas where Hutu were being threatened by advancing RPF soldiers. While Prunier argues that perhaps 13,000–14,000 people were saved by Opération Turquoise,[71] the action had little to do with stopping people from being killed in a genocide. Rather, it was about supporting a long-time ally. By protecting Hutu areas, the French troops protected the *génocidaires* and allowed them to escape to neighboring countries.[72]

The RPF took Kigali on 4 July and declared a unilateral cease-fire on 20 July. The genocide was over. The international community had done nothing to stop it. This fact, and the manner in which it was ended, ultimately resulted in an even larger human conflagration in Rwanda's next-door neighbor, Zaire.

Could the Genocide Have Been Stopped?

There is a debate about what the UN and states could have actually done to prevent or stop the genocide. A report to the Carnegie Commission on the Prevention of Deadly Conflict argued that 5,000 troops "could have made a significant difference in Rwanda." The most pessimistic analysis, by Kuperman, argues that because of limitations in airlift capability, the international community could only have reacted fast enough to save at most 125,000 lives—calculated as 25 percent of an estimated 500,000 people killed.[73] There were plenty of warning signs that the situation was unstable and significant violence was possible. When UNAMIR was first created, the UN Security Council could have authorized a larger force with a more robust mandate. This would have required the agreement of Rwanda. A reflection of the "Somalia Syndrome" and a more cautious approach to peacekeeping and associated activities was to be found in Presidential Decision Directive 25[74] signed by President Clinton just weeks after the genocide began. The United States wanted to reduce the percentage of UN peacekeeping expenses it paid, indicating a financial imperative in limiting the extent of UN peacekeeping—and also more restrictive criteria for when the U.S. would support—and participate in—Chapter VI and Chapter VII operations.[75] Support by the U.S. and other countries for a large operation was not forthcoming. Michael Barnett argues that there were three other moments when the international community failed to act when it could have to prevent the massive loss of life: (1) when UN headquarters declined to allow UNAMIR to take more robust action against those suspected of planning a genocide; (2) failure of the Secretariat to provide significant information in its possession and argue for an early intervention based on that information; (3) Security Council refusal to authorize action in the weeks in April immediately after the genocide started.[76]

Once UNAMIR began to be deployed, other warning signs became apparent. The 11 January "genocide cable" was only one of many points where relevant information was made available to the UN and other actors. This cable was shared with the ambassadors from the United States, France, and Belgium. Dallaire provided other information to UN headquarters. He was finally given the go-ahead to search for weapons, but given the restrictive terms of UNAMIR's mandate, including that any such operations be done in cooperation with the police, few weapons were found. Again, the UN could have acted more forcefully on early warning information to prevent the genocide, but it did not. There was not sufficient interest on the part of key players.

Once the killing started, it was not possible to ignore the killing itself, but there were strenuous efforts to avoid recognizing the import of the killings. Portraying the killings as part of a civil war or age-old tribal hatreds seemed to make it "normal," just one of those things that happens in Africa periodically. Beefing up UNAMIR would entail crossing the Mogadishu Line. Yet we also perhaps see the first glimmers of the working of the "never again" norm. This norm identifies genocide as the most egregious of all international crimes and creates pressure to act. The verbal contortions used to avoid using the term genocide represent simultaneously the moral pressure to intervene and the unwillingness on the part of most of the global power elite to actually do so. It was only once the term genocide started to be uttered from the mouths of those representing the major powers that there was discussion and action toward putting a beefed-up force into place, although the West was able to avoid any meaningful action since UNAMIR II was not deployed until August, and without proper support. The French Opération Turquoise, rather than reflecting the "never again" norm, was a reflection of pure national interest. The intervention came too late and was focused on protecting French allies. The French use of "never again" rhetoric illustrates the power of the norm—not to force timely action to stop genocide, but rather to enable non-normatively based action—that is, to serve as a cover for other action. It is only in the aftermath of the genocide that international norms began to peer above the parapet—if only briefly.

From Genocide to Humanitarian Crisis

By the time the genocide ended, the focus had moved from the genocide itself to the humanitarian aftermath. If the international community did not seem interested in stopping 800,000 people from being killed, it was much more worried about the large numbers of refugees generated by the conflict. The humanitarian crisis illustrated the dilemmas and dangers of responding to large-scale humanitarian situations.

The first mass exodus of refugees occurred in late April when 170,000 people fled to Ngara in western Tanzania in twenty-four hours. They kept fleeing, with an additional 500,000–800,000 fleeing to North Kivu in eastern Zaire on 14–17 July, after the RPF had taken control of most of the country.[77] These refugees were not Tutsi fleeing the Hutu *génocidaires*, however. Rather, they were Hutu fleeing the oncoming RPF fighters. In the end, more than two million Hutu refugees fled Rwanda to escape the RPF. About half of these fled to eastern Zaire, with the rest spread among neighboring countries—in particular Tanzania and Burundi.

These Hutus included *génocidaires*—those who had participated in the mass slaughter—and many ordinary Rwandans who played no role in the genocide. The reason why the former group fled is obvious—they feared what would happen to them if the Tutsi RPF caught up with them. The second group had more, and more complex, reasons for leaving. First, some, like refugees around the world, simply fled the brutal fighting. Second, they were afraid the RPF would indiscriminately go after any and all Hutu. This fear was exacerbated by propaganda put out by the *génocidaires*. Third, many Hutu were forced into refugeehood by their fellow Hutu, to serve as shields for the leaders who planned and executed the genocide. They were intimidated by the *génocidaires*. Further, the refugees stayed as a result of a defining feature of Rwandan society—pervasive top-down control and decision- making. The individuals were not used to making decisions on an individual basis; rather, decisions were made for them, as part of a group.[78] This combination of factors led to one of the central dilemmas of the crisis. How should humanitarians deal with humanitarian action that could possibly prolong or expand a conflict, or, alternatively, be used as an excuse for others not to engage in actions that address the situation?

Supporting Hope, Covering Up Inaction or
Supporting Génocidaires?

Although the United States was loath to be involved in, or support, any effort to stop the genocide or protect civilians during the genocide, it did participate in a very significant—and public—if somewhat short-term, response to the aftermath of the genocide. By late July the story had moved from genocide to cholera. The camps in eastern Zaire were the perfect breeding ground for disease. At least 50,000 people died in Goma, Zaire, within a month after the mass exodus. J. Brian Atwood, the head of the U.S. Agency for International Development, described the situation as "chaos."[79]

Before discussing the actual U.S. response, let us pause to consider the import of these words. Apparently the mass murder of 800,000 people over one hundred days is not worthy of being called chaos, but the same number of people crammed into refugee camps, combined with disease, does rise to this level. The refugees are victims of "chaos." They are not victims of the aftermath of the most intense period of mass killing the world has ever seen. This is the same as saying that "mistakes were made." It passively depoliticizes the situation and avoids apportioning blame or responsibility. "Chaos" has no political antecedent; rather, it is a state of being that apparently arrives fully formed out of nowhere. Refugees died because of "chaos," not because of disease that was the direct result of a mass exodus in the context of a genocide in which the United States and other actors refused to lift a finger. Further, "chaos" acquires a further descriptor—cancer—and the U.S. had arrived to provide palliation and possibly a cure. By preventing the cancer of chaos from spreading, it would prevent further death from the chaos. Yet, returning to the discussion in Chapter 1, we can see that Atwood had the diagnosis wrong. The cancer that was killing refugees was not "chaos"—the apolitical and meaningless term used when one wants to avoid a correct diagnosis. By treating the symptoms of the chaos—the United States and the rest of the world did not even try to treat the "chaos" itself—USAID and the U.S. military were global hospice workers engaged in superficial palliation. They kept some people alive permanently, while others were kept alive for a while, only to die as a result of disease once the hospice workers left, or at the hands of either the Hutu militants who were running the camps or the Tutsi-supported troops who came to eject them.

What did this palliation look like? Operation Support Hope[80] involved 3,000 troops—troops that might have been used earlier to stop the genocide, or might have been used to address the growing insecurity in the camps. Instead, they were used to help provide food and water and shelter. In 1994, the United States spent $231.9 million on humanitarian assistance for the region outside Rwanda (vs. $73.3 million within Rwanda). This assistance amounted to $242.2 million in 1994 and $177.9 million in 1996.[81] The aid was brought in via highly publicized airlifts. On 22 July 1994, five days after the first cases of cholera were reported, President Clinton announced he would send troops to the region to help carry out the humanitarian mission. By the time U.S. troops left Goma on 25 August—just a month after they had arrived—the U.S. military had airlifted in massive amounts of equipment and aid.[82] These actions undoubtedly saved many lives. But even if the war on cholera had been temporarily won by the U.S., as it supported hope, the suffering that was relieved was just a drop in the ocean of the suffering that had occurred and was yet to occur in Zaire.

Operation Support Hope was pure and unadulterated palliation. Given the speed with which the U.S. military responded to provide humanitarian assistance, it could have also deployed to protect people during the genocide. The United States used this very public operation to show the world that it cared and was doing something about the situation in the Great Lakes region. But it was just a mop-up operation, dealing with the loose ends—the "chaos"—after the genocide. Yet, the chaos was decontextualized and depoliticized. Furthermore, although Atwood called for war criminals to be tried, the U.S. troops had no mandate to arrest anyone. It was purely humanitarian: palliation but no prosecution, even though a few months later the U.S. would help set up an international court to try those who participated in the genocide. This palliation without prosecution had a devastating long-term effect. More than one million refugees were still in Zaire. Most would stay there for two more years, allowing growing insecurity to fester.

This large numbers of refugees allowed the approximately 50,000 former Rwandan soldiers of the Forces Armées Rwandaises (FAR) and militia[83] to hide out and organize themselves for a return to Rwanda to retake power. Exile was "the continuation of the war by other means."[84] Former high-ranking officials in the Rwandan government, ex-FAR, and militia controlled the camps, prevented refugees from going back home, and organized the military actions that ultimately destabilized the border area and beyond.[85] The massive refugee camps provided cover for the *génocidaires* and those who wanted to regain power in Rwanda. Thus, a main responsibility for the leaders was to keep the refugees from returning. This task was facilitated in a couple of different ways. It was very hard for individual refugees and families to make the decision to return home, absent such a decision by the leaders, because of the collective decision making in Rwandan society. This situation was further reinforced by the propaganda spread by the leaders, which misrepresented the situation in Rwanda at the time.[86] While the new government might have wanted to marginalize the returning Hutus,[87] it was the Hutu leaders who were in the most danger. Yet, in order to scare the refugees, the situation was made to sound significantly more dangerous than it actually was.

The Rwandan government did not help the situation, however. There were contradictory statements regarding how and when the refugees should return. As the RPF consolidated its hold on power, it seemed that the Hutu population was being systematically marginalized, and the government was not making it easy for the refugees to return.[88] The RPF had engaged in massacres at the end of the war, and as one NGO worker observed, "Bodies appeared regularly in the Kagera River until May 1995, long after the RPF gained control of the country."[89] Further, the Rwandan jails were overflowing with suspected *génocidaires*, and the refugee leaders were able to capitalize on this to demonstrate the danger of returning.[90] They were thus able to maintain and tighten their grip on the camps, which served as the staging ground for destabilization.

Early Efforts to Return the Refugees

Within a couple of months after the refugees left, it was clear to most of the main actors in the region that the refugees needed to return. The camps were likely to become destabilizing. It was also felt that reconciliation would be easier if the refugees returned sooner rather than later because there would be less time for further hate and suspicion of the refugees to develop within Rwanda. The debate revolved around when. UNHCR argued for an early return.[91] On 23 July 1994, High Commissioner for Refugees Sadako Ogata stated that UNHCR wanted to encourage refugees to return.[92] UNHCR offered to take a group of twenty camp leaders from Goma back to Rwanda so they could see for themselves the conditions the refugees would be returning to and report back to the camps. They refused—an indication of the resistance and defiance among the leaders.[93] UNHCR first tried to repatriate refugees from Goma on August 23. This was stopped by the militias and camp leaders. Yet many thousands of refugees did repatriate from Goma during the last part of 1994, accompanied by a Zairian security escort to the border. At the same time, UNHCR suspended its repatriation assistance to Rwanda in September because of alleged human rights abuses there.[94]

Two issues permeated discussions within UNHCR about return. The first was the actual conditions in Rwanda. That is, was it safe for the refugees to go back? Conditions varied throughout the country, UNHCR did not have access to significant portions of Rwanda, and there was much contradictory information. It was thus hard for it to make a firm decision.[95] The second issue was that of the voluntary nature of the return. The principle of voluntary repatriation is generally recognized.[96] Yet, given the situation in the camps and the fact that the refugees, for the most part, were not able to make the decision to repatriate because of the intimidation and violence on the part of the militants, this principle took on new meaning. If the refugees themselves are not able to make the decision whether or not to return, almost by definition any returns, particularly on a large scale, will not be "voluntary."

By October it was clear that the militants were expanding their organization and consolidating their grip over the camps.[97] That month, Ogata said: "The aim [of the camp militants] appears to be to control the refugee population, block their voluntary return to Rwanda and build resistance against the Government in Kigali."[98] By the end of the year, some NGOs pulled out of Goma and Ngara in Tanzania because of the worsening situation. UNHCR considered this, although, as Dennis McNamara, director of the UNHCR Division of International Protection, stated: "the agency's mandate and the humanitarian imperative of caring for the majority of vulnerable and needy civilians, women and children, made a withdrawal impossible."[99] Both MSF France and the International Rescue Committee decided that the consequences of continuing to provide assistance—allowing the militants continued safe haven—overrode the humanitarian imperative.[100] The realization of the effect humanitarians might have turned out to be a significant turning point. While most other organizations stayed—including MSF Holland and MSF UK[101]—the debate about withdrawal highlighted how embedded the humanitarians were in the situation. One official from CARE UK suggested that CARE should continue to provide assistance only if the *génocidaires* were brought to justice, a somewhat naïve position given the reality on the ground in the camps, the lack of international support for separating out the *génocidaires* so they could be arrested, and the sheer number of those to be brought to justice. Another CARE UK official, however, disagreed, focusing solely on feeding people.[102] This also led to a much wider debate about whether or not the humanitarian imperative could be absolute, and whether humanitarians need to focus more on the "do no harm" principle. While the debate at the time varied widely within and among NGOs, Fiona Terry identifies five main justifications used by NGOs to continue their work:

(1) humanitarian imperative;
(2) attempts to affect the way the camps were administered from within and minimize the aid diverted to militants through "résistance humanitaire";
(3) focus on technical issues of relief provision, ignoring ethical issues;
(4) the "institutional logic" of NGOs, which prioritized the media coverage and funding that having a presence in the camps would generate;
(5) sympathy with the Hutu militants, in particular on the part of Catholic organizations.[103]

The obvious first step was to separate out the *génocidaires* and militant leaders from the rest of the population. Various plans to accomplish this were floated as early as mid-August 1994, when the Zairian prime minister requested that 20,000 ex-FAR be relocated away from the border. When family members were included, the total number of people to be relocated climbed to 80–90,000. Identifying all the ex-FAR would have been problematic. This plan would have been very costly, estimated at $90 to $125 million (whereas it was estimated that the solution ultimately adopted cost only about 2 percent of what a full-fledged peacekeeping operation would have).[104] Furthermore, such an undertaking would have entailed deploying a significant number of troops. The international community showed almost no support for this, and by January 1995 the Secretary-General admitted defeat in his attempt to put such a force together. Further, he put the responsibility for addressing the security issue on UNHCR, thus abdicating the responsibility of the UN to maintain international peace and security to its humanitarian arm.[105] The palliators were asked to act as protectors, which of course they could not do.

A lesser option was then pursued—deploying a security force in the camps. Its mandate would not include separating extremists. Rather, its focus would be to maintain security in the camps for the refugees and make sure relief supplies could be distributed unhindered. However, it was hoped that the security force would undermine the hold the extremists had in the camps, making it possible for the refugees to make the decision to go home. This was the main reason UNHCR Goma requested this deployment. UNHCR negotiated with Zaire to create the Zairian Camp Security Contingent (ZCSC). Deployed in February 1995, it was comprised of 1,500 elite Zairian troops and paid for by UNHCR. The Zairian minister of defense referred to them as "'Ogata's troops.'" Yet, they were not, and could not be, under the command of UNHCR. While it could try to exercise influence in how the troops carried out their mandate, the orders came from the government. Obviously, however, the government wanted to be able to place the blame on UNHCR in case anything went wrong.[106] Furthermore, Ogata, as head of a humanitarian agency, did not have a mandate for controlling military forces of any kind. This abdication of its security role by the Security Council highlights the fact that UNHCR, and humanitarian actors more generally, are being called upon to carry out functions that they are not equipped to do and which are the purview of international security actors, like the Security Council. The international community had proven itself incapable of providing the support necessary for humanitarian agencies to carry out their work or, indeed, to obviate the need for humanitarian action in the first place. Furthermore, some felt that the ZCSC was a bad idea, precisely because it was not under UNHCR control, and when the war broke out, some of the troops fought, rather than providing protection to the refugees.[107] Although the ZCSC did arrest a few "small fry" leaders, most leaders, although known to the ZCSC, remained untouched by the force.[108] Further, the Zairian government provided resources to the militants, and rather than undermining their position, worked to strengthen it.[109] Given the lack of support from all quarters to separate the extremists, there seemed little prospect for a quick return of the refugees.[110] A massacre of 2,000 people at the Kibeho internally displaced camp in Rwanda on 22 April 2005 (during which UNAMIR was ordered not to intervene, even though it had a mandate to protect displaced persons) further supported the militant's arguments that it was unsafe to go back.[111]

The first forced repatriation from Zaire occurred in August 1995. A Human Rights Watch report[112] in May 1995 stated that arms were reaching the militants, and Zaire felt implicated. Further, Security Council Resolution 1011 of August 16, lifting the arms embargo against Rwanda, directly contravened Zaire's position in favor of continuing the arms embargo. Consequently, approximately 12,000–15,000 refugees were expelled from the Kivu region to Cyangugu and Gisenyi in Rwanda over several days, beginning 19 August.[113] It is unclear why the repatriations stopped. One senior UNHCR official claims it was the result of international pressure.[114] The head of the UNHCR office in Goma at the time maintains that the repatriation was not seriously supported by the central government and that while it might have instigated the repatriation, the local officials were on their own. Under these conditions, there was no way that the repatriation could be sustained, and on 20 August the forcible returns ended.[115]

Although the forced repatriation was condemned as a violation of human rights, and UNHCR could not support it because it contravened its mandate and other international law, some palliators saw it as a possibly positive development.[116] There was relatively little violence, and the refugees, for the most part, seemed to move of their own free will. Yet, the hoped for momentum for further voluntary returns did not materialize, and some officials, particularly in Kigali, were coming to the conclusion that forced repatriation was the only way to get the refugees back. In other words, UNHCR should just allow this to happen, and then help the refugees when they were back in Rwanda. Some coercion, probably by Zairian forces, was necessary to break the stranglehold of the extremists to allow the refugees to make their own decision (although it was assumed most of them would decide to return).[117]

Soon thereafter, Zaire announced a deadline of 31 December 1995 for all the refugees to leave Zaire. UNHCR did not oppose the deadline, and was roundly criticized.[118] Yet some felt that the only way to deal with the situation and allow the refugees to exercise what was assumed to be their preferred option to return to Rwanda was to, in fact, force them to exercise that option.[119] This was, at least on the surface, a significant breach of international norms, and it was shocking that UNHCR would not vigorously oppose such an eventuality. Yet it also highlighted the difficulties and conundrums faced by humanitarian actors in a situation where the international community is not willing to act. The deadline came and went without the hoped for returns. On 26 November, after a meeting with former President Carter, President Mobutu Sese Seko announced the deadline was being suspended. The voluntary return of refugees, which had increased significantly during the previous month, declined precipitously.[120]

The Return of the Refugees

Throughout the first part of 1996, other strategies were pursued. The Zairian government restricted travel on the part of refugees. Further, much economic activity was quashed by Zairian troops, including the closing of shops. This was very short-lived, however.[121] The problem of repatriation appeared intractable. While attempting to implement voluntary repatriation, UNHCR Goma also followed another tactic. Recognizing that there was no prospect of the refugees returning to Rwanda soon, it decided to investigate another durable solution—moving those refugees who did not wish to go back to settlements farther from the border. UNHCR recognized that this would not be looked on favorably by Zaire. Further, it would undermine efforts to encourage voluntary repatriation. It would help the leaders gain greater control over the refugees and a firmer position within Zaire from which to mount their hoped for return to power in Rwanda. Yet UNHCR hoped that it might put more pressure on Zaire to arrest the leaders as it had promised. However, it was difficult to envisage the entire refugee population moving to new locations, and just moving the camps without addressing the issue of the militants would not help the situation. UNHCR considered moving some of the camps closest to the border away from the border to deprive the militants of easy access for their raids into Rwanda. One camp considered was Kibumba, which had a relatively weak internal structure. Many in Kibumba wanted to stay there because they had easy access to their interests, such as property, in Rwanda. UNHCR hoped that moving the camp would undermine the camp structure and induce many of the refugees to repatriate. In turn, it was hoped, this would build momentum for repatriation from other camps. Yet relocation could also have the effect of making staying in Zaire appear like a realistic possibility for the refugees, undermining UNHCR's position that stability in the region could only be attained by the return of the refugees. Such a strategy would allow the international community to continue to abdicate its responsibility. In the end, none of these options were implemented.[122]

At the same time, the security situation in eastern Zaire was getting worse. By October a widespread civil war had emerged in eastern Zaire as a result of an attempt by the government to expel approximately 400,000 local Tutsi—the Banyamulenge. The Banyamulenge, and other forces hostile to the Mobutu regime, constituted themselves as the Alliance of Democratic Forces for the Liberation of Congo-Zaire (ADFL) and counterattacked. The ADFL, which will figure prominently in the next chapter, was also supported by Rwanda and Uganda, who were concerned with ending the infiltrations from Zaire. As the ADFL swept through eastern Zaire, they attacked refugee camps, since they saw ex-FAR and militia as enemies and the camps as enemy bases. Thousands of refugees died, probably at the hands of all parties involved in the conflict—ADFL, ex-FAR and militia, and Zairian troops. And, from late 1996 onwards, all the major camps were emptied.[123]

As the conflict spread, and the pressures on the refugees from many different quarters increased, it was clear that UNHCR was involved in a situation far beyond its normal operating parameters and that it could not hope to adequately deal with the situation. It was marginalized as events overtook its capabilities. The High Commissioner told UNHCR's Executive Committee on October 7 that "probably never before has my office found its humanitarian concerns in the midst of such a lethal quagmire of political and security interests."[124] Refugees fled before their camps were destroyed, and eventually all international aid workers were evacuated from Bukavu and then Goma by 2 November, thus losing access to information and the refugees themselves. On 7 November UNHCR called on the international community to raise a force to ensure humanitarian access. UNHCR supported the proposed, but ultimately doomed, multinational force.[125] The High Commissioner also encouraged the refugees to return in a radio address in October.[126]

The "lethal quagmire" Ogata referred to held the potential for even greater disaster.[127] A summit of regional leaders held in November 1996 recommended a "'neutral force'" to protect refugees and humanitarian assistance and facilitate the return of refugees.[128] Some NGOs, such as Save the Children, argued that such an intervention might make the situation worse, while others, such as MSF, said that there should be a robust force, with a Chapter VII mandate, to provide security for the area, rather than just protecting humanitarian workers.[129] France was very supportive of a force, but given France's previous relationship with the old Rwandan regime, and its less than balanced Opération Turquoise, the motives of the French government were questionable.[130] The U.S. and UK took longer to come around. Memories of Mogadishu lingered. Indeed, one particularly prescient officer in the State Department forecast in 1993 that a conflict in Zaire "'could easily turn into a Somalia and Rwanda rolled into one.'"[131] On 9 November, the Security Council took the preliminary step of laying the basis for the future authorization of a peacekeeping force,[132] and did, indeed, authorize a force on 15 November.[133] The mandate did not include arresting the militants[134] (which, by this time, would have been a much more difficult and dangerous exercise than in 1994) and sending them to the International Criminal Tribunal for Rwanda, which had just been established by the Security Council. Operation Assurance[135] was to be a purely palliative exercise, aimed at dealing with a dire security situation the UN had let fester for more than two years. Canada had agreed to lead the force.[136] It was likely relieved when events obviated the need for the force.[137]

In the period 15–20 November 1996, as a result of an ADFL offensive on Goma, approximately 600,000 refugees repatriated to Rwanda from the Goma area, with UNHCR and other aid organizations virtually helpless to do anything until the refugees actually entered Rwanda. UNHCR transported some of the refugees, although for most of them it was easier to walk. The sheer number of people, as well as their relative proximity to the border, mitigated against a significant UNHCR role until the refugees crossed the border. At that point, UNHCR returned the refugees to their communes of origin. At least 200,000 more refugees fled farther into Zaire. The aim of the ADFL was to destroy the camps, thus depriving the Hutu militants of bases from which to launch their infiltrations. There is speculation that the ADFL may actually have wanted to push the refugees farther into Zaire, away from the border, making it harder for the militants to operate and, more generally, to prevent the return of an extremely large number of Hutus. Another group, the Mai Mai, who wanted to get rid of all Kinyarwanda (the language spoken in Rwanda and parts of eastern Zaire/DRC and Uganda) speakers from the Kivu region, prevented most of the refugees from fleeing into Zaire.[138] Some did, however, go farther into Zaire, sometimes pushed by the Hutu militants who were, yet again, using them as human shields.[139]

Palliation Undermining Protection

The presence of the militants in eastern Zaire set the scene for ongoing destabilization and misery in the region, the likes of which the world has rarely seen, and illustrates both the palliative nature of the international response and the conundrums faced by humanitarian actors. It was clear early on that the large refugee population on the periphery of Rwanda would pose a significant security threat.[140] Yet the response to the security threat was palliation, first with Operation Support Hope, which helped to create the environment where the Hutu militants were able to consolidate their destabilization. Once the destabilization was firmly in progress, the palliators were called on by the international community to address the *security* situation. This they obviously could not do.

Furthermore, put in such a situation, they face practical and moral conundrums that may conflict with their humanitarian mandate. Humanitarians saved a lot of lives. Yet the question remains—did their actions just perpetuate the insecurity, providing shelter and resources to militants who destabilized the region and creating a population of "well-fed dead" who were at the mercy of the militants and ADFL? MSF France thought they were doing more harm than good, and decided that they should leave. Yet, since most other organizations decided to stay there was little impact from their departure. This highlights a bigger issue. While humanitarian organizations may, at times, have a very large impact on a situation, they cannot always know—or control—that impact. Their job is helping people in immediate need. They are not there to end a conflict or stabilize a security crisis. Yet they are called on to do so—or at least used as an excuse for others not to take necessary action. They create the illusion of protection. They were criticized for being there, for setting up and supporting the camps—camps that hid *génocidaires*.

But if they had not been there how many more people would have died? Initial deaths were likely fewer than if the camps had not existed. But how can one adequately make a decision that might lead to more short-term deaths in the hope of preventing more deaths later on?

Nor can militarized humanitarianism, to the extent the military is only there to deliver assistance, accomplish this goal of preventing killing. Yet airdropping food from C5s provides a reasonable, if superficial, simulacrum of action. Opération Turquoise had little to do with humanitarianism or human rights, but France was able to call on the "never again" norm to justify protecting those who carried out the genocide. Operation Support Hope had a dual function—to cover up the fact that the United States did not do anything to stop the genocide and also provide cover for inaction in the aftermath as eastern Zaire became increasingly unstable. It created the illusion of protection, thereby reducing the prospects of real protection, and contributed to the continuation of the conflict.

Prosecution as Action

At the same time it was withdrawing peacekeepers from Rwanda, the Security Council condemned violations of international humanitarian law in Rwanda. On 1 July, when the genocide was all but over, the Security Council, in Resolution 935, set up a Commission of Experts to investigate the massacres. The Commission found clear evidence of genocide against the Tutsi,[141] and recommended in October 1994 than an international tribunal be set up by the Security Council. Rwanda also requested a court, although on its terms. For the Security Council, a court was necessary to divert attention from the lack of response to the genocide. It was also seen as important for regional peace and security. John Shattuck, U.S. assistant secretary of state for democracy, human rights, and labor, thought that quick arrests of the *génocidaires* in the camps and subsequent trials in an international court could alleviate the threat of continued violence and instability. Thus, international justice would be part of a wider conflict prevention and management strategy.[142] As this, however, it utterly failed.

After the genocide Rwanda faced many pressing issues. First, the government needed to establish and shore up its legitimacy. It needed to convince the world that it was not just a Tutsi-dominated government intent on oppressing the Hutu population and engaging in revenge killings. Some of this obviously happened, but the government did not want this to undermine its international image. It had massive goodwill as a result of international guilt over the genocide. An international tribunal would continue to put the focus on the genocide and exacerbate international shame. Second, it needed to deal with the demands for justice. More than 100,000 genocide suspects were in jail in Rwanda,[143] although the core members of the *géno-cidaires* were outside the country. After the genocide Rwanda lacked the judicial infrastructure to deal with the demands for justice in any substantial way. An international tribunal could directly address the massive caseload. It could also help facilitate the rebuilding of its domestic justice system.[144] In addition, it knew that most of the major perpetrators who were outside of the country would not be extradited to Rwanda. An international court would be a neutral institution that could accept and try these perpetrators in a way that Rwanda could not. Further, the government wanted to neutralize the former government and its potential to challenge it from eastern Zaire.[145] Thus, as with other cases in this book, the government tried to use the tribunal as a front in a broader conflict with forces that could threaten it.

Since Rwanda was sitting on the Security Council at the time, it played a significant role in shaping the court. However, even though it had called for the establishment of an international tribunal, in the end it voted against it when it came to a vote on 8 November 1994—seven months after the genocide began. It was not able to get enough concessions from the other Security Council members to allow it to shape and control it in the way it wanted, although it did get a couple of major concessions that greatly affected its ability to use it for its own ends. The government objected to the lack of capital punishment. Without it, lower level perpetrators who would be tried in domestic courts would face the death penalty, while the architects of the genocide, who would be more likely to be tried at the ICTR, would only face a prison term. Given the evolution of international law and norms, however, having the death penalty was never a serious option. In addition, there was concern about the lack of clarity about whom the tribunal would prosecute. Would it only try the main perpetrators of the genocide, or might it also turn to members of the RPF suspected of massacres against Hutus? The government obviously would want to prevent the latter. Rwanda did not want any French judges on the court, given France's support for the former regime, and it wanted war criminals to be imprisoned in Rwanda, rather than in other countries, as was originally stipulated in the ICTR statute (this was eventually changed to allow imprisonment in Rwanda). It wanted the ICTR to be based in Rwanda, rather than at its eventual home of Arusha, Tanzania. If the ICTR was in Rwanda, the Rwandan government would be better able to control it and use it to bolster its legitimacy. However, the Security Council decided that its impartiality would be compromised if it was based in Rwanda, although it eventually gave the court the ability to hold trials in Rwanda if it wanted. Rwanda was concerned that it would not have enough institutional capacity, particularly since initially it only had two chambers (eventually expanded to three). It also was concerned that the ICTR would be just a subsidiary organ of the ICTY, given that they would share a chief prosecutor and appeals chamber. In the end, though, the deputy prosecutor was based in Kigali, giving the tribunal a greater presence in the country than the ICTY enjoyed in the former Yugoslavia.[146]

The biggest issue, however, relates to the aftermath of the genocide, including the actions to address the situation in eastern Zaire. The Security Council proposed giving the ICTR jurisdiction over crimes committed from 6 April 1994 to the end of 1994. Rwanda wanted the jurisdiction to start on 1 October 1990 to allow prosecution of those suspected of planning the genocide earlier, and to end on 17 July 1994, when the genocide ended. This would prevent prosecution of RPF atrocities after the war ended. It would also prevent any future actions it might take to deal with the Hutus in eastern Zaire from being covered by the court. In the end, the ICTR was given a mandate to look at crimes committed during the entirety of 1994—1 January to 31 December 1994. This allowed for prosecution of genocide planning in the immediate run up to the genocide. And while it still covered crimes committed by the RPF immediately after the war ended, it essentially gave the government impunity for what it was to do later on in eastern Zaire (as well as in Kibeho and elsewhere). No RPF leaders have been prosecuted by the ICTR, although a number have been pursued by other countries—mostly in Europe—under the principle of universal jurisdiction.[147] Indeed, Rwanda was able to manipulate the ICTR through threats of, and actual, noncooperation with the court to block investigations of RPF crimes and to ensure prosecution of its enemies.[148] Rwanda also had significant support from western countries who shared guilt over the failure to act, and especially the U.S. and UK, who also perceived the Tutsi-led government as "good," leading the country toward democracy. This gave Rwanda significant power to manipulate the ICTR for its own ends. It was seen as an "authoritative victim," able to write its own narrative.[149]

The ICTR has worked very slowly and has faced significant criticism from Rwanda regarding its inability to successfully prosecute significant numbers of defendants.[150] While the Prosecutor and others at the ICTR share some of the blame for this perceived ineffectiveness, some of the blame must be shared with Rwanda, which has manipulated the court and put obstacles in its way, as well as the UN, which has not adequately funded[151] and otherwise supported the court.

Rwanda also attempted to address the question of impunity in a less formal way. Recognizing that it could take up to two hundred years to prosecute all those held in Rwandan prisons on suspicion of genocide,[152] it set up an alternative justice mechanism called *gacaca*, which could try all but the top level of genocide related crimes—including organizing the genocide and sexual offenses. It sat between formal criminal court proceedings and truth commissions, and was supposedly a more local or "African" form of justice, based in local traditions of dispute resolution.[153] It also involved a much wider portion of the community in the proceedings than is found in normal criminal trials, with 260,000 judges elected in October 2004.[154] The *gacaca* courts were partially retributive and partially restorative.[155] Like the South African Truth and Reconciliation Commission, it encouraged accused *génocidaires* to provide full disclosure of their actions. In return, the accused would receive significantly reduced sentences.[156] This would, theoretically, provide a fuller account of the genocide and allow victims and the families of victims to have their suffering acknowledged. However, what kind of truth they provided and whether this was always helpful in reconciliation and community building is in question.[157] Indeed, it appears that there were a significant incidence of lies and half-truths, and *gacaca* was used a form of personal revenge.[158] This brief mention of *gacaca* highlights the problems and limitations of international criminal justice mechanisms. Such proceedings can hope to try only a few people of many thousands, tens of thousands, or indeed hundreds of thousands who might have participated in a genocide or other situation of mass atrocity. The ICTR sat uncomfortably alongside national formal genocide trials in Rwanda. But neither could accommodate the large numbers of people involved in the genocide. Further, neither could address in any significant way the necessity of reconciliation and community building in Rwanda. Indeed, both national trials and the ICTR helped to reify the power of the winning side. The "local" forms of justice had ambiguous results. This occurred postconflict, which differs from the situation in Uganda, to be discussed in Chapter 5, which occurred in the midst of conflict and which raised more significant issues of conflict management.

R2P³ in Rwanda

Rwanda happened before R2P was given a name or was recognized in any way by the international community. Yet, it occurred in the midst of a developing conversation about humanitarian intervention and laid the groundwork for R2P. So perhaps it is unfair to claim that it is a failure of R2P. Yet, even without the name, the precursor to R2P—"never again"—existed and obviously played a role in discussions on how to respond. The great rhetorical contortions deployed to avoid using the word "genocide" demonstrate the potency of "never again." The vast array of human rights and genocide-specific international law and norms did little to induce action. Rwanda was perceived as an inconsequential country in an out of the way corner of the world, and so it was easy to ignore the situation, or at least to create a narrative that allowed inaction. Yet the "never again" norm would not go away. A few brave souls started calling the genocide for what it was. For most, however, the term was just too dangerous. To speak it would be to acknowledge responsibility— maybe not in terms of the responsibility to protect, but in terms of the Genocide Convention and "never again." Thus, there was denial of genocide and then awkward constructions such as "acts of genocide." This was, of course, meaningless, intended to cover up reality. Yet it also highlighted a curious situation that, to a certain extent, exists to this day. It was clear that mass killings were going on. Whether this was an orchestrated campaign of mass extermination of a particular group of people, or less coherent violence, should not have mattered. Yet it was only when the magical term "genocide" was uttered that states would feel pressure to act. Failing to invoke genocide perhaps let states off the hook, but the people who were killed in Rwanda were dead nonetheless. The "never again" norm could have its intended effect only when the specific word was uttered. By the time the word was said, it was far too late. But, luckily for the West, a humanitarian crisis in the form of cholera appeared. This allowed the United States, in particular, to put on a big show of using its troops to battle cholera—the same troops that might have been used to stop the genocide. Here, the "never again" norm has an effect, but not necessarily the effect one might hope for. A further effect came with

Table 2.1. Responsibility Conundrums in Rwanda

	Protectors	Prosecutors	Palliators
Protection	−failure to act to stop the genocide −Operation Turquoise only protected one side −failure to separate militants		+some called for intervention to separate out the militants
Prosecution	−took no action to arrest militants	+contributed to basis for ICC −took a very long time to prosecute relatively few *génocidaires* −Rwandan government used ICTR for its own purposes	−some linked palliation to prosecution
Palliation	+provided some assistance −did little to protect refugees—left to palliators		+assisted two million refugees −some protection activities −supported conditions for continuation of conflict

the creation of the ICTR, although, coming after the genocide had ended, it had no effect on the genocide itself, and had minimal effect on the ongoing security crisis on the periphery of Rwanda.

   After the troops left, leaving the humanitarians—the palliators—to fend for themselves, the international community—the supposed protectors—called on the palliators to deal with a security crisis. This of course they could not do. But even though the members of the Security Council knew the potential outcome of the increasing insecurity in eastern Zaire after the genocide, they could not bring themselves do what they did not do during the genocide—deploy relatively small numbers of troops to head off a greater disaster. The results would be felt for years to come. Many palliators also knew what might become of the mass of humanity on the border with Rwanda, and they faced an awful choice—continue to feed hundreds of thousands of people, knowing that the very situation they enabled by their humanitarian acts was destabilizing the region, or pull out. Most decided to stay; a few left, but their withdrawal made little difference. Although they certainly did not intend this, their actions, combined with the West's cowardice in dealing with the refugee population, set the scene for one of the worst conflagrations since World War II.

Yet this highlights one of the main conundrums faced by humanitarians. While they save innumerable lives, their actions may also contribute to the continuation of conflict. There was a lot of soul-searching after Rwanda on the part of humanitarians, and there was a greater awareness of potential downsides of humanitarian action, but even though new standards were created, one fact was inescapable. Humanitarians can be used as highly imperfect substitutes for proactive robust civilian protection and as scapegoats for failure by the international community to protect people. Blame for protection failures must be placed at the feet of the highest reaches of global political power, but this does not reduce the frequently unresolvable quandaries in which palliators find themselves.

CHAPTER 3

Democratic Republic of the Congo: Protecting Civilians?

The international community has a certain
responsibility. . . . It tends to pass on responsibility for
African crises on to Africans and bodies like the OAU
that lack the means to handle these crises.

Peacekeepers may not only be operationally justified in
using force but morally compelled to do so.

You can have a helicopter one day used to deliver the
Force Intervention Brigade troops to attack a village
and next day to deliver aid to that same village.

The conflict in eastern Zaire had continental repercussions, including the
overthrow of Mobutu, regional intervention from across sub-Saharan Africa,
and continued widespread human misery.[1] It also led to the largest UN peacekeeping mission to date, the application of the protection of civilians concept, and the first conviction by the International Criminal Court. It also
posed significant questions about the international community's strategies
and will to address situations of mass atrocity. In the end, what we see is a
muddled mess where precursor and proto R2P activities debuted, international criminal justice gained prominence but was also problematized, and
the dilemmas for humanitarians continued. Yet, for all this, the DRC remains
a "stealth conflict," "undetected—absent from international consciousness,"

"consistently absent from policy, media, public and academic agendas."[2] Unlike Darfur, it has no international social movement. And, except for the occasional revelation of peacekeeper misdeeds,[3] there is little media coverage. There are no viral videos about the DRC, and the Twitterverse seems silent. During the course of what came to be known as Africa's World War, Kosovo, Sudan (first the country as a whole, then Darfur, and, most recently, South Sudan), Somalia, Afghanistan, Iraq, and Palestine have all captured column inches, television time, and computer screen space. Even its brave Nobel nominee Denis Mukwege, who has worked for years to treat rape victims,[4] is shunted aside so the world can embrace the latest media darling, Nobel Peace Prize winner Malala Yousafzai, demonstrating yet again that its millions of dead pale in comparison to anything related to the global "War on Terror." Yet, the numbers of people who have died in these conflicts pales in comparison to the human misery found in the DRC.

From Spillover to Coup

Séverine Autesserre argues that a significant portion of the violent conflict that occurred in Zaire/DRC—and especially in the eastern part which most concerns us here—had at least part of its roots in local conflicts that significantly predate the genocide in Rwanda and the ensuing violence across the border. This includes extremely complex ethnic politics and conflicts over land and resources. She argues that the way this conflict was understood by international peace builders—including the UN peacekeeping operation—negatively affected attempts to bring peace to the troubled country.[5] Gérard Prunier states that the violence in eastern Congo, while "it preexisted the war, had been made worse by the war, and would not stop even if the war ended,"[6] and notes the broader east African origins of the war.[7] However, the presence of more than one million Rwandan refugees who brought their ethnic politics with them provided kindling for latent and not so latent tensions to explode. It also provided the context for international perception and response. Thus, the following discussion takes the expanding conflict in Zaire (soon to be the Democratic Republic of Congo) as inextricably intertwined with the Rwandan genocide and its aftermath. It will also focus more on the macro level of the conflict and response rather than the micro foundations.

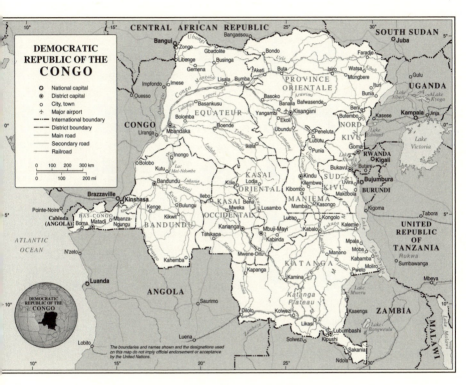

Map 3. Democratic Republic of the Congo, Map No. 4007
Rev. 10, July 2011. United Nations.

While the ADFL was battling Hutu militants in eastern Zaire and break-ing up the camps, it also had a larger goal—Kinshasa. The ADFL, which was an artificial conglomeration of four different movements, and which had the support of Uganda as well as Rwanda,[8] expanded the conflict westward, all the way to the capital 1,500 kilometers away. It also had the tacit support of the United States, which, although it was becoming increasingly worried about Laurent Kabila's intentions and his ability to run Zaire if the ADFL overthrew Mobutu,[9] was supporting both Rwanda and Uganda to further its interests against Mobutu and Sudan.[10] The ADFL took Kinshasa on 17 May 1997 and Kabila took power.

In a fundamental sense, the fall of Mobutu did not change anything in the region. The status of the Banyarwanda was not resolved and regional secu-rity issues still existed. Rwanda and the new government in Kinshasa signed an agreement to cooperate in military efforts against the Hutu militants and the Mai Mai in eastern DRC. The Rwandan Patriotic Army (RPA) maintained a presence in eastern DRC, not paying attention to borders, expanding its presence in late 1997 and early 1998, when both militants and civilians were killed.[11] Kabila gradually turned against his patrons to the east, leading to in-creased tensions with Rwanda—and Uganda—by the first part of 1998, as well as increasingly hostility to Tutsi present in the eastern DRC.[12] Conflict also continued in Rwanda. The repatriation of the refugees had served to partly reimport the civil war back into Rwanda, with increased attacks throughout the country. Thousands of civilians were killed—many by the RPA—and humanitarian workers were also targeted.[13] With continuing instability and lack of resolution of fundamental regional issues, the stage was thus set for a resumption of violent conflict.

Africa's World War

This happened with a vengeance on 2 August 1998, when the leader of a bri-gade of the Forces Armées Congolaises (FAC) announced the intention of overthrowing Kabila for corruption and misrule. On 27 July Kabila had called for Rwandan and Ugandan troops to leave and increased attacks against Tutsi, further escalating the explosive situation.[14] On 3 August, another brigade, based in Bukavu, joined the rebellion and swiftly took over the main towns in the eastern part of the Kivus. This was supported by Rwanda. The newly formed Rassemblement Congolais pour la Démocratie (RCD) was, like the

ADFL, a Rwandan proxy. Rwanda put forth both a security rationale—the continuing threat of Hutu militants in eastern DRC—and a humanitarian one—a supposed genocide against Tutsi by Kabila. While outside actors had intervened during the first war in 1996–97, this second war—or second phase of the same war—quickly drew in many more regional actors. Uganda justified its involvement on lack of security along the border. More broadly, however, it wanted to continue to play a part in the regional geopolitical game centered in the DRC. Angola, Zimbabwe, and Namibia also quickly joined the fray, on Kabila's side, armed with a mandate from the Southern African Development Community (SADC). A Burundian rebel group, the Forces pour la Défense de la Démocratie (FDD), sided with Kabila and was trained by Zimbabwe. This brought in Burundi. Sudan supported Kabila, in the context of its conflict with Uganda. Other countries also became involved at one point or another, including Chad and Libya on the side of Kabila, as well as Zambia, Tanzania, Kenya, and Congo-Brazzaville in much more ambiguous positions. South Africa never intervened, but it had interests in the conflict. While regional geopolitics and security issues were at the core of many of the interventions on one side or another, access to resources—including gold, diamonds, copper, and coltan (a key component in mobile phones)—also served to perpetuate the fighting.[15] As the fighting expanded, the rebel groups expanded and splintered into a bewildering array of groups for and against the government, serving as proxies for various state actors, in particular Rwanda and Uganda, as well as acting as little more than criminal groups existing for the sole purpose of mineral extraction.[16] Thus, the DRC became the center of a Hobbesian[17] conflict of all against all, involving state actors stretching from southern Africa through to Sudan as well as a variety of nonstate actors. The conflict became known as Africa War One.[18]

This brought horrible human suffering, as civilians became caught in the middle of conflict and became the direct object of violence themselves, and large numbers of people flowed across borders or became internally displaced.[19] By 3 February 1999, there were 500,000 IDPs in the DRC, with 190,000 in the Kivus.[20] Sexual violence became a dominant part of the Congo narrative, but all sectors of the population were subjected to violence. The government—and rebels—started recruiting (or rerecruiting) child soldiers.[21] The international response included, eventually, the largest peacekeeping mission at the time, and the development of the protection of civilian concept. The ICC also came to prominence through its pursuit of cases in the

DRC, although its involvement demonstrated the weaknesses and contradictions of the ICC.

From Disengagement to MONUC

During the time of "peace" between the fall of Mobutu and the resumption of all out war in August 1998, the UN was relatively unengaged. On 18 February 1997, the Security Council called for refugees and displaced persons to be protected,[22] although it did not provide the means to do so. This was the sole resolution the Security Council passed on the crisis during 1997. In 1998 it passed a resolution on the flow of arms into the region and condemned incitement to genocide,[23] and three generic resolutions on "the situation in Africa"[24] that did not refer specifically to the Great Lakes region. On 19 November, the Security Council passed Resolution 1208, which, following on from a report by the Secretary-General on "Protection for Humanitarian Access to Refugees and Others in Conflict Situations," noted the responsibility of states to protect refugees and "noted," without specifying, the "range of measures" the international community could use to support African states to ensure the security of refugee camps. The Secretary-General's report argued that the international community needed to step in when states did not live up to their responsibilities to protect refugees and others in the midst of conflict.[25] Yet, although there was recognition of the responsibility of the international community to address civilian protection, little happened.

On 9 April 1999, the Security Council passed Resolution 1234, which, while "expressing its concern" about human rights violations in the DRC, did little but condemn massacres and exhort states to stop fighting. Instead of taking robust action to deal with its "concern," it "call[ed] for safe and unhindered access for humanitarian assistance." That is, it called in the palliators to get on with their jobs and for states (i.e., the DRC) not to get in their way. Resolutions 1258 and 1273, too, did little to concretely address the situation.

Most of the main parties to the conflict signed a peace agreement in Lusaka[26] on 10 July 1999. While, as an initiative of SADC, it was a reflection of the African solutions for African problems mantra, it put the burden of implementing the agreement on the UN, including disarming the foreign rebel groups within thirty days. The UN was requested to "track down" all the armed groups in the DRC and then send *génocidaires* to the ICTR. Given the expected timeframe, the task at hand, and the previous UN experience in the region, this was wildly optimistic, and the Lusaka agreement soon became increasingly irrelevant as various parties violated it with impunity.[27] In response, the UN created the United Nations Mission in the Democratic Republic of Congo (MONUC) in Resolution 1279 on 30 November. This resolution was limited, renaming the group of liaison personnel already there and indicating that it would further deploy MONUC personnel after another decision. Such deployment was seen as months away.[28] Resolution 1279 also called on states to donate more money. In February 2000, the Security Council, in Resolution 1291, finally recognized the situation in the DRC as a threat to international peace and security, and authorized phased deployment of 5,537 military personnel under MONUC.[29] It called on MONUC to facilitate the delivery of humanitarian assistance and gave it a Chapter VII mandate to "protect civilians under imminent threat of physical violence"— although the main part of the mandate came under Chapter VI[30] and the PoC mandate was secondary to the main role of MONUC.[31] Indeed, although the Secretary-General's report on the DRC the month before had included the words "atrocity" and "massacre," and had noted serious concern over the human rights situation,[32] UN forces "would not have the capacity to protect the civilian population from armed attack."[33] Rather, MONUC would "escort humanitarian assistance convoys only within the limits of their means and under favourable conditions."[34] Resolution 1291 also called on parties to the conflict to help bring to justice those who engaged in genocide, crimes against humanity, or war crimes, although it did not give MONUC a mandate to facilitate this. This protection of civilians mandate—the second of its kind[35]—presaged the influential Brahimi Report, or the Report of the Panel on United Nations Peace Operations, of August 2000. The report stated that

> peacekeepers may not only be operationally justified in using force but morally compelled to do so. Genocide in Rwanda went as far as it did in part because the international community failed to use or to reinforce the operation then on the ground in that country to oppose obvious evil.... If a United Nations peace operation is already on the ground, carrying out those actions may become its responsibility, and it should be prepared.[36]

A couple of observations should be made at this point. First, the leaders from the countries involved in the conflict had called for a force of 15,000—20,000, and France wanted 10,000. The Clinton administration was concerned about the ability of the UN to handle a large force and had a hard time convincing Congress to fund such a force.[37] More generally it did not want to give the UN a "blank check."[38] The United States also did not want MONUC to have a mandate to disarm nonstate actors, the Somalia Syndrome obviously operating in the background. Thus, second, MONUC was not to be an interpositional force. The only robust element of the resolution concerned the protection of civilians, but given that this was a relatively new thing for the UN, it was unclear exactly what this meant. In sum, MONUC was destined to be an observer to the conflict.[39] There was a recognition that something needed to be done, but little will to commit the resources necessary to do it. Thus, MONUC, rather than being a sort of proto-R2P action was, rather, another façade. The Security Council called on humanitarians to palliate and prosecutors to prosecute, but did little to enable either, or to actually protect people.[40]

MONUC, which took three years to deploy its initial 5,537 troops,[41] did not get off to an auspicious start. In the second half of 2000, fighting between Ugandan and Rwandan forces broke out in Kisangani, and various rebel groups expanded fighting, particularly in the Kivus and Equateur Province, displacing another 400,000 people and leading to a total of 1.8 million people displaced by the end of the year. The government restricted MONUC flights, thus impairing its ability to do its job.[42] Given that MONUC was deployed with the consent of the government, and was too small and weak to robustly challenge any of the parties, there was little MONUC and the Security Council could, or would, do—except for "*stressing* the need for increased humanitarian assistance to the Congolese population."[43]

Turmoil continued in Kinshasa. On 16 January 2001 Laurent Kabila was killed by a bodyguard. He was succeeded by his son, Joseph. The new president appeared to have a different perspective and was more willing to talk with opposing factions. He announced the opening of the Inter-Congolese Dialogue mandated under the Lusaka peace agreement and intended to bring together various government, opposition, and armed groups for negotiations. The Dialogue soon collapsed,[44] as did the Lusaka agreement more generally, with widespread fighting throughout the country.[45]

On 22 February, while condemning the massacres and atrocities[46] occurring in the DRC, and reaffirming the mandate of MONUC, which included the protection of civilians, the Security Council also accepted[47] a revised concept of operations from the Secretary-General that removed the protection of civilians element.[48] The focus was on protecting UN personnel and facilities, even though the Secretary-General noted massacres, torture, and widespread killings.[49] The Secretary-General also noted that the total number of displaced was more than 2,335,000, and that less than half these were receiving assistance. And, the report relayed that there were "16 million people with critical food needs" tied directly to the war.[50] Thus the initial experiment with protection of civilians faltered even before it began. MONUC was partially depleted even before it was deployed,[51] dictated by financial worries and a concern that the UN not take on something at which it might fail. This was certainly not an auspicious time to implement the "curtain of troops" called for in Resolution 1417. The idea was to create a demilitarized zone along the border. Given the troop numbers this would require, the idea was one of many ideas and initiatives consigned to the dustbin.

While some foreign troops were withdrawn, many of the armed groups consolidated their hold in eastern DRC.[52] The Security Council expanded MONUC to 8,700 troops, but did not expand its mandate even though it expressed "deep concern" over the humanitarian situation—particularly in Ituri—as well as ethnic violence.[53] Preventing regional destabilization was prioritized over protecting civilians. The lack of support for protecting civilians was all too evident in May 2002. A mutiny against one of the rebel groups, RCD-Goma (RCD-G), in Kisangani led to significant violence against civilians, with up to at least fifty[54]—and probably more than a hundred[55]—civilians being killed. MONUC did not intervene militarily to stop the killing, relying solely on diplomatic measures,[56] although it did depart from customary neutrality and blamed the killing, which it estimated at 183 people, on the RCD-G.[57] The Secretary-General subsequently noted that while the Security Council had given MONUC a PoC mandate, it had not made it possible for it to carry out that mandate.[58] The first couple of years of MONUC were not an auspicious start for implementing meaningful PoC. Finally, in language that presaged the World Summit Outcome document, the secretary-feneral noted that "the basic responsibility of providing protection to civilians rests with the local authorities, who must act in a manner consistent with internationally accepted standards of human rights."[59]

Another peace agreement was signed on 30 July 2002, this time between Kabila and Kagame. It was focused on disarming ex-FAR and *interahamwe* and the withdrawal of Rwandan troops. MONUC and the DRC government would cooperate to identify, disarm, and repatriate the militants to Rwanda within ninety days. Yet by the end of October, although

Rwanda had withdrawn 21,000 troops,[60] only a few hundred militants had been repatriated. Indeed, both Rwanda and the militants had an interest in keeping the conflict going.[61]

MONUC was not up to the task. It was not given the resources or mandate to adequately address the situation. Thus, by spring 2004, there were still 10,000 ex-FAR and *interahamwe* in eastern DRC.[62] In ten years, the international community had failed to address a situation it had allowed to grow and fester, but which was now vastly more complex than in 1994. There was general insecurity throughout eastern DRC and human insecurity on an almost incomprehensible scale. A broader peace agreement between the government and a number of rebel movements was reached in December 2002, which included a new push by the government to reassert control in the east. Yet MONUC was not given any new mandate to facilitate this,[63] although on 26 December the EU called for an enhanced force of up to 16,000 troops.[64] This would change when things got even worse in the northeastern part of the country.

The International Community Finds (a Few) Teeth

The human disaster in the eastern DRC was described by Refugees International as "a slow motion holocaust."[65] In October, the Secretary-General had noted the "precarious" human rights situation in eastern DRC, with "Widespread and grave violations of human rights and international humanitarian law."[66] He noted that "Humanitarian conditions in the Democratic Republic of the Congo remain deeply disturbing. Civilians continue to bear the brunt of the crisis."[67] Of a population of 53 million, 17 million needed food aid and 2.2 million people were displaced. There was an increase in harassment of aid workers.[68] Overall, "the situation demands greater protection of civilians under imminent threat of physical violence."[69]

This was particularly so in the northeastern region of Ituri, which had been described as "the bloodiest corner of the Democratic Republic of Congo."[70] Uganda was the dominant external actor in the district, although Rwanda also had proxies in Ituri.[71] It was there to control and extract natural resources.[72] As part of its strategy of control, it fanned ethnic conflict, particularly between the Hema and Lendu,[73] exacerbating preexisting tensions over land,[74] leading to widespread violence, with 50,000 people dead and 500,000 people displaced between 1999 and 2003.[75] The ICG described a "progression . . . from land-based communal violence, to land-related operations of ethnic cleansing, to repeated acts of genocide by both Hema and Lendu."[76] Further, various armed militias and rebel movements fought, expanded, and splintered into at least twelve militias.[77] The leaders of four of these groups would later have arrest warrants issued against them by the ICC—Jean-Pierre Bemba[78] of the Mouvement de Libération du Congo (MLC), Thomas Lubanga of the Union des Patriotes Congolais (UPC), Germain Katanga of the Force de Résistance Patriotique en Ituri (FRPI), and Mathieu Ngudjolo Chui[79] of the Front de Nationalistes et Intégrationnistes (FNI).[80] Officials from the UN, U.S. and EU saw a possible genocide in the making.[81] MONUC was unable to deal with the complex conflict dynamics in Ituri.[82] It was also not prepared for the rapid withdrawal of Ugandan troops in late April; the resulting power vacuum led to the massacre of hundreds, and to tens of thousands fleeing Bunia.[83]

On 30 May 2003, via Resolution 1484, the Security Council finally gave a full Chapter VII mandate to a peace enforcement mission, including protection of civilians—although not to MONUC. Rather, an EU-sponsored force, led by France,[84] was authorized as an Interim Emergency Multinational Force (IEMF). It was to help stabilize the security and humanitarian situation in Bunia, protect the airport and IDPs, and protect civilians.[85] It was only to last three months. Since the IEMF was just a temporary measure—and only in one small corner of the country, the Security Council also beefed up MONUC on 28 July, again with more personnel (10,800) and a full Chapter VII mandate to, among other things, "protect civilians and humanitarian workers" in Ituri and the Kivus (the latter "as it deems within its capabilities").[86] While the Security Council was strongly in favor of a more robust PoC mandate, Italy inserted a note of caution. It noted that a strong Chapter VII mandate could lead to a situation where peacekeepers would become parties to a conflict, thus changing the nature of peacekeeping activities.[87] Indeed, while PoC is supposedly a more palatable, nonpolitical concept than R2P, certain PoC activities can become extremely political and inadvertently veer into R2P-like activities.

Operation Artemis arrived heavily fortified, including heavy armor and helicopter gunships.[88] It did have an appreciable impact in Bunia itself by reestablishing security and weakening the Hema and Lendu militias. However, given that it was restricted to Bunia,[89] this tended to push the violence against civilians beyond the town.[90] Further, given the strict three-month limit of the deployment, the militias could just wait out the operation unless

MONUC was very dramatically reinforced and empowered at the end of the three months.[91] The force commander issued an ultimatum for the various militias to leave or disarm, and eventually engaged in significant fighting to enforce this edict.[92] Eventually, thousands of refugees returned to Bunia,[93] although MSF noted at the time that "security in Bunia remains extremely precarious."[94] Operation Artemis did little to protect people beyond Bunia—including the 150,000 residents who had fled[95]—or to address the wider issues in Ituri, which continued to experience widespread atrocities.[96] It also served to skew the balance in favor of one of the militia—Lubanga's UPC—since Lubanga could redeploy forces he might have otherwise needed to protect Hema in Bunia.[97] As a joint EU operation, it also served to redirect focus in Europe on Africa. At the end of 2003 the EU decided to spend €250 million in support of African peacekeeping, and France and the UK floated the idea of creating an EU rapid reaction force.[98]

The newly reempowered MONUC began to deploy while Artemis was still on the ground, with Task Force II (or the Ituri Brigade) coming up to a strength of 4,500 troops by November. The Ituri Brigade was the first UN peacekeeping operation to include protection of civilians in its concept of operations (CONOPS) mission statement.[99] It, too, had attack helicopters and armored personnel carriers,[100] and began to act more robustly than previous MONUC missions.[101] The interim Ituri Brigade Commander recognized a shift from "keeping peace" to "enforcing peace."[102] The special representative of the Secretary-General, William Lacy Swing, indicated that the goal was "to stop the killing and end the violence."[103] Overall, "MONUC was showing signs in Ituri of becoming the force it should have been over the previous four years."[104]

Yet the same could not be said for MONUC in the Kivus, described as the "crucible" of conflict,[105] which by 2003 had been "on fire"[106] for close to ten years and had been experiencing a "cancerous metastasis of armies and militias."[107] The International Rescue Committee had estimated in a report in April 2003 that between 1998 and the end of 2002, 3.3 million "excess deaths" had occurred as a result of the war, which was the largest death toll in any war since World War II.[108] In a previous report, it had noted that more people had died in the DRC than in all wars in the world in the same period.[109] The majority of these deaths were the result of disease and malnutrition brought on by the conditions of the war, including mass displacement, although more than 80 percent of homes had experienced violence.[110]

Though its numbers were beefed up, MONUC acted passively into 2004, allowing forces led by Laurent Nkunda,[111] a dissident from RCD-Goma, to take over Bukavu in June 2004.[112] And while some of its high-visibility patrols did contribute to stability and localized protection, once the patrols left an area, the violence returned.[113] The UN argued that once there was no peace to keep, "the role of peacekeepers end,"[114] although there also seemed to be a conflict between the military and political leadership of MONUC.[115] This reflected the fact that MONUC was not given adequate resources to carry out a robust PoC mandate,[116] as well as continuing confusion about the role of peacekeepers in situations that seemed to hover between peace and war. More important, perhaps, it was a reflection of the lack of guidance given to peacekeepers on how to carry out their PoC mandate.[117]

The Security Council reiterated MONUC's PoC mandate on 1 October in Resolution 1565, which authorized MONUC "to use all necessary means, within its capacity and in the areas where its armed units are deployed." This was in line with the recent report from the Secretary-General, although it included far fewer additional troops—5,900 versus 13,100—than he had requested.[118] By early 2005, MONUC began engaging in more robust activities, including an operation in South Kivu to protect villages from nighttime attacks.[119] This was clearly needed, since at the end of 2004, 31,000 people were dying each month as a result of the conflict, even though the war had theoretically been over for eighteen months.[120] At the same time, reports began to emerge of sexual exploitation and abuse on the part of peacekeepers. While a horrible violation of trust itself, it was doubly ironic given that sexual violence was to become a defining element of violence against civilians in the DRC.[121] MONUC's mandate was further strengthened in March 2005 in Resolution 1592, which reiterated that "MONUC is authorized to use all necessary means, within its capabilities and in the areas where its armed units are deployed . . . to ensure the protection of civilians under imminent threat of physical violence, from any armed group, foreign or Congolese . . . and to disrupt the military capability of illegal armed groups."[122] MONUC was encouraged "to make full use of its mandate under resolution 1565."

The more forceful response was sporadic. In the first half of 2005, MONUC indicated that it would take more forceful action to disarm the Forces Démocratiques de Libération du Rwanda (FDLR)—yet another reincarnation of the Rwandan *génocidaires*—both by itself and in association with the Congolese army, the Forces Armées de la République Démocratique du

Congo (FARDC).[123] There were few results.[124] Indeed, MONUC indicated that it would not engage in forcible disarmament itself. That would be left up to FARDC. MONUC did not feel that it was its duty, as a peacekeeping operation, to engage in "targeted warfare," and it was worried about possible repercussions for civilians.[125] The FDLR remained an intact, if somewhat diminished, fighting force. MONUC engaged in some other innovative activities, which had some effect on civilian protection,[126] although massacres still occurred.[127] The Ituri Brigade had a bit more success, such that, at the same time that five militia leaders were arrested by the government—including Thomas Lubanga, who would later become the first person convicted by the ICC—15,000 of approximately 20,000 militia were disarmed.[128] However, even as the threat of violence—although still present[129]—receded a bit, FARDC became a new source of insecurity.[130] MSF documented a precarious security situation for civilians.[131] It also raised questions about the relationship between MONUC and humanitarian actors,[132] which will be discussed below. Because of the lack of security, MSF had to withdraw from the outskirts of Bunia in late July 2005.[133]

On 21 December 2005, the Security Council reemphasized the robust POC mandate.[134] It also seemed to make a link between the security of civilians and the political process.[135] It followed this up with a resolution[136] in April 2006 that authorized a European Union Force in the DRC to help provide security in Kinshasa for the elections. It included a PoC mandate "in the areas of its deployment," although given that the worst violence was in the east, this was not a particularly relevant mandate,[137] but it did serve to reinforce the principle, and EUFOR itself did generally contribute to the security of the elections.[138]

During this period the focus of political activity turned to the elections in 2006. This also became a focus for MONUC. The peace agreement in 2002 led to the official end of the war with a new transitional government installed on 30 June 2003, which included senior posts for leaders from various rebel and opposition groups. According to Autesserre, this shifted the entire mindset of MONUC from peace enforcement to peacekeeping as the DRC became "postconflict."[139] Given the amount of fighting documented above, however, this would seem to have been a less than accurate assessment of the situation—certainly in the east.[140] The "election fetish"[141] reoriented the focus away from security and the protection of people. In mid-2005 the Secretary-General requested additional troops for Katanga Province—eventually authorized in 2006—to secure the elections rather than secure the territory or the population.[142] In "postconflict" DRC, protection of civilians became subordinate to other interests—with just a few exceptions.

The first five years of MONUC were characterized by a piecemeal response that reflected the lack of interest and political will to actually address the situation. It also called into question the focus on PoC. While armed with a PoC mandate, the peacekeepers did not know what to do with it, and did not have the resources for widespread protection of civilians. While the punctuated robust responses from 2003/4 were perhaps somewhat encouraging, the need was far greater. Two observers note that "a weak operation still creates the impression, among the local population, that something is being done to protect civilians and keep the peace, when in fact that is not the case."[143] Weak, ineffective peacekeeping thus operates in the same way as humanitarianism to create the illusion of action—not only for the local population but also internationally. While the phased nature of the buildup and deployment of MONUC may have been lauded by some, it was also a reflection of lack of international will to actually take the required action to protect people in a robust, ongoing, and meaningful way.[144] Although the PoC concept is portrayed as nonpolitical, the experience in the DRC made it very clear that it is not. When PoC requires taking robust military action—including killing people—against military and political actors, this is political and requires political will, which was lacking in April 1994 when the genocide in Rwanda started, later in 1994 and beyond when insecurity started to grow as a direct result of the fallout of the genocide, and in 1998 when the civil war in eastern DRC, directly tied to the genocide, erupted again. It took several years for even a modicum of will to assert itself.

A Renewed Focus on Protection of Civilians

MONUC did start to take PoC more seriously as an overarching concept or "umbrella framework" for all actors. It acted as a "force multiplier"[145] for humanitarian actors, facilitating the delivery of humanitarian assistance and expanding humanitarian space by "initiating" humanitarian access (rather than just accepting it), "challenging military contingents to take on their responsibilities, conducting joint assessments, providing military protection to humanitarian convoys, physically taking civilians out of danger, demining, and establishing field hospitals."[146] These activities belong, perhaps, under the heading of humanitarian protection, although the military element provides a more robust side and demonstrates some of the issues of conceptual clarity surrounding the concept of protection. MONUC accrued more respect than did the humanitarian coordinator precisely because of the military might it represented, and it could use this respect to negotiate access. Further, the humanitarian coordinator acquired more authority because of his position as the deputy special representative of the Secretary-General, rather than his humanitarian position per se.[147] Palliators thus drew on the power of the protectors. MONUC did, however, also take more robust, R2P type measures to directly protect civilians in a wider area through the deployment of military personnel outside the context of humanitarian support action.[148]

This more robust action came at a cost. First, there were instances of retaliation on the part of the FDLR against civilians.[149] Second, FARDC engaged in widespread human rights violations.[150] This was put down, at least partly, to the government not paying the troops, in particular the newly integrated rebel troops.[151] Indeed, MONUC identified FARDC as responsible for 40 percent of human rights abuses.[152] Third, there were negative humanitarian consequences. The robust activities sometimes pushed rebel groups farther into the bush, destabilizing new areas and leading to greater displacement of the civilian population. Furthermore, aid groups were worried about being seen as collaborating with armed peacekeepers, which could lead to decreased access to populations in need of assistance,[153] and some left South Kivu.[154]

Yet, even with the above issues, FARDC was seen as the only game in town, and continued cooperation with FARDC was prescribed in the Secretary-General's report of 20 March 2007.[155] Given the vast territory and limited resources of MONUC, it had little choice but to cooperate with FARDC.[156] The Security Council concurred, and in Resolution 1756 it extended the mandate of MONUC, which at this point had grown to an accepted troop strength of 17,030, until the end of 2007, clearly putting protection of civilians at the top of its responsibilities and priorities.[157] It also focused particular attention on the issue of sexual violence.[158] The Secretary-General's report on 2 April 2008 noted a "bleak" humanitarian situation.[159] It also noted significant issues of humanitarian access, harassment of aid workers, and the necessity of armed escorts.[160] The report also included a section on protection of civilians, citing the direct protection by MONUC of 150,000 civilians in North Kivu.[161] They would certainly need such protection given the release of an updated report from the IRC in January calculating that 5.4 million people had died in the DRC between 1998 and 2007, with 2.1 million of the deaths occurring since 2002—that is, when the DRC entered its "post-conflict" phase. Eastern DRC had a death rate 85 percent higher than the average across all sub-Saharan Africa.[162] The fighting resumed at the end of August in North Kivu, which produced 100,000 IDPs within a few days, and an additional 250,000 IDPs overall. Around one hundred civilians were killed in the following couple of months, and there was widespread sexual violence, with thousands or tens of thousands of cases. Humanitarian organizations had to suspend their activities in the face of being targeted and general insecurity.[163] In contrast, Ituri seemed like a peaceful haven, with MONUC having reduced the risk of renewed violence and breaking up some of the armed groups.[164]

MONUC's relationship with FARDC, and its credibility in protecting civilians, were further strained in the second half of 2008 in the wake of expanded fighting near Goma. FARDC used MONUC troops as human shields. In one attack on 4 November, 150 civilians were killed by the Congrès National pour la Défense du Peuple (CNDP, a group created by Laurent Nkunda in December 2006[165]) even though MONUC troops were nearby. MONUC used its resources to protect aid workers, a journalist, and military observers rather than the local population.[166] MONUC could protect civilians only in major population areas; elsewhere, it could only protect itself.[167] Human Rights Watch called for more peacekeepers.[168] The Security Council responded by temporarily increasing the overall strength of MONUC by 3,085. These were to be deployed immediately, with an initial mandate until the end of the year, although there was clear indication that this would be extended.[169] However, as HRW noted, it could take up to four months for the troops to be deployed, and it thus endorsed a call for an EU bridging force to be deployed until the additional troops arrived,[170] which was not forthcoming. The following day the Secretary-General noted that "The humanitarian toll on the civilian population has been immense."[171]

He also noted "that the lack of capacity of FARDC is a major impediment to peace and to the fulfillment by MONUC of its mandate."[172] In other words, the region was in flames, large numbers of innocent people were dying, and the government was incapable of addressing the situation. Again, this was little different than the situation in eastern Zaire fourteen years earlier. The UN continued to respond incrementally.

The expanded fighting highlighted the role of Rwanda in eastern DRC. The CNDP was a proxy of Kigali. There was suspicion that Rwandan troops were fighting again in Congolese territory. While unproven, it did seem clear that Rwanda was using its territory to support the CNDP, including recruiting child soldiers and providing equipment.[173] This was the first time that Rwanda's allies in the West openly implicated Rwanda for its support for the CNDP.[174] Kabila asked for a multinational force from SADC, with no success. The EU discussed a possible EU force in the interim while the additional MONUC forces deployed. Yet EU countries were wary of Rwanda's response and did not want to risk European lives.[175] A mandate given to the UN Secretary-General's special envoy for the Great Lakes Region, former Nigerian president Olusegun Obasanjo, "to focus on addressing the challenges to peace and security posed by the continued presence and activities of illegal armed groups in the eastern part of the country and on building confidence between the Democratic Republic of the Congo and its neighbours"[176] seemed like 1994 all over again.

The Security Council further focused MONUC's mandate on protection of civilians on 22 December in Resolution 1856. Belgium and Burkina Faso wanted MONUC to be able to act against armed groups independently of FARDC.[177] Given the problems with FARDC, this would be a crucial empowerment of MONUC. The Security Council noted "that a major obstacle to lasting peace in the Kivus is the presence and activities of illegal armed groups on Congolese territory"—fourteen years after it refused to do anything about other illegal groups on Congolese territory. It extended the deployment of MONUC until the end of 2009 at a total strength of 22,016. The resolution stated that, acting under Chapter VII, the Security Council authorized the use of "all necessary means" (i.e., military force) to protect civilians, support security of humanitarian operations, and "cooperate in national and international efforts to bring to justice perpetrators of grave violations of human rights and international humanitarian law." It thus gave MONUC a mandate to contribute to all elements of R2P[3], although it listed PoC as the top priority.

This was an unequivocal statement of support for PoC. By putting this at the top of MONUC's agenda, and calling for robust rules of engagement, the Security Council was mandating a muscular response to violence against civilians. Yet it took a long time for PoC to become a top priority for MONUC. MONUC itself, and the PoC mandate in particular, were ratcheted up incrementally, with only periodic robust action to protect civilians. Further, it should be noted that the most robust mandate to protect civilian populations occurred during a period of notional "peace."

Yet the dangers to civilians were to escalate.[178] In January 2009 Kinshasa and Kigali decided to put aside their differences and cooperate to deal with the FDLR.[179] This included joint military action in North Kivu named Umoja Wetu. A small number of both CNDP and FDLR combatants were disarmed. Yet a significant portion of the FDLR was pushed westward, in a situation reminiscent of 1996. And, again, civilians bore the brunt of the operation. By mid-February more than 100 civilians had been killed, and by early March UNHCR had registered an additional 160,000 IDPs.[180] Sexual violence continued unabated, with an average of thirty-six reported rapes every day.[181] The toll on civilians would increase as MONUC joined FARDC for renewed action against the FDLR in an operation called Kimia II. The two operations combined led to the displacement of 1.5 million people by August 2009.[182] In July, Oxfam warned of FDLR reprisal attacks against civilians,[183] and access for humanitarian organizations became more difficult.[184] FARDC was seen as the main perpetrator of sexual violence in some areas, as well as engaging in other "grave abuses."[185] The Secretary-General also noted the negative effects on humanitarian access.[186] The situation was exacerbated by the rapid integration of militia groups into the military, including not paying the former militia. Given that, as one observer pointed out in 2010, "the Congolese army is now a melting pot which includes 56 rebel groups, successively 'integrated' since the 1980s,"[187] one can understand the impediment to creating a coherent, disciplined fighting force. The local population also felt that MONUC was having a limited impact in providing security. The 3,000 extra troops had yet to be deployed.[188] In November, Human Rights Watch noted killings and reprisals by FARDC "in a military operation backed by the United Nations."[189] A report the month before cited "more than 1,000 civilians killed, 7,000 raped, and 900,000 forced from their homes."[190] These abuses were well known to MONUC, which theoretically was involved to minimize the potential harm to civilians. It took eight months for MONUC to announce that it would suspend support for one army brigade. Further, one of those deemed responsible for many of the abuses was Bosco Ntaganda, former leader of CNDP (and former member of the RPF and RPA),[191] who became a general in the FARDC, and who had an outstanding ICC arrest warrant that the government refused to implement.[192] Thus, instead of contributing to the protection of civilians, MONUC appeared complicit in abuses against civilians. And the international community was reluctant to criticize Ntaganda's promotion and role in Kimia II,[193] or the broader fallout from the various initiatives.[194]

The Security Council weighed in again on the DRC on 7 December, giving the DRC government the diplomatic equivalent of a slap on the wrist by "*strongly encouraging* the Government of the Democratic Republic of the Congo to implement its 'zero-tolerance policy' against criminal acts and misconduct in the armed forces."[195] Two weeks later, citing resolutions 1674 and 1894 (which it had just passed the previous month, and which reaffirmed the responsibility to protect) on the protection of civilians, it again decided that PoC should be MONUC's top priority. It also gave explicit direction to MONUC regarding conditions for its support of FARDC operations, including the possibility of MONUC withdrawing its support from units that committed grave violations of international humanitarian, human rights, and refugee law.[196] MONUC had also developed such a policy,[197] although it would turn out to be toothless.[198] At the same time, the Secretary-General noted "innovative measures to protect civilians from attacks by illegal armed groups and FARDC elements"[199] although he also noted 125 attacks on aid workers and a restriction on humanitarian operations.[200] By the end of 2009, only 2,050 of the 3,085 additional troops the Security Council had approved more than a year earlier had arrived.[201]

Kimia II, which reduced FDLR ranks by around half, was formally ended in December 2009, to be replaced by another operation, Amani Leo. Even with reduced numbers, however, the security situation was still precarious.[202] The Secretary-General noted "significant challenges."[203] The human rights situation continued to be "problematic," with a "high level of human rights violations" and a "high level of displacement."[204] The rate of sexual violence increased to forty-two incidents each day,[205] leading the UN special representative on sexual violence in conflict to call the DRC the "rape capital of the world."[206] At the same time, there was discussion of drawing down MONUC forces, with a target date of June 2011. MONUC would be reconfigured to focus more on capacity-building and peacebuilding, although PoC would also remain a priority.[207] The Security Council, in renaming MONUC the UN Organization Stabilization Mission in the Democratic Republic of Congo (MONUSCO), agreed to an initial withdrawal of 2,000 troops by the end of June 2010 while also keeping PoC at the top of its priorities.[208] The rebranding of the peacekeeping operation coincided with a broader shift toward "stabilization." This included creation of the Stabilization and Reconstruction Plan for Eastern DRC (STAREC) and the International Security and Stabilization Support Strategy (ISSSS).[209] This shift from "pacification" to "stabilization" seemed as inappropriate as labeling post-2003 DRC "postconflict." And what stabilization meant was unclear. As Oxfam noted, "the nature of stabilisation is still 'vague and uncertain' and understandings of it vary. . . . In the DRC this uncertainty is particularly evident."[210] In addition, there can be conflict between mitigating conflict and providing assistance, as well as between military stabilization and PoC: "Stabilisation might move the UN aid agencies closer to the security agenda of the mission, thus reducing humanitarian space."[211]

In October 2010, the Secretary-General noted that while most of the country was free of conflict[212] (and there were fewer civilian casualties in the DRC[213]), the eastern part of the country was still wracked with violence, with increasing attacks against civilians.[214] He noted the need for further improvement in PoC, and in particular the need for more helicopters.[215] Two years after the rapprochement between the DRC and Rwanda, and subsequent action against the FDLR, the FDLR was not significantly weakened,[216] although the arrest in France, and subsequent transfer to the ICC, of Callixte Mbarushimana, the vice-president of the FDLR, did help disrupt some of its activities.[217] The credibility of MONUSCO was called into question based on its inability to protect civilians.[218] The under Secretary-General for peacekeeping operations, Atul Khare, recognized the failure of MONUSCO to stop mass rapes in Walikale.[219] Both the FARDC and rebel groups continued to recruit child soldiers.[220] The number of IDPs in the Kivus rose, with 90,000 IDPs being generated as a result of one FARDC offensive against ADF rebels on the border with Uganda, although as a result of the change in operating area of the militias, many IDPs were able to return to their home areas.[221] Yet the number of IDPs in South Kivu more than doubled, with people fleeing attacks as well as possible retribution.[222] Humanitarian insecurity increased significantly in the first half of 2010, with 120 incidents involving aid workers, which affected their ability to deliver assistance and evaluate needs.[223]

Security Council Resolution 1991 of 28 June 2011 reiterated the priority of the protection of civilians by MONUSCO. While focus turned to the elections, rebels and FARDC were still engaging in widespread abuses.[224] In June and July there were a total of 620 human rights abuses attributed to militias (300) and FARDC (320).[225] In the space of four days in June at least 387 civilians were raped in one part of North Kivu.[226] By July, MONUSCO was left with no attack helicopters, and only ten utility and four observation helicopters, leaving it unable to protect civilians or go after armed groups.[227] There were continuing restrictions on humanitarian access, with 133 incidents against humanitarian workers in the Kivus the first nine months of the year.[228] Heading into 2012, violent conflict continued, with more than 100,000 people displaced between November 2011 and January 2012.[229] The renewed violence included the reactivation of a group led by Gedeon Kyungu Mutanga, which was supported by the government until the end of the war in 2003, at which time it became, like many others, a criminal gang. Gedeon was convicted by a military court in 2009 and sentenced to death. However, he escaped from prison in September 2011, likely with the help of the government so he could engage in election-related violence.[230]

The situation took another turn for the worse in April 2012. Bosco Ntaganda, former protégé of Thomas Lubanga and general in the FARDC, deserted, along with several hundred of his soldiers, from the army. Ntaganda had previously been protected by Kabila, who refused to arrest him and turn him over to the ICC. After the desertion, Kabila called for his arrest but said he would not turn him over to the ICC.[231] The deserters called themselves M23 (Mouvement de 23 Mars—referring to the failed[232] 2009 peace agreement),[233] and the fighting led to renewed movements of refugees to Rwanda and Uganda,[234] with up to 200,000 displaced in two months,[235] and reports of forced recruitment of child soldiers.[236] The activities of M23 were exacerbated by renewed attacks by Mai-Mai militias targeting Kinyarwanda speakers.[237] At the end of May a UN report[238] was leaked that accused Rwanda of supporting the M23 group, as well as other armed groups in eastern DRC— which Kabila described as an "'open secret'"[239] and which Rwanda denied. In talks held between Rwanda and the DRC, Rwanda requested impunity for Ntaganda and other mutineers.[240]

On 27 June, the Security Council passed Resolution 2053, noting the abuses of M23. It did not, however, criticize Rwanda for its support of M23. The resolution also cited the need to bring Ntaganda to justice. In a press statement on 16 July, the Security Council condemned outside support for armed groups in the DRC, although, again, it did not name Rwanda,[241] while the EU made a half-hearted attempt to call on Rwanda to stop "any" support of such groups.[242] However, the United States, which initially sought to prevent the release of the report criticizing Rwanda, along with the UK[243] and other donor countries, began to withhold aid from Rwanda, and the U.S. war crimes ambassador, Stephen Rapp, indicated that Rwanda's leaders might be investigated by the ICC, demonstrating perhaps that the "genocide credit"[244] that had protected Rwanda from criticism was starting to run out.[245] Uganda was also implicated in supporting M23.[246] There were talks among the various countries with a view toward implementing a "neutral" force to address the M23 (and an initial agreement on a 4,000-person force by the International Conference on the Great Lakes Region [ICGLR][247]), although they foundered partly on the question of whether it should include Rwandan forces, which the DRC rejected.[248] In October, a UN report was leaked that claimed that the Rwandan defense minister, James Kabarebe, had effective control over M23.[249] On 12 November the report was submitted to the Security Council, confirming allegations of Rwandan and Ugandan support for M23.[250] The Security Council responded with two resolutions condemning M23,[251] the first one the same day Goma fell to M23 as "far better armed and more numerous"[252] peacekeepers watched.[253]

In late February 2013, a regional "framework" agreement was announced that was intended to bring peace to the DRC.[254] At the same time, M23 fractured[255] and Ntaganda fled, eventually turning himself in to the U.S. Embassy in Kigali to be turned over to the ICC.[256] Immediately after the framework was presented, and in the context of this new agreement, the Secretary-General submitted a report that noted the multiplicity of armed groups operating in eastern DRC.[257] He recognized that the first step in "stabilizing" eastern DRC was to deal with these groups. As part of this strategy, he recommended the creation of an intervention brigade within MONUSCO that would be tasked with "neutralizing" these armed groups.[258] A month later, the Security Council endorsed the creation of an Intervention Brigade within MONUSCO's existing structure and troop limits, and reiterated that its top priority was protection of civilians.[259]

The resolution, which also authorized the use of unmanned aerial vehicles, clearly stated that this brigade—which "highlights the reluctance of some to implement the mandate [of MONUSCO] to its fullest extent"[260]—would not be a precedent. Challenging core peacekeeping principles such as impartiality and consent, and using force only in self-defense,[261] the force would essentially repurpose about 3,000 existing South African, Tanzanian, and Malawian MONUSCO troops to engage in even more forceful activities against M23 and other groups.[262] Many humanitarian organizations expressed fear that it could exacerbate the humanitarian situation.[263] The Intervention Brigade had some early success against M23, but, as the commander of MONUSCO, Lieutenant-General Carlos Alberto Dos Santos Cruz, said when it began to deploy, "it is not a magic solution to all the problems."[264] Indeed, with forty armed groups present in eastern DRC, and the bewildering complex international context of the conflict, any final solutions to the conflict will also be complex. Further, while on the one hand it appears to represent a renewed commitment to the principles of R2P in its focus on stopping atrocities, it is also a reflection of disagreement among troop-contributing countries over how far such missions should go. As this is being written, it appears that M23 has been defeated, but it is too soon to evaluate the staying power of the revitalized international efforts to address the two-decades-old conflict in the DRC.

R2P³ in the DRC

The reports of the Secretary-General sound like a broken record. "Persistent violations of human rights." "Sexual violence." Restrictions on humanitarian access. Violence by FARDC and militias. Increasing numbers of IDPs. "Innovative" approaches to PoC.[265] Although advances are cited, "robust" action is taken, and "innovations" implemented, it is difficult to see fundamental change. There are claims about numbers of civilians protected, but while certainly important, they are but a drop in the ocean of "human misery" regularly cited. MONUC/MONUSCO did, eventually, make it up to the 20,000 troops requested by countries in the region ten years earlier, but this seemed miniscule compared to the required 100,000 troops cited in a UN report in 1999, or downright stingy compared to the more than 100,000 troops deployed by the United States in both Iraq and Afghanistan.[266] The billion dollars per year spent on MONUC sounds like a lot, until, again, it is compared to Afghanistan or Iraq. And the shortage of helicopters in the later years is a reflection of where the West's priorities lay.

In the final pages of this chapter I will analyze in more depth how the three responsibilities have been implemented, how they have interacted, and how the DRC illustrates many of the dilemmas discussed in Chapter 1.

Palliation

The amount of money spent on humanitarian aid over the course of the conflict has been significant. Yet, much of the need has been unmet, and it has paled in comparison to the amount spent on peacekeeping. The figures in Table 3.1 reflect the amount requested and received via the UN Consolidated Appeals process. This does not capture all bilateral and non-UN

Table 3.1. Total Consolidated Appeals 2000–2013 (US$)

Year	Original requirements	Revised requirements	Total resources available	Unmet requirements	Percent covered
2000	71,363,897	37,039,207	13,109,710	23,929,497	35.4
2001	139,464,891	122,856,090	83,132,706	39,723,384	67.7
2002	194,140,365	202,201,192	98,431,642	103,769,550	48.7
2003	268,645,326	229,407,473	108,782,190	120,625,283	47.4
2004	187,094,868	162,602,463	118,811,355	43,791,108	73.1
2005	185,394,640	219,757,245	142,656,881	77,100,364	64.9
2006	644,929,808	696,024,728	354,195,238	341,829,490	50.9
2007	686,591,107	686,591,107	463,818,035	222,773,072	67.6
2008	575,654,173	736,511,765	607,264,789	129,246,976	82.5
2009	831,005,682	946,252,242	644,401,677	301,850,565	68.1
2010	827,616,628	827,616,628	521,026,865	306,589,763	63.0
2011	719,289,671	735,754,098	487,391,703	248,362,395	66.2
2012	718,555,610	791,331,026	589,870,347	201,460,679	74.5
2013[a]	892,643,970	892,643,970	489,949,241	402,694,729	54.9

Data from OCHA Financial Tracking Service, http://fts.unocha.org/, as of 24 October 2013.
[a]Partial year, through 24 October 2013.

multilateral aid, but it represents the largest amount and will serve to indicate trends.

As can be seen, in every year the need was much greater than the resources made available. Further, the absolute figures say little about how much was accomplished, given the scale and magnitude of both the need and the problems associated with operating in the DRC, including the lack of infrastructure; the lack of roads, which necessitated the use of air transport; and, of course, the complex security and actor environment, where humanitarians had to negotiate a minefield of ever-shifting and contradictory alliances and hostile groups.[267]

There was a very substantial increase in both requested aid and actual aid provided in 2006 and following years. This was during and after the transition. Thus, just when the country was supposed to become more stable as a result of the elections and the inclusion of government opponents in the government as a result of the peace deal, the situation seemed to have gotten worse, at least in the eastern part of the country. In addition to comprising the world's largest peacekeeping force, the DRC was consuming a substantial portion the world's humanitarian assistance, accounting for 15 percent of funds from the Central Emergency Relief Fund in 2006 and 2007. The east accounted for 80 percent of external resources.[268] Palliation still seemed to be the order of the day.

Protection Cluster

The DRC witnessed the most significant development of the concept of protection of civilians, with significant interaction between palliators and protectors in implementing PoC. A new element in the focus on PoC—the protection cluster—was introduced in 2006. In 2005 the Inter-Agency Standing Committee created the cluster system "to strengthen system-wide preparedness and technical capacity to respond to humanitarian emergencies by ensuring that there is predictable leadership and accountability in all the main sectors or areas of humanitarian response."[269] One organization would take the lead in coordinating action among various humanitarian actors in each of nine particular areas of activity, such as food, refugees, and education.[270] UNHCR was designated the lead agency for the global protection cluster.[271] The cluster approach was created to coordinate the *humanitarian* response. However, as noted in Chapter 1, many humanitarians conceptualize their work as entailing protection. A further claim, however, came in December 2006 when the UNHCR assistant high commissioner for protection, Erika Feller, tied it directly to R2P, maintaining that "The 'cluster approach' now being introduced in situations of internal displacement . . . [has] been formulated as a means of operationalizing the notion of a 'responsibility to protect.'"[272] While humanitarians frequently shy away from using R2P terminology,[273] this was an explicit attempt to tie the PoC agenda to R2P, while at the same time making a distinction between the *humanitarian* response and the *human rights* response.[274] The IASC also foresaw the need to coordinate with other actors, including peacekeepers.[275] However, the application of the protection cluster in the DRC went beyond coordination led by UNHCR.

The Protection Cluster began in the DRC at the beginning of 2006. Given that the entire population was under threat of displacement, the cluster was given responsibility for the entire population, rather than just IDPs.[276] This represented a significant expansion of the mandate for humanitarian actors like UNHCR. Further, however, UNHCR was to share cluster lead responsibilities with MONUC because of its PoC mandate.[277] There was a recognition that PoC might require military action.[278] Thus, a humanitarian actor, which, while still embedded within the global political milieu of the UN, and which is supposed to act according to a humanitarian ethos, was paired with a military actor, also embedded within UN (and DRC) politics with a mandate to kill people—a rather different mandate and working method than UNHCR. They had two different understandings of protection and two different ways of approaching and carrying out that mandate. The potential for the conundrums outlined in Chapter 1 to become reality was great.

There would be situations where the only way to address immediate threats to civilians would be through military action[279]—an acceptance of the limitations of humanitarian protection. Constraints on the Protection Cluster also became clear early on, including the scale of the situation and the fact that in order to address root causes of protection violations—for example, the various militias and armed groups—a high-level political strategy was needed. The former constraint required many more resources than were available to both MONUC and humanitarian actors such as UNHCR, while the latter illustrated the limits of humanitarian action. UNHCR is not designed to deal with such issues, and MONUC as a peacekeeping operation—albeit one with an evolving and strengthening mandate—could only do so much. Jaya Murthy thus concluded that "the Protection Cluster will ultimately be unsuccessful in protecting civilians at risk" until the "highest political agents in the international community"—that is, the Security Council—become more engaged in a sustained manner.[280]

Even though "there seemed to be genuine progress in achieving coherence between the military and civilian approaches to protection,"[281] MONUC's coleading of the Protection Cluster did not last long. In addition to arguments that clusters should not be led by two UN bodies, there were significant concerns surrounding MONUC's impartiality and neutrality,[282] particularly in the context of its support of FARDC military operations. By 2009 MONUC had begun to move away from its cluster coleading activities throughout the country.[283] One report noted that "too close an alignment between humanitarian agencies and UN political or peacekeeping actors may undermine the perceived neutrality and impartiality of humanitarian action and pose a threat to humanitarian space."[284]

The UN Secretary-General observed in July 2010 that "The support of MONUC to FARDC also seems to have led to negative perceptions of United Nations humanitarian organizations, and incidents of targeting escorted United Nations humanitarian convoys were reported."[285]

Tensions between Security Council mandates and humanitarian principles were noted by one observer,[286] as were concerns that "politics would always 'trump' humanitarianism."[287] And, while there were concerns that humanitarian actors would be perceived as being connected to political agendas, "there is evidence that actors on the ground do draw distinctions between humanitarian actors and other parts of the UN. Maintaining such a distinct identity can play an important role in ensuring humanitarian space in ongoing conflict situations."[288]

There is clear recognition of the political milieu in which UNHCR works. Thus, "UNHCR should seek to influence and contribute to the Secretary General's report and to mission mandates," including "political engagement with member states and Security Council members" on Security Council resolutions.[289] If a humanitarian agency is involved in the political process of drawing up a political document that authorizes a peacekeeping operation to, among other things, kill people in the process of "keeping" or "enforcing" peace, or protecting civilians, and to potentially take sides (e.g., cooperating with FARDC), it becomes embedded within the political goals of the operation, and it becomes hard for it to claim impartiality and neutrality. Although this level of engagement with the political process would not be apparent on the ground, and thus would not necessarily affect perceptions, the fact that it is a UN agency still creates potential problems. And if UNHCR is linked to politics/partiality, other humanitarian organizations may be, too.

The challenge for other humanitarian actors is to avoid being tainted in this way. Some NGOs felt that many individuals did not understand the difference between NGOs and the UN,[290] while others thought there was greater understanding of the difference between NGOs, ICRC, and UN. The ICRC, in particular, has been active in disseminating information about its work, and this openness has led to a certain amount of trust of the ICRC in the DRC.[291] Oxfam, recognizing that the security of aid workers depends on being accepted by the locals,[292] in an attempt to distinguish itself from other actors and thus maintain its impartial humanitarian brand identity, took two superficial yet effective actions. First, instead of using Toyota Landcruisers, the vehicle of choice of the modern humanitarian,[293] Oxfam uses Land Rovers. Second, to set them apart from other actors in an even more strikingly visual manner, they were painted purple. This was saying to the armed groups: we are different, we are not the UN, we are not tied in with their agendas, we are just here to help you. Oxfam vehicles were not shot at because everybody knew about their "funny cars."[294] On the other hand, Tasneem Mowjee claims that, with a few exceptions, "aid workers were targeted, not due to the nature of their work, but as a result of the resources they represented,"[295] although this applied more to international staff. National staff had many more problems in this regard.[296]

Other concerns regarding UNHCR's and NGOs' relationship to MONUC include requests from MONUC to the Protection Cluster for "detailed protection information (e.g., the whereabouts of civilian populations, individual cases of sex- and gender-based violence (SGBV)"[297] to help it carry out its PoC mandate. This conflicts with the humanitarians' desire to protect sources and victims. Further, when members of the Protection Cluster participate in the filling in of the protection matrix, which indicates where MONUC must, should, or could protect civilians, they are taking part in hostilities.[298] ICRC did not formally participate in the cluster. It was an observer, so its name did not appear on any official cluster documents.[299] It could thus claim distance between the politics of, and robust actions resulting from, the Protection Cluster. A related issue arose in the context of the Secretary-General's 29th-report. UNHCR wrote to the special representative on behalf of the protection cluster to express concern over some confidential information that had appeared. Besides noting this particular issue, it also helped to create distance between the cluster as an independent entity and MONUC.[300]

In January 2010, the UN issued the "UN System-Wide Strategy for the Protection of Civilians in the Democratic Republic of Congo." It involved not only MONUC but UNHCR and other UN agencies. The idea was to bring together the wide variety of UN agencies present in the DRC under one coherent strategy. Given that it involves a very wide array of actors with different mandates, modes of operating, and understandings of protection, the concept of PoC might be stretched so much that it is meaningless.[301]

According to the UN Department of Peacekeeping Operations' (DPKO) "United Nations Peacekeeping Operations: Principles and Guidelines,"

> An integrated mission is one in which there is a shared vision among all United Nations actors as to the strategic objectives of the United Nations presence at the country-level. This strategy should reflect a shared understanding of the operating environment and agreement on how to maximize the effectiveness, efficiency, and impact of the United Nations overall response.[302]

Thus, all parts of the UN should have the same understanding of the goals of the UN mission in a country and how to achieve these goals. And different parts of the UN can support each other.[303] Yet, integration could also affect perceptions of neutrality of NGOs.[304] Thus, MONUC can be an advocate for humanitarian action and provide direct protection, such as through secure corridors and mobile operating bases.[305] Indeed, in 2009 UN agencies were reliant on MONUC escorts to reach 94 percent of North Kivu because of insecurity.[306] At the same time, since MONUC was considered a party to the conflict,[307] this could affect the perception of the neutrality of UN humanitarian agencies and other humanitarian actors. Indeed, UNHCR feels ill at ease with the concept of "One UN" at times, precisely because of its need for the appearance of neutrality, which can be affected by the actions of other parts of the UN. And its cochairing of the Protection Cluster was "not an easy fit," given their different needs and priorities.[308] Further, while all UN agencies are supposed to have the same goals and priorities, this frequently does not happen in practice. UNHCR was frequently dependent upon MONUC to reach remote areas. But UNHCR staff were not accorded priority on these flights, thus undermining UNHCR's ability to carry out its mission. Vicky Tennant recommends a separate flight service for UNHCR. While this might have the positive effect of gaining a bit of distance from MONUC, it also calls into question the idea of an integrated UN mission with common priorities.[309]

Further, at times when NGOs asked for protection, they were told to go to FARDC. Receiving protection from FARDC would make them even more of a target than if they were protected by MONUC.[310] Given that FARDC was also responsible for civilian deaths, this would further undermine confidence on the part of NGOs.

Humanitarian Conundrums

Thus, while MONUC played a positive role at times in supporting humanitarian action, and humanitarian actors and MONUC did engage in a positive way in many situations,[311] some of the potential problems highlighted in Chapter 1 are also in evidence. In particular, by being perceived as a party to the conflict, MONUC's relationship with humanitarian actors could call into question such actors' neutrality and independence, making it more difficult for them to do their jobs. Yet humanitarians can run into problems even when connection to the UN or other actors is not an issue.

An incident in Ituri in 2001 serves to highlight one of the main conundrums of humanitarian aid—the limits of impartiality. On 26 April 2001, six

ICRC staff were murdered—four local and two expatriate staff.[312] As part of its aid efforts, the ICRC had initially prepositioned supplies in Hema areas. After doing further surveys, it decided to move a significant portion of the resources to Lendu areas.[313] The Hema did not like the fact that the ICRC was helping its enemies and decided to retaliate.[314] The ICRC left the region. As I have previously written about this situation:

> To the ICRC, moving the resources seemed like a reasonable action—take the resources to where they are most needed. To the Hema, it appeared that the ICRC was taking sides. The ICRC was being impartial, but was being impartial the politically savvy thing to do? In the end, six aid workers were killed and the ICRC lost access to affected populations. Was impartiality relevant in this situation? Should it have left more resources in the Hema areas to "buy off" the dominant group?[315]

This case highlights a fundamental paradox in the humanitarian ethos. Humanitarians want to provide aid where it is most needed. Yet such aid can be perceived as providing resources to one's enemy.[316] It—and humanitarian actors themselves—thus become politicized and embedded within the conflict. Humanitarians thus have to deal with alternate perceptions of what they do, which can constrain their freedom of movement and their ability to do what they perceive to be their mission. They are acting in a particular context that may be incompatible with their ideology and methods.

Another case illustrates how humanitarians, following normal procedures, can run afoul of local micropolitics:

> in Bunia, there was a conflict between two different ethnic groups over property and assets. An INGO, new to the area and unaware of this, hired a car from one of the groups. It put its stickers on the car and then used it when conducting a household survey. When members of the other group saw the car, they recognized it as their enemy's car. They forced the INGO staff members out of the car and were going to kill them. Fortunately, the INGO staff were able to radio MONUC for assistance and were rescued by the military.[317]

Mowjee further illustrates how NGOs, by following their humanitarian mandate of impartiality, could be perceived as taking sides:

The risk of a community not perceiving humanitarian organizations as neutral has been demonstrated in South Kivu. The local
population had been terrorized by an armed group called the
Rastas. Since international NGOs were negotiating access and
working in rebel-held areas, the local population suspected them of
supporting rebel groups with food and medicines. They found the
idea of support to the Rastas "a bitter pill to swallow" in light of the
atrocities committed by this group. So, they reported this to the
newly elected Governor, who decided to stop humanitarian agencies
from traveling to the area on security grounds—the FARDC was
going to start operations against the Rastas and the government
could not guarantee the safety of humanitarian agencies. The
humanitarian community felt that the NGOs negotiated access in a
principled and transparent way but this transparency may have
been vis-à-vis the international community—reporting their
activities at OCHA meetings and discussing them with donors—
rather than local communities. The restriction was lifted only after
intervention by MONUC and the HC [High Commissioner] and
extended discussions with the Governor.[318]

The NGO approach to the Rastas also conflicted with MONUC's. MONUC
cited evidence that the Rastas were linked to the FDLR, and thus wanted to
take action against the FDLR if it did not stop supporting the Rastas. The
NGOs, which had more direct communication with the armed groups on the
ground, had a more nuanced understanding of the situation, indicating that
while there may have been some complicity between the two groups, they
were not the same, and that going after the thousands of FDLR soldiers to
stop one hundred Rastas could lead to greater suffering as a result of retaliation and displacement. Thus, an R2P-like protection activity could actually
make the situation worse and endanger humanitarian activities.[319]

Prosecution

On 3 March 2004, the government of the DRC referred the situation in Ituri
to the ICC,[320] although the following month the ICC indicated that this referral applied to the entire country—not just Ituri.[321] Although the ICC Prosecutor, Luis Moreno Ocampo, had indicated that he would have initiated a

case under his *proprio motu* powers,[322] he preferred to have the case referred by the government itself.[323] Indeed, he actively sought the referral, as with Uganda.[324] This would indicate greater support and potentially greater cooperation by the government for the ICC. Such cooperation would only be partially forthcoming as the government tried to use the ICC for its own political purposes against its enemies, and tried to protect its allies from the ICC. Theoretically, according to the Prosecutor, self-referrals "increase the likelihood of important cooperation on the ground."[325] This is important because "Absent coercive means at its disposal, the ICC's dependence on state cooperation becomes an important factor in its effectiveness."[326] Thus, on the one hand, if a state refers itself to the ICC for investigation, it would have an interest in facilitating investigation and other activities by the court. On the other, there is a danger that the ICC would become politicized, or perceived as such by many on the ground, particularly if the ICC did not fully investigate possible violations by the government and its allies.[327]

In June 2004, the Prosecutor indicated his decision to open an investigation in the DRC, with the focus "on the perpetrators most responsible for the most grave crimes."[328] This was the first official investigation for the ICC. The Prosecutor indicated that he would focus on Ituri because it was "'the most urgent situation to be followed.'"[329] The first arrest warrant was issued,[330] under seal, on 10 February 2006, and unsealed on 17 March. It accused Thomas Lubanga of enlisting and conscripting children to fight for the Union des Patriotes Congolais/Forces Patriotiques pour la Libération du Congo (UPC/FPLC).[331] Lubanga had been arrested in 2003, and had been in custody in Kinshasa since 2005, although the Prosecutor was worried he might be released soon.[332] Lubanga was transferred to The Hague on 16 March on French military aircraft, aided by MONUC.[333] The charges were confirmed in January 2007, and the trial began on 26 January 2009. In the intervening period, however, an example of one of the conundrums noted in Chapter 1 arose. In June 2008, the proceedings were suspended because Ocampo refused to turn over potentially exculpatory evidence to the defense.[334] The issue involved confidential information provided by MONUC and some NGOs. The Prosecutor did not want to reveal the information to protect his sources, and most of the sources had refused to allow the information to be revealed. Indeed, of 212 undisclosed documents, there were 156 documents provided by the UN that the UN refused to allow to be revealed.[335] The proceedings were stayed for months while legal wrangling and discussions with the UN went on. The UN put forth various options for letting the ICC judges determine whether the information was, in fact, exculpatory and should be turned over to the defense. The UN provided information to the ICC under the terms of the Relationship Agreement between the UN and the ICC.[336]

MONUC has provided information and assistance to the ICC in this context.[337] Commenting on this situation, Mona Rishmawi, legal advisor for the UN High Commissioner for Human Rights, argued, "But whatever decision the Court will take, it will have serious implications on the future cooperation between the UN and the ICC, this approach could seriously hamper the flow of information."[338]

In the end, a compromise was reached and the trial went forward.[339] However, right from the beginning we see tensions between actors and practices. The Prosecutor requires information. Sometimes this information is held by people on the ground who are participating in a response to the conflict, such as MONUC. In order to do their job properly these individuals and organizations require anonymity if they are to provide required information. If this anonymity cannot be guaranteed, they either cannot provide the information or will endanger their protection (or humanitarian) mission.

While there have been criticisms regarding the Lubanga case, including whether or not the charges of child recruitment were of sufficient gravity vis-à-vis other violations,[340] the case was extremely important as the first case to be prosecuted (successfully) by the ICC.[341] It also established child recruitment as a particular class of activities liable for punishment. There is also anecdotal evidence that this case has had at least a mild deterrent effect on militia leaders in the DRC who have had second thoughts about recruiting child soldiers and may have stopped the practice,[342] thus creating a "Lubanga Syndrome."[343] This is hardly a robust deterrent effect, and the practice of recruiting child soldiers continues in the DRC[344] and elsewhere, and the "Lubanga Syndrome" may have also just induced commanders to lie about the age of their recruits.[345] And there are significant methodological issues in demonstrating such a deterrent effect—that is, demonstrating that something has not happened because of a case tried before the ICC. As William Schabas has argued, "while we can readily point to those who are not deterred, it is nearly impossible to identify those who are."[346] And although some argue that the benefits of using child soldiers outweigh the possibility of being punished,[347] it points to one ray of hope for the positive use of the ICC in conflict to alter the behavior of combatants. The Lubanga case also, however, points to continuing conundrums regarding providing evidence to the ICC and maintaining a veneer of neutrality and impartiality on the part of protectors and palliators. To the extent that the UN is seen as providing information against perpetrators, this affects its ability to do its job and can also endanger specific individuals as well as the mission as a whole.

The second individual to have an arrest warrant issued against them was Bosco Ntaganda. It was issued under seal on 22 August 2006 and unsealed on 28 April 2008. It, too, was focused on recruiting child soldiers in Ituri[348] (although as we have seen he is implicated in activities in the Kivus). As noted above, Ntaganda became a general in the FARDC. He helped to remove Nkunda as the chairman of the CNDP in January 2009. He was reported to have "received important sums of money from Kinshasa, encouragement from Kigali and a guarantee that the Congo would grant him amnesty and protect him against International Criminal Court (ICC) prosecution."[349] Kinshasa thought that Ntaganda would be more accommodating than Nkunda as head of the CNDP. Kigali also provided pressure to get rid of Nkunda.[350] Rwanda was deeply implicated in supporting the CNDP, and Rwandan leaders could have been charged as accomplices if Nkunda had been indicted by the ICC. Thus, the removal helped both governments and helps to explain the submergence of international criminal justice to other concerns.

It also raises important questions regarding the use and abuse of the ICC by state actors. The Prosecutor postulated that self-referrals would mean better cooperation by the government doing the referring. Yet, at least in the case of the DRC, this appears not necessarily to be the case. Ntaganda evolved from an enemy to an ally in the eyes of the government in Kinshasa. He was important in bringing CNDP rebels over to the government side and was rewarded. The government was worried that without protecting Ntaganda from the ICC, Ntaganda would have little incentive to end, or at least tone down, his destabilizing efforts. Given Ntaganda's complicity in human rights violations during Kimia II and other operations, it had a negative outcome in terms of human rights and protecting civilians. But the case illustrates the fact that states who sign on to the Rome Statute may attempt to subvert or manipulate the ICC for their own ends, undermining the principles and purpose of the ICC. Indeed, after Ocampo reiterated his call for Ntaganda to be arrested in April 2012, Kabila noted his irritation with such pressure from the ICC, saying "I do not work for the international community."[351] He further stated, though, that Ntaganda could be tried in the DRC.[352] But Kabila had one big reason not to arrest him—the fear that such a move could undo efforts, however ambiguous and ineffective, to incorporate CNDP rebels into FARDC.

The Prosecutor's choices for prosecution have raised suspicions of partiality on the ground. For example, as alluded to above on the point of gravity in the Lubanga case, questions were raised as to why Lubanga was prosecuted for recruiting child soldiers[353] but not for atrocities committed by the UPC. And there are serious questions regarding the lack of prosecutions against other militia leaders who have been integrated into FARDC, as well as government officials. As noted above, foreign governments—in particular in Kigali and Kampala—are also deeply implicated in the activities of various militia groups in eastern DRC; yet there has been no attempt to hold political and military leaders of Rwanda and Uganda to account by the ICC.[354] Doing so would undermine the cooperation the ICC currently receives (in some cases anyway) by those two countries. Indeed, as Schabas points out, self-referral "has the practical consequence of establishing a degree of complicity between the Office of the Prosecutor and the referring state."[355] And self-referrals become "not even really self-referrals, but referrals of one's own rebel groups."[356]

The other two cases from the DRC also concern Ituri—Germain Katanga[357] and Mathieu Ngudjolo Chui.[358] The arrest warrants were both issued under seal in July 2007. They were charged with war crimes and crimes against humanity in relation to attacks on Hema in the village of Bogoro in Ituri in early 2003. Katanga was the leader of the FRPI, and had been in custody in Kinshasa at the time of the arrest warrant. Ngudjolo was the leader of the FNI who had gone on to become a colonel in the FARDC, based in Bunia. The cases were subsequently joined and they went on trial in November 2009. Ngudjolo was eventually found not guilty, while Katanga's trial continues.

Finally, in August 2010, the ICC issued an arrest warrant under seal for Callixte Mbarushimana,[359] executive secretary of the FDLR-FCA (Forces Démocratiques pour la Libération du Rwanda-Forces Combattantes Abacunguzi), for war crimes and crimes against humanity committed during attacks against civilians in both North and South Kivu in 2009. He was arrested by French authorities two weeks later and sent to The Hague in January 2011. However, the Pre-Trial Chamber declined to confirm the charges against him and he was released.[360]

The above discussion points to the possibility that states could use the ICC for their own ends. Indeed, Phil Clark argues that "the Congolese and Ugandan governments have proven adept at employing state referrals to the ICC for their own political and legal gain."[361] Further, the ICC has "empowered the Congolese and Ugandan governments in this regard by actively pursuing state referrals and, in the process, affording states substantial influence over the Court's investigations and prosecutions."[362] During his time as Prosecutor, Ocampo indicated that he would only pursue a few individuals in each case, and that these would be those with the greatest responsibility for crimes.[363] Other evolving criteria for prosecution included encouraging national prosecutions for the "small fish" to complement the focus on a small number of "big fish," as well as focusing on cases where there is enough evidence to warrant a significant likelihood of successful prosecution. In addition, the Prosecutor would take into account the possibility for political and social destabilization.[364] This latter point might be perceived as related to the question of the "interests of peace" that has figured so prominently in the debate over the role of the ICC in Uganda. If a prosecution interfered with a peace process, it could affect the political and social stability of a country.

Ocampo engaged in a campaign to persuade the government to refer the situation to the ICC, both publicly and through discussions with the government itself.[365] Yet this may have compromised the ICC's standing and impartiality. Clark notes four problems with the Prosecutor's strategy in the DRC. First, by focusing on Ituri—where obviously many crimes have been committed—Ocampo pursued cases that were less likely to directly implicate government officials, and thus less likely to destabilize the situation. This was because the conflicts in Ituri were the most isolated from politics in the capital, and there was less evidence to connect Kabila to atrocities in Ituri—although there is suspicion that he had supported rebel movements including the FRPI led by Katanga. Further, as noted above, FARDC has been implicated in a variety of war crimes, including in Ituri. Nonetheless, focusing on Ituri would avoid implicating government officials, which was particularly important heading into the elections.[366] Yet the case selection risks creating a situation of impunity for government officials. Once Ntaganda became an enemy of the government, and the government decided to arrest him, the difficulties and tensions became even more apparent. Kabila wanted Ntaganda to be tried in the DRC. Under the principle of complementarity, whereby states have primary responsibility for prosecuting the crimes covered in the Rome Statute, and only if the Prosecutor determines that the state in question is unable or unwilling to undertake such investigations and prosecutions can the ICC become involved, this would normally be encouraged. However, given that the ICC has issued a warrant for his arrest, combined with the previous immunity the government had provided, this is rendered problematic. Since it was obvious that the government was not willing to prosecute Ntaganda, could it now turn around and say that it had changed its mind? Undertaking its own prosecution would allow the government to control the process, and in doing so could possibly preclude potential evidence of its own complicity in some of Ntaganda's actions from coming out. Ocampo pushed the idea of positive complementarity—the idea that the ICC can help foster robust domestic judicial systems, or "a proactive policy of cooperation aimed at promoting national proceedings."[367] This is necessary given the inability of the ICC to try more than a few cases in any one country. Yet in the DRC the ability and will of the government to undertake such prosecutions is in serious doubt.[368] This is particularly the situation in a case like Ntaganda's where there are multiple competing pressures that may mitigate the government's interest in trying him.

Second, as noted, Lubanga was only tried and convicted on charges related to recruiting child soldiers, while many other potential crimes were avoided. Including the other crimes could implicate members of the Rwandan and Ugandan governments, thus potentially destabilizing regional politics. The Pre-Trial Chamber noted that the Prosecutor had provided insufficient evidence regarding the international nature of the crimes, forcing the Prosecutor to withdraw charges related to an "international" conflict, and focusing instead on the "internal" nature of the conflict and the charges. Further, as Clark notes, Lubanga is a "middle-ranking perpetrator," and others have more responsibility for atrocities. Given that the conflicts in which Ocampo initially pursued charges are linked in numerous and complex ways, he needs to maintain good relations with all governments in the region. Thus, from a political perspective, one can understand not wanting to implicate members of the various governments. Yet, this raises significant issues with regard to impartiality and government impunity. By not pursuing a wider array of charges and focusing on lower level perpetrators, the prosecutor avoided uneasy questions related to the Ugandan government's involvement in atrocities.[369]

Third, Ocampo pursued a narrow set of charges that were more likely to lead to a speedier trial and conviction. This meant that the broader range of crimes committed were not highlighted, which might partially undermine any potential (if still slight) deterrent function, as well as avoiding those responsible for the worst crimes.[370] Fourth, the Prosecutor's focus on Ituri raises issues regarding complementarity, since Ituri had a more developed judiciary, which could have tried Lubanga and others itself.[371] However, there are still problems in Ituri, including the inability to protect prosecutors, judges, and defense attorneys,[372] and one militia leader in Ituri, Yves Kahwa, who was initially convicted and sentenced to twenty years in jail, ended up with amnesty.[373] By focusing on Ituri, the prosecutor got some "easy"[374] cases, and the government got a pass since the ICC was investigating crimes, but in a way that precluded potential government culpability. The government was thus able to manipulate the ICC for its own ends.

Further, by focusing on militia leaders, the Prosecutor has allowed FARDC members to escape justice. FARDC is deeply implicated in significant widespread human rights abuses. However, the Prosecutor has not gone after any FARDC commanders or others with command responsibility of the military. The only exceptions to this are Ntaganda and Ngudjolo, who were charged as militia leaders and then subsequently joined FARDC. Although a few members of FARDC have been charged and convicted within the DRC, many have been able to escape justice. Even going after relatively low-level offenders can lead back to the pinnacle of power, while going after FARDC commanders would even more directly implicate the government. Even if it did not touch Kabila and other government ministers, it could still interfere with government strategy to deal with militias, as is evident in the Ntaganda case.

This reliance on the DRC government is further evident in the decision by Ocampo in May 2012 to add an additional seven charges to the arrest warrant for Ntaganda—three for crimes against humanity and four for war crimes. These all relate to his activities with the FPLC in Ituri in 2002 and 2003, thus continuing to avoid charges related to the CNDP in Kivu in 2006–9. While the charges increased diplomatic pressure on the Congolese government to arrest Ntaganda, they do not tie into the Kivus, where the Congolese army and government are implicated. Further, given Rwanda's support for Ntaganda, it avoids connecting him to Rwanda, since the Rwandan army was much less active in Ituri during the earlier period than it has been in the Kivus. Thus, neither government, upon which the Prosecutor is reliant to actually capture and turn over Ntaganda, is directly implicated. The charges are broader than those for Lubanga, but narrow in temporal and geographical scope.[375]

As Payam Akhavan notes, "The ICC is a utopian aspiration that must function amidst the hellish nightmares that surround the periphery of privilege and power in the world."[376] He argues that where the state is a victim—where it cannot control the nonstate forces arrayed against it—self-referrals can be a positive act, helping to strengthen the state against its "tormentors."[377] He further argues that in such cases of self-referral, "there should not be an assumption of bias or politicization simply because the accused are members of a non-state entity in conflict with a state."[378] This may be true, although Akhavan also notes that states might be "villains" where "the prospects [for cooperation] are bleak."[379] Further, however, the more likely case is that the state might be both "victim" and "villain," which calls for further nuance. Such is the case in the DRC. The state is, in one sense, a "victim," since it has not been able to control the vast expanse of the eastern part of the country, where militias and foreign troops have run rampant. From this perspective, the self-referral is a good thing, helping to rein in at least a few of those most responsible and stigmatizing others who bring death and destruction. Yet the Congolese state is also most certainly a "villain," supporting some of these groups, protecting some of the accused, and directly tormenting many of its residents through the actions of FARDC. It is these situations, which are likely to be much more numerous than any situations of pure victimhood, that pose the most danger for the ICC and highlight the unresolved issues inherent in the Prosecutor's cooperation dilemma. The Prosecutor requires cooperation from states—in particular those states in which atrocities have occurred and which he would like to prosecute—but states are not going to cooperate unless it is in their interest to do so. "Victim" states have such an interest, while "villain" states do not. Victim/villain states have an interest in cooperating where it hurts their enemies, but not where it threatens the government or its allies.

The Prosecutor has an interest in getting the state's enemies behind bars in The Hague. He or she also has an interest in getting state perpetrators behind bars, but this is tempered by the interest in cooperation. By pursuing cooperation in the DRC, the Prosecutor has contributed to a perception of bias and unequal justice, highlighting the potential for abuse on the part of state parties to the ICC. Of course, the situation is further complicated when, as with Ntaganda, a former militia "tormenter" becomes a state "tormenter." In complex and fluid situations such as the DRC where individuals and groups regularly change allegiances, and where former militia leaders are needed to ensure a peace deal, the Prosecutor becomes embedded in conflicts in which they may have some effect, but which they cannot control. And the need for cooperation—combined with the realities of state power—leads to an ambiguous situation where the only possible outcome, even in the circumscribed world of the ICC, is highly imperfect justice, which frequently serves the interests of states rather than the "interests of justice."

Protection

The DRC represents both the normative promise of R2P and the actual on the ground realities of R2P and PoC, which can be significantly divergent. The Security Council has given MONUC/MONUSCO a progressively more robust mandate. By 2008, MONUC had the most robust mandate ever given to a peacekeeping operation. Protection of civilians was listed as the top priority, and it was given a robust Chapter VII mandate. On paper, this was the area of overlap between PoC and R2P, with a mandate to use robust military force to protect civilians. Theoretically, this was the implementation of paragraph 139 of the World Summit Outcome document collective action under Chapter VII "to protect . . . populations from genocide, war crimes, ethnic cleansing and crimes against humanity." Yet it was certainly not done "in a timely and decisive manner." Even though there was a recognized need to protect civilians, from the start MONUC was not given the resources necessary, and "The conceptualisation of the mission failed to take into account the complexity of the conflict, the size of the country as well as the needs on the ground."[380] It was hampered by the lack of troops provided for, and their slow deployment. The deployment was "slow and reactive . . . [resulting] in an increase of troops only after a previous protection crisis had erupted."[381]

As the years wore on, MONUC's troop strength was slowly increased in a piecemeal fashion, but even at its height, it lacked the numbers required for such a vast area. In 2011 MONUSCO had one peacekeeper for every 1,100 inhabitants of North Kivu, or one peacekeeper per twelve square kilometers.[382] This contrasts with the rule of thumb that somewhere between two and ten peacekeepers are required per 1,000 inhabitants. MONUC also failed another test—that it should be at least as big as the largest indigenous armed force. The first test would have required a force of 10,000–50,000 troops in North Kivu; the second would have required 20,000. The actual size in December 2008 was 6,000.[383] It did not have enough helicopters to rapidly transport troops. Furthermore, many of the troop-contributing countries did not have particularly professional armies, which affected their ability to take action.[384] Just as important, however, there was misunderstanding of the mandate—focusing on the Chapter VI element. There was a lack of concrete

Table 3.2. MONUC/MONUSCO Expenditures by Year

Year (1 July–30 June unless otherwise noted)	Expenditures (US$)
6 August 1999–30 June 2000	55,271,000
2000–2001	246,472,000
2001–2002	401,302,000
2002–2003	508,122,000
2003–2004	665,059,000
2004–2005	940,946,000
2005–2006	1,078,498,000
2006–2007	1,135,261,000
2007–2008	1,129,624,000
2008–2009	1,222,639,000
2009–2010	1,346,584,000 (estimated)
2010–2011	1,365,000,000
2011–2012	1,489,390,000 (approved)
2012–2013	1,402,278,000 (approved)
2013–2014	1,456,378,000 (approved) (plus $140,000,000 for Intervention Brigade)

MONUC Facts and Figures, http://www.un.org/en/peacekeeping/missions/past/monuc/facts
.shtml; MONUSCO Facts and Figures, http://www.un.org/en/peacekeeping/missions/monusco
/facts.shtml; Enough Project, "The Democratic Republic of Congo: Taking a Stand on Security
Sector Reform (16 April 2012), 18, http://www.enoughproject.org/files/DRC_SSR-Report
_2012_0.pdf; UNGA, "Financing of the United Nations Organization Stabilization Mission
in the Democratic Republic of the Congo," A/66/584/Add.1 (14 June 2012).

guidance to peacekeepers on what PoC actually entailed, and lack of will on the part of troop-contributing countries to actually use the troops in conformity with the mandate.[385] The international presence in the DRC significantly predates the 2005 World Summit and the recognition of R2P. Indeed, it goes back to one impetus for R2P—the Rwandan genocide. It has evolved in conjunction with the evolution of R2P. PoC mandates and activities, including those under Chapter VII, predated R2P, although the strongest direction from the Security Council came in the years after the World Summit.

Looking at funding and staffing figures for MONUC and MONUSCO, we see an operation that grew to be one of the largest peacekeeping operations in the world. From the very modest level of $55 million in 1999–2000, the budget for MONUSCO for 2013–14 was around $1.5 billion, making it the most expensive peacekeeping operation. As of the end of October 2013,

MONUSCO had 21,485 uniformed personnel, including 19,557 military personnel. Yet, this paled in comparison to the needs of the DRC, which were almost limitless. In such a situation it is perhaps thus impossible to adequately meet the needs, but much more could have been done—both in terms of sending more troops and other resources in a timely manner and in terms of what MONUC did with what it had.

The development of MONUC has closely followed the development of the idea of protection of civilians, with an increasingly robust PoC mandate. And it has, on occasion, engaged in significant military activities—more robust than most peacekeeping missions—which did protect civilians and facilitate humanitarian access. Yet, the limits of R2P were evident, particularly in the absence of the use of R2P language. While R2P was used in the resolutions on Libya, and, as we shall see, has been at the forefront of discussions—if not resolutions—in Darfur, the Security Council has been notably silent on the connection between R2P and PoC in the DRC. Perhaps this is a reflection of the slow-burning nature of the conflict, which started before the language of R2P came into vogue, and which only rarely rises to near the top of the international agenda. It is also perhaps a reflection of the relatively depoliticized nature of the context. While there are obviously political considerations for the great powers—in particular with Western insistence on supporting Rwanda—the consensus on the DRC is broader than in many other situations. This is perhaps helped by the lack of core national interests of the great powers in the region. Lack of interests is also the enemy of action. With no interests, there is no urgent need to respond to the ongoing catastrophe in eastern DRC. PoC allows (or is a reflection of) greater political (and less politicized) consensus, but it is this quality of the lack of political urgency that distinguishes PoC from the potentially more robust R2P. Operation Artemis demonstrated what a robust R2P-like deployment could accomplish. The Security Council was happy enough to provide a full Chapter VII mandate to a peace enforcement mission, as long as it was not responsible for it financially and in terms of manpower. But it was limited in territorial scope and duration. It also ended up inadvertently skewing the balance in favor of one of the combatants.

With regard to the conundrums outlined in Chapter 1, we can say that the UN, and the EU through Artemis, engaged in some robust military action in isolated spaces, which, for a time, protected civilians, as did the Intervention Brigade. MONUC/MONUSCO also facilitated the provision of humanitarian assistance. At the same time, some of the activities MONUC carried out with FARDC were highly dubious. Certainly many FARDC activities led to significant civilian casualties. Furthermore, while facilitating the provision of humanitarian assistance at times, its role in the Protection Cluster and its broader relationship with humanitarian actors also demonstrated the potential for peacekeepers to endanger humanitarian operations, or at least the difficulty in supporting such operations, especially when peacekeeping operations trumped humanitarian operations.

It did not play a role in apprehending Ntaganda, and its role in providing information to the ICC in the Lubanga case highlighted the ambiguous role the military might play in such situations. At the same time, there is a developing, if yet still conflicted, relationship between the ICC and MONUSCO. A memorandum of understanding (MoU) between the ICC and MONUC was agreed to on 8 November 2005, which followed a broader agreement between the UN and ICC in 2004.[386] The MoU stated that MONUC would, as Margherita Melillo argues, rather than directly supporting the ICC, *support the government of the DRC in its support to the ICC.*"[387] MONUC was thus one step removed from the ICC. It would "give consideration" to assisting the government in arresting individuals sought by the ICC. The MoU was permissive rather than directive. And although there was a reluctance on the part of MONUC to participate directly in arresting suspects, and while MONUC was criticized for not assisting in the arrest of Ntaganda,[388] MONUC did participate in the arrest of both Lubanga and Katanga, as well as other suspects who were turned over to DRC authorities.[389]

This indirect cooperation was rendered potentially more direct in 2013. In Resolution 2098—the same resolution that created the Intervention Brigade—the Security Council directed MONUSCO to use "all necessary measures . . . through its regular forces and its Intervention Brigade" to "Support and work with the Government of the DRC to arrest and bring to justice those responsible for war crimes and crimes against humanity in the country, including through cooperation with States of the region and the ICC."

While it is still supporting the DRC government, it can now work more directly with the ICC. The government has the main responsibility to protect civilians, and MONUSCO is there to help it. The government also has the main responsibility to cooperate with the ICC. Thus, MONUSCO would still be helping the DRC carry out its responsibilities vis-à-vis the ICC, but with a more direct mandate. The awkward construction of this and previous resolutions and the MoU can be at least partly attributed to non-Rome Statute

Table 3.3. Responsibility Conundrums in the DRC

	Protectors	Prosecutors	Palliators
Protection	+relatively robust mandate with some protection of civilians −civilian casualties in joint operations −Artemis affected balance among combatants	+deterrence of crimes—Lubanga Syndrome −difficulties using information from MONUC	+some protection of humanitarians +highlight abuses −create illusion of protection −reduce prospects of needed protection
Prosecution	−little success apprehending suspects	+punish perpetrators +uphold idea of human rights/ rule of law −conflict with peace efforts/ military integration −used as weapon by government −at mercy of governments −narrow charges	+support human rights −endanger humanitarian activities/ neutrality undermined
Palliation	+support humanitarian assistance −endanger humanitarian assistance/ undermine neutrality	+protect humanitarians −endanger humanitarian assistance/ undermine neutrality	+keep people alive −well-fed dead

party permanent members of the Security Council who did not want to create a direct connection between UN peacekeeping and the ICC and thus further support the ICC as an independent institution.[390] Yet these developments do indicate the evolution of closer links between protectors and prosecutors, however difficult the relationship may continue to be.

The DRC, while representing a very large portion of UN expenditure on peacekeeping and humanitarian assistance, and witnessing the most activity at the ICC, has stayed under the R2P radar. It has played a significant role in the development of the doctrine and practice of protection of civilians,[391] but in a way that has kept it out of the media and political spotlight, contributing to the DRC's status as a "stealth conflict." And the practice of PoC in the DRC has been contradictory—with some positive advances but also a multitude of situations where the protectors have not protected civilians adequately or have engaged in activities (in particular with FADRC) that undermine protection, taking a much more reactive posture[392] than might be needed to protect civilians.

CHAPTER 4

Uganda (and Beyond): Testing the International Criminal Court

The LRA is devouring the lives of children in northern Uganda.

[T]here can be *no* political compromise on legality and accountability.

Traditional justice mechanisms . . . shall be promoted . . . as a central part of the framework for accountability and reconciliation.

If the focus in the DRC was on the protection of civilians, Uganda highlighted a separate set of concerns. While still embodying the full range of R2P[3] conundrums, the most prominent concern has revolved around the role of the ICC and the peace process. The situation in Northern Uganda encapsulates the many challenges the ICC, and the international community more generally, face in prosecuting individuals who are involved in an ongoing conflict. The government referred the situation in Northern Uganda, and specifically, the Lord's Resistance Army (LRA), to the ICC in 2003. It soon found that it could only refer the entire country, not a particular actor, thus raising the possibility that individuals in the Ugandan military might also be prosecuted. Further, once it was perceived that the arrest warrant for LRA leader Joseph Kony might be hampering the peace process, Uganda found that it did not have the ability to withdraw the referral. This shows that states may become enmeshed in international institutions that limit their actions as sovereign states. The Ugandan referral also illustrates how states may use the ICC for their own purposes, as Uganda used the referral to gain legitimacy for its continued military actions against the LRA.

The situation in Northern Uganda has also had regional implications, as the LRA has moved out from Uganda and expanded its fighting to Sudan, the Democratic Republic of the Congo, and the Central African Republic. This complicates the task of constructing a comprehensive narrative of the conflict. A significant amount of violence in northeastern DRC was directly associated with incursions by the LRA and the Ugandan army in pursuit of the LRA in the DRC. Reference has already been made to some of this activity in the previous chapter, but will be more directly pursued in this chapter. While the conflict that started in northern Uganda has spread across borders, it has had specific implications in Uganda. Further, as will be seen, the role of humanitarian organizations has been deeply ambiguous, highlighting the potentially problematic role of humanitarianism. Yet, this was not typical palliation; rather humanitarian organizations took over functions which the Ugandan state could have undertaken and as a result played a role in facilitating the humanitarian crisis itself.

The Origins of the Conflict in Northern Uganda

The focus of the conflict in Uganda has centered on the LRA and its fight against the government (and, indeed, the population). The common narrative of a brutal, insane leader depoliticizes a movement and a conflict that is, in fact, deeply political. Further, both the actions of the ICC and the global popular movements that have arisen to shine a light on LRA brutality elide any brutality on the part of government forces.

The roots of the conflict are based in ethnic politics that were at least partly constituted during the colonial period and which have resulted in a north-south divide. In the northern part of Uganda, which was to become known as Acholiland, the British imposed an administrative rule that replaced traditional power structures with a new set of appointed rulers. At the same time, they imposed a concrete Acholi identity and political unity where such structures had been much more diffuse.[1] Acholi district, which has been at the core of the conflict, was created in 1937 in the context of creating power structures that, it was hoped, would bring anticolonial segments of society into the system. Many Acholi found work in the civil

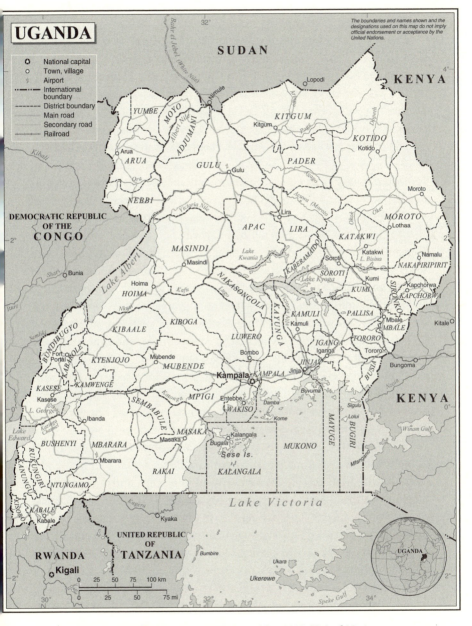

Map 4. Uganda, Map No. 3862 Rev. 4, May 2003. United Nations.

service, as well as the police and army. The Acholi thus held a position of privilege under colonial rule that would set the scene for anti-Acholi sentiment
postindependence.[2]

Uganda's first prime minister, Milton Obote, although he wanted to move
away from the tribal politics of preindependence Uganda and instead create
a national political identity, ended up doing the opposite. He brought in many
northerners to the central government and created a system of patronage in
northern Uganda (where he was from). This ended up creating a north-south
divide and reified tribal political differences. Obote eventually ended up ban-
ning all parties but his own Ugandan People's Congress, and continued to
favor northern tribes—the Acholi and the Langi (his own tribe). In 1971, Idi
Amin took power in a coup, and he immediately set about to undermine
northern ethnic privilege, purging the military, and then the civil service, of
Acholi and Langi. He then wiped out the Acholi political class (dividing the
country in the process).[3] When Obote came back into power following the
Tanzanian ouster of Amin in 1979, he again brought Acholi and Langi into
the Ugandan National Liberation Army (UNLA), in large numbers. This did
not last, and the Acholi overthrew Obote, who they accused of favoring Langi.
During the same period, a new insurgency appeared. In response to the violent and corrupt elections of 1980, the National Resistance Army (NRA) took
up arms under the leadership of Yoweri Museveni. Most of the NRA were
from the south; there were also some Rwandan Tutsi refugees, including future Rwandan president Paul Kagame.[4] As part of his strategy to gain support for his movement, Museveni built up a regional ethnic identity in the
Luwero Triangle in the south, which became his stronghold.[5] The movement
became about southerners ejecting northerners from power.[6]

When Museveni took power in 1986, the remnants of the UNLA retreated
to the north, and eventually many went to Sudan.[7] Acholi were prevented
from sharing in national power while local power structures were undermined. And the National Resistance Movement (NRM), the only political
actor given any room to operate,[8] engaged in a brutal counterinsurgency campaign against the north, portraying Acholi as the enemy. This crackdown
against an imaginary enemy resulted in the very thing it was supposed to
stop—an armed rebellion. This new rebellion came in the form of the Ugandan People's Democratic Army (UPDA),[9] made up of three to four thousand
former UNLA troops who had reentered Uganda from Sudan, and which co-
alesced around Acholi identity and gained support among the population.
The counterinsurgency expanded, intensifying the feeling of ethnic target-

ing among the Acholi, while at the same time preventing any local political leadership from developing, thus opening the way for local armed groups.[10]

Thus the stage was set for the forerunner of the LRA, the Holy Spirit Movement (HSM), to emerge. Embedded within local spiritual traditions, which drew from Pentecostal Christianity, Islam, and indigenous practices, and which emphasized the need for spiritual cleansing and healing, an Acholi spirit medium named Alice Auma (later known as Alice Lakwena) emerged as a potent force. Claiming to be possessed by a number of spirits, including a particularly powerful spirit named Lakwena, she was said to be able to cleanse people of bad spirits. She claimed it was her power that allowed a 1985 coup to succeed. She healed retreating UNLA soldiers of bad spirits, and, with the help of UNLA soldiers, freed from prison many people said to have been kidnapped by the NRA. This was the start of a violent movement against the Museveni regime that came to be known as the Holy Spirit Movement.[11] Building upon both Acholi identity and a discourse of cleansing, and stepping into a religious lacuna in northern Uganda,[12] Lakwena mobilized an army numbering as many as 10,000 soldiers,[13] although she claimed to have as many as 18,000.[14] She claimed she could address the local political crisis through cleansing returning Acholi soldiers and fight the NRA. She also came into direct violent conflict with the UPDA,[15] and also engaged in violence against the Acholi (justified as part of a campaign to move the Acholi away from their "evil ways of life"[16]). She soon moved into the national context, taking thousands of soldiers south toward Kampala in 1987 in a bid to liberate the Acholi from the Museveni regime. Her forces collapsed a few miles from Kampala.[17] Infighting expanded among armed groups in Acholiland. The UPDA was brought into negotiations with the government. Many took advantage of an amnesty,[18] while the rest joined factions from the former HSM.[19]

The most prominent of these factions was led by Joseph Kony. Kony claimed to be related to Alice Lakwena, although the exact relationship is unclear. He claimed to have been possessed by a number of spirits, and engaged in healing and divining.[20] By 1990, Kony's group, which he had named the Lord's Resistance Army, had become the only effective rebel group,[21] even as the government engaged in increasingly more violence in the north.[22] Kony fought against the NRA, but also those seen as collaborators.[23] He failed to get significant popular support since many Acholi were tired of the fighting, and increasingly relied on violence against local populations for survival, while portraying the Acholi collaborators he fought against as "false" Acholi.[24] Kony used religious language to ground his claim to legitimacy, and although many have described the LRA as bizarre and beyond comprehension,[25] based partly on this religious language, Adam Branch argues that religion was used to bind the group together, and in particular to bind the troops to the LRA leadership, and thus it should not be given nearly as much emphasis as it has received in the popular imagination.[26] As the NRA further expanded its violence against the Acholi population[27] in its attempt to find the rebels, it seemed that rather than fighting each other, both the NRA and LRA were fighting civilians.[28] By early 1991 the LRA began significant attacks against civilian targets like clinics and schools, and expanded its child abductions.[29] After failed peace talks in 1993–94, the LRA set up bases in southern Sudan. The Sudanese government, which had been providing some support to the LRA, significantly expanded its support as the LRA was used as a proxy against the Sudanese People's Liberation Front (SPLA), which had been fighting the government in Khartoum for years.[30]

The (Neo)Humanitarian Turn

In 1996, the government began to forcibly move civilians into camps it called "protected villages" as a way to control the population. Anybody outside of the camps was labeled a rebel and killed. Within a few months there were a few hundred thousand people in the camps, expanding to one million within ten years,[31] most of the rural population of Acholiland, and by 2005 there were two million displaced Ugandans, including 90 percent of the Acholi.[32] This military strategy[33] created its own humanitarian crisis. By concentrating the population, it was easier for the LRA to attack the civilian population, and the government did little to protect the camp populations,[34] which were periodically attacked by the LRA.[35] The "appalling"[36] conditions in the camp, with "virtually no provision for sanitation or sustenance,"[37] led to disease and excess deaths of around 1,000 per week by the middle of the first decade of the twenty-first century (with most dying from malnutrition or curable diseases)[38]. By cutting the population off from its usual forms of subsistence, the camps created need and aid dependency where there was none before.[39]

Many camp inhabitants left the camps for their villages, undeterred by the threat of violence from the government. The government thus began to integrate humanitarian organizations into its internment efforts, asking the World Food Program (WFP) to feed 200,000 people. Other aid agencies ramped up their efforts in the camps. The humanitarian community faced a dilemma—should it cooperate with the government in its counterinsurgency strategy by providing food to those the government was trying to suppress? Although some organizations initially withheld assistance,[40] any hesitation was short-lived as the agencies started providing large quantities of aid.[41]

One might argue that the humanitarian impulse overrode problematic questions about collaborating with the government. Yet Branch also argues that the camps were "particularly attractive to aid agencies" with "a concentrated, easily surveilled, accessed, and controlled population."[42] Further, the dominant discourse by this point of the "good" Museveni government fighting the "evil" LRA made it easy for donors, aid agencies, and the UN to engage in and support the government agenda.

Yet, although the ethics of the situation seemed to recede into the background, humanitarian organizations were complicit in government counterinsurgency efforts that created a humanitarian crisis. In Rwanda, UNHCR and other aid organizations were castigated for supporting the refugees in eastern Zaire, with critics claiming that they created the security crisis emanating from the camps. And aid agencies agonized over whether or not they were fueling insecurity. Yet the refugee populations and camps materialized as a result of the aftermath of the genocide, even if the militants played a role in the exodus. The refugees would not necessarily have spontaneously repatriated. In Uganda, the displacement was government policy. Most of the displaced did not want to move to the camps in the first place and wanted to return home. The government created the humanitarian crisis. If humanitarian organizations did not provide aid, the government would not have been able to continue its policies. It was not able to support the camps itself. When the organizations provided food and other resources, they relieved pressures on people to leave the camps, thus enabling the government's forced displacement strategy and perpetuating a humanitarian crisis they were there to alleviate.[43] This was palliation in support of one side in a conflict that was waging a war on its own people. It enabled government violence. The WFP recognized in 1999 that the "WFP may have too readily fallen in line with government policy, in effect becoming both provider and legitimizer of a villagization policy."[44] If the WFP had instead provided resources to help people return to their homes, the aid could have had the opposite effect, providing a positive response to a humanitarian crisis created by the government. Instead, the displacement became routinized.[45] The aid agencies were thus complicit in "political mass persecution" or "'social torture'" on the part of the government,[46] and their veneer of neutrality disappeared.[47]

Further, the aid agencies were dependent upon the Ugandan military—the Ugandan People's Defence Force (UPDF)—for access and security, protected by large military convoys and at times paying UPDF officers for protection or access.[48] They paid for fuel for army vehicles and food for the troops protecting the WFP convoys,[49] thus creating a "protection racket."[50] Even with the payments, the UPDF would not go to places it felt were too dangerous.[51] Humanitarian actors regularly face threats to access from nonstate actors, whereas in Uganda, while the LRA did attack humanitarian organizations,[52] including food convoys,[53] some of the threats came from the state. This situation also allowed the United States to provide military aid to the government under the pretext of protecting humanitarianism.[54] Finally, by supporting the government and providing cover for its forced displacement policy, humanitarian organizations "normalized" the forced displacement and internment, thus undermining the possibility of naming it as a war crime.[55] In other words, humanitarians provided palliative cover for a government to undertake potential war crimes—certainly an unintended, but potentially foreseeable, consequence.

Child Soldiers

While the government engaged in its campaign to pacify the Acholi population, the LRA continued its reign of terror in the north[56] with sometimes little response from the government. While the LRA was not a serious threat to the government, neither was it so weak that it could be completely eliminated.[57] The LRA "turned Gulu and Kitgum into permanent battle zones,"[58] although the government was a full participant in the violence in the north. The LRA preyed on the local population, killing large numbers of civilians, with hundreds if not thousands dying every month.[59] In less than one week in January 1996, for example, four hundred civilians were killed during an LRA attack in Kitgum.[60] The LRA became known for abducting children to serve as soldiers or to support the rebels in other ways, such as carrying supplies or as "wives."[61] The government responded with Operation North, a violent campaign that, while failing to wipe out the LRA, terrorized and exacerbated tensions with the civilian population in the north.[62]

It was the child soldiers that provided the lens through which the world viewed the conflict in northern Uganda.[63] The LRA is portrayed as evil men who abduct and enslave children. While this is true, Branch argues that the reality is more complicated, particularly given the multiple reasons children might have for joining or staying with the LRA, including escaping the dire situation created by the government in the north.[64] More important, government actions are shoved aside and ignored. Indeed, while the LRA is recognized as recruiting child soldiers, the government has engaged in similar activities, recruiting children into Local Defense Units (LDUs). LDUs were supposed to ensure the security of villages or camps, but many children were sent to the front lines to fight the LRA.[65] Some of the children recruited into the UPDF were former LRA child soldiers.[66] The recruitment of child soldiers by Ugandan security forces appears to have coincided with the start of Operation Iron Fist,[67] an operation in southern Sudan to go after the LRA, conducted with the consent of the Sudanese government,[68] and continued for several years.[69]

This lens of child soldiers is evidenced in the paucity of UN Secretary-General reports on Uganda. Between 1995 and 2012, there were only three reports specifically on Uganda (Uganda figured in a number of other reports in the context of the conflict in the DRC)—in 2007,[70] 2008,[71] and 2009.[72] These reports all focused specifically on children and armed conflict.

Museveni was perceived by Western governments as one of the new leaders of Africa, the face of the African Renaissance. As a result of its adherence to neoliberal economic policies and its attempts to deal with AIDS, Uganda was seen in a positive light and, as with Rwanda under Kagame, was given a pass on the less positive aspects of its governance, including the brutality in the north. It was also perceived as an ally in the War on Terror.[73]

Thus, the "official discourse"[74] of the LRA as incomprehensible, bizarre, pseudo-Christian child kidnappers—a reflection of the "heart-of-darkness"[75] paradigm where Africa is perceived as incomprehensibly violent—drowned out the rest of the reality of the conflict in Uganda. This included the fact that the LRA did produce political manifestos[76] and some in the north saw the LRA as freedom fighters[77] (although in 1997 90 percent of the Acholi in Gulu and Kitgum indicated they did not support the LRA[78]). While they may not necessarily have supported the LRA, or thought it could realize its political goals, some in the north did think the LRA "puts words to their experiences"[79] of marginalization and violence. The official discourse not only depoliticized the LRA; in conjunction with the new African leader narrative, it deified Museveni and obscured the widespread human rights violations being committed by the government. This official discourse allowed the conflict to be seen in humanitarian terms rather than in political terms[80]—reinforced by the statement in 2003 by UN Undersecretary-General for Humanitarian Affairs Jan Egeland that northern Uganda was the worst humanitarian situation in the world[81]—which could justify the humanitarian support discussed above. And it led to the Western view that Kony should be "eliminated,"[82] undermining support for negotiations. Museveni thus was not only not constrained in his conduct of the war in the north, but was also able to pursue his militaristic policies in Sudan and the DRC.[83]

Museveni was given another boost in December 2001 when the LRA was identified as a terrorist organization by the U.S. government.[84] In the wake of the 9/11 attacks by Al-Qaeda, those perceived as fighting terrorism were given military and diplomatic support by the United States. Given the LRA's connection to the hardline Islamist Sudanese government, it was easy to identify the LRA as terrorists, even though it did not threaten the U.S. in any way.[85] As an ally in the "War on Terror," Uganda was given significant military support to help fight the LRA.[86] There were also reports that the U.S. had previously given Uganda military assistance which was then passed on to the SPLA.[87] The aid given to fight the LRA supported the strengthening of the military and the government. In addition, around 50 percent of the government's budget was provided by development agencies.[88] Yet much of this was not used for its given purpose. With all of the resources at its disposal, the government in 2002 launched Operation Iron Fist against the LRA. It took an immense human toll on the local population,[89] with widespread torture, ill-treatment, rape, sexual abuse, arbitrary arrest, and extrajudicial killings reported on the part of the UPDF and paramilitary bodies.[90] On 2 October 2002, the military issued an order to evacuate "abandoned villages" in three northern districts, thus creating across the north a "military operational zone."[91] The number of people in IDP camps increased from 350,000 to 1.8 million. The war spread, thus providing further reasons for the West to provide military support to eliminate the LRA.[92] Iron Fist was "a catastrophe for the people of northern Uganda."[93]

The violence wrought by the LRA also expanded in southern Sudan. The Sudanese government reduced the assistance it gave to the LRA under pressure from the United States. As a result, the LRA engaged in attacks in government-controlled territory in addition to its attacks in SPLA areas. Its attacks in Sudan also increased as a result of Iron Fist. As the UPDF began to operate in southern Sudan, the LRA had to move around more, thus expanding its area of terror and forcing more people to become displaced. It also attacked Sudanese refugee camps in Uganda.[94] The expansion into

Sudan was the start of a trend whereby the LRA was eventually pushed out of Uganda almost entirely, transferring the problem to other countries. The UPDF also exported its violence against civilians to southern Sudan, including recruiting Sudanese to fight.[95]

Using the ICC

On 16 December 2003, President Museveni referred the situation in northern Uganda to the ICC. On 29 January 2004 he and ICC Prosecutor Ocampo appeared at a joint news conference.[96] This moment was a triumph for the ICC. This was its first case, five and half years after the Rome Statute was signed, and it represented the potential of international institutions playing a positive role in upholding international human rights norms. At the same time, it raised disquiet. Ocampo had lobbied for this referral,[97] and indeed had begun preliminary investigations. Even though a state cannot refer only one party to the ICC, this is what Museveni tried to do, asking the ICC to investigate the LRA. It seemed that Ocampo was happy to oblige, setting aside concerns about atrocities by the UPDF, thus calling into question the impartiality of the ICC. Further, it raised a significant question—what is the proper role of the ICC in the midst of an ongoing conflict? The LRA was still active, even though the government had instituted an amnesty in 2000[98] to try to induce members of the LRA to leave the group. How would this independent international judicial process affect the local peace process? Would the "interests of justice" undermine the "interests of peace"? Is such a stark trade-off inevitable? Furthermore, how would the ICC interact with local traditional justice mechanisms?

That press conference on 29 January was important for the ICC. And it was important for Museveni. The focus was on the LRA—no mention was made of the UPDF. Thus began the instrumentalization of the ICC. The referral made it easier for Ocampo to gain the cooperation of the government—a key consideration in any investigation. The price for this cooperation was a statement by the ICC that only mentioned the LRA. In his 29 January 24 statement, Museveni indicated that he would amend the amnesty law "to exclude the leadership of the LRA, ensuring that those bearing the greatest responsibility for crimes against humanity committed in Northern Uganda are brought to justice." Indeed, this was in accord with the Office of the UN High Commissioner for Human Rights, which had stated in 2001: "The issue of a blanket amnesty, particularly where war crimes and crimes against humanity have been committed, promotes a culture of impunity and is not in conformity with international standards and practice."[99] It further recommended that "The international community should take the necessary steps to isolate further the top leadership of the LRA and to hold it accountable for the gross human rights violations for which it is responsible."[100]

Payam Akhavan, who served as an advisor to the government, claims that "International trials were also viewed [by the Ugandan government] as a depoliticized venue for justice . . . the ICC could also become an instrument for national reconciliation."[101] But was this really an act of depoliticization, or was it, in fact, the exact opposite? Museveni was handing Ocampo his first case on a silver platter, (seemingly) removing impediments to prosecuting the LRA,[102] while steering the Prosecutor away from the many human rights violations committed by his own troops.[103] Although many of these violations had taken place before 1 July 2002, before which no violations could be prosecuted, there were plenty of war crimes committed after that date, in particular in the context of Operation Iron Fist—as well as in the DRC. Some of Ocampo's own staff urged him not to appear with Museveni to avoid an appearance of partiality,[104] and a few days after the press conference, Human Rights Watch stated that "the ICC prosecutor cannot ignore the crimes that Ugandan government troops have committed."[105] The clear message was that Ocampo was not being impartial, which could significantly undermine the credibility of the ICC. The lack of impartiality was further underlined when various Ugandan officials indicated that they would not be subject to the ICC jurisdiction, including the attorney general, Amama Mbabazi, who declared that the UPDF had not engaged in any war crimes and thus would not be tried by the ICC. There were threats to withdraw cooperation if the UPDF was investigated.[106] Not wanting to undermine a "new" African leader, the U.S. pressured the ICC not to investigate the UPDF.[107] The ICC was thus instrumentalized by both the domestic regime and a powerful international actor (which is not even a member of the ICC), creating strong partiality, which the ICC seemed more than happy to embrace.

Although Museveni would say a few weeks later that he would cooperate with the ICC if it investigated the army for war crimes,[108] he reinforced this partiality,[109] positioning the conflict as an international issue, indicating that it was only because the LRA was outside its borders that Uganda was calling in the ICC. Museveni continued to position Uganda as not only a victim but also a good international citizen, asking for cooperation from international institutions to help it solve the LRA problem, while also shoring up its democratic credentials, which had been tarnished by its conduct of the war.[110] And by cooperating on the LRA, Museveni hoped to push aside any action by the ICC against Uganda for its activities in the DRC.[111] This was a way to further bring in the international community. Who will go after Kony to arrest him? According to the Ugandan minister of defense, "It is not Uganda; if they ask us we shall lend a hand, but actually it will be international forces."[112] As Sarah Nouwen and Wouter Werner argue, "The ICC could turn the LRA from enemies of the Ugandan government into enemies of the international community as a whole."[113] Ocampo reiterated the requirement for international cooperation, including from Sudan, while also seeming to tie the case into the "War on Terror": "The case is so awful I don't think any state would be against co-operating . . . I believe all the states in the world would co-operate [against] these terrorist attacks."[114]

Less than three weeks later, Sudan affirmed that it would cooperate with the ICC. The Sudanese ambassador to Uganda predicted that "Kony's days are numbered,"[115] citing the peace process in Sudan and the havoc the LRA had wrought in southern Sudan. The ambassador indicated that Sudan would comply with an ICC arrest and surrender order. While citing the problems Kony had created in southern Sudan, Sudan was probably also hoping that its stated intention to cooperate would divert attention from Darfur.[116] As will be seen, these hopes were in vain. A month later, Sudan and Uganda signed an agreement—Iron Fist II—to allow the UPDF to go after the LRA in southern Sudan, which contributed to a weakening of the LRA.[117]

Six months later, on 29 July, the ICC announced that it was opening an investigation.[118] On 6 May 2005, Ocampo asked the Pre-Trial Chamber to issue arrest warrants for Kony[119] and four of his top deputies, which it did on 8 July, under seal. The arrest warrants were unsealed on 13 October. Akhavan argues that the fact that it took seven months for the Prosecutor to make this decision, "despite Uganda's need for swift action,"[120] is an indication of the safeguards in place to prevent states from using the ICC for their own political purposes. Yet this period of time says little about the politics involved. Ocampo obviously wanted the case. Yet the case for the investigation—including the gravity threshold—needs to be made. While the Office of the Prosecutor (OTP) argued that the greater "gravity" lay with the LRA actions,[121] there were still many UPDF abuses,[122] and the OTP made a calculated decision to go after only one side in the situation, for the reasons noted above. However, as Tim Allen points out: "Forcible displacement of population is a war crime under the Rome Statute, and it has obviously oc-curred on a massive scale. It is hard to see how it lacks gravity."[123] Partiality and political calculation seemed clear.

Yet the referral did seem to have had a couple of effects. First, it put more pressure on Sudan to cut off support of the LRA. This weakened the LRA, and forced it to abandon some of its bases in southern Sudan, and led to in-creased attacks within Uganda.[124] Second, it had a "sobering" effect on the LRA.[125] Two senior leaders of the LRA—chief negotiator Sam Kolo, and chief of operations Onen Kamdulu—defected in February 2005. Although this seemed to indicate splits in the leadership, the LRA also responded by reor-ganizing its leadership.[126] It also seemed to create pressure—at least for a while—on the LRA to engage in peace negotiations.[127] More LRA foot sol-diers were leaving, likely to take advantage of the amnesty.[128] The government was at the same time pursuing both peace negotiations and a military vic-tory, seeming to prefer the latter.[129] The ICC investigation helped to legitimate its military actions. The military pressure might have, in turn, worked with the ICC to push the LRA toward negotiations.[130] The arrest warrant also seemed to have another effect. In October and November the LRA attacked five humanitarian workers in retaliation for the arrest warrants, thus con-necting the palliators to the prosecutors.[131]

Peace Versus Justice?

The ICC investigation, and eventual arrest warrants, complicated two inter-twined dynamics. First, while the ICC may have created an incentive for peace negotiations, it also created a disincentive. Without firm guarantees that they would not face prosecution for their actions, why would senior LRA leaders negotiate a settlement and reenter society? The government perhaps could give such assurances for domestic prosecution—although it had committed itself to removing the amnesty so as not to interfere with the ICC—but nei-ther it nor the Prosecutor could give such assurances for the ICC. Only the Pre-Trial Chamber could permanently suspend proceedings—although the Prosecutor can determine that a prosecution is not in the "interests of jus-tice" and request that the Pre-Trial Chamber stop the case.[132] In 2005 Ocampo indicated that in order to comply with the requirement that a prosecution be in the interests of justice, "the Prosecutor will follow the various national and international efforts to achieve peace and security, as well as the views of witnesses and victims of the crimes."[133] Although this was written in the context of Darfur, it would equally apply to Uganda. Ocampo appeared to rule out stopping prosecutions just two years later.[134] The UN Security Council could indefinitely suspend proceedings on a yearly basis, but could not do so permanently, and given the place of the LRA on the U.S. terrorism list, a deferral was unlikely. Both the U.S. and EU supported the ICC position.[135] Indeed, in November 2006, the U.S. supported the arrest warrants, while also discouraging the ICC from looking at the UPDF.[136]

Second, in addition to the effects on the formal peace process, there were questions about how the ICC might undermine local and national reconciliation, especially the reconciliation ritual known as *mato oput*. Further grounding these concerns was the fact that the origins of the LRA in the HSM were supposedly tied to cleansing and reconciliation. Taken together, these concerns came to be defined under the peace vs. justice debate. That is, would the ICC, as the embodiment of global retributive justice, undermine local and national efforts—as found in the amnesty and *mato oput*—toward ending the conflict and reconciling those who had fought with the LRA with rest of the Acholi people? Although it was frequently put in such stark terms, the reality of the situation was much more nuanced, as the ICC seemed to have both positive and negative effects on the peace process, the amnesty possibilities for the leaders of the LRA were ambiguous, and the so-called traditional ceremonies and informal justice mechanisms also seemed to have more dubious foundations.

Amnesty and Negotiations

The government had engaged in negotiations and reconciliation with a number of groups from the late 1980s to as late as 2003,[137] which included amnesties under the Amnesty Statute of 1987. Like the 1987 amnesty law, a 1998 amnesty bill was introduced to encourage Ugandans in exile to return home, while also excluding some crimes, such as genocide.[138] The 2000 Amnesty Act (which had been driven by civil society groups, including the Acholi Religious Leaders Peace Initiative, and opposed by Museveni[139]) did not have any such restrictions. While the amnesty initially had little effect on top LRA commanders, eventually, in conjunction with the ICC referral, it did provide the framework for at least a few high-level LRA soldiers to come in.[140] More broadly, as Zachary Lomo argues, "the amnesty law provided a framework with which they can woo back the conscripts in the LRA to come home."[141] By 2004, thousands of LRA fighters had applied for amnesty, but then there was a significant reduction in amnesty applications,[142] and then a renewed rate of applications, with 20,592 amnesty applications by April 2006.[143] Indeed, the fighting capacity of the LRA had begun to be reduced significantly, with up to five fighters lost on average every day—either through being killed, being captured, or defecting—leading many commanders to favor negotiating with the government.[144] At the same time, the government amended the Amnesty Act in April 2006 to allow top LRA commanders to be excluded from the amnesty. In the following months, there would be confusion about whether Kony and other commanders were, indeed, excluded. Three days after the amendment, Museveni said that those who had been indicted by the ICC were excluded from the amnesty, which was reiterated by the security minister in June. In July, Museveni reversed course and offered amnesty to Kony and the others, while Uganda internal affairs minister Ruhakana Rugunda indicated that since a list had not been approved by parliament yet, Kony and the others would still be eligible for amnesty.[145] Rugunda also stated that alternative reconciliation and accountability mechanisms were a "logical modality that will supplement discussions."[146] Museveni further pledged that no LRA member would be turned over to the ICC, while his security minister, Amama Mbabazi, had not made a formal request for withdrawal of the warrants.[147] The Ugandan government thus had a very confused position on the ICC, making it that much more difficult for the LRA commanders to know where they stood.

Ocampo, on the other hand, was not ambiguous. While the ICC may have worked very deliberately and held off on the execution of arrest warrants to give space for former Ugandan state minister Betty Bigombe to engage in mediation and negotiations,[148] Ocampo stated in July 2006 that "The best way to finally stop the conflict is to arrest the top leaders."[149] International leaders also indicated support for the ICC warrants over amnesty, including the UK ambassador to the Security Council, Emyr Jones Parry.[150]

However, while the ICC may have been a useful way of regaining international credibility for the government and legitimizing the war against the LRA, it soon appeared to be a barrier to peace. Given the inability to arrest or militarily defeat the LRA, lack of international support, and a need to shore up its image after flawed elections and the continued humanitarian situation in the north, the government decided to attempt to get the LRA to participate in peace talks in the middle of 2006[151] (this followed on previous attempts to engage the LRA, led by Betty Bigombe[152])—even though Museveni had previously and subsequently expressed skepticism about, or indeed opposed, peace talks.[153] Negotiations began on 14 July 2006, mediated by the Government of South Sudan (GoSS),[154] leading to a cessation of hostilities on 26 August.[155] The semiautonomous GoSS was created after the signing of the Comprehensive Peace Plan in January 2005, which brought to an end decades of conflict between the government of Sudan in the North and the South, and was highly motivated to end the LRA attacks in South Sudan.[156]

As a result of the cessation of hostilities, most LRA fighters left northern Uganda. This opened up some restrictions on movement, and within a few months 230,000 civilians left the IDP camps (although most of those did not actually go home). There were some violations of the cessation of hostilities, which expired on 28 February 2007, and LRA fighters failed to gather at designated places in southern Sudan.[157] In addition to southern Sudan, the LRA also had a significant presence in the DRC, having previously established itself in Garamba National Park, beginning in September 2005, with hundreds appearing in the following months.[158] In April 2006 Uganda had asked the Security Council for permission to enter the DRC to strike against the LRA in Garamba, and in August the chief of the Ugandan Defence Forces, General Aronda Nyakirima, indicated that if the LRA did not take "advantage of the peace talks, Uganda will go to [Congo] with or without the government's authority."[159] Thus, even as talks continued in Juba between the government and the LRA, the LRA itself was becoming more a regional pest, and the Uganda-focused negotiations seemed less able to address regional concerns. Further, it appeared that the government was just using the peace talks as leverage to gain support for military action in the DRC if and when the talks failed.[160]

Although there were continuing violations of the cessation of hostilities, talks resumed in Juba on 26 April 2007, leading to two agreements. The first, on 2 May, focused on comprehensive solutions, providing a general framework to address long-term social, political, and economic grievances in Northern Uganda. While a positive step, it was very vague, did not directly address many of the issues raised by the LRA, and put off concrete implementation for further negotiation. More fundamentally, however, there were continuing questions as to whether the LRA was a legitimate interlocutor to negotiate over long-standing issues in Northern Uganda.[161]

The second agreement, on 29 June, was on reconciliation and accountability.[162] The agreement recognized the necessity of producing an impartial history of the conflict. Traditional justice mechanisms were seen "as a central part of the framework for accountability and reconciliation," and would include "alternative sentences, reparations, and any other formal institutions or mechanisms." State actors (e.g., the military) were exempted from special procedures set up by the agreement and would only be subject to existing criminal justice processes (which had exempted the military from any significant accountability for years). Domestic courts would address the most serious crimes, including international crimes, with the government agreeing to "Address conscientiously the question of the ICC arrest warrants relating to the leaders of the LRA/M." An annex, which made reference to ICC complementarity, specified that there would be a special division of the Ugandan High Court set up for this purpose.[163] Alternative penalties and sanctions, intended to promote reconciliation and reparations, would replace existing penalties.

The agreement thus seemed designed to address questions of local accountability and justice and the concerns of the LRA leadership with regard to the ICC arrest warrants, which it had demanded be rescinded.[164] And it seemed to reflect the government's (conflicted) preference for amnesty over prosecution. While the agreement seems to indicate that LRA leaders would face criminal proceedings, it also appears that they might just face traditional justice, which would not involve the usual penalties such as incarceration, or indeed the death penalty. The mixed messages from the government on amnesty were detailed above, but are encapsulated in the following two statements from Museveni. First, in May 2005, he stated that " 'If we capture him, he would be tried under our law, since he refused amnesty. We have the death penalty, the ICC doesn't."[165] This may have been an attempt to encourage the LRA to come to an agreement to end the conflict as soon as possible. A month after the conclusion of the annex, Museveni said that Uganda had invoked the ICC because the LRA was outside of Uganda, and that if they returned and asked for amnesty, Uganda would ask the ICC to withdraw the case. Kony and others would be given amnesty.[166]

Did this represent just a straightforward trade-off between peace and justice—a reflection of Museveni's long-standing strategy of reaching peace deals by offering impunity[167]—or was it an attempt to create a more nuanced approach to justice? The issue of traditional justice will be addressed in more depth in the next section, but given the government's flip-flopping on the issue of amnesty, the former seems more plausible.

It was clear that Ocampo would have nothing to do with attempts to evade ICC jurisdiction. In June 2007 he stated that "the drafters [of the Rome Statute] were well aware that rendering justice in the context of conflict or peace negotiations would present particular difficulties and they prepared our institution well to meet those challenges."[168] He noted that he was given a clear mandate "to apply the law without political considerations," and that amnesties, immunity, and withdrawal of indictments for "short-term political goals . . . are not compatible with the Rome Statute."[169] He saw no incompatibility between the ICC and peace processes, noting the deterrence value of the ICC and the role of arrest warrants in bringing parties to a conflict to the negotiating table, and maintaining that national mechanisms could be used for all except those which bore the greatest responsibility—those indicted by the ICC.[170] He said

> It is the lack of enforcement of the Court's decisions which is the real threat to peace. Allowed to remain at large, the criminals exposed are continuing to threaten the victims, those who took tremendous risks to tell their stories; allowed to remain at large, the criminals ask for immunity under one form or another as a condition to stopping the violence. They threaten to attack more victims. I call this extortion, I call it blackmail. We cannot yield.[171]

He reaffirmed his stance in March 2008.[172]

There were also significant questions regarding how arrest warrants might be suspended or withdrawn in practice. The Security Council could suspend the proceedings for a year, indefinitely renewable. The Security Council was not interested.[173] Furthermore, the Security Council would have to make a positive decision every year for the rest of the lives of those with arrest warrants against them to suspend the warrants. It seems unlikely that Kony and the others could count on that. Furthermore, the experience of other mass murderers, such as Augusto Pinochet and Charles Taylor, who thought they had achieved permanent impunity, should give any mass murderer who has become the target of international criminal justice mechanisms pause.

The second avenue for stopping proceedings is for the Prosecutor to apply to the Pre-Trial Chamber for the arrest warrants to be withdrawn. Under the principle of complementarity the Ugandan government could claim that it was able to carry out investigations and prosecutions where necessary. It would have to show that it had the necessary legislation to prosecute individuals for the relevant individual crimes (which Uganda did not have at that point), the necessary impartial judicial institutions, and the intent to actually prosecute the relevant individuals. The contradictory statements from the Ugandan government, as well as the language in the accountability agreement and the annex, would have called this into significant question. If the government did defer to nonlegal, nonformal, nonpunitive measures such as traditional justice, this also would not satisfy complementarity (although some argue the opposite[174]). The Prosecutor argued that withdrawing the arrest warrants would not be in the interests of justice. Although ICC officials had indicated in 2005 that the investigation could be halted in the interests of justice, even after arrest warrants had been issued,[175] given Ocampo's previous statements, there seemed little chance of this happening.

In September 2007, the Office of the Prosecutor released a Policy Paper on the Interests of Justice, which laid out the thinking of the OTP on this issue. It noted that "the text and purpose of the Rome Statute clearly favour the pursuit of investigations" and that "it is clear that only in exceptional circumstances will the Prosecutor of the ICC conclude that an investigation or a prosecution may not serve the interests of justice."[176] Three specific factors were to be considered: the gravity of the crime, the interests of victims, and the particular circumstances of the accused.[177] In the case of the LRA, the gravity criteria were clearly met, and there were no issues relating to the accused—for example, age or infirmity. The interests of the victims were cast in terms of the protection and safety of the victims in the context of an investigation.

One might argue that a situation where fighting had stopped, people could stop living in fear of attack from the LRA, and 1.5 million IDPs could go home might be a form of justice. There is no mention of the interests of peace in the Rome Statute, and the Policy Paper specifically noted "that there is a difference between the concepts of the interests of justice and the interests of peace and that the latter falls within the mandate of institutions other than the Office of the Prosecutor."[178]

With respect to peace processes, the OTP noted that "The ICC was created on the premise that justice is an essential component of a stable peace,"[179] citing the UN Secretary-General: "Justice, peace and democracy are not mutually exclusive objectives, but rather mutually reinforcing imperatives."[180] While recognizing the necessity of comprehensive solutions, it stated that "The Office . . . will pursue its own judicial mandate independently."[181] The clear message was that the "concept of the interests of justice . . . should not be conceived of so broadly as to embrace all issues related to peace and security."[182] The latter is the mandate of the Security Council—and others—and the Security Council could take it on itself to defer an investigation or prosecution if it saw fit. Peace and security are political matters best left to others.

While one cannot say that the ICC is not a political body, at its most fundamental level it was designed to be independent of outside political influences. And even though they may intrude (for example via an Article 13 referral or Article 16 deferral by the Security Council), it would be very difficult for the Prosecutor to claim the expertise and wisdom to decide when one peace process justified stopping proceedings and another did not (although he did feel confident to say that if Kony was arrested, "we will have peace tomorrow"[183]). Further, in the case of the LRA, while it started in Uganda, is has now spread far beyond Uganda, operating in South Sudan, the DRC, and the Central African Republic. The focus on peace in Uganda ignores these other contexts. Thus, recognizing an amnesty in Uganda could do a significant disservice to victims in other countries.

The question of amnesty became moot as the agreement fell apart. There was internal dissension within the LRA (including the execution of Kony's second in command, Vincent Otti, who had been the lead negotiator, by Kony in October 2007) and confusion over a number of points, including disarmament, demobilization, and reintegration of LRA fighters, as well as LRA accountability. After several delays, it was announced on 25 May that Kony would not sign the final agreement. In the ensuing months, even as peace began to come to northern Uganda with the exit of the LRA, preparations for more fighting occurred. Indeed, it appeared that Kony was using the negotiations to rearm and regroup,[184] which was facilitated by humanitarian aid provided to the LRA during the negotiations[185] (which the ICC called for an end to[186]), and after one more deadline on 30 November, at which Kony failed to show, the UPDF attacked the LRA in Garamba. Although supposedly a joint operation between Uganda, the DRC, and the GoSS, Operation Lightning Thunder was dominated by the UPDF.[187] Museveni indicated in 2009 that he would not reopen negotiations with Kony.[188]

Yet the issue of amnesty remained alive. Between 2000 and 2011, more than 26,000 former LRA members received amnesty.[189] In 2010, the Directorate of Public Prosecutions initiated its first prosecution against a former LRA colonel, Thomas Kwoyelo, denying him amnesty. This was overturned in September 2011.[190] However, the amnesty expired in May 2012. This had particular significance for a recently captured LRA commander, Major General Caesar Achellam, who, unlike Kwoyelo, appeared to face trial. The lack of amnesty could potentially undermine efforts to induce other LRA soldiers to surrender.[191]

The ICC and (Traditional) Justice—Incompatible Concepts?

While the government wanted to end the war, it seemed more concerned about ending it on its own terms, potentially through a military victory. It offered amnesty, but its statements were contradictory, as was its position on justice. The ICC held a clear and firm understanding of justice as retribution. The people most affected by the LRA—the inhabitants of northern Uganda—held nuanced yet ambiguous and contradictory perspectives on justice. After the insertion of the ICC into the conflict, a dominant discourse developed that pitted the ICC against peace and traditional justice. They were described as being "on a collision course . . . rais[ing] a number of questions related to issues of legitimacy and sovereignty."[192] The ICC was perceived and framed as an outside force—"a third independent actor in the civil war"[193]—which interfered with the quest for peace and centuries-old indigenous accountability and conflict resolution mechanisms.[194] Traditional justice, and especially the *mato oput* ceremony of the Acholi, became reified and romanticized.[195] The amnesty in Uganda, with its connections to local justice, was portrayed as without precedent, and thus not understandable by outsiders.[196] International (retributive) and traditional (restorative) justice became dichotomized. "Traditional justice" was instrumentalized by local leaders to buttress their power and by the government to help it regain control of the justice debate after it invited the ICC in. The whole of northern Uganda was held to believe in the primacy of traditional justice, although the reality was significantly more complicated.

The one thing people in northern Uganda did agree on, though, was the need for peace so that people would not need to live in fear and would be able to go home. According to one study, in 2005 there was "overwhelming support for the amnesty process throughout the country,"[197] which was seen as a way to achieve the above goal. Further, there was a perception that the involvement of the ICC had undermined the amnesty process.[198] The confluence of the amnesty law, various traditional justice mechanisms, and the ICC involvement raised a couple of important questions: "Who should drive

the process of justice within this context? How should international understandings of justice influence local perceptions, and which should take
precedence?"[199]

In February 2005, a group of Acholi community leaders released a statement calling on the ICC to "'suspend its investigation and refrain from
planned issuance of arrest warrants until peace is achieved in Northern
Uganda.'"[200] They hosted a delegation of Acholi community leaders in
March 2005. They again asked that the ICC respect the traditional justice and
reconciliation processes of the Acholi.[201] Another meeting was held the next
month, with a more representative group from across northern Uganda. The
response from both meetings seemed to undermine the argument that local
leaders were completely opposed to the ICC intervention.[202] Local NGOs, and
some international NGOs working in Uganda, such as Save the Children,
voiced dissent against the ICC investigation.[203] Yet, in 2005, a year after the
original Save the Children statement, it released another statement that supported the work of the ICC while also raising some concerns. While it recognized that there had not been an increase in attacks as a result of the
preliminary investigation, it was still worried that the issuance of warrants
might lead to such attacks.[204] The ICC was also identified as a neocolonial
intervention that ignored local practices.[205] These practices are purported to
be core to the identity of those in northern Uganda, and in particular the
Acholi. Yet there are significant questions about the status of these practices
and the level of support they garner, so we must ask what are these practices,
how traditional are they, and is there indeed a significant conflict between
them and the ICC?

While there are a variety of traditional justice mechanisms identified in
northern Uganda,[206] the focus has been on the Acholi, and one particular process called *mato oput*—drinking the bitter root. It is intended to allow "for
reconciliation with compensation, rather than revenge."[207] Advocates of this
ceremony focused on the religious—and specifically Christian—question of
forgiveness. A report written by Dennis Pain in 1997 for International Alert,
after a meeting of government officials, church leaders, and representatives
from the LRA, helped to focus the discussion on how to facilitate reconciliation (as well as promote Acholi unity). The report was entitled "The Bending of the Spears," which referred to another traditional (if rarely used)
ceremony called *gomo tong*, "bending the spears," and was framed in an explicitly religious manner. It supported a combination of amnesty and *mato
oput*, along with *gomo tong*, to facilitate reconciliation.[208] As Branch observes,

the report "reduced [the war] to an internal social crisis brought about by the breakdown of traditional authority, to be resolved through rebuilding traditional Acholi order,"[209] noting that Pain (and the World Bank) "ignore the violence used by the LRA and the government against each other and ignore the violence of the government against civilians, in favor of focusing on LRA violence against civilians, defining it as intra-Acholi violence."[210]

Although there were also many historical practices that supported retribution rather than reconciliation, *mato oput* was quickly supported by local activists and religious leaders as well as international organizations. By the middle part of 2005, numerous *mato oput* ceremonies were performed. These were sometimes attended by journalists and aid workers, and were claimed to be very effective.[211]

These ceremonies were concentrated in and around Gulu. Further afield, and particularly in the IDP camps, there was less support for *mato oput*. Non-Acholi were particularly unenthusiastic, asking why it should be only Acholi who did the forgiving.[212] One might also point out that the LRA had expanded far beyond Uganda (and a significant portion of the LRA was made up of Sudanese,[213] as well as Congolese and Central Africans), and it is difficult to see how one group of people in one country could make a decision on how those who carried out the violence should be treated. While this might be more understandable for those—especially child soldiers—who were being reintegrated into their former communities, it would be harder to make the case for Kony and other senior commanders who bore the greatest responsibility for the death and destruction wrought by the LRA. Many wanted Kony and others prosecuted, while there was worry about security issues related to the arrest warrants. Furthermore, many *mato oput* ceremonies performed had to do with local murders, perhaps encouraged by the international funding provided for compensation. And those that did involve former LRA rebels were not performed in the way they were supposedly performed in the past.[214] As Linda Keller points out, "Reconciliation and reintegration places very difficult burdens on Acholi victims, who are asked to 'welcome home' those who butchered their family and maimed them."[215] Many will not want to engage in such forgiveness. As Joyce Neu observes, one would have to be "superhuman" to forgive in this situation.[216]

Further, these "traditional" ceremonies seemed to harken back to a past that did not exist, or at least not in the way imagined, and seemed to be more tied in to supporting and reifying certain power structures. The word Acholi itself dates back to British colonial times in the late nineteenth century, thus

highlighting the role of "nontraditional" forces in creating "traditional" identities. The practice of many rituals has been tied into the creation of new
classes of "traditional" leaders by the colonial administration.[217] This continues to the present day as "traditional" chiefs maneuver for power, using "traditional" rituals to shore up that power.[218] This is not to argue that there may
not be value in these ceremonies, or that they are entirely constructed from
the outside or completely instrumentalized, without any authenticity. Rather,
whereas many outside observers romanticized and essentialized *mato oput*
specifically, and a culture of forgiveness more generally, among the Acholi,
it must be recognized that there are a multiplicity of voices in northern
Uganda on the issue of amnesty, forgiveness, and traditional justice.

In a survey conducted in April and May 2005, 66 percent wanted punishment for the LRA, while only 22 percent preferred forgiveness or reconciliation, 91 percent of those who had heard of the ICC thought it would
facilitate peace, and 89 percent thought it would support justice. Only 10 percent felt that traditional leaders could bring peace and justice. Between
50 percent and 70 percent thought that traditional ceremonies were useful in
dealing with the LRA.[219] In the same study, when asked what justice is, 31 percent identified trials, 18 percent said reconciliation, 11 percent said truth
and fairness, 10 percent said assistance to victims, 8 percent said compensation, and 7 percent said traditional justice.[220]

Another survey conducted two years later revealed concern about the effect of the ICC on the peace process and support for peace with amnesty
while simultaneously demonstrating support for accountability, and specifically for the ICC.[221] Indeed, 58.5 percent said it was important that the LRA
be put on trial, and 64 percent said that the international community should
conduct the trials. In addition, 76.1 percent indicated that trials at that point
(mid-2007 when the Juba process appeared to hold out hope of ending the
conflict) might endanger the peace process. When given the choice of national
trials, international trials, or no trials, 44.3 percent indicated a preference for
international trials, 24.7 percent for national trials, and 31.1 percent for no
trials; 67 percent felt the ICC should be involved in responding to the atrocities in northern Uganda (even as 44.1 percent said the ICC should stop its
arrest warrants).[222]

Overall, then, people in northern Uganda wanted peace and a better life
and were concerned about the best way to achieve this. There was strong support for punishing at least the main leaders of the LRA, preferably through
the ICC, although concern about how this would affect the peace process was

present. There was also support for traditional justice, in particular for those lower down the LRA hierarchy (including the children of northern Uganda who had become child soldiers). This demonstrates how both the ICC and traditional justice can exist side by side. *Mato oput* and other similar ceremonies can be used to facilitate healing and reconciliation for many who have been caught up in the fighting and facilitate the reintegration of LRA fighters back into the community. At the same time, those with the most responsibility for the conflict—Kony and a few other top commanders—can be pursued by the ICC to provide a different type of justice. The one thing missing from this equation, of course, is the government and UPDF (55 percent indicated the UPDF should be punished[223]). There is little prospect of any significant form of justice for crimes committed by the government and UPDF, particularly given the ICC's refusal to pursue such crimes.

In addition, as the International Crisis Group points out, "Traditional reconciliation ceremonies receive tepid support in part because they are insufficient to the scale and nature of the conflict."[224] The "traditional" *mato oput* ceremony involves an individual admitting guilt, asking forgiveness, and paying compensation to the clan of the victim. While Kony had asked southern cultural leaders for forgiveness, and has indicated a preference for traditional justice,[225] he repeatedly denied attacking the Acholi.[226] The former LRA commander Sam Kolo said that he would not ask for reconciliation and pay compensation to his victims, but said he would engage in the *mato oput* ceremony performed by the paramount chief.[227] Kony sees the killing as justified, and so would be unlikely to admit guilt and ask for forgiveness.[228] This seems to indicate, first, that senior LRA commanders are not serious about reconciliation, and second, that the "traditional" ceremonies carried out may, in at least some circumstances, fall far short of the robust reconciliation process attributed to them. *Mato oput* was designed to deal with disputes between clans up to "simple murder," and was generally not used in the case of killing in war[229] (perhaps recognizing, as does international humanitarian law, a difference between killing, or at least many types of killing, during war, and killing outside of war) or the other kinds of crimes committed by the LRA.[230] If the ceremony is supposed to be about individual reconciliation, how does one scale this up to a situation where the LRA has killed more than 100,000 people and abducted between 60,000 and 100,000 across a vast area of central Africa over twenty-five years?

It may be possible to engage in individual reconciliation at a very local level of individuals who have come from an Acholi village, killed or abducted people from that village, and then come back to that village to ask for forgiveness. The people in the village can forgive that person for what they have done to the people in that village. They cannot forgive what the LRA has done in other parts of northern Uganda, or indeed in other countries. Traditional justice mechanisms can only deal with direct victims, whereas "Indirect victims include all of Uganda and indeed the entire world; international crimes are thought of as crimes against the international community as a whole. The general trend in the international community is for prosecution."[231] How can a village forgive Kony and others of his inner circle who have directed this swath of destruction across central Africa? How can an entire country forgive? While other soldiers might sit down with a paramount chief, who could Kony sit down with? Museveni? Given the government's role in the misery brought to northern Uganda, those from the region would hardly accept him speaking on their behalf. Further, as the ICG argues, "Peace deals without accountability have generally not worked in Uganda,"[232] with grievances not addressed.

Thus, while local justice mechanisms such as *mato oput* might deal with a significant number of former LRA fighters, for those most responsible for the killing—including those with arrest warrants from the ICC—traditional mechanisms are likely not enough, for five reasons identified by Keller:

(1) "the unprecedented complexity of perpetrators needing reconciliation";

(2) "the traditions themselves have atrophied and lack legitimacy";

(3) "the ceremonies require 'acknowledgement and truth telling' as a 'vital part of the process' ";

(4) "the Acholi require compensation prior to reconciliation ceremonies. Compensation is difficult if the perpetrator is unknown. . . . [and] Given the brutality, depravity, and scale of the atrocities, it might be impossible to compensate for the crimes"; and

(5) "there is currently confusion over the ceremonies, with some calling any tradition '*mato oput*' and others confusing the various ceremonies."[233]

Furthermore, an amnesty would still leave an international mass murderer walking free among his victims. There is little evidence that this would lead to a stable situation where his victims felt that they received any kind of real justice. Indeed, a survey carried out in eastern DRC in 2008 revealed that

85 percent believe "it is important to hold those who committed war crimes accountable and that accountability is necessary to secure peace."[234] In fact, in March 2010, victims of an attack in Faradje in northeastern Congo led by LRA Lt. Col. Charles Arop, who was responsible for the so-called Christmas massacres in 2008 (discussed below),[235] asked the Congolese justice minister to prosecute Arop. Arop had surrendered to Ugandan soldiers the previous September and requested amnesty in Uganda.[236] Is it reasonable for Uganda to override the wishes of Arop's victims in the DRC by granting amnesty—which eventually occurred?[237] Yet Congolese hopes for justice seemed to be in vain, with no plans to prosecute LRA in the DRC.[238]

Even if an amnesty was granted, there would still be the ICC warrants to deal with. While, superficially, the warrants seemed to have pushed Kony to the negotiating table and then away again, the situation appears more complex. There is little evidence that Kony would have signed the peace agreement if the warrants had been suspended or rescinded—and little international support for rescinding them. Museveni provided assurances in 2006 that he would not turn Kony over to the ICC,[239] but would this have actually provided permanent insulation from the ICC? The only other option would be to grant Kony safe haven in a country not a party to the ICC and unlikely to become one any time soon. While many in northern Uganda might have supported this option,[240] unlike Idi Amin, Kony would not necessarily be as certain that this would last permanently, as Charles Taylor found out.[241] Indeed, there has been a permanent shift in the calculations of dictators and mass murderers. It is decreasingly possible to escape the reaches of the international criminal justice regime, even in "safe" countries.

The Depoliticized and Instrumentalized ICC

What does this discussion tell us about the role of the ICC in the northern Ugandan (and now beyond) conflict? The ICC was portrayed by its supporters as a savior of Uganda. It would help the people get rid of Kony, and bring justice to an area that has known little justice for decades. This has not occurred, and once the Acholi realized that the ICC does not have an army or a policy force to arrest Kony, their support for the ICC waned.[242] Its role has been much more ambiguous. By being portrayed as a savior, it ties into the so-called "savage-victim-savior" structure identified by Makau Mutua[243] and developed by Adam Branch. As Branch argues, "The *savage* is the African violator of criminal justice. . . . outside the pale of politics, and even humanity," while "The *victim* is individualized but anonymous, defined in terms of a universally applicable set of basic rights. . . . [and] depoliticized."[244] The victim thus requires "the *savior* [who is] the self-proclaimed enforcer of global law"[245] who pushes aside any alternative approaches to justice. The depoliticized savior rushes in to protect the depoliticized victim who is suffering at the hands of the depoliticized savage. If all actors are depoliticized, it is easier to avoid the political context in which the savagery occurs, and it allows the savior to avoid looking into other potential savages (i.e., the UPDF) since it was the government that called in the savior in the first place. Further, since the savage has been depoliticized and dehumanized, and other potential savages identified as the savior, it is easier to justify the use of force against the savage.[246] The ICC is thus instrumentalized by one political actor to go after another political (if depoliticized) actor, as well as to use force against the victims themselves (for their own good). The use of the ICC to legitimate the use of force has been noted by the special advisor to the Prosecutor,[247] and can clearly be seen in Uganda. The ICC arrest warrants legitimated not only military action within Uganda against the LRA (as well as against the citizens of Northern Uganda),[248] but also in Sudan, the CAR, and the DRC. It also legitimated circumscribing and cracking down on internal political dissent.[249]

Further, as a dominant (depoliticized) global political actor, the ICC is able to define the justice narrative. It shoves aside local justice alternatives. The supporters of these local justice alternatives—"traditional justice" such as *mato oput*—in turn attempted to portray their approaches as indigenous and apolitical, threatened by a neocolonial outsider whose very presence threatened the possibility of peace and undermined local culture. Neither of these narratives capture the full reality. The ICC is limited in what it can do. It cannot arrest and bring to The Hague those against whom it has issued arrest warrants. It must rely on other actors—usually states, or maybe international peacekeeping forces. Ocampo has argued that "'coalitions of the willing'" and "'special forces'" are needed to arrest those sought by the ICC, led by the United States—the same country that was pressuring the ICC not to investigate the UPDF. So, special forces are needed to go after illegitimate political actors, but legitimate, Western-friendly governments are exempted from the reach of the special forces. Further, states can constrain not only its ability to arrest perpetrators but also limit investigations if the ICC does not act in a way that accords with their wishes. Thus, Uganda can threaten to withhold cooperation if the ICC (a supposedly depoliticized actor) does not act in a politically sensitive manner.

Neither the ICC nor other forms of transitional justice can actually bring justice if there is no transition.[250] Certainly Museveni's entire strategy was to avoid a transition. There was no serious prospect that any type of political realignment would be allowed. If the top LRA commanders were allowed to return to Uganda and given amnesty, it would be the government, as the sole legitimate political power, which granted the amnesty. There would be no inclusion of the LRA in the political process. By branding Kony and other senior leaders outlaws, the ICC undermined any possibility of political inclusion of the LRA. Similarly, there seemed little interest in responding to the demands of the people of Northern Uganda, which the LRA claimed to represent. The only justice would be, in the end, that given by the government. There would be no change in power relations, and certainly there would be no real prosecutions of senior military and government figures who were responsible for much of the suffering in Northern Uganda, an impunity effectively supported by the ICC as part of the bargain to be able to investigate the LRA.[251] While the amnesty may have provided space for many LRA to come back home, and *mato oput* may have helped integrate some of those back into society, they have not brought relief to the conditions under which those in Northern Uganda have suffered for years. And while the LRA violence may have left Northern Uganda, it has been displaced across the border to other countries in the region. The government still enjoys significant impunity for what Olara Otunnu calls the "secret genocide" of the Acholi,[252] bolstered by the ICC and nations like the United States that rely on "new" African leaders like Museveni to provide a modicum of stability and a veneer of democracy.

Further, even though Ocampo relied on a quantitative analysis of gravity to buttress his decision to go after the LRA but not government forces, it is precisely those government forces for which the ICC was created—a situation where the government is unwilling to prosecute. Yet the ICC has allowed itself to be diverted from such situations, essentially acting as a surrogate for the government against its enemies, while allowing the government to act as it likes—resulting in a so-called "asymmetric" referral.[253] As William Schabas asks, "in a domestic justice setting involving ordinary crime, would we countenance a national prosecutor who ignored clandestine police death squads on the grounds that gangsters were killing more people than the rogue officials?"[254]

Peace and/or/via Justice

The dominant discourse in Uganda has put peace and justice in opposition,[255] while others argue that one gets peace *via* justice—that there can be no peace without justice. Yet the relationship between the two is more complex. As Priscilla Hayner argues, "Working for both peace and justice requires a broader and more holistic view of how both of these aims are achieved and the important connection between them."[256] We also need broader understandings of both concepts, which recognize that peace is more than absence of violence[257] and justice goes beyond trials.[258]

Thus, "peace" means an absence of physical conflict, but it also means a broader context in which there is a lack of political oppression or fear of such, as well as a lack of fear of a return to violence. "Justice" can involve both retributive and restorative forms. It can facilitate the absence of violence or a return to violence by removing from society—or by reintegrating perpetrators back into society and removing their ability to return to harm—those who carried out the violence. Returning LRA have been reintegrated into society via the amnesty and *mato oput*, while the top leaders of the LRA (and others) have been marginalized and excluded from Northern Uganda via the ICC warrants and the military campaign. That this has displaced the violence to other countries does not undermine the effect of this marginalization. Yet, a significant element of peace—a broader political reconciliation or transition—has not occurred. This will likely continue to be the case unless there is "justice"—of the retributive kind—for members of the UPDF and government who were responsible for significant widespread suffering on the part of the civilian population. Peace and justice are not inherently dichotomous.[259] In Uganda they have been portrayed as such, but we have seen both imperfect and partial peace and justice in Uganda precisely because they have not been better integrated and because justice has been manipulated for short-term, partial peace, which leaves intact existing political and social inequalities.

Branch argues that the ICC is too narrow, ignoring the role of Western states, aid agencies, and corporations in creating and maintaining political and humanitarian crises as exemplified in northern Uganda. And it ignores broader concepts of global justice.[260] This is true, although how to realistically craft a court that could address all of these concerns is a difficult question to answer. Schabas notes that soon after the warrants were issued, the International Court of Justice found Uganda liable for international crimes in the DRC: "The international legal regime looks incoherent."[261] Incoherent indeed. Both our concepts and institutions thus seem too narrow, too easily diverted from looking at the sui generis aspects of particular situations, but also too easily diverted from examining broader contexts in which these particular situations operate and the multiple culpabilities of multiple actors and the multiple dimensions of peace and justice embedded within such situations.

Hunting Kony—and Protecting Civilians?

As the peace process collapsed, the focus returned to the attempt to find Kony, either to capture him or to kill him. This military response acquired a more international element, as the United States, in particular, became more involved. And this effort had a much more international scope. The LRA had essentially decamped from northern Uganda,[262] taking up residence, first in Garamba National Park, and then spreading further across northeast DRC and the CAR, establishing itself at the confluence of the Sudan, the DRC, and the CAR, in an area where it was less likely to be attacked, and in the process becoming harder to disarm.[263] Kony had approximately six hundred soldiers and six hundred abducted civilians in Garamba by mid-2008, and had stockpiled food and other resources. The LRA also began cultivating fields in the area.[264] And it began attacks against civilians in the immediate region of Garamba.[265] Ocampo had supported a suspension in international activities to arrest Kony during the Juba negotiations, a decision he said he regretted in 2008.[266] The UN Mission in Sudan had indicated in 2006 that it would not arrest LRA leaders who participated in the Juba peace talks.[267] Yet it is unclear whether this made any difference.

As discussed in the previous chapter, MONUC had its hands full in eastern DRC with a wide variety of armed groups. It did not have the resources to undertake any sustained efforts against the LRA. While MONUC signed a memorandum of understanding with the ICC to assist in efforts to arrest Kony and the other LRA leaders with arrest warrants,[268] it was severely constrained, with other priorities (in particular the Kivus),[269] and has been ambiguous on its commitment to undertake the necessary activities. In January 2006 the LRA killed eight Guatemalan peacekeepers in Garamba.[270] As the International Crisis Group noted, "Military operations against the LRA would be complicated by the densely forested terrain, poor infrastructure and lack of effective armed capacity in the area,"[271] and MONUC was "Hamstrung by a mandate to protect civilians and support the Congolese army,"[272] as well as its focus on the elections.[273] After the death of the peacekeepers, MONUC had few troops near Garamba, and those that were in the area were for logistical support;[274] FARDC did not have a presence either,[275] not viewing the LRA as a major threat.[276] In 2007, a MONUC official said that "MONUC does not have the capacity or the mandate to be on the front lines of getting rid of foreign armed groups in Congo."[277] This was particularly true with regard to the LRA in Garamba, which had expanded its attacks in the area and along the DRC-South Sudan-CAR border.[278] MONUC and FARDC signed a joint directive on 30 May that focused on protecting civilians, containing the LRA, and encouraging demobilization, although MONUC's limitations were clear.[279]

In September 2008 MONUC and FARDC engaged in Operation Rudia, which was intended to contain the LRA, prevent attacks on civilians, and encourage defections. Although some defections occurred, the operation was not very successful and resulted in renewed LRA attacks on civilians.[280] An estimated 50,000 people fled as a result of these attacks.[281]

The UPDF, along with Congolese and south Sudanese forces, attacked Kony's camp in December 2008.[282] Kabila had initially been resistant to allowing outside forces back in, but gave in after pressure from the United States.[283] The operation failed because the attack was leaked, which allowed Kony and his soldiers to leave.[284] This was the Operation Lightning Thunder referred to previously. It was intended "to destroy or occupy LRA camps, to 'search and destroy' LRA forces, to 'search and rescue' persons abducted by the LRA, and to capture or kill LRA leaders, particularly those indicted by the ICC."[285] Although MONUC had a civilian protection mandate, it was not involved in planning the operation, and was only informed hours before the operation began. Camps were destroyed, but it led to more LRA attacks and further displacement,[286] and both FARDC and MONUC were criticized for not better protecting civilians.[287] The LRA was also further dispersed into South Sudan and the Central African Republic,[288] splintering into seven to ten groups.[289] The LRA attacks became known as the Christmas Massacres. The LRA killed more than 865 civilians while abducting at least 160 across a swath of northeastern DRC from just east of Garamba to Doruma to the northwest, as well as in southern Sudan. Between December 2008 and February 2009 more than 140,000 fled. These were a continuation of attacks that began in September 2008, when Kony was still holding out hope that he would sign the peace agreement.[290] These contradictory actions further called into question Kony's commitment to sign the peace agreement if the ICC warrants were withdrawn.

In March 2009 the UPDF formally withdrew from the DRC at the request of the Congolese government (although its military activities in northeastern Uganda continued covertly with the approval of Kinshasa, with UPDF soldiers—estimates ranged from 2,000 to 7,000—operating in northern Uganda).[291] While the EU only called on Kony to stop fighting,[292] the UN Security Council issued a presidential statement on 22 December 2008 commending the military actions and noting the ICC warrants and the Security Council's support for promoting justice. And while it condemned the actions of the LRA, no further practical support was forthcoming to address the continuing threat from the LRA.[293] At least the United States provided intelligence and funding in the form of $1 million in fuel to the botched military operation. This was the first time the U.S. had supported a specific operation (as opposed to the counterterrorism training it has provided to the Ugandan military), and represented the beginning of more robust U.S. engagement via its new Africa Command (AFRICOM).[294]

The attacks continued, with 1,200 people killed, 1,400 abducted, and 228,000 displaced between September 2008 and June 2009. Lightning Thunder was replaced by Operation Rudia II in May 2009, with FARDC again taking the lead, with logistical, fuel, and food aid supplied by MONUC.[295] Although the presence of MONUC expanded in the following months, it was hardly adequate, focused as it still was on the Kivus.[296] The UN Secretary-General urged the government to ensure that protection of civilians was integrated into all FARDC operations, an implicit recognition that FARDC was not adequately protecting civilians as it carried out its military operations.[297] Humanitarian aid was targeted. In particular, the LRA attacked displaced populations receiving aid, leading humanitarian organizations to provide "assistance to populations in areas where a military presence could be assured during and after the distributions."[298] Attacks continued, and another massacre occurred in December 2009, when more than 321 civilians were killed and 250 abducted in Makombo, with MONUC having no capacity to prevent or respond to the attacks, with more attacks occurring in other areas.[299]

Although LRA numbers had been significantly depleted, with an estimated 305 soldiers killed and 81 defectors, it was still a very significant threat, notwithstanding Ugandan and Congolese statements to the contrary.[300] One estimate put the number of LRA fighters toward the end of 2010 at approximately four hundred, spread out among three countries.[301] There was little progress against the LRA in the DRC,[302] even though there were less than one hundred LRA fighters left in the DRC.[303]

The UPDF continued its activities, chasing the LRA into South Sudan and the CAR, although this effort began to peter out by mid-2010. The LRA was no longer a threat to Uganda, and Museveni had other priorities, including increasing support to the African Union Mission in Somalia (AMISOM) and elections in Uganda in 2011 in which he was reelected. The UPDF was also restricted in its ability to act in the DRC by the Congolese government, particularly in light of the ramp up to the 2011 Congolese elections, as well as general mistrust of Uganda. This mistrust is symptomatic of wider regional mistrust among the neighboring countries, but in particular of Uganda.[304]

United Nations

During this period, other international actors started to become more prominent. MONUC (now MONUSCO) had been relatively ineffective, given lack of resources and competing priorities. While the Security Council had made a few statements, it was relatively unengaged. The Secretary-General issued three reports related to the LRA—one each in 2007,[305] 2008,[306] and 2009[307]—but these all focused on the particular issue of children in armed conflict, and only on Uganda.[308] The next report, in 2011, finally turned to the broader regional impact of the LRA, noting that, by late 2011, 440,000 had been displaced as a result of LRA attacks, with 335,000 in the DRC, while in Uganda, all but 80,000 of the 1.8 million IDPs had left the camps.[309] While the report noted MONUSCO's PoC mission,[310] its ability to carry out that mission continued to be hampered by lack of resources and issues of access. The UN had also begun to act more regionally, with the UN missions in the CAR, the DRC, and Sudan meeting and agreeing to establish "LRA focal points in each mission."[311]

MONUSCO began to engage in more active operations in Orientale Province, where the LRA still had a presence, beginning with Operation Rudia

Umbrella on 30 November 2010, aiming to deter more LRA attacks. This was followed up by Operation Kimiana Lombango, which was intended to facilitate access for humanitarian organizations as well as deter LRA attacks.[312] These operations did not have the desired effect of deterring LRA attacks.[313]

In March 2011, the UN Regional Office for Central Africa (UNOCA) was established in Gabon to "support the efforts of countries in the Central African region to consolidate peace, prevent conflict, and tackle cross-border challenges to peace and stability," and to "act as the regional focal point for the LRA issue."[314] The Security Council held two meetings specifically on the LRA in 2011—21 July and 14 November—during which they commended the military activities taken by the four affected countries and called for support of the AU in its actions against the LRA.[315]

Heading into 2012, there were indications that the LRA had further dispersed and weakened, and attacks in the DRC decreased, although it still remained a threat. During the latter part of 2011, MONUSCO had engaged unilateral and joint actions in Garamba, aimed at deterring LRA attacks during the Christmas period.[316] By May 2012, it was estimated that there were only sixty LRA soldiers left in the DRC, although they still created insecurity (including for humanitarian operations)[317] in and around Garamba, as well as in other countries, especially the CAR. In the first part of the year, MONUSCO engaged in further operations to protect civilians and undermine the LRA.[318] In June, the Secretary-General put forth a "Regional Strategy to Address the Threat and Impact of the Activities of the Lord's Resistance Army,"[319] which identified gaps in the response to the LRA and laid out the actions that the UN should take to address the issue, including support for the AU and protecting civilians. By the end of the year, however, an evaluation of the plan noted that little had been done to implement the plan and little on the ground had changed, although it did note effective action by MONUSCO to protect civilians—if not to stop LRA attacks.[320]

The humanitarian situation remained precarious. Indeed, the Office for the Coordination of Humanitarian Assistance noted the geographic, infrastructure, and security difficulties faced by those attempting to provide humanitarian assistance and to deal with the LRA more generally.[321]

There were significant sections of the area that were not accessible in both the DRC and the CAR, and in some places most humanitarian organizations refused to travel without a military escort.[322] Funding also lagged significantly behind requirements—42, 35, and 65 percent of the need in CAR, DRC, and South Sudan were funded.

African Union

The AU started to make the LRA threat more of a priority in August 2009,[323] followed by a decision at its Assembly of the African Union in July 2010 to facilitate regional action against the LRA. In 2011, AU ministers agreed to an "AU authorised mission" to go after the LRA. Pushed by the United States as well as by some of its member states, this was a significant departure for the AU. It had previously authorized four peacekeeping missions in Burundi, Darfur, Somalia, and the Comoros islands (although the mission in Somalia featured more robust peace enforcement activities).[324] This mission, however, was "an ongoing multinational military campaign."[325] While it would still be dominated by Uganda (and thus would not be a full-blown peace mission like AMISOM), the AU imprimatur would it give it a veneer of legitimacy which might make it easier for the DRC and the CAR to allow Ugandan forces on their territory. Yet the fact that it was an authorized mission rather than a full AU action raised questions about legality and authority, particularly given that it crossed international borders. It also did not fit within the AU's longer-term strategy of developing regional standby forces under the African Peace and Security Architecture (APSA). The EU, as the AU's primary donor, was skeptical, since it saw the Ugandan military as the most promising way to defeat the LRA. The four countries involved—the CAR, the DRC, South Sudan, and Uganda—were less interested in the coordination aspects and more interested in what funds might flow into their military coffers.[326]

In March 2012, the AU announced a new military operation to go after the LRA. It was to be headed by Uganda, which would contribute 1,500 of the 5,000 regional troops.[327] It encountered problems from the beginning. The difficult relationship between Uganda and the DRC, and a general lack of political support by all countries involved hampered progress. The DRC refused to contribute troops, and Uganda threatened to pull out its troops from counter-LRA activities (as well as AMISOM) because of allegations regarding its involvement with M23.[328] In addition, a lack of funding, a coup in the CAR, and the DRC forbidding Ugandan troops from entering the DRC further undermined the coherence and effectiveness of the AU efforts.[329] According to a joint NGO report, the Regional Task Force "exists only on paper and cannot be considered operational."[330] No concept of operations, which would provide a coherent vision for the mission, as well as a chain of command, had been agreed to, nor had the troops involved received adequate training on protection of civilians. Political issues also hindered access to some LRA-affected areas in the DRC and in a disputed area (Kafia Kingi[331]) on the border between Sudan and South Sudan.[332] By March 2013, the military component of the African Union Regional Cooperation Initiative for the Elimination of the LRA,[333] the Regional Task Force, numbered about 2,000 (out of a projected 2,800), mostly Ugandan, which continued to act independently of the AU command. Furthermore, there were serious questions about how effective the troops could be in the LRA-affected area, which was around 115,000 square miles.[334] Indeed, between April and June 2013 there were 30 LRA attacks in the DRC and 8 attacks in the CAR.[335]

United States

The United States became the most important nonregional state actor in the fight against the LRA. Dealing with the LRA featured as part of the Bush administration's counterterrorism policy in the Great Lakes region. It added the LRA to the Terrorist Exclusion List in 2001, and in 2008 Kony was added to the U.S. Treasury's list of "specially designated terrorists."[336] On 24 May 2010, President Obama signed the Lord's Resistance Army Disarmament and Northern Uganda Recovery Act of 2009,[337] stating the necessity "to protect and assist civilians caught in the LRA's wake . . . and to support efforts to bring the LRA to justice,"[338] noting the ICC arrest warrants.

It called for the creation of a strategy by the United States to support LRA disarmament. This strategy was published by the White House on 24 November 2010.[339] It had four strategic objectives: protecting civilians, arresting or removing Kony and his senior commanders, promoting defections and reintegration of LRA soldiers, and providing humanitarian assistance. The strategy explicitly cited the responsibility to protect—tying it to the 2010 National Security Strategy of the United States—in the particular context of holding those who target civilians accountable for their actions.[340]

As part of the strategy, Obama sent in one hundred soldiers to provide military advice, logistics and other support. The first troops arrived in Uganda on 12 October 2011, with the rest following over the course of a month.[341]

This was to be a short-term deployment, with no direct participation in fighting, although U.S. officials were vague about exactly how long U.S. soldiers would be deployed, and also refused to foreclose the possibility of direct combat.[342] Seventy of the soldiers were based in Uganda while the other thirty were based in the CAR.[343] It had also provided $23 million to the UPDF for Operation Lightning Thunder by the end of 2010[344]—and $500 million overall to the UPDF by 2011. These troops were part of AFRICOM, the U.S. Africa Command, created in 2008 to form a more coherent response to perceived threats on the continent.[345] The creation of AFRICOM was driven by three agendas—counterterrorism, gaining access to Africa's resources, and a broader agenda focusing on weak/failing states, poverty, and environmental crises.[346] AFRICOM is not headquartered in Africa (although it initially tried to negotiate to place its headquarters on the continent, resulting in strong resistance from almost all African countries, save Liberia).[347] Instead, it has established Offices of Security Cooperation in several countries,[348] while setting aside plans for regional integration teams to work with subregional organizations (which also received significant skepticism in Africa).[349] While the public focus has been on the human security aspects of its work, AFRICOM represents a militarization of U.S. policy toward Africa, with the intention of erasing the distinction between military and civilian. This loss of distinction can be seen in the U.S. military presence in northern Uganda, with the military providing, for example, medical services.[350] This would seem to be a natural extension of practice in Afghanistan, where U.S. military personnel would engage in civilian activities *in civilian clothing*, thus attempting to soften the presence of the military by winning the hearts and minds of the local population.[351] The militarization of U.S. policy can be seen clearly in the fact that in 2010, AFRICOM received $763 million, while the Africa Bureau of the State Department received $226 million.[352]

The LRA disarmament act was successful in making its way through Congress in no small measure because of support from civil society organizations like the ENOUGH Project and Invisible Children. Indeed, soon after Obama signed the Act, the executive director of Human Rights Watch, Kenneth Roth, advocated "the humanitarian use of force . . . to arrest Joseph Kony."[353] Branch notes the irony of such groups supporting the use and spread of the U.S. military (and indeed the CIA) in a part of the world that had previously suffered at the hands of the CIA (in the Congo).[354]

The public campaign to address the LRA issue gained significant prominence in 2012. A group named Invisible Children launched a campaign called

Kony 2012[355] with a video[356] that went viral[357] in March of that year. It called
for the United States and other governments to use their resources to help
capture Kony and bring him to The Hague to stand trial. It created a public
sensation, attracting the usual support from famous people,[358] but also bringing into public consciousness a long-running conflict in a far-flung corner
of the world of which Americans (or indeed most people around the world)
had little or no knowledge. It was criticized for a simplistic view of the
conflict—seeming to suggest that the war was still going on in Uganda, years
after Kony had left—and simplistic prescriptions for action—essentially
suggesting that Americans could make a significant difference by wearing
bracelets and throwing fund-raising parties.[359] Invisible Children called for
Obama to come to the rescue, and in one video called for "a plan to arrest
Joseph Kony while limiting the casualties to the child soldiers. It's possible.
We have the technology, we have the intelligence, we have the resources."[360]
While ignoring all of the logistical and political impediments to this action,
it made stopping Kony seem to be a simple matter of applying U.S. technology while legitimizing U.S. action in the region, which, according to the head
of the U.S. detachment contributing to the hunt for Kony, is to be achieved
via "'innovative, low-cost, and small-footprint approaches to achieve our security objectives on the African continent.'"[361] A lot of small footprints can
be funded with $763 million. In April 2013, under its War Crimes Rewards
Program, the U.S. offered a reward of $5 million for information leading to
the arrest of Kony and the other two remaining LRA ICC indictees.[362]

R2P³ in Uganda and Beyond

As this book is being completed, the situation in Uganda and the wider area
is extremely ambiguous. The UN Secretary-General, citing a forthcoming report from the UN High Commissioner for Human Rights, sums up the devastation wrought by the LRA:

> LRA systematically violated international human rights and
> humanitarian law by subjecting civilians to summary executions,
> attacks, torture, cruel, inhuman and degrading treatment, abduc-
> tions, forced conscriptions, sexual violence, slavery, displacement,
> widespread pillaging, poor living standards, lack of access to health
> care, education and work, as well as the outright denial of the

freedom of conscience, thought and religion . . . . LRA is responsible for more than 100,000 deaths, that from 60,000 to 100,000 children are believed to have been abducted by the rebel group and that 2.5 million civilians have been displaced as a result of its incursions.[363]

More than 420,000 were displaced in the CAR, the DRC, and South Sudan as of May 2013, including 320,000 IDPs in Orientale Province. This does not include the 80,000 IDPs still displaced in Uganda (and 10,000 missing in northern Uganda[364]). Attacks continued in the DRC and the CAR. The last reported attack in South Sudan was in June 2011, at least partly attributable to the presence of the UPDF.[365] Except for the remaining IDPs, continuing issues related to demobilization and reintegration of former LRA soldiers, Uganda is peaceful. It seems to have successfully exported its LRA problem to neighboring states. There were unconfirmed reports in November 2013 that Kony—or at least some of his soldiers—were in contact with the government of the CAR to discuss surrender.[366]

This case is in many ways the most complex of all of the cases in the book, transcending multiple borders and theaters of conflict. Indeed, the LRA has, according to Kevin Dunn, "creat[ed] an insecurity complex that has grown in geographical size over the past two decades."[367] All the various aspects of R2P[3] feature, although one aspect dominated the local, diplomatic and academic narrative (prosecution) for a number of years, to be overtaken by a new public and diplomatic narrative (protection). The third aspect, palliation, has remained hidden but provides a significant cautionary tale for palliators.

Beginning with palliation, the Ugandan government created the "protected villages"—camps for the forcibly displaced—as part of its anti-LRA strategy, as well as a broader crackdown on those in northern Uganda. This created an "appalling" situation, which humanitarian organizations, acting on their humanitarian imperative, stepped into to help. They kept people alive, but also supported a government anti-insurgency policy that created the problem in the first place, thus perpetuating the humanitarian crisis, which was at its core political. People were in need and humanitarians decided to help them, with little consideration of the broader context in which they were operating. It was pure palliation, but palliation that enabled some very unhumanitarian activities by the government. The humanitarians were dependent on the UPDF for access and so could not criticize the government. Thus, as we saw with both the prosecution and protection responses, international action on behalf of human rights and humanitarian ideals actually empowered a government to undertake human rights abuses similar to those it was supposedly fighting against.

Two issues emerged with the ICC. First, as with the humanitarian response, the ICC, ostensibly an organization dedicated to supporting human rights, appeared to empower the Ugandan government in its human rights abusing campaign against the LRA and the people of northern Uganda. Labeling Joseph Kony and his associates as major international criminals legitimized whatever action the government saw fit to conduct in order to deal with the scourge of the LRA. Since the Prosecutor refused to investigate the UPDF and properly label some of its actions as war crimes, the UPDF had nothing to fear, and could justify its actions as necessary to deal with a wanted international criminal. It was able to instrumentalize the ICC for multiple domestic and international political purposes.

Second, the role of the ICC was cast in very stark peace vs. justice terms. But it was, in fact, much more complicated. The ICC warrants may have played a role in bringing the LRA to the bargaining table as well as driving it away, although there were other factors at play.[368] The bigger question, however, was who gets to speak for the victims? Arguments against ICC involvement came most forcefully from many within the Acholi community who advocated for traditional justice. There was a divergence of views among the Acholi—as well as others in northern Uganda who had also been significantly affected by the conflict. There were different interpretations of justice put forth. Most forceful, perhaps, was the argument that peace was more important than anything else. Yet, others in northern Uganda advocated retributive justice. International NGOs argued that there could be no peace without justice. The government was ambiguous on the issue. It passed the amnesty law, offered amnesty to all LRA—including Kony—and, most recently, Museveni has become a vocal critic of the ICC.[369] But it also flip-flopped, attempting to deny amnesty to one LRA commander and ultimately allowing the amnesty law to lapse. The "international community" in the guise of the ICC was firm—the warrants must stand, and retributive justice must take its course. The ICC represented global morality, which laid claim to the dominant narrative. Which community should we listen to? The community of victims? But which victims? The Acholi, who became cast as the sole victims in the conflict, but who had split opinions on the role of the ICC? Other communities of victims in northern Uganda, who might have leaned more toward retributive justice? The government, which was less victim and more perpetrator, but which claimed victim status to justify its own victimization of others? The ICC, which while claiming to represent the victims in Uganda, also claimed to represent the international community as victim of international crimes? People in communities outside of Uganda who were also affected by the LRA, and some of whom very forcefully demanded justice of the retributive kind? Just as the LRA created a regional insecurity complex, so did it, along with other local, regional, and international actors, create a regional justice complex, where multiple and overlapping justice claims and counterclaims existed, raising questions about the proper locus of judicial authority. Such authority has been transnationalized through the Rome Statute, as well by as the multiple local and transnational claims for justice by individuals and groups.

Protection all too often seemed to have the opposite effect. The Ugandan government's efforts to "protect" its population from the LRA created more hardship and misery for the people of northern Uganda, which was then exported to the people of southern Sudan, Orientale Province in the DRC, and southeastern CAR. While actions such as Operation Lightning Thunder were cast in protective terms, they resulted in further attacks by the LRA, perpetuating a recurring dynamic. While MONUC/MONUSCO at times engaged in some protective activities, it was hopelessly underfunded and undersupported, with too few troops and other priorities. Its interactions with FARDC, as in the DRC more generally, were ambiguous and problematic. The African Union, while attempting to implement African solutions for African problems, was not able to marshal enough resources and overcome regional mistrust and issues of sovereignty. Nor did its troops receive adequate training in civilian protection. The United States used the mantle of protection to extend its military reach and implement antiterrorism strategies. And regional governments were more than happy to oblige, given the resources being made available to them.

The idea of protection became more dominant just as the actual threat from the LRA was decreasing. The LRA is estimated to be responsible for 100,000 deaths, most of which occurred before the failed peace talks. So why did hunting Kony and protecting his victims rise to the top of the agenda of the world's remaining superpower, as well as feature prominently on the agendas of the UN and the African Union? Did the continued engagement of the ICC create international pressure to stop the LRA—or did it, as asserted above, enable actions that had little to do with civilian protection? Did the newly established responsibility to protect discourse play a role? R2P was coming into its own at the same time as the Juba talks. Perhaps the failure of

Table 4.1. Responsibility Conundrums in Uganda

	Protectors	Prosecutors	Palliators
Protection	+UN provided some robust PoC +UPDF credited with supporting PoC in some areas −UN significantly undersupported, significant gaps in protection −UPDF, FARDC responsible for significant abuses	−little support for carrying out arrest warrants −justified anti-civilian "protection" activities	−undermined protection in Uganda
Prosecution	−no success apprehending suspects	+push LRA to negotiating table −prolong conflict/undermine peace process −instrumentalized by govt.	
Palliation	+protected some humanitarian activities −endangered humanitarians by association	+palliators attacked in retaliation	+fed people in Uganda −contributed to perpetuation of large-scale forced dis-placement

Juba was the spur for the international community to finally get serious, with organizations like Invisible Children providing the final prod? Or, did R2P provide the normative justification for actions more related to antiterrorism—and, more generally, to expanding U.S. global and regional military reach?

The very idea of protection itself becomes confused and complicated. R2P is supposedly about protecting civilians from their governments or others who threaten them. This happened in very small doses, mainly by the UN, which was significantly overburdened. Instead, protection came to be equated with hunting down and arresting or killing one man. Joseph Kony became the epitome of existential threat to civilians in Uganda and beyond, although by the time of the advent of various international LRA strategies, he, and the rest of the LRA, were not much of a threat to governments. Does this mean that people have become the new locus of concern for governments and the international community? Or does it mean that people become instrumentalized as governments use the evil individual or group as justification for rather unprotective activities? Can removing one man by force actually result in protection? Is this what the responsibility to protect means? Mareike Schomerus[370] and Ronald Atkinson et al.[371] raise serious questions about the efficacy of military force to end the LRA threat, pointing out that military action against the LRA has resulted in increased attacks against civilians. In the event of further strikes against the LRA, there would thus need to be enough troops in place to fully protect civilians, or to fully cordon off all LRA troops. Either option would require a very large number of troops—far higher than what has been committed to date,[372] particularly given the 115,000 square mile operating area of the LRA. Atkinson et al. assert that "The moral hazard in this case is particularly high."[373]

What does this say about the responsibility to protect? While we have the normative framework, is it possible to carry out R2P activities in many of the places where it might be needed—particularly remote, out of the way, ungoverned spaces—in a way that can guarantee civilian protection if related activities may increase the insecurity for civilians? And if theoretically possible, what are the chances that the necessary resources will be provided and used in the appropriate manner? The critics have no answer as to how to stop the LRA. The critiques must be taken seriously, but can we go beyond the critiques? Does this require an assumption that there is always an answer beyond the critique—that just because we have a norm that says the international community should protect people, it actually can? I am not sure, but it does seem clear that all the actors involved could act in a manner that better contributed to protection, however imperfect that protection might be.

CHAPTER 5

Darfur: The Post-World Summit Test

It's a tribal war.

Bashir is dividing us.

Save Darfur.

Though starting two years before the UN formally recognized R2P, the conflict in Darfur became the first test of R2P. Hundreds of thousands of people have been killed and millions displaced as a result of the fighting between the Sudan Liberation Army (SLA), the Justice and Equality Movement (JEM), the Sudanese government in Khartoum, and the government-backed *janjaweed*. There has been much hand-wringing, large amounts of money have been given to humanitarian efforts, war criminals have been indicted, multiple cease-fires and peace deals have been signed and ignored, a weak African Union peacekeeping force was sent to Darfur to monitor a nonexistent peace, and an equally toothless UN peacekeeping force has been deployed.

R2P formed the background to the discussion over how the international community should respond to Darfur. However, it proved less than decisive, as no muscular intervention or other similar activity has occurred to deal with what has variously been identified as genocide, war crimes, and crimes against humanity, even as a global social movement arose to "Save Darfur." The ICC has become a prominent element of the international response, but became embroiled in controversy as charges of neocolonialism were leveled against the ICC when Sudanese president Omar al Bashir was indicted by the ICC. Humanitarianism has also played a role even as palliators became caught up in the conflict as a result of the ICC investigation. Darfur has thus represented normative developments in the areas of human rights, international criminal justice, and humanitarianism while also highlighting the main R2P[3] conundrums.

Responsibilities in Darfur

In February 2003, the Sudan Liberation Army, a group of rebels in the province of Darfur in western Sudan, attacked government forces in response to a perceived marginalization and underdevelopment of the "black" region by the "Arab" government in Khartoum.[1] The government labeled them bandits[2] and engaged in further repression, including supporting the *janjaweed* (Arab nomad militants) who attacked villages. This movement has deep historical roots. Darfur has a long history of marginalization by the government, short-lived low intensity conflict, and regional interference.[3] Mahmood Mamdani identifies the distribution—or maldistribution—of land, dating back to colonial times, as a key element driving the conflict, exacerbated by drought and desertification.[4]

The conflict rapidly expanded, and by April refugees began arriving in Chad to escape the fighting. *Janjaweed* attacks amounted, according to many observers, to ethnic cleansing. The Fur, Zaghawa, and Masalit ethnic groups—the same groups from which the rebels came—were attacked by rival ethnic groups (with the support of the government). In July the government "unleashed the *Janjaweed* on a grand scale,"[5] with the apparent aim to displace civilians.[6]

Palliative Responses to "Tribal Conflict"

The first cease-fire between the rebels and the government came in September 2003, and rapidly fell apart. There were 65,000 Darfurian refugees in Chad, and on 1 September UNHCR issued an appeal for humanitarian assistance. At the same time, the UN resident coordinator estimated that there were 400,000 IDPs in Darfur.[7] The government tried to prevent assistance from reaching those in need. It prevented a U.S. Agency for International Development (USAID) mission from visiting parts of Darfur, stopped the first U.S. shipment of food aid arriving at Port Sudan, and declared that there was no food crisis. At the end of December, the government denied that there was an

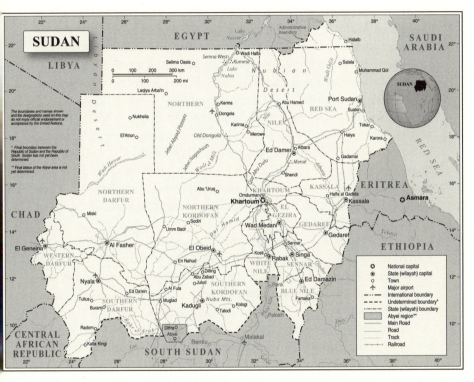

Map 5. Sudan, Map No. 4458 Rev. 2, March 2012. United Nations.

insurrection in Darfur, labeling it a local tribal conflict (although just a few days later President Omar al Bashir did identify it as a rebellion).[8]

As in Rwanda, by identifying it as tribalism, the international community was able to obfuscate the situation, depoliticize the context, evade its responsibilities, and fend off pressure to intervene to stop the killing. The tribalism discourse allowed states to focus on humanitarian aid and the effect of the government-sponsored violence in Darfur rather than dealing with the underlying causes of the conflict.

The palliative discourse continued into 2004 as UNHCR characterized the situation as "a race against time" to feed the refugees and IDPs.[9] The first aid did not reach the camps in Chad until mid-February, and most of the IDPs were still out of reach because of insecurity. The palliative discourse initially allowed Western states to pursue their interests, which were twofold. First, ensure that the peace deal between Khartoum and the southern rebels succeeded. Second, avoid direct military involvement, since there was little upside in terms of cold, hard traditional state interests in sustained engagement. Given the post-9/11 interest in Sudan as an ally in the "War on Terror," U.S. interests might have been negatively impacted.[10] Portraying it in terms of humanitarian disaster made it possible for the United States and other countries to argue that they were doing something by providing humanitarian assistance without affecting other interests.

In March 2004, a year after the conflict erupted, Western editorial pages started using the "G" word—genocide. For the previous year, the "never again" norm had been safely in the background. However, once more information started coming out and editorial writers and the public had a better idea of what was going on, there was pressure to start addressing the situation. February and March brought a series of massacres, which represented a turning point. The United States, focusing on the humanitarian aspect of the conflict, said that food production in Darfur would decrease by 60 percent over the course of the year.[11] A chorus of calls to do "something" began to erupt. One of the first was an opinion piece by Nicholas Kristof in late March, using the previously unspoken word "genocide."[12] Other editorials followed. The UN humanitarian coordinator for Sudan, Mukesh Kapila, who was leaving Sudan, spoke out forcefully, comparing Darfur to Rwanda.[13] April 2004 was the ten-year anniversary of the beginning of the Rwandan genocide, and it was impossible to ignore the parallels—U.S. president George Bush talked about the "atrocities" in Darfur, and UN Secretary-General Kofi

Annan (on whose watch as head of UN peacekeeping the Rwandan genocide had occurred) talked about possible "military action."[14]

In April, the AU came to an agreement with the government and other parties to the conflict to deploy a small force—the African Union Mission in Sudan (AMIS)—to monitor a humanitarian cease-fire, which fell apart almost immediately. It did not have a mandate to stop the fighting, or even to protect civilians and use force.[15] Yet it was the first concrete action taken by the international community to address even a small portion of the security situation. The mandate expanded a bit in October when the AU Peace and Security Council gave AMIS a mandate to protect civilians and humanitarian operations "within resources and capability."[16] It also called on the government to bring perpetrators to justice. However, the mandates were significantly circumscribed. Given that the government was supporting mass atrocities, it could hardly be counted on to ensure justice. Furthermore, there was no invocation of Article 4h of the AU Constitutive Act which allowed for R2P-like intervention by the AU. Rather, it was subservient to Sudanese sovereignty. The AU recognized its responsibilities, and chastised an African government in a way that had not been seen before, but carried out its responsibilities in a rather meek manner that avoided violating the norm of nonintervention. Sudan was able to determine the terms of AU engagement, and it held a seat on the AU Peace and Security Council (PSC) at the time.[17] This situation raised eerie parallels with the seat Rwanda held on the Security Council during the genocide. AMIS was also constrained by its size. The October resolution provided for a total of 3,320 personnel, and even though it eventually deployed up to 7,000, this was hardly enough to cover an area the size of France. Further, it was constrained in the equipment it had access to, particularly given the reluctance of states to provide more support in the form of armored personnel carriers and other transport and communications equipment.[18] Thus, while the Security Council (especially the permanent members, P5) was relieved that the AU was doing its job, it did not want to provide much support to allow it to actually carry out its mission.

In July, the UN Security Council finally got into the act when it passed Resolution 1556. It "reiterat[ed] its grave concern at the on-going humanitarian crisis and widespread human rights violations, including continued attacks on civilians," identified the conflict in Darfur as a "threat to international peace and security and to stability in the region," and noted "that the Government of Sudan bears the primary responsibility to respect human rights." It called on the government to facilitate humanitarian aid as well as to disarm the *janjaweed* by the end of August. Yet there was little prospect that this would or could happen. Resolution 1564 of 18 September suggested that the AU send in more troops and set up a commission to investigate whether or not genocide was taking place. It had little practical value, nor did Resolution 1574 in mid-November. Security Council members thus felt international pressure to address a situation acknowledged as going beyond a simple humanitarian disaster, but they did little to address it.

Yet, the "G" word would not go away. Andrew Natsios of USAID had described the situation in Darfur as genocide, and the U.S. House of Representatives passed a resolution declaring Darfur a genocide in July 2004 and asked President Bush to consider intervening. The following month, a group of evangelical Christian leaders representing 45,000 churches called on Bush to send troops to Darfur to stop the "genocide."[19] In September, U.S. secretary of state Colin Powell uttered the "G" word. Yet he stated that this did not require the United States to take any military or other action to stop the genocide. Thus, the "never again" norm found verbal expression at the highest reaches of the U.S. government. At the same time, however, its lack of normative force was demonstrated by Powell's disclaimer. Yet the very fact that the disclaimer had to be made illustrated the growing salience of the nascent responsibility to protect.[20] The same month, the European Parliament passed an almost unanimous resolution saying that Darfur was "'tantamount to genocide.'" Although there is no meaningful distinction between something being labeled as "genocide" or "tantamount to genocide," using such terminology serves as an escape hatch from the responsibility to protect and the (disputed) obligations that flow from the Genocide Convention. Moral outrage can be expressed while interests such as avoiding military entanglement can be upheld. Both the German foreign minister and the British foreign secretary also identified Darfur as genocide, with little further action.[21]

The debate over whether or not Darfur amounted to genocide allowed the international community to evade calls for concrete action. In Europe, some countries provided a lot of money and said nothing (Scandinavia and the Netherlands). Further, some European countries seemed to tie Darfur in with disapproval of the U.S. invasion of Iraq and opposed U.S. initiatives to condemn Sudan (France claimed that it was a civil war rather than genocide or ethnic cleansing).[22] The AU said, in the words of Gérard Prunier, that it was "a case of mass-murder without any known perpetrators."[23] In January 2005, the UN Commission of Inquiry released a report finding crimes against humanity but not genocide.[24] This set off a firestorm of debate, and even though there was very little functional difference between genocide and crimes against humanity, there was much discussion about why the UN had not found genocide and whether the "lesser" crimes against humanity also qualified under the emerging responsibility to protect norm.

Mamdani notes that those who identified what was going on in Darfur as genocide contributed to three outcomes: first, the broader context of the conflict was shoved to the background; second, the rebels gained impunity since they were seen as fighting genocide (although the subsequent arrest warrants for some rebel leaders at least partially undermine this view); third, the conflict was further racialized and punishment was allowed to trump reconciliation.[25] One might add that the side debates over what to call it allowed states to obscure possible and necessary responses. The availability of palliation allowed states to evade their responsibility to protect.

Prosecuting Genocide

During the first few months of 2005 the international community debated referring Darfur to the ICC. A number of countries wanted to support the fledgling ICC and further develop international justice norms. This would also help deflect pressure for intervening in Darfur. The Bush administration was implacably opposed to the ICC, and argued vociferously against this, maintaining that Darfur could be added to the ICTR mandate in Arusha. Yet, it faced a conundrum. There was very great pressure to "do something" in Darfur. And, having identified it as genocide, there were increasing expectations to put something behind the words. Furthermore, the administration had come under a lot of pressure after it "de-signed" the Rome Statute in 2002. So, there was pressure from the "never again" norm and from the international justice norm. Although caving in to either one was not palatable to the Bush administration, it went for the lesser of two "evils"—support the ICC while forestalling further action.

The Security Council voted to refer Darfur to the ICC on 31 March 2005.[26] The ICC officially began an investigation in Darfur in early June 2005.[27] However, the referral to the ICC, and the eventual investigation, had, at best, a short-term effect on the course of the conflict and the extent of the fighting.

While the first part of 2005 saw somewhat diminished fighting and an improved humanitarian access situation,[28] fighting began in earnest again by September. Attacks on civilians increased, creating more displacement and decreased humanitarian access, particularly in West Darfur where NGOs were forced to withdraw and humanitarian organizations were able to reach only 45 percent of the population.[29] The tribalism discourse continued. Robert Zoellick, U.S. deputy secretary of state, said in November 2005 "It's a tribal war, that has been exacerbated by other conditions, and frankly, I don't think foreign forces ought to get themselves in the middle of a tribal war of Sudanese."[30] This would, on the one hand, appear to be a repudiation of previous government statements labeling the situation genocide. However, it was perfectly consistent with attempts to preclude any military involvement. Further, given that his remarks were made in Khartoum, his comment would also be a way to placate the Sudanese government, an important ally in the "War on Terror."

In addition to government, and government-sponsored *janjaweed*, attacks, infighting occurred within an increasingly fractious rebel movement. The SLA split into two more or less ethnically based groups, and another rebel group, the Justice and Equality Movement, had previously spawned a splinter group, the National Movement for Reform and Development (NMRD). These groups made various alliances with each other and fought each other at times. The conflict spread to Chad as refugees crossed the border, Chad hosted Darfurian rebel groups, and Sudan hosted Chadian rebel groups that aimed to overthrow President Idriss Deby.[31]

Avoiding Responsibilities: Peacekeeping with No Peace to Keep

As the fighting continued and it became obvious that the ICC referral was having little effect on its intended targets, and that the AU was not up to the job of imposing peace in Darfur,[32] there was renewed focus on a UN peacekeeping force with a more robust mandate and greater resources than the AU to stop the fighting. A partial recognition of the inadequacy of AMIS came in January 2006, and again in March, when the AU voted, in principle, to transfer its operations to a UN peacekeeping operation under pressure from Western countries. A deadline of 30 September was set to end the AMIS mandate and transfer to a UN peacekeeping operation,[33] although this transfer did not take place.

Further AU-sponsored peace talks occurred in Abuja, with a 30 April deadline. The Darfur Peace Agreement (DPA)—was finally signed on 5 May 2006 between Khartoum and one group of rebels. It began to fall apart almost as soon as it was signed. Other rebel groups continued their attacks, and the government never seriously reined in its own attacks, launching a new offensive against the nonsignatory rebel groups in August. Pressure continued to mount for a UN force. To derail such proposals, Khartoum proposed to use its own forces to stop the killing.[34] Since it was responsible for much of the violence, this was not taken seriously.[35] On 31 August, the Security Council passed a U.S.- and UK-sponsored resolution extending the mandate of UNMIS, which was created to monitor the North-South peace agreement, to Darfur to help implement the DPA, thus taking over from AMIS. Resolution 1706 referred to the R2P provisions in the 2005 World Summit Outcome document. It also invoked Chapter VII and used the term "all necessary means" to provide for the ability for UNMIS to use force to, among things, "protect civilians under the threat of physical violence." Yet the resolution also indicated that the consent of the government would be required. The Security Council was still kowtowing to the government, and thus not living up to the ultimate responsibility to protect, including in cases of government nonconsent, which it recognized in the second paragraph of the resolution. It also stated that the force in Darfur should have a "strong African participation and character," another concession to Khartoum, which did not want non-African troops on its soil.

Yet the United States continued rhetorical support for a UN mission. On 20 September, President Bush criticized Khartoum for impeding the UN force, staking the credibility of the UN on approving a peacekeeping mission.[36] However, Bush did not specify exactly what the UN should do if Sudan did not accept UN peacekeepers in Darfur, and any attempt to impose a force in Darfur without Khartoum's approval would have been vetoed by China and Russia. He shifted the responsibility from individual states to an amorphous international community, as personified by the UN. Domestic political forces with a normative agenda and the international "never again" norm created pressure for Bush to react in some way, although not to the extent the promoters of the norms might prefer. UNMIS never deployed in Darfur, a result of the opposition of Khartoum to having non-AU troops in Darfur, and the unwillingness of the Security Council to stand up to the government. By giving Khartoum a veto over the deployment of UN troops in Darfur, the international community ensured that it would not have to actually carry out its purported responsibilities under the R2P norm.

Inching Toward Responsibility?

Khartoum continued to resist attempts to get a UN force into Darfur. A compromise in the form of a hybrid UN-AU force was proposed and initially accepted in principle by Khartoum in November 2006,[37] although the United Nations Force in Darfur (UNAMID) was not officially created by the Security Council until 31 July 2007 with Resolution 1769—eleven months after passing resolution 1706. This resolution affirmed previous support for R2P while authorizing UNAMID under Chapter VII to, among other things, "protect civilians, without prejudice to the responsibility of the Government of Sudan." Thus, it recognized that Sudan was not fulfilling its responsibilities and so the international community was stepping in to fulfil them instead. The United States specifically noted the Chapter VII mandate to protect civilians.[38] However, the greater focus appeared to be on humanitarian assistance. Indeed, the resolution noted that "humanitarian efforts remain a priority." It also mentioned the necessity of bringing perpetrators to justice. The final draft removed a reference to "seizure and disposal" of arms in favor of a reference to monitoring arms, thus reducing its capability to remove from the ground weapons that could be used to kill civilians. Further, the resolution made the implementation of the peace agreement, rather than the protection of civilians, a higher priority, even though previous AU-UN planning had noted that PoC was crucial to the success of any political solution.[39] There was thus confusion in the conceptualization of the mandate of UNAMID as to whether the political process or civilian security was the greater priority.

This resolution was followed by several months of torturous negotiations with the Sudanese government that called into question the Security Council's full acceptance of R2P. In the weeks following the resolution, the killing in Darfur increased, although with a somewhat different character. In addition to government-supported attacks, and the fighting among some rebel groups, some of the "Arab" groups began engaging in tribal fighting to divide the spoils of war.[40] This was further evidence that there was, in fact, no peace to keep in Darfur as the UN prepared to insert

26,000 peacekeeping troops into Darfur. An attack on AU peacekeepers by rebels that killed ten AU soldiers also highlighted the chaotic situation in Darfur.[41]

Planning for the mission, and especially the protection of civilians portion of the mandate, was integrated, with a wide variety of UN humanitarian agencies involved (although in the end the mission itself was not particularly integrated)[42]. Yet there appeared to be tensions between the humanitarians, who were advocates of PoC, and the military and police elements, who were seen as those with the primary responsibility for protecting civilians, with little understanding of how these two sets of actors were to coordinate,[43] raising the question of which actors can and should engage in PoC activities. Further, there appeared to be significant deference given to the government, with a recognition that "the relationship with the authorities, particularly the military and the police, is fundamental to the sustainability of the Mission's protection efforts."[44] While this is the norm in traditional peacekeeping efforts, it is evidence of a lack of will to adequately stand up to the government, and thus the Security Council was allowing sovereignty to get in the way of its responsibilities to protect civilians. Humanitarian actors tried unsuccessfully to have this caveat removed from the mission description. They were successful, however, in changing the focus from "protect civilians from harm" to "protect civilians," thus enlarging the understanding of what PoC means.[45]

As the months wore on, Khartoum (as well as the AU, to a certain extent[46]) balked at allowing non-African troops to deploy in Darfur. It also failed to approve UNAMID's list of troop contributions, failed to allocate necessary land for UNAMID bases, asked for unacceptable provisions in the status of forces agreement, and refused permission for night flights by UNAMID. This had the effect of delaying the deployment of necessary elements of UNAMID and undermining UNAMID's ability to do its job, essentially giving Khartoum a de facto veto over the force.[47] The international community itself was not supportive. Twenty-four requested helicopters were not forthcoming from member states[48]—even though there are approximately 12,000 military helicopters worldwide.[49] The UN took over from the African Union on 31 December 2007, with a troop strength of about 9,000 soldiers (just over one-third of the approved strength of 26,000, and only 2,000 more than AMIS) with no helicopters, which are crucial for troop transport and other duties related to protecting civilians.[50]

UNAMID deployment had only reached 10,000 nine months later, and continued to be affected by a lack of resources like helicopters. As Secretary-General Ban Ki-moon noted, the situation was getting more dangerous, with attacks on UN and other international personnel, and nine peacekeepers being killed in three months. A continuing lack of will to directly address the security situation in Darfur was evident.[51] While the government had committed to blanket clearance for airlifting in equipment and daytime operations by UNAMID in Darfuri airports, as well as promising protection of convoys, government harassment of UNAMID personnel and operations continued, and it initiated new offensives against rebels. Rebel groups also put restrictions on and harassed UNAMID and humanitarian agencies. By the end of August, there had been 208 hijackings of humanitarian vehicles and 153 abductions of humanitarian personnel.[52] On 31 July, the Security Council, in Resolution 1828, reiterated the protection of civilians mandate and directly cited the World Summit Outcome document (previously there had been an indirect reference to Resolution 1674 on the protection of civilians, which mentions the relevant paragraphs in the outcome document).

Even as there was an increase in diplomatic activity with the appointment of Djibrill Bassolé as the AU-UN joint chief mediator for Darfur[53] and increased activity on the part of the United States by Ambassador Scott Gration,[54] and even as the UNAMID deployment expanded to 12,541 military personnel and 2,639 police personnel by the end of January 2009, the fighting had also expanded and the government had increased restrictions on the movement of UNAMID and humanitarian personnel.[55] An "Agreement of Goodwill and Confidence-building for the Settlement of the Problem in Darfur" was signed between the government and JEM on 17 February,[56] although this rapidly fell apart.

Prosecuting Bashir: Peace Versus Justice?

At the same time, the issue of justice became prominent. The ICC issued its first arrest warrants in Darfur in April 2007—for Sudanese minister of state for humanitarian affairs, Ahmad Haroun, and *janjaweed* leader Ali Kushayb. In response, the government indicated that it was undertaking its own investigations of war crimes in Darfur (but not including these two),[57] although the court set up in West Darfur only prosecuted individuals for murder not related to the Rome Statute and theft.[58] This was just a cynical ploy to avoid further pressure. Yet it was feeling vulnerable in the face of international pressure, and this may have been one contributing factor to its eventual agreement to the deployment of UNAMID.[59] At the same time, the government showed its defiance by naming Haroun as head of a committee to investigate human rights violations in Darfur, and then to a committee that oversaw the deployment of UNAMID.[60] The pressure increased significantly in July 2008 when Ocampo asked the ICC Pre-Trial Chamber to issue an arrest warrant for President Bashir.[61] This set off a fierce debate about the effect this might have on efforts to end the conflict (as well as the North-South peace accord). Some argued that this action would further entrench the Sudanese government, making it even more reluctant to stop the killing in Darfur.[62] It might also embolden the rebels. The Justice and Equality Movement said that, given the genocide charges, it would "not negotiate with a war criminal."[63] There were also concerns that this might imperil the humanitarian mission, as well as endanger the UNAMID peacekeepers.[64] Others argued that it would demonstrate that there was no impunity for those who commit atrocities, and that it could put further pressure on the government to stop the killing. The Security Council could indefinitely delay the prosecution, thus providing an incentive to the government.[65] Pressure could be seen in the government's plan to revive the previously mentioned investigations into Darfur, a thinly veiled attempt to avoid international scrutiny.[66]

The AU and the Arab League called on the Security Council to suspend proceedings against Bashir. Russia concurred,[67] as did China.[68] The Non-Aligned Movement argued that going after Bashir "could be conducive to greater destabilization with far-reaching consequences for the country and the region."[69] President Thabo Mbeki of South Africa indicated fears for the peace process.[70] South Africa, Libya, China, and Russia lobbied to have the proceedings against Bashir set aside in the context of negotiations to renew the mandate of UNAMID in July 2008.[71] The Arab League and the Organization of the Islamic Conference both condemned the proceedings against Bashir, as did the African, Caribbean and Pacific Group.[72] Perhaps the most intriguing response came from the United States. While it is not surprising that European and other associated countries would support the ICC,[73] it is more curious that the United States, which abstained on the vote to renew UNAMID's mandate, was much more outspoken in supporting the ICC investigation. According to Alejandro Wolff, deputy U.S. ambassador to the UN, "The U.S. abstained in the vote because language added to the resolution would send the wrong message to Sudanese President Bashir and undermine efforts to bring him and others to justice."[74] France suggested possible criteria for consideration of a deferral: ending the conflict with Chad, deployment of UNAMID in full, negotiations with the rebel groups, removal of Haroun from power, and engaging with the ICC. Sudan only partially fulfilled some of the criteria, most notably not removing Haroun from power, and so this initiative went nowhere.[75] The Security Council responded by "taking note" of an AU Peace and Security Council communiqué[76] that requested the deferral and "having in mind" the concerns of the AU over the Prosecutor's request.[77]

This became tied up in broader discussions about the evolving international criminal justice regime. At the AU Assembly on 30 June and 1 July 2008, the member states passed a resolution that called on non-African states to stop using the principle of universal jurisdiction to try Africans for mass atrocities. While recognizing that those who commit grave offenses should be brought to justice, and citing Article 4h, the resolution stated that "The abuse of the Principle of Universal Jurisdiction is a development that could endanger international law, order and security," and any attempt to exercise universal jurisdiction against African leaders "is a clear violation of the sovereignty and territorial integrity of these states."[78] There were accusations of a "legal campaign" against Africa.[79] Although the Rome Statute is not based on universal jurisdiction, AU rhetoric blurred the two. The animosity against universal jurisdiction was driven, in particular, by a number of Western countries trying Rwandans for their role in the genocide, which exacerbated tensions noted in Chapter 3. This further escalated when France and Spain indicted current Rwandan government officials for their role in the genocide and indicated that they had evidence against Paul Kagame.[80] Rwanda has gone to great lengths to fend off accusations of crimes committed by the RPA during the genocide and human rights violations since the genocide on the part of the RPF government. The Rwandan justice minister and attorney general, Tharcisse Karugarama, described the West's actions as a "neo-colonial judicial coup d'état."[81] There was a meeting between the AU and the EU to discuss the issue, which led to a joint report,[82] but this stance was just a precursor to a much bigger standoff over the issue of the ICC and Africa, with Bashir at its center.

A week after the Prosecutor's request for an arrest warrant, the AU Peace and Security Council passed a resolution that asked the Security Council to defer the ICC process against Bashir. It argued that "approval by the Pre-Trial Chamber of the application by the ICC Prosecutor could seriously undermine the on-going efforts aimed at facilitating the early resolution of the conflict in Darfur" and Sudan more broadly, and thus result in greater suffering. It also called on Sudan to investigate and bring perpetrators to justice, citing the principle of complementarity, which gives states primary jurisdiction.[83] If Sudan would undertake serious investigations it could avoid further action by the ICC. This was not particularly realistic since one of those being investigated by the ICC was the Sudanese head of state. In addition, the PSC asked the AU Commission to establish a high-level panel to investigate options for dealing with the situation in Darfur. This induced Sudan to create a special war crimes prosecutor[84] and to arrest *janjaweed* leader Ali Kushayb. Given that Sudanese law does not cover genocide, crimes against humanity, or war crimes, this was an attempt to appear to be cooperating with the ICC and head off attempts to go after Bashir.[85]

The year 2009 began with a renewed request for the Security Council to defer the Bashir investigation.[86] This became even more urgent for the AU when the ICC issued an arrest warrant for Bashir on 4 March.[87] The PSC reacted the next day by calling, yet again, for the Security Council to defer proceedings, while also reiterating its commitment to combating impunity and calling on the "Sudanese authorities to exercise utmost restraint."[88] So here we see a contradiction. On the one hand, Africa has a commitment to international justice, and wants Bashir to stop his human rights abuses. Many African countries saw that Bashir was just causing them problems.[89] At the same time, it wanted the proceedings against Bashir suspended—but not necessarily ended altogether. This latter stance was based on the argument that the investigation and arrest warrant against Bashir could undermine the prospects for a peaceful resolution of the conflict in Darfur. The AU also asked for help from the League of Arab States to stop the investigation. In June, the African state parties met to discuss the situation. Libya, which is not a state party to the ICC, as well as Senegal, Djibouti, and Comoros, which are, tried to pressure the rest of the countries to withdraw from the ICC.[90] This did not occur, although most of the state parties did reiterate the call for a suspension of the arrest warrant.[91]

Almost immediately after the arrest warrants were issued, Sudan retaliated by ejecting thirteen international NGOs, on the pretext that they had provided the ICC with false evidence.[92] They comprised 40 percent of the 6,500 local and international humanitarian staff in Darfur and provided food for 1.1 million people,[93] and two of the organizations were used by the World Food Program to distribute 80 percent of the food it provided.[94] Overall, they were responsible for half of the aid distribution. The Security Council was unanimous in its criticism.[95] Julie Flint and Alex de Waal assert that Ocampo had claimed repeatedly that he received information from humanitarian organizations,[96] a claim that humanitarian organizations denied. The expulsion had a significant negative impact, but not as bad as some had feared. Other NGOs on the ground filled in some gaps, and some of the expelled NGOs "rehatted," with other chapters of the NGOs coming back. Oxfam US, which had been in other parts of Sudan, was able to move in to Darfur to replace Oxfam UK, which had been expelled.[97] Mercy Corps Scotland replaced Mercy Corps US. And the Swiss chapter of CARE replaced CARE USA.[98] The organizations made clear that these were separate organizations and did not have a policy of trying to avoid restrictions through such substitutions.[99] UNAMID also had to step up some of its humanitarian-related activities, such as guarding warehouses and vehicles previously used by the expelled NGOs.[100]

After the expulsion, the JEM announced it would pull out of peace talks,[101] while also demanding that the thirteen international and three domestic NGOs be reinstated,[102] as well as insisting that JEM prisoners be released by the government.[103] Thus, the arrest warrant provided an excuse for both the government and the rebels to flex their muscles. For Bashir, the arrest warrant delegitimized the NGOs and the international community even further, and for JEM and the other rebel groups the arrest warrant delegitimized Bashir.[104] The government also announced on 16 March that all international NGOs would have to leave within a year. A further targeting of NGOs was seen on 11 March when three MSF expat workers were kidnapped, with demands that the arrest warrant be cancelled. Other attacks against NGOs followed.[105] Sudan came under pressure from some of its supporters, including Egypt, to reverse the expulsion.[106] This was followed by increased pressure on the part of the United States, which eventually resulted in Sudan allowing in three new NGOs.[107] In addition to the direct humanitarian impact, the Secretary-General expressed concern over the potential impact on UNAMID, including its ability to carry out its protection mandate.[108] The continuing insecurity placed "considerable strain on the Operation's protection capacity."[109] Since UNAMID's deployment, it had lost fourteen peacekeepers to the fighting, "reminding us of the great danger of deploying a peacekeeping operation in an environment with no peace to keep."[110] The Secretary-General reiterated his call for the provision of helicopters, which were necessary for its ability to provide protection and generally move around the region.[111]

The situation reached its logical conclusion the following month when the AU Assembly, in addition to its usual condemnation of the abuse of universal jurisdiction[112] and call for the Security Council to suspend proceedings against Bashir, went a step farther and called for African states not to cooperate with the ICC. It said that the Assembly regretted that the Security Council had not acted on the deferral request, called for AU member states not to cooperate with the ICC in the Bashir case, called for the Assembly of States Parties of the ICC to draw up guidelines on prosecutorial discretion, and reasserted African sovereignty.

This was a very significant development, particularly given that at the time thirty African states were parties to the Rome Statute. They seemed to indicate that they were repudiating their obligations.[113] Why? Some were bullied by AU chairman Libyan president Moammar Qaddafi and AU commission chair Jean Ping, both of whom were hostile to the ICC.[114] But beyond this, there were broader issues with regard to feeling ignored by the Security Council. If there had been some response from the Security Council, the outcome might have been different. Instead, there was silence.[115] Yet, there was dissent from this decision by a number of countries, including Botswana,[116] Benin,[117] Chad,[118] South Africa[119] and Uganda,[120] thus indicating that the decision was far from unanimous.

Three months later, the African Union High Level Panel on Darfur issued its report.[121] The report, named after the panel's chair, former South African president Thabo Mbeki, characterized the situation as "Sudan's crisis in Darfur"[122] and argued that there were three pillars to addressing the situation—peace, reconciliation, and justice.[123] It made a number of recommendations, including strengthening the special courts, creating hybrid courts with Sudanese and non-Sudanese judges, strengthening the criminal justice system, removing immunities for all state actors in Darfur, and establishing a Truth, Justice and Reconciliation Commission.[124]

The report argued that Sudan had a "duty to deal with the crimes that have been committed in Darfur"[125] within its national legal system, thus recognizing the responsibility to prosecute, as well as Sudan's responsibility to protect its people. Through the creation of hybrid courts, it attempted to "Africanize" the international criminal response. Yet, while it was not explicit on this issue, there was no question that Bashir would be tried by the hybrid courts. Given the government's role in the conflict, how could he be? It was also questionable that others in his government could be tried transparently in this manner.[126] The ICC was the default option, even though much of

Africa appeared to be against this. Yet it is important to point out that the requests to defer the proceedings against Bashir did not try to deny Bashir's guilt, and some AU actors argued that Bashir would need to be tried at some point—just not while the conflict was ongoing.[127] This brings up the same dilemma as posed by Kony—how to bring to justice a major player in a conflict while the conflict is ongoing without creating disincentives for the individual and undermining the peace process. In this case, however, as with Slobodan Milosevic, the individual in question is a state official rather than a nonstate actor, raising broader questions about sovereignty and sovereign immunity.

In November 2009, the Assembly of States Parties of the ICC (ASP) took place in The Hague. Immediately before this annual gathering, the African members of the ICC held another meeting in Addis Ababa—also attended by fifteen nonstate parties. They decided to ask that the question of peace be included in prosecutorial guidelines in addition to the question of justice. They also wanted Article 16 to be amended so that the General Assembly could act when the Security Council failed to act. Finally, they asked for further clarification on the immunities of state officials.[128]

At the ASP, South Africa put forth two proposals, based on these decisions, on behalf of the AU. First, the Prosecutor should take into account the interests of peace in making prosecutorial decisions. Second, the General Assembly should be allowed to act on a request to defer an investigation when the Security Council has not acted on such a request.[129] The proposal regarding the interests of peace engages with the same issues raised with regard to Uganda. Can a judicial body determine on its own whether its investigations will undermine a broader political process—and should it? Would this not just politicize the ICC and undermine the independence of the Prosecutor? The Prosecutor argues that such a determination belongs to the Security Council. The UNSC has not acted on requests to defer the proceedings against Bashir. This power was given by the Rome Statute signatories, including a majority of African states. Yet, beyond the fact that the UNSC had not acted, there is broader dissatisfaction with the Council throughout Africa. African countries argue that it is undemocratic and ignores Africa's needs, and there has been a push to get more seats for African and other developing countries, with South Africa, Egypt, and Nigeria all making claims for a permanent seat.[130] The AU has demanded two permanent seats for Africa.[131] Moving such decision making to the General Assembly would, theoretically, address the power imbalance, since African states have much greater representation, and developing countries more generally have a majority. Yet giving the power to the General Assembly would likely politicize the ICC even more and undermine its ability to do its job. Neither of these proposals was likely to succeed, and indeed both failed, with only two African state parties supporting the proposal to amend Article 16, and only four supporting the proposal on prosecutorial guidelines.[132]

The fourth decision from the pre-ASP meeting—on immunities—relates directly to the new issue raised by the arrest warrant against Bashir. Article 27 removes all immunities from nationals of state parties—including heads of state—while Article 98 appears to provide some immunity for nationals of nonstate parties. By referring the situation in Darfur to the ICC, the Security Council seems to have removed that immunity.[133] This was the first time that the ICC had gone after a sitting head of state. Previously, the ICTY had gone after Milosevic while he was still president of Serbia. Charles Taylor, former president of Liberia, was tried by the Special Court for Sierra Leone, and there has been an ongoing process to try Hissène Habré, the former president of Chad—supported by the AU.[134] Yet trying one of their own seemed to be too much—even to some who had agreed to such a possibility when they signed the Rome Statute. Further, some leaders began to realize that they might be next. Even those heads of state who come from nonstate parties might be vulnerable if the Security Council decided to go after them—as Moammar Qaddafi found out.[135]

Attempts to create an ICC liaison office in Addis Ababa also became a victim of the dispute. Since all of the active cases at the time were in Africa, the ASP decided to establish an office to liaise with the AU,[136] but given the anti-ICC views of the chair of the AU Commission at the time, Jean Ping,[137] the prospects for such an office receded,[138] thus inhibiting the development of ICC activities.

The situation between the ICC and AU became even more tense in 2010. The original arrest warrant for Bashir was for war crimes and crimes against humanity. On 3 February, the ICC Appeals Chamber ruled that the Pre-Trial Chamber should take another look at this decision.[139] The AU cast this as "detrimental to the search for peace."[140] Ocampo, who was perceived as extremely arrogant and generally hated by many African leaders,[141] did not help the situation when he compared upcoming elections in Sudan to elections under Hitler.[142] At the ICC Review Conference in Kampala in June, in a much more measured statement, the legal counsel to the AU Commission, Ben Kioko, made a more specific caution regarding the potential negative effects of the ICC arrest warrants. He noted that after the arrest warrant was issued, rebel groups put more conditions on peace talks.[143] Yet, regardless whether or not this should be a consideration, once Bashir was labeled a war criminal, it would be rather difficult to put that genie back in the bottle.

On 16 July, the Pre-Trial Chamber issued an additional arrest warrant for Bashir, adding the charge of genocide.[144] In response, the PSC reiterated the call for African states not to cooperate with the ICC, and the AU Assembly rejected "for now" the ICC request to open a liaison office.[145] Yet the AU summit also revealed a significant split between African countries—those generally supportive of the ICC, such as South Africa, Botswana, and Ghana, and those against, in particular nonstate party countries such as Libya, Egypt, and Eritrea, but also some countries that are state parties. On the one hand, Thandi Modise, ANC deputy general secretary, stated: "If Bashir were to come to South Africa today, we will definitely implement what we are supposed to in order to bring the culprit to Hague. . . . We can't allow a situation whereby an individual tramples on people's rights and gets away with it. . . . The perpetrators of war crimes should be tried at all costs."[146] On the other, the chair of the AU at the time, Bingu wa Mutharika, the president of Malawi (a state party), said: "To subject a sovereign head of state to a warrant of arrest is undermining African solidarity and African peace and security that we fought for for so many years."[147]

Here we see the competing political currents that support the development of transnational international criminal justice while simultaneously arguing for retaining the prerogatives of sovereignty. Yet even Mutharika was slightly equivocal on the topic, saying Bashir would not be tried outside Africa while simultaneously stating he "would not sweep the issue of El Bashir under the table."[148] There is thus not a complete rejection of bringing Bashir to account at some point. The issue of peace vs. justice remains, but the geopolitical moment, with an increasingly assertive Africa being frustrated by its attempts to claim a bigger seat at the apex of global power, got in the way.

In the following months, a few states made good on the resolve of the AU not to cooperate with the ICC. Even though as state parties they are required to arrest and surrender to the ICC an individual with an outstanding arrest warrant on that state's soil, Chad,[149] Djibouti,[150] Malawi,[151] Kenya,[152] and Nigeria[153] allowed Bashir to visit without arresting him. Chad claimed that since Bashir was a sitting president there was no obligation to arrest him. The response from Kenya was somewhat more conflicted. The Kenyan president,

Mwai Kibaki, invited Bashir, but the prime minister, Raili Odinga, disagreed. He cautioned that Africa seemed to be going back to its policy of noninterference, saying that "when [Africa] formed the AU, we said goodbye to sovereignty."[154] A couple of months later, a meeting Bashir was scheduled to attend in Kenya was rescheduled after the ICC reminded Kenya of its duties under the Rome Statute.[155] The politics surrounding Kenya's relationship became much more complex when the ICC issued arrest warrants for several people involved in election violence in 2007, including the future president, Uhuru Kenyatta, and the deputy president, William Ruto. In September 2013 the Kenyan parliament debated withdrawing from the ICC.[156] The AU has followed suit by discussing mass African withdrawal from the ICC,[157] and although the AU called for no sitting head of state to face charges before the ICC, it did not in the end call for mass withdrawal.[158] Bashir was due to address the UN General Assembly in New York in September 2013, but withdrew after significant protest and efforts by the United States, which as the host of the UN has obligations to allow foreign leaders to visit the UN, to persuade him not to come.[159]

Protecting Civilians?

As the debate about the Bashir arrest warrant raged, the conflict on the ground continued and UNAMID slowly ramped up its capabilities. Security Council resolutions continued to cite the World Summit Outcome document, although they did not cite the responsibility to protect by name. Resolution 1881 of 30 July 2009 focused on PoC as well as ensuring humanitarian access. The concept of operations (CONOPS) for UNAMID specifically stated that "The principal objective of UNAMID is the protection of the civilian population."[160] The required robust force[161] failed to materialize, with a consequent failure to carry out its PoC mission. Troops were slow to deploy. By June 2009, only 68 percent of the planned 19,555 military personnel had been deployed. Even lower percentages applied to police and civilian personnel.[162] And even if deployed, logistical issues surrounding moving equipment and people were significant impediments to action.[163] Helicopters failed to materialize, thus significantly undermining UNAMID's ability to travel around the vast area of Darfur and respond quickly to instances of violence. The excuse provided by the potential helicopter-contributing countries was that there was a global shortage of military-grade helicopters because they were needed elsewhere, and in particular in Iraq and Afghanistan. The "War on Terror" thus negatively affected the ability of UNAMID to adequately do its job. UNAMID received its first five helicopters only in February 2010, more than two years after it began to deploy.[164] Yet even these could not be used for a while. The government engaged in significant obstructionism about when, where, and how UNAMID could operate. A few months after the helicopters arrived, the government banned UNAMID helicopter flights for a couple of weeks.[165] Even when this restriction was lifted, UNAMID still had to negotiate with the government over when and where it could fly its aircraft or where its troops could go. This was nothing new, since the government had previously prevented AMIS from importing helicopters and armored personnel carriers,[166] as well as engaging in other obstructionist activities.[167] Each new report from the Secretary-General seemed to detail new restrictions and other impediments to the deployment and use of personnel and equipment. It has also suffered numerous attacks, losing a number of personnel in the process.[168] In rare cases only, such as an instance in 2009 where UNAMID refused to leave Muhairiya in order to protect the 30,000 residents and IDPs, has it defied the government.[169] This situation was a far cry from that envisioned under R2P and illustrates the very halting steps the international community has taken in Darfur to implement R2P. It demonstrates the significant differences between R2P and PoC. If UNAMID had been given a true R2P mandate and capabilities, it would not have been so subservient to the Sudanese government (although, as we saw in the DRC, having a strong mandate does not necessarily lead to robust action—there must be political will and the capabilities to carry out the mandate).

There was a lot of international pressure to act more robustly on Darfur. The conflict in Darfur has spawned its own global social movement—certainly one of the most visible civil society movements since the antinuclear movement in the 1980s. This has included single-focus NGOs such as the Save Darfur Coalition and the Darfur Consortium. The Genocide Intervention Network, and its student wing STAND, and Enough, founded by the Center for American Progress[170] and the International Crisis Group, are focused more broadly on stopping genocide around the world. Justice for Darfur aims to support the ICC in bringing cases in Darfur. Many of these organizations use the language of R2P. Indeed, Darfur has become the first post-World Summit R2P cause. And Darfur has attracted its own celebrities who have advocated for more robust action—including George Clooney, Mia Farrow, and Bob Geldof.[171] In the same way Invisible Children reduced the situation of the LRA to very simplistic Manichean terms, they repeat the message from the movement that the conflict is simple—the bad government against the people of Darfur, with international aid workers and activists the heroes.[172] Yet the conflict has evolved as rebel groups have fractured and become responsible for some of the killing and attacks on humanitarians and UNAMID—which is a harder war to sell on the global stage.[173] Furthermore, in the same way that the actions of the ICC emboldened the rebels, the support of such visible public figures further emboldened them, and may have undermined the peace process as rebels hoped for an international intervention that could deliver what they had been unable to achieve on the battlefield,[174] thus illustrating the moral hazard inherent in R2P advocacy. Conflicts are seldom as simple as one bad party (usually the government) and one aggrieved party (some group of people), especially if they are allowed to fester for a long period.[175] The more complicated they get, with more actors representing various shades of gray in terms of responsibility for atrocities, the harder it is to identify a simple course of action in the R2P framework. Even as the "Save Darfur" movement continued to ramp up, some observers (including one of the "fathers" of R2P, Gareth Evans) were arguing against any further robust action in terms of a military intervention in Darfur, maintaining that by 2008 the situation had changed significantly, such that the violence was not nearly as bad as in the first year or so of the conflict, or that expanded military action beyond the peacekeeping mandate of UNAMID would create dangers for humanitarian activities.[176]

Mamdani provides a trenchant critique of the Save Darfur movement,[177] which, he argues, engaged in religious and racial stereotyping, reduced the conflict to "Arab perpetrators and African victims," depoliticized and decontextualized the conflict, and put the conflict in good vs. evil terms where Americans could feel good about themselves for standing up to evil and being saviors. This undermined the possibility of a political settlement. Since the "Arabs" have been identified as the perpetrators of genocide, it is easy to make the connection to the "War on Terror," and thus Mamdani concludes that "the movement to Save Darfur . . . [was] the humanitarian face of the War on Terror."[178] This unwarranted racialization also, Mamdani argues, calls into question ICC allegations against Bashir, and in particular the charge of genocide, thus highlighting the politicization of the ICC.[179]

Yet, while the rate of killing had definitely decreased, the conflict was far from settled, there were still millions of displaced people, and the humanitarian situation overall remained dire. Although UNAMID had increased its capacity to protect humanitarian activities, the ICRC had to suspend many of its activities in Darfur because of abductions of ICRC staff in West Darfur as well as in Chad.[180] In July, the Security Council, while extending UNAMID's mandate for another year, expressed concern about the humanitarian situation, including restrictions on humanitarian access.[181] Even as UNAMID continued to expand its protection activities, it experienced continuing restrictions on its freedom of movement by the government as well as rebel groups.[182] And even though the humanitarian situation was described as "stable" for IDPs—at least for those in "well-established camps"—4.2 million people were receiving food from the World Food Program.[183] Two million Darfuris were displaced in mid-2010—a quarter of the population of Darfur,[184] more or less the same number of Rwandans who fled the country after the genocide. And the military component of UNAMID was only at 88 percent of its authorized strength—17,308 of 19,555—two and a half years after it took over from AMIS. What troops were there were severely constrained in what they could do. Between March and June, 90 of 94 helicopter flights by an Ethiopian tactical helicopter unit were disallowed by the government.[185] The stability was periodically upset, as in December 2010 when 40,000 people were forced from their homes as a result of fighting.[186] The world was in full palliation mode in Darfur. In each report, the Secretary-General continued to note fighting between government and rebels, large numbers of people requiring humanitarian assistance, and restrictions on the movement of UNAMID forces and humanitarian actors. And Bashir continued to be protected by the African Union, which was a partner to a peacekeeping mission that had as a core part of its mandate to protect civilians—including from the government. The situation was "stable" in the same way that a patient who is not getting any worse—or any better—is "stable."

On 14 July 2011, the government signed a peace agreement as part of the multiyear Doha peace negotiations with the Liberation and Justice Movement (LJM),[187] a shifting coalition of splinter rebel groups brought together for negotiating purposes.[188] This followed cease-fire agreements (violated on numerous occasions) with the LJM and JEM the previous year.[189] The 2011 agreement did not include JEM or two factions of the Sudanese Liberation Army—SLA-Abdul Wahid and SLA-Minni Minawi.[190] And the agreement was slow to change the situation on the ground, as conflict and displacement continued, with no significant progress toward final status talks, although the creation of the Darfur Regional Authority was a welcome move toward power sharing.[191] While some displaced persons returned, the humanitarian situation was still of concern, and humanitarian and UNAMID personnel continued to be harassed and faced restrictions on movement.[192]

By October 2012, conflict had increased again in Darfur.[193] Meanwhile, the Security Council, while noting the increase in violence and insecurity in parts of Darfur and delays in bringing all actors into, and implementing, the peace process, decided to reduce the military component of UNAMID, which had never reached full deployment, to 16,200, while also reducing the other police components.[194] We can see parallels with MONUC/MONUSCO, as that peacekeeping force was reduced somewhat in a move toward "stabilization" even though the situation was far from stable. Conflict further expanded in 2013,[195] and at the time of writing, more than ten years after the start of the conflict in Darfur, the Secretary-General's most recent report noted that "intercommunal fighting significantly increased the risk of physical violence perpetrated against the civilian population. . . . result[ing] in an estimated 300,000 people being displaced, more than the combined total displaced in Darfur within the past two years."[196] Overall, the current displaced population is 2–2.5 million, and perhaps 300,000–500,000 people have died as a result of the fighting.[197] There are 1.4 million people living in IDP camps in Darfur, and 3.2 million people require humanitarian assistance.[198] The Secretary-General noted that "Efforts to secure a comprehensive and inclusive peace agreement for Darfur have yielded limited results"[199] and "The pace of implementing the Doha Document continued to lag behind the revised timetables."[200] Further, "access to populations in conflict-affected areas remained constrained,"[201] and "only 33 percent per cent of the $624 million required in the United Nations and Partners Work Plan for Sudan humanitarian projects in Darfur has been covered."[202] Overall, the Secretary-General was "deeply concerned about the prevailing security situation in Darfur, which has, without a doubt, deteriorated over the past six months."[203] The Security Council observed the deteriorating situation at the end of July 2013 and extended UNAMID's mandate at the lower troop levels through August 2014. It noted UNAMID's Chapter VII mandate to protect civilians and humanitarian workers, although it felt it had to demand, yet again, that the government allow freedom of movement for UNAMID; obviously the Chapter VII mandate was not having the desired effect.[204]

R2P³ in Darfur

As in the other cases in this book, Darfur exhibits many of the conundrums of R2P³. All three types of global responsibilities and responses to mass atrocities are present. And, as with the other cases, all three were imperfectly implemented and seemed to raise as many questions as answers. Darfur became the first real test of the newly christened R2P—a test that the international community failed miserably. The referral to the ICC seemed to further herald a revolution in international accountability for mass atrocities, while it spurred a counterreaction from Africa that seemed to indicate the limits of normative acceptance of an expanding international criminal justice regime. A poorly funded humanitarian response became entangled in broader realpolitik concerns, and humanitarians became part of the conflict.

It took a long time for the international community to recognize the scope of the situation, but by 2005 the identification of genocide and war crimes eventually led to increased pressure to respond, although there were two parallel pressures in this regard. The first came from the "never again"/evolving R2P norm to "do something" to stop the international crimes. Having little interest in doing something substantial, the major powers were happy to support an ineffectual African Union peacekeeping effort that had no peace to keep and made little difference on the ground. The second pressure came from the nascent international justice regime with the new ICC at its core. Yet the turn to the ICC relieved some of the pressure to intervene, although the eventual pressure led to a weak PoC peacekeeping operation rather than a robust R2P action.

AMIS was ineffectual in stopping the violence or protecting civilians. It had neither the resources nor the mandate to stand up to parties to the conflict—in particular the government. Humanitarians kept people alive with food, water, and medical supplies, but this was obviously not enough to protect people. UNAMID was severely underresourced—it never reached its full deployment strength, did not have necessary equipment such as helicopters, and even at full strength would have been incapable of adequately covering a territory the size of France. And even though it had an increasingly robust protection of civilians mandate, its lack of resources hampered this function—even though the head of UN peacekeeping operations, Hervé Ladsous, declared in July 2013 that UNAMID "has the robustness to deal with the situation."[205] Perhaps more important, it was still subservient to Khartoum. The Bashir regime was able to constrain its movements, as were other parties to the conflict. This was hardly the kind of operation advocates of R2P had envisioned. At the time of writing, UNAMID is beginning to wind down, even though there is no secure comprehensive peace in Darfur. In the end, rather than providing comprehensive civilian protection, it essentially acted as a multiyear stopgap measure. Fighting and killing continued almost unabated, although at a significantly lower level. And it was at this much lower level that the Save Darfur movement seemed to hit its stride, in the same way that Kony 2012 came significantly after there was any real threat to Uganda, and its regional impact had diminished (although not disappeared).

The injection of the ICC into the conflict revealed many contradictions and tensions. It highlighted how humanitarians can find themselves wrapped up in external processes to which they have no direct connection—or at least over which they have no real control. Was it really a perception that humanitarians were helping the ICC that promoted Bashir to expel the organizations? Or were they a convenient scapegoat? Or both? In one sense it does not matter, since the on and off restrictions the government put on their operations demonstrate how little control humanitarians may have over their actions. More fundamentally, the ICC investigation raised a couple of questions with regard to the functioning and acceptance of the ICC. First, as with Uganda, the question of peace versus justice came front and center, as some argued that the investigation and eventual arrest warrants for Bashir imperiled the peace process.[206] African leaders argued that a deferral by the Security Council would allow a peace process to progress. Yet was this really the case? There had been failed attempts at peace agreements before—agreements that fell apart as much as a result of actions by the government as by others. Bashir was responsible for a very significant amount of the violence. There was little evidence that he had all of a sudden changed his mind and was ready to come to terms with the rebels in Darfur. Further, while there were a few intemperate statements on the part of African leaders, the AU did not suggest that any deferral be permanent; nor did it suggest Bashir should not have to face justice at some point. Indeed, some very clearly stated that he should. The argument is that Bashir would have had no reason to make peace with the threat of a trial in The Hague awaiting him at the end. Yet that threat would always be there. The Security Council cannot defer proceedings indefinitely. Even if it did defer temporarily, Bashir could not count on deferral being a permanent state of affairs—he would be very foolish to expect to be protected in this way indefinitely.

The bigger question surrounds the referral in the first place. The referral served big power interests, by allowing them to, at least for a while, avoid greater military involvement in Darfur. It probably did not make Bashir less likely to conclude a peace deal. Instead, it put pressure on him, constrained him—a bit anyway—and, perhaps more important, sent a broader signal to all parties to the conflict, although this signal was interpreted in various ways. On the negative side, the rebels may have taken this as a sign of international support for their cause, hardening their position. Certainly, they attempted to use it as a way to delegitimize the Bashir regime. At the same time, however, ICC action was not completely one-sided, with rebel leaders being investigated—and in fact appearing before the ICC in The Hague. The Pre-Trial Chamber refused to confirm the charges against Bahar Idriss Abu Garda,[207] the head of JEM and the coalition of rebel groups United Resistance Front (URF), which splintered in 2008. Two other rebel leaders who appeared before the ICC, Abdallah Banda Abakaer Nourain and Saleh Mohammed Jerbo Jamus, were killed before the trials could begin.[208] The reaction to the eventual charges against Bashir also highlighted the potentially soft support for the ICC by states parties when it appears to go against other interests—international criminal justice norms do not necessarily trump other norms and perceptions of interest. And while the outcome might not have been very different had the referral not occurred, the ICC can make conflict management more difficult. Yet continued impunity also undermined efforts to establish long-term peace. Further, Darfur demonstrates the limits of Security Council referral in the absence of real Security Council support to follow up on the referral and eventual proceedings. Indeed, Louise Arbour, former high commissioner for human rights and member of the UN Commission of Inquiry on Darfur, has indicated "that it was a very bad idea" to refer Darfur to the ICC, precisely because of the lack of support, arguing that it had served to undermine the ICC.[209]

Humanitarians became caught up in global power politics as a result of the Bashir arrest warrant. And their ability to function was restricted in many ways by the government and rebels. Yet, as Don Hubert and Cynthia Brassard-Boudreau argue, "But the fact that there were massive humanitarian operations taking place within the sovereign territory of an Islamic state in the

Table 5.1. Responsibility Conundrums in Darfur

	Protectors	Prosecutors	Palliators
Protection	+AMIS and UNAMID deployed +UN provided some robust PoC −AMIS and UNAMID significantly constrained by Sudanese government, significantly undersupported, significant gaps in protection		−lack of adequate protection of humanitarians
Prosecution	−no action in carrying out arrest warrants	+sent signal that government's conduct was unacceptable +some action against rebels −criticized for undermining peace process −emboldened rebels −backlash against ICC	−discussion of relationship with ICC undermined palliation
Palliation	+protected some humanitarian activities −limited in protecting humanitarians by lack of resources and willingness to confront various actors in conflict	−endangered by ICC −government used ICC activities to constrain humanitarian action	+assisted millions in Darfur and neighboring countries +some protection activities −served as diversions

midst of the US-led war on terror is an indication of how far the normative goal-posts in favour of humanitarian access have shifted."[210]

This may be true, but the palliators' position is less than secure. While Darfur represents the largest humanitarian operation in the world (with 13,000 humanitarian workers in 2008),[211] humanitarians are caught between both local (governments and rebel groups) and international (peacekeepers and ICC) forces.[212] While there are not the same accusations that they have made the situation worse, as in Rwanda/Zaire (or, indeed, in Uganda),[213] their situation is still precarious, and they have to work extra hard to maintain neutrality, although that will not always help them. Expanding violence has significantly undermined humanitarian operations. Eric Reeves noted in August 2013 that "Virtually no international (expatriate) staff remain in Darfur, certainly not in the field or in remote locations—either for critical assessment work or to provide oversight for aid distribution."[214] He cites "lawlessness and a deliberately chaotic violence . . . encouraged by Khartoum" against civilians as well as UN and NGO officials, which even the government cannot control. Forty-seven aid workers have been killed, 139 injured, and seventy-one abducted in Darfur—almost half since UNAMID came on the scene. Humanitarian neutrality has not helped these people, nor has UNAMID been able to provide the necessary humanitarian security.

What, then, can we conclude about the case of Darfur? The international community failed its first R2P test. While there was a large peacekeeping force, it was chronically underresourced and did not have an adequate mandate to challenge the biggest purveyor of violence—the government—or engage in robust enough protection of civilian activities. Sovereignty thus reared its ugly head, even in this supposed postsovereign world we inhabit. The insertion of the International Criminal Court seemed to rescue this postsovereign world, but in reality it made somewhat of a muddle of things. Humanitarians may have been able to work in the middle of a complex and violent conflict, but they, like UNAMID, were constrained by a very wide variety of actors on the ground. Recognition of responsibilities abounded at the international level, but the implementation of these responsibilities was severely lacking.

CHAPTER 6

Realizing R2P³: Labeling, Institutions, and Authority

[G]enocide must not be tolerated. It is a moral
imperative that states must take action to prevent and
punish genocide.

You can't stop every bad thing from happening.

These quotes reflect the vexing nature of the evolving global human rights regime. On the one hand, we attach great hope that its underlying norms will, one day, help stop mass atrocities. On the other hand, we are confronted with the reality time and again of the all too often ambiguous and ambivalent manner in which those same norms are implemented. The grave human rights situations discussed in this book are directly tied to difficult questions of international peace and security and entail a broader range of responses than those discussed in the book, including political pressure, sanctions, and military action of a different type than envisaged under the heading of R2P. However, while bound up in larger dynamics, protection of human rights is frequently the most urgent issue to be addressed in these situations. Further, the cases addressed here have provided a series of tests for the international community and the norms and institutions it has created in recent years. The responses to these conflicts also raise questions about how we understand and conceptualize the international community.

Three sets of questions emerge that will be addressed in this chapter. First, at the most basic level, does the way people die, or the motivations of the people who are killing them in these situations, matter? That is, do (or should) labels matter? Second, have the international community's ideas—international norms—concerning human rights protection outstripped its ability to engage in such protection? Are global institutions up to the task they have set for themselves? Do states need to recognize limits to their responsibilities? Third, should authority and decision-making procedures be reconceptualized to ensure appropriate and timely responses to mass atrocity situations? Or is the issue one of generating more political will to exercise authority and make decisions that actually result in the protection and rescue of victims of mass atrocity crimes?

Labels

In the Introduction I defended my use of the term "mass atrocities" as a catch-all phrase to cover a variety of international crimes. Yet the perceptions and actions of diplomats and activists do not necessarily correspond to this term. Labels do matter. Words matter. In Rwanda, the word "genocide" seemed to be the key to action, and so it was avoided. Yet, in Darfur, the word was used with an explicit disclaimer that it did not demand action. Then lawyers, diplomats, and activists debated rather heatedly the lack of the use of the term by the UN. Hundreds of thousands of people died unnecessarily as a result of these acts of omission and commission. Should deaths as a result of crimes against humanity or widespread war crimes be less important or noteworthy than deaths at the hands of perpetrators ascribed with the intent to wipe people out as a group, rather than as individuals? Identifying actor intent may help to shape and influence political responses—understanding motivations obviously helps to underpin appropriate diplomatic and other initiatives. Yet, in situations of rescue,[1] such legal niceties are not as relevant—and can get in the way of appropriate responses designed to save lives.

The media coverage of the crisis in Darfur has far exceeded that of the DRC, even though the human calamity in the DRC is much greater than in Darfur. And this is where labels matter. The genocide discourse applied to Darfur, for example, has overshadowed the brutal reality of wars that fall short of being labeled "genocide," such as the conflict in the DRC. This is not to say that the international community's response should be based predominantly on numbers of people killed. However, this paradox demands that states and other actors involved in formulating effective responses to such situations seek a greater, more nuanced appreciation of the facts on the ground. Exaggerating numbers of people killed, as happened in Darfur, might generate headlines and help to start social movements, but it does not help create adequate policy—nor does creating a media frenzy based on a situation from five or ten years earlier, as in the case of the LRA. The numbers of deaths resulting from the DRC crisis has been staggering, exceeding the deaths in all the other cases discussed in this book put together. Importantly, the situation in the DRC has never been labeled a genocide, and most people have died as a result of the secondary effects of protracted crises, especially disease and malnutrition, rather than being targets of direct violence. While shocking evidence of endemic sexual violence earned the DRC the label "rape capital" of the world, it was a temporary theme that did little to generate the kind of political will necessary under R2P or other doctrines to halt these atrocities. The slow burn of this chronic emergency seems to matter less than other crises, such as Darfur. Death at the hand of crazed horse-riding *janjaweed* or the weird cult-like LRA makes for attention-grabbing headlines and generates the public's compassion. An imminent attack on Benghazi activates our mass atrocity radar—particularly since the would-be perpetrator was an Arab leader once labeled a "mad dog" by former U.S. president Ronald Reagan. The daily slog of disease, forced displacement, rape, and death in the DRC does not capture the imagination in quite the same way. Media coverage of peacekeeping in the DRC is much more mundane than coverage of the telegenic air strikes on Tripoli. But both conflicts have been extremely important in defining how the international community addresses atrocities.

One other issue demands mention here. All too often diplomats, activists, and the media portray Africa as the "heart of darkness," riven with tribalism and crazed killing that defies explanation[2] and seems to spring out of nowhere, thus leading to crisis. This, along with a focus on the humanitarian aspects of a situation, significantly depoliticizes these situations. Mass atrocity situations are intensely political and are frequently the result of significant calculation on the part of one or more actors—whether states or rebel groups and other violent nonstate actors. Thus, they require political responses, rather than just apolitical palliative ones. The way African conflicts are portrayed frequently makes it too easy for publics and policymakers to look away, and leads to misdiagnosis and inadequate responses. This book has focused on responses to crisis, but we must also recognize that the focus on "crisis" undermines adequate analysis and responses that might avert crisis or prevent a crisis from recurring.

Norms and Institutions

The world has witnessed a sea change in human rights norms since 1945. Sovereignty means something different now than when it could be used as an almost absolute shield against condemnation of human rights abuses and action to stop those abuses. Paragraphs 138 and 139 of the World Summit Outcome document and Article 4h of the AU Constitutive Act reflect this fact. Leaders are, in word, no longer allowed to indiscriminately kill their own people—and yet in deed, they do. When such atrocities are perpetrated, whether by national authorities or nonstate actors, the international community is supposed to step in—and yet it rarely does so in time or in an adequate fashion. Sovereignty is compromised, but so is political will. The very intergovernmental institutions states task with enforcing or upholding these norms are imperfect and only able to engage in piecemeal response. Moreover, there seems to be little thought given among decisionmakers to how the various responses work together. While the concepts seem clear and worthy of merit—protect people from harm, prosecute those who do harm, and feed people who are caught up in harm situations—the reality of concrete, on-the-ground practice differs widely from the theory.

While this book was being written, a dramatic instantiation of the responsibility to protect occurred in Libya. The UN uttered the words "responsibility to protect," and within less than one month's time a NATO-authorized no-fly zone was established, which spelled the end of the Qaddafi regime and Moammar Qaddafi himself. While this played well on TV, and has been used as a pretext to oppose robust response in Syria, there are serious questions about the outcome of this attack, and such actions constitute a least likely response to mass atrocity situations. Rather, international responses are likely to bear greater resemblance to the operations in the DRC or Darfur than to Libya. For all the talk of its demise, the Westphalian notion of sovereignty unencumbered by outside forces is still a powerful idea. Sovereignty was no bar in Libya, but it has ostensibly been in Syria, particularly as great power interests have prevented action. Sovereignty was not the key impediment to responding in Rwanda—rather, it was will to act. In Darfur, both the UN and

AU have been reluctant to challenge directly Sudanese state authority. Efforts to address the cross-border threat posed by the LRA have been impeded partly because of sovereignty issues. In the DRC, the international response has been consensual (at least with the state), and thus poses no challenges to state sovereignty. Yet, as in other cases, the issue has been the will to act. MONUC deployed far too slowly without adequate resources for the mandate given to it, and its commanders were reluctant to use the robust protection of civilians mandate they were provided by the Security Council. Operation Artemis and the Intervention Brigade are small but important examples of what can happen when the will is there, but they do not necessarily presage a dramatically new era in R2P and PoC.

And as this conclusion is being written, another mass atrocity situation has erupted in the CAR, which sits adjacent to the countries discussed in this book. As with the other cases, the CAR conflict has long, complicated roots. The response by the international community through the Security Council has followed a familiar pattern. There has been discussion of genocide and "never again" by activists, while diplomats have been much more measured in their use of language. UN Secretary-General Ban Ki-moon described "mass violence,"[3] U.S. ambassador to the UN Samantha Power referred to "atrocities,"[4] and French ambassador to the UN Gérard Araud stated that the CAR was "'on the brink of mass atrocities.'"[5] UN Deputy Secretary-General Jan Eliasson described the situation as "a vicious cycle that could very easily turn into mass atrocities,"[6] while John Ging, director of operations for OCHA, dared to say that "we see the seeds of genocide here."[7] The December 2013 UN Security Council resolution authorizing an African-led "support mission" cited the domestic authorities' responsibility to protect, referred approvingly to its previous resolutions on PoC, noted the fact that the CAR is a party to the Rome Statute, and raised concern about the humanitarian situation. Thus the triumvirate of R2P³ was invoked—although the incantation of R2P was watered down to PoC. Thousands of (underresourced) African troops have deployed in and around the CAR capital, Bangui, joined by 1,600 French troops. The ICC, which through the Bemba case was already involved in the CAR, has commented on the new situation. OCHA has issued "flash updates," noting that the crisis has created more than 500,000 IDPs, just as the CAR crisis was nudging into prominence on NGO websites. It is too early to say whether this response will significantly affect the human rights and humanitarian crisis in the CAR, but it does seem to be an indication that international community reaction to mass atrocity situations is becoming more routinized, which further strengthens and reaffirms R2P[3] norms.

Yet R2P[3] responses are problematic and paradoxical. Peacekeeping has been adapted in the DRC and elsewhere in a way that exposes its inherent weaknesses and shortcomings. The first weakness is the reliance on consent. This has undermined effective response in Darfur, as the government in Khartoum has been allowed to impose significant restrictions on what the peacekeepers can do. The second weakness is its transitory nature and reliance on fluctuating political will. While a fifteen-year presence in the DRC may not seem transitory, the fact that new mechanisms need to be reinvented and implemented each time a new crisis erupts further undermines its effectiveness. Except for outlier responses like Libya, which featured direct action by the most powerful international actors, most military-based conflict responses rely on troops from poor countries funded by the rich countries. This means that for each new mission, the DPKO has to go around hat in hand begging for donations and cajoling states to send troops—troops that, in some cases, may not be adequately prepared for the tasks at hand. Even assuming these issues are resolved, peace operations are still plagued with the challenges of integrating into an effective command and control structure the troops, military observers, and civilian police contributed from sometimes dozens of countries. Then there must be political will to sustain the mission until it is completed. This is difficult when commanders from different countries are given different understandings of their mission parameters by their political masters back home. An obvious answer to this ad hoc approach would be to create some sort of standing, rapid response force. This has been discussed in UN circles for decades, with little prospect of being realized. In Africa, there seems to be more enthusiasm to create an African standby reaction force, but in practical terms this will take substantially more work. We are thus left with much more modest expectations of what PoC and R2P will look like in the future—and more nuanced understandings of what we mean by protection.

The challenge posed to states by the ICC referral in Darfur is no less a threat to traditional notions of sovereignty than the military action in Libya. The ICC is an international institutional revolution, even if expectations remain tempered for the time being regarding its ability to transform international criminal justice. While the ICC Prosecutor is independent, she or he is not omnipotent. The Rome Statute empowers the Prosecutor to determine which situations to investigate, the judges in the Pre-Trial Chamber decide which arrest warrants to issue, and the judges in the trial and appeal chambers make the final decisions on guilt and innocence. The ICC faces significant constraints and tensions. The Prosecutor is reliant on state, state-based, and nonstate actors for the information needed to prosecute individuals. This can put those actors in very difficult situations and endanger, for example, the provision of humanitarian assistance. It is also reliant on state and state-based actors (e.g., peacekeepers) to execute its arrest warrants and physically transfer indictees to The Hague. This might make the Prosecutor beholden to these actors, in particular where states refer situations in their own countries to the ICC. Should the Prosecutor avoid investigating state actors—for example, government leaders and military personnel—to ensure state cooperation in apprehending the state's enemies? If so, does this make the Prosecutor partial, which in turn would undermine his or her credibility? If not, does this doom prosecutions? As we have seen, misperception concerning the court's impartiality is a real risk. Yet, even in such cases, this does not guarantee state cooperation, as states have repeatedly endeavored to use and manipulate the ICC for their own ends.

The ICC is not immune to pressure from international actors, either. While it is independent, it is also a product of an international political process, and thus remains subject to the whims of international politics. While select states parties have tried to get the ICC to change the basis on which it makes prosecutorial decisions, these efforts have thus far failed; there is little chance the states parties would agree, for example, to mandate the Prosecutor to consider issues of peace in his or her prosecutorial decision-making. Yet, this does not eliminate the fact that the ICC may be embedded in ongoing conflicts where its actions could help or hinder peace, even if the peace vs. justice dichotomy is far too simplistic.[8] It is clear that in Uganda, for example, where the Acholi supposedly value peace over justice, the reality is much more complex. And previous attempts by the Ugandan government to resolve conflicts through amnesty have not led to a stable political situation.

Further, these same states can make life difficult for the Prosecutor in other ways, including through various types of noncooperation, which may violate their obligations under the Rome Statute. The Security Council can also affect the ICC, namely by deciding to refer some cases, but not others, or by deferring ongoing proceedings as it attempts to use the ICC as a peace-making tool—thus transforming the basis for international criminal justice from a normative one to a consequentialist one.[9] Under this scenario, the ICC becomes just another part of the conflict response "toolkit." This is a threat to the independence of the ICC, but it is woven into the fiber of the court and reinforces its political underpinnings—which, in some ways, is no different from any other judicial body. Just as humanitarians may be criticized for providing aid on the basis of need alone, the ICC has been labeled as biased for not being more geographically diverse in the cases it has chosen for its docket. The institutional design of the ICC leaves it open to criticism and pressures from a variety of quarters, which create real conundrums. This is not helped by the fact that in situations where the international community turns to the ICC, it does not, as in the case of Darfur, provide it with the necessary support to implement fully its mandate. It is further constrained by the fact that its limited resources constrict the range of alleged perpetrators it can actually prosecute in any given case. Thus, the ICC is both independent of, and dependent upon, a variety of actors. Yet states may also be subject to ICC pressure and find themselves enmeshed in an institution that they want to control for their own purposes, but which might interfere with their own plans.

Palliators are buffeted from all sides. The dangers and constraints are different for UN humanitarian actors, such as the UNHCR, than for NGOs. Humanitarian organizations rely on neutrality to gain access to those in need, although adhering to this principle is seldom sufficient to guarantee access. For the UNHCR, just being part of the UN system can make it a target. It must constantly balance the tensions inherent in fulfilling its mandate, which could mean speaking out publicly about atrocities, as well as ensuring that its actions do not jeopardize other actors (e.g., peacekeepers) working in the same crisis environment. Providing aid impartially is also no guarantee that actors on the ground perceive humanitarianism as an impartial act. Much like the principle of neutrality, impartiality is in the eye of the beholder and, where it is questioned, can actually result in accusations against humanitarian actors of partiality and bias. Moreover, NGOs often discover that neutrality has a thin veneer in settings that require their staff to work closely with military actors (e.g., in integrated missions) or necessitate negotiation with multiple rebel groups in addition to government and local communities. Humanitarian actors also have to be careful that their resources are not used by the conflict parties themselves to continue that conflict. They must thus "do no harm." But does supplying "a bed for the night" mean turning a blind eye to human rights abuses? If so, the potential for harm is real. If not, they risk endangering not only their principles but also the safety of their staff if they speak out about abuses. Assertions of a humanitarian imperative, therefore, do not necessarily obviate other imperatives at work in crisis zones marked by atrocities. Further, although humanitarians generally tend to use the language of PoC rather than R2P, humanitarianism has also been tied directly to the R2P project.[10] The implications of connecting a supposedly apolitical practice driven by the principle of humanity to a highly politicized construct embedded in the highest levels of global politics and international peace and security requires much further debate and strategic response.

All these actors and institutions, while working to better the human condition in the most extreme situations imaginable, do not necessarily share the same goals. Protectors want to keep people from being harmed—although given their connection to international peace and security, there will be other agendas and priorities at play. Prosecutors want to punish those who commit the most heinous of crimes—but they may not be able to go after all sides in a conflict if they hope to get state cooperation. Palliators want to keep people alive, a day at a time, in the middle of conflict—but their actions could help to fan a conflict, ultimately resulting in more deaths. These are all focused on what some would say rather modest goals—helping people in the moment or responding to specific crises on an emergency basis. Yet they are all part of a much larger political project to restructure relations between individuals, governments, and the international community. Even palliators, who may claim no political project beyond a bed for the night, would like to see something more (indeed humanitarian actors have been among the most vocal supporters of the ICC). And by inserting themselves into conflict where they might not necessarily be accepted by all groups, they are, in effect, directly challenging state wishes.

Authority

Those who advocate for the responsibility to protect envision a new relationship between people and power. Prosecutors directly challenge the powerful. And, as the president of MSF-France has written, "humanitarian action . . . will inevitably clash with the established order."[11] They wish to move the traditional locus of authority and decisionmaking in mass atrocity situations and humanitarian crises away from the state and resituate it beyond the state. While a lengthy discussion of the implications of this fall outside the scope of this project, a few points are in order. On the basis of timeliness and decisiveness, there are inherent tensions in the Security Council's claimed monopoly of authority to authorize and legitimate military measures to protect civilians. First, and with the possible exception of the Libya case, the Security Council generally does not act in a timely manner in responding decisively to mass atrocity situations, which violates the spirit of R2P as articulated in paragraph 139 of the World Summit Outcome document. Second, the working methods of the Security Council constrain rather than empower consensus in achieving timely and decisive response to mass atrocity cases. The threat or actual use of the veto power by the permanent members allows politics to dominate decision-making and in practice has tended to reify rather than problematize sovereignty over human rights.

Third, and related, not all states and other actors have the same goals; thus, even when a superficial consensus exists on R2P, deep divisions remain. Fourth, an increasingly restive world resents the undemocratic concentration of power in the Security Council, where decisions concerning UN member states rest with just five countries. This is most prominent in Africa, where the AU argues for more representation on the Security Council and has asserted its own right to authorize R2P-like missions in Africa, even in the absence of Security Council approval. This raises significant international legal issues.[12] While there is broad agreement on implementing more consensual peacekeeping activities, and a recognition that the UN needs to work with the AU, African crises require both regional and global involvement, and this raises questions of resources.[13] The AU has very ambitious plans in the realm of peace and security, and has demonstrated a willingness to deploy in situations where others will not, but its visions outstrip its capabilities and resources. Moreover (and like the UN itself) the AU has demonstrated a lack of willingness to stand up to governments when necessary to advance human rights goals—such as in Darfur. Ultimately, the responsibility to protect represents universal claims to protect human rights, but in practice that protection is far from universal. The tensions between global and regional organizations will continue, although the recent cooperation between the UN and AU in the CAR is a hopeful sign.

The ICC also has a claim to global, if not universal, authority—although that authority can be universalized through Security Council action—which, like R2P, aims to uphold expanding notions of human rights. Yet, as the reality of its actions and potential has become clearer over time, states are evincing second thoughts and raising questions about why and how this global institution has come to be focused on one particular continent, comprising only 15 percent of the world's population. It is not surprising that the implementation of this new authority has not been smooth, and that there has been pushback against the ICC—even by those who had initially signed up to it.[14] However, these dynamics, including incentives or disincentives to prosecute certain cases over others, raise significant issues for how the ICC operates and its credibility. Further, although the ICC's authority has been constituted by states, it is significantly, if not completely, independent of their control—in a much more robust manner than the UN's independence from its state members. The AU has attempted to blunt ICC authority by proposing and expanding African human rights institutions that could take over the court's functions. The actual international legal effect, as with the AU's assertion of the right to authorize military action without Security Council approval, is unclear—as is the decision to provide immunity for sitting heads of state or other senior officials while in office.[15] And again, in parallel with choppy implementation of the African Peace and Security Architecture,[16] these efforts are unlikely to bear significant practical fruit in the short term, even as both represent broader attempts to shift authority from the global to the regional level.

The actions of palliators—and especially NGOs—raise a different set of issues. These organizations have no independent legal authority to make decisions and impose their will on others in the way that the UN or ICC does—and in fact they very often appear to operate at the whims of others. Yet they have also become embedded within contemporary conflict and mass atrocity situations in a fundamental way. In their actions they are both independent of, and dependent on, states and other actors, and affect key international security situations in profound ways. Although there have been attempts from different corners of the international community to increase NGO accountability,[17] these actors still have power and authority over the lives of millions who have been abandoned by their states.

All these observations lead to the conclusion that our current international institutions are in flux, and understandings of how the international community operates are far from complete. Even as global institutions make universal claims to power and authority, their exercise of that power and authority is neither comprehensive nor satisfactory. This has led to a push by regional organizations to challenge global authority, which, in addition to calling into question the proper locus of international authority in the areas of human rights and international peace and security, raises further serious issues about democratic accountability and effective decision-making in mass atrocity cases. The role of nonstate actors in this process also demands more attention as they are often left to fill in the gaps of international implementation of human rights and humanitarian norms, and as they continue to put pressure on states to live up to their responsibilities.

Continuing Conundrums

What comes through most clearly from the analysis in this book is that while significant developments have occurred in the areas of human rights and humanitarian norms and principles, the application of those norms has fallen significantly short of the idealism behind the norms. Further, while springing from similar, if not identical, ideational fountains, they do not necessarily always mutually support each other. There are questions of trade-offs, overlapping authority, and institutional design and implementation that have yet to be managed and reconciled effectively. Further, the international community's responses to mass atrocities all too often feel like half measures, and most cases are left to resolve themselves or burn themselves out, to the very significant detriment of the millions who die or are displaced. The goal becomes creating "a livable situation"[18]—livable at least for those making the decisions in New York or Geneva, if not for those caught in the middle of conflict. So, even though states have committed themselves to extremely robust norms for the protection of human rights, recent experience teaches us that we should be more modest in our expectations of what these norms and institutions might, in reality, accomplish—at least in the short term. The focus needs to be on generating political will to implement the norms we have and fully supporting the institutions and organizations created in parallel with these norms.

This does not mean that we should throw up our hands in despair. Indeed, the fact that we can have these discussions at all indicates significant progress in global attempts to protect human rights. Rather, given that situations such as those described in the book are intimately tied into the highest levels of global politics, we ought to cultivate a realistic understanding that those authorities residing at the apex of global power are unlikely to change their practices overnight. Further, we need to ensure that adequate analysis is provided alongside the activism that has arisen to address mass atrocities. This includes better analysis of potential endgames—how do these situations get resolved versus just creating "livable situations"? Part of this involves a clear examination of the positives and negatives of the responses available to

the international community to address mass atrocities, as well as the conundrums faced when attempting to implement one or more of them indi-
vidually or collectively.

These responsibilities need to be seen as part of an integrated whole of
conflict response—all appropriate, but accomplishing very different things.
Palliation is a key short-term response to keep people alive until a conflict
ends. It cannot be used as a way to resolve the situation. Doing so will likely
prolong a conflict and make the situation worse. Yet the humanitarian imperative provides little defense against such manipulation. Being vocal about
human rights abuses undermines attempts at silence and obfuscation by political leaders, but risks access to people in need.

Prosecution can hold people to account for their actions, and can help
undermine impunity, which might otherwise allow mass atrocity perpetrators to maintain positions within postconflict society and engage in further
destabilization. Yet, it is a double-edge sword, since the threat of prosecution,
while creating pressure to end a conflict, can have the opposite effect—
creating incentives to continue fighting. Some suggest sequencing—holding
off on prosecution until a peace deal has been struck. Yet there will be pressure
to prevent postconflict justice, reinforcing impunity, in peace negotiations.
Naming names and starting investigations can prevent this dynamic. Further, identifying those most responsible for mass atrocities can delegitimize
them, hopefully undermining their support. Such delegitimization can also
contribute to support for stronger protective efforts. Institutional naming
and shaming by the ICC can create pressure to act to stop atrocities, although
giving something its proper name does not necessarily lead to proper action.
Further, the justice mechanisms must be scrupulously impartial; otherwise,
they might empower one perpetrator and, as with palliation, contribute to
the continuation of conflict. Prosecutors need to ensure that their actions do
not undermine the key job of palliators. Yet, even with the best of intentions, this may not be possible in some situations where all outside actors are
viewed through the same lens, and thus the actions of one may taint others.
Supporters of the ICC point to the potential deterrence value of the ICC.
This is in little evidence to date, but there will be no prospect for deterrence
unless an increasing number of mass atrocity perpetrators end up behind
bars in The Hague.

Protection can come in many forms. Yet, whether it comes in the form of
robust peacekeeping or dramatic military action as in Libya, it requires will—
will on the part of the international community to provide a mandate to

stand up to perpetrators, potentially transgressing sovereignty; will to provide the necessary resources to carry out the mandate; and then will to actually use those resources. Such will has been in evidence only rarely. Further, while protectors have the potential to help palliators reach affected populations, the potential for compromising the neutrality of palliators is great. In addition, protectors have a potential role to play in apprehending ICC suspects. While peacekeepers are understandably wary about engaging in firefights to carry out arrest warrants, they have at times allowed the worst leaders to carry on human rights abuses within their areas of operation, which ultimately undermines protection. Being more proactive in this area could, at times, support the protection mission, as well as help to undermine future conflict by removing leaders who might reignite conflict—and by creating a demonstration effect for potential agitators.

Responsibilities to respond to mass atrocities have been recognized by states and other international actors. Protection, prosecution, and palliation have all been brought to bear in various situations, with extremely varying results. Yet a more concerted effort to implement them in a more timely and more thoughtful manner is required to live up to the promise of protecting human rights.

NOTES

Introduction

1. Convention on the Prevention and Punishment of the Crime of Genocide.

2. UN High Commissioner for Human Rights, Democratic Republic of the Congo, 1993–2003, Report of the Mapping Exercise documenting the most serious violations of human rights and international humanitarian law committed within the territory of the Democratic Republic of the Congo between March 1993 and June 2003 (August 2010), 259, www.ohchr.org.

3. UNSC, "Final Report of the Commission of Experts Established Pursuant to Security Council Resolution 780 (1992)," S/1994/674 (27 May 1994): 33.

4. Ibid., 37.

5. Martha Minnow, "Naming Horror: Legal and Political Words for Mass Atrocities," *Genocide Studies and Prevention* 2, 1 (2007): 40; William A. Schabas, "Semantics or Substance? David Scheffer's Welcome Proposal to Strengthen Criminal Accountability for Atrocities," *Genocide Studies and Prevention* 2, 1 (2007): 36.

6. Sarah Sewall, Dwight Raymond, and Sally Chin, *MARO—Mass Atrocity Response Operations: A Military Planning Handbook*, Carr Center for Human Rights Policy, Harvard Kennedy School and U.S. Army Peacekeeping and Stability Operations Institute (May 2010), http://www.hks.harvard.edu.

7. David Scheffer uses the term "atrocity crimes." David Scheffer, "Genocide and Atrocity Crimes," *Genocide Studies and Prevention* 1, 3 (2006): 229–50.

8. Linnea Bergholm, "The African Union, the United Nations and Civilian Protection Challenges in Darfur," Refugee Studies Centre, Oxford University, Working Paper Series 63 (May 2010), 15.

9. Kevin C. Dunn, "The Lord's Resistance Army and African International Relations," *African Security* 3, 1 (2010): 58.

10. Gareth Evans, *The Responsibility to Protect: Ending Mass Atrocity Crimes Once and for All* (Washington, D.C.: Brookings Institution Press, 2008).

11. See Kurt Mills and David Karp, eds., *Human Rights Protection in Global Politics: Responsibilities of States and Non-State Actors* (Basingstoke: Palgrave Macmillan, 2015). See also Toni Erskine, ed., *Can Institutions Have Responsibilities? Collective Moral Agency and International Relations* (Basingstoke: Palgrave, 2003).

Chapter 1. Interrogating International Responsibilities

Epigraphs: French government, quoted in Michael Barnett and Jack Snyder, "The Grand Strategies of Humanitarianism," in Michael Barnett and Thomas G. Weiss, eds., *Humanitarianism in Question: Politics, Power, Ethics* (Ithaca, N.Y.: Cornell University Press, 2008): 143; UN Security Council, "Statement by the President of the Security Council," S/PRST/2006/28

(22 June 2006); UN General Assembly, 2005 World Summit Outcome, A/Res/60/1, 15 September 2005.

1. It was identified as such by the counsel for Bosnia and Herzegovina before the International Court of Justice. Martin Mennecke, "What's in a Name? Reflections on Using, Not Using, and Overusing the 'G-Word,'" *Genocide Studies and Prevention* 2, 1 (2007): 57.

2. Michael Barnett, *Empire of Humanity: A History of Humanitarianism* (Ithaca, N.Y.: Cornell University Press, 2011), 10.

3. David Kennedy, *The Dark Sides of Virtue: Reassessing International Humanitarianism* (Princeton, N.J.: Princeton University Press, 2004).

4. David Rieff, *A Bed for the Night: Humanitarianism in Crisis* (New York: Simon & Schuster, 2002).

5. Barnett and Snyder, "The Grand Strategies of Humanitarianism," 145–55.

6. Rieff, *A Bed for the Night.*

7. Fiona Terry, *Condemned to Repeat? The Paradox of Humanitarian Action* (Ithaca, N.Y.: Cornell University Press, 2002).

8. Michael Barnett and Thomas G. Weiss, "Humanitarianism: A Brief History to the Present," in Barnett and Weiss, *Humanitarianism in Question*, 13.

9. David Forsythe, *The Humanitarians: The International Committee of the Red Cross* (Cambridge: Cambridge University Press, 2005).

10. Ibid., 161.

11. See Gil Loescher, *The UNHCR and World Politics: A Perilous Path* (Oxford: Oxford University Press, 2001), for a history of UNHCR.

12. For an overview of the breadth of activities UNHCR is involved in, see UNHCR, *State of the World's Refugees 2006: Human Displacement in the New Millennium* (Oxford: Oxford University Press, 2006).

13. Thomas G. Weiss and Amir Pasic, "Reinventing UNHCR: Enterprising Humanitarians in the Former Yugoslavia," *Global Governance* 3, 1 (1997): 41–57.

14. Erin D. Mooney, "Presence, Ergo Protection? UNPROFOR, UNHCR and the ICRC in Croatia and Bosnia and Herzegovina," *International Journal of Refugee Law* 7, 3 (1995): 415.

15. Michael Barutciski, "Tensions Between the Refugee Concept and the IDP Debate," *Forced Migration Review* 3 (1998): 11–14.

16. Barnett, *Empire of Humanity*, 179; Bill Frelick, "'Preventive Protection' and the Right to Seek Asylum: A Preliminary Look at Bosnia and Croatia," *International Journal of Refugee Law* 4, 4 (1992): 439–54.

17. Barnett, *Empire of Humanity*, 179.

18. Ibid.

19. Adam Roberts, "NATO's 'Humanitarian War' over Kosovo," *Survival* 41, 3 (1999): 102–23; Larry Minear, Ted van Baarda, and Marc Sommers, "NATO and Humanitarian Action in the Kosovo Crisis," Thomas J. Watson, Jr. Institute for International Studies, Brown University, Occasional Paper 36 (2000), http://www.watsoninstitute.org/pub/OP36.pdf.

20. Sarah Kenyon Lischer, "Military Intervention and the Humanitarian 'Force Multiplier,'" *Global Governance* 13, 1 (2007): 99–118.

21. "The War Against Terrorists of Global Reach Is a Global Enterprise of Uncertain Duration," *National Security Strategy of the United States of America* (September 2002): iv.

22. Kurt Mills, "Neo-Humanitarianism: The Role of International Humanitarian Norms and Organizations in Contemporary Conflict," *Global Governance* 11 (2005): 165.

23. Ibid., 166.

24. Conor Foley, *The Thin Blue Line: How Humanitarianism Went to War* (London: Verso, 2008), 16–18.

25. Mills, "Neo-Humanitarianism," 167.

26. Mary B. Anderson, *Do No Harm: How Aid Can Support Peace or War* (Boulder, Colo.: Lynne Rienner, 1999).

27. See Katrina West, *Agents of Altruism: The Expansion of Humanitarian NGOs in Rwanda and Afghanistan* (Aldershot: Ashgate, 2001), 13–37, and Elizabeth G. Ferris, *The Politics of Protection: The Limits of Humanitarian Action* (Washington, D.C.: Brookings Institution Press, 2011), 91–125, for an overview of the humanitarian system. See Hugo Slim, "International Humanitarianism's Engagement with Civil War in the 1990s," *Journal of Humanitarian Assistance* (June 2002), and David Chandler, "The Road to Military Humanitarianism: How the Human Rights NGOs Shaped a New Humanitarian Agenda," *Human Rights Quarterly* 23 (August 2001): 678–700, for a discussion of the development of rights-based humanitarianism.

28. WHO, "WHO Definition of Palliative Care," http://www.who.int/cancer/palliative/definition/en/.

29. Marc Dubois, "Protection: The New Humanitarian Fig-Leaf," presented to the conference Protecting People in Conflict and Crisis, Refugee Studies Centre, Oxford University, 22–24 September 2009, 2, http://www.rsc.ox.ac.uk/pdfs/endnotemarkdubois.pdf

30. Nicholas Berry argues that the ICRC actually works to undermine the institution of war itself, although David Forsythe denies there is any evidence of such a policy on the part of the ICRC. Nicholas O. Berry, *War and the Red Cross: The Unspoken Mission* (New York: St. Martin's, 1997); Forsythe, *The Humanitarians*.

31. Alex de Waal, *Famine Crimes: Politics and the Disaster Relief Industry in Africa* (Woodbridge: James Currey, 1997).

32. Kurt Mills, "The Postmodern Tank of the Humanitarian International," *Peace Review* 18 (April–June 2006): 261–67.

33. Michael Hardt and Antonio Negri, *Empire* (Cambridge, Mass: Harvard University Press, 2000), 36.

34. Barnett and Weiss, "Humanitarianism," 29.

35. Mary Kaldor, *New and Old Wars: Organized Violence in a Global Era*, 2nd ed. (Stanford, Calif.: Stanford University Press, 2007).

36. Barnett and Snyder, "The Grand Strategies of Humanitarianism," 143.

37. Eric K. Leonard and Steven C. Roach, "From Realism to Legalization: A Rationalist Assessment of the International Criminal Court in the Democratic Republic of Congo," in *Governance, Order and the International Criminal Court: Between Realpolitik and a Cosmopolitan Court*, ed. Steven C. Roach (Oxford: Oxford University Press, 2009), 59–63 .

38. Steven R. Ratner, Jason S. Abrams, and James L. Bischoff, *Accountability for Human Rights Atrocities in International Law* (Oxford: Oxford University Press), 6.

39. Benjamin N. Schiff, *Building the International Criminal Court* (Cambridge: Cambridge University Press, 2008), 24–25; Ratner et al., *Accountability for Human Rights Atrocities in International Law*, 6.

40. Raphael Lemkin, *Axis Rule in Occupied Europe: Laws of Occupation, Analysis of Government, Proposals for Redress* (Washington, D.C.: Carnegie Endowment for World Peace, 1944).

41. Prosecutors did use the term, however. William A. Schabas, *An Introduction to the International Criminal Court*, 4th ed. (Cambridge: Cambridge University Press, 2011), 99.

42. Literally "guilty mind."

43. Schabas, *An Introduction to the International Criminal Court*, 8–10.

44. Samantha Power, *"A Problem from Hell": America and the Age of Genocide* (New York: Perennial, 2002), 288.

45. James C. Hathaway, "New Directions to Avoid Hard Problems: The Distortion of the Palliative Role of Refugee Protection," *Journal of Refugee Studies* 8, 3 (1995): 288–94; Jennifer Hyndman, "Preventive, Palliative, or Punitive? Safe Spaces in Bosnia-Herzegovina, Somalia, and Sri Lanka," *Journal of Refugee Studies* 16, 2 (2003): 167–85.

46. Power, *"A Problem from Hell"*, 391–441.

47. The Princeton Principles on Universal Jurisdiction, Princeton Project on Universal Jurisdiction, 28 (2001), http://lapa.princeton.edu/hosteddocs/unive_jur.pdf.

48. Julia Geneuss, "Fostering a Better Understanding of Universal Jurisdiction: A Comment on the AU-EU Expert Report on the Principle of Universal Jurisdiction," *Journal of International Criminal Justice* 7, 5 (2009): 946.

49. Naomi Roht-Arriaza, *The Pinochet Effect: Transnational Justice* (Philadelphia: University of Pennsylvania Press, 2006).

50. Christopher C. Jalloh, "Universal Jurisdiction, Universal Prescription? A Preliminary Assessment of the African Union Perspective on Universal Jurisdiction," *Criminal Law Forum* 21, 1 (2010): 15–16. See also *AU-EU Technical Ad Hoc Expert Group on the Principle of Universal Jurisdiction Report* (15 April 2009), http://www.africa-union.org/.

51. Kurt Mills, "'Bashir Is Dividing Us': Africa and the International Criminal Court," *Human Rights Quarterly* 34, 3 (2012): 404–47.

52. Jalloh, "Universal Jurisdiction, Universal Prescription?" 56.

53. Schabas, *An Introduction to the International Criminal Court*, 18, 21.

54. For more on the creation of the ICC see Schiff, *Building the International Criminal Court*; Schabas, *An Introduction to the International Criminal Court*; Eric Leonard, *The Onset of Global Governance: International Relations Theory and the International Criminal Court* (Aldershot: Ashgate, 2005); Steven C. Roach, ed., *Governance, Order, and the International Criminal Court: Between Realpolitik and a Cosmopolitan Court* (Oxford: Oxford University Press, 2009).

55. While the crime of aggression was included in the Rome Statute, the Court's jurisdiction was suspended until the states parties agreed to a definition and the scope of application of the crime. The states parties agreed to a definition at the Review Conference of the Rome Statute in June 2010, but its actual application has been suspended until at least 2017. ICC, "Review Conference of the Rome Statute Concludes in Kampala," ICC-ASP-20100612-PR546 (12 June 2010), http://reliefweb.int/node/357833.

56. Kurt Mills and Anthony Lott, "From Rome to Darfur: Norms and Interests in U.S. Policy Toward the International Criminal Court," *Journal of Human Rights* 6, 4 (2007): 497–521.

57. David P. Forsythe, "U.S. Foreign Policy and Human Rights: Situating Obama," *Human Rights Quarterly* 33, 3 (2011): 785; Alexander Dukalskis and Robert C. Johansen, "Measuring Acceptance of International Enforcement of Human Rights: The United States, Asia, and the International Criminal Court," *Human Rights Quarterly* 35, 3 (2013): 593–95.

58. Author interviews.

59. ICC, Situations and Cases, http://www.icc-cpi.int/Menus.

60. ICC, Office of the Prosecutor, Report on Preliminary Examination Activities 2012 (November 2012): 42–43, http://www.icc-cpi.int/iccdocs.

61. Marlise Simons, "Karadzic Accuses His Accusers," *New York Times*, 2 August 2008.

62. Kurt Mills and Cian O'Driscoll, "From Humanitarian Intervention to the Responsibility to Protect," in *The International Studies Encyclopedia*, ed. Robert A. Denemark (London: Wiley-Blackwell), 2532–52.

63. Gary J. Bass, *Freedom's Battle: The Origins of Humanitarian Intervention* (New York: Knopf, 2008).

64. Kurt Mills, *Human Rights in the Emerging Global Order: A New Sovereignty?* (Basingstoke: Macmillan, 1998), 135–36; Nicholas J. Wheeler, *Saving Strangers: Humanitarian Intervention in International Society* (Oxford: Oxford University Press, 2000), 55–136.

65. Kaldor, *New and Old Wars*.

66. Cited in Mills, *Human Rights in the Emerging Global Order*, 147–48.

67. Wheeler, *Saving Strangers*, 141–43.

68. Kurt Mills, "United Nations Intervention in Refugee Crises After the Cold War," *International Politics* 35 (December 1998): 391–424.

69. Roberts, "NATO's 'Humanitarian War' over Kosovo," 113.

70. Kofi Annan, "Two Concepts of Sovereignty," *Economist* 352 (18 September 1999); Francis Deng, *Sovereignty as Responsibility: Crisis Management in Africa* (Washington, D.C.: Brookings Institution, 1996); Mills, *Human Rights in the Emerging Global Order*; Thomas G. Weiss and Jarat Chopra, "Sovereignty Is No Longer Sacrosanct: Codifying Humanitarian Intervention," *Ethics & International Affairs* 6 (1992): 95–117.

71. International Commission on Intervention and State Sovereignty (ICISS), *The Responsibility to Protect* (Ottawa: International Development Research Centre, 2001).

72. High-level Panel on Threats, Challenges and Change, *A More Secure World: Our Shared Responsibility*, United Nations, 2004, http://www.un.org/secureworld/.

73. Kofi Annan, *In Larger Freedom: Towards Development, Security and Human Rights for All*, Report of the Secretary-General, United Nations, 2005 A/59/2005, http://www.un.org/larger freedom/.

74. UNGA, 2005 World Summit Outcome.

75. See Alex Bellamy, *Responsibility to Protect* (Cambridge: Polity Press, 2009), 98–131, for a critique of prevention.

76. Ibid., 106–30.

77. Bellamy, *Responsibility to Protect*, 42.

78. Frequently humanitarian practitioners label their activities *interventions*. However, for conceptual clarity, it is necessary to separate forceful actions from nonforceful ones. The former can be undertaken only by states and state-based entities, while the latter can be undertaken by a much wider variety of entities. Further, the former usually indicate a violation of sovereignty, while the latter frequently (although not always) do not. See Mills, *Human Rights in the Emerging Global Order*, 128–30. A commonly cited definition of humanitarian intervention comes from Holzgrefe: "the threat or use of force across borders by a state (or group of states) aimed at preventing or ending widespread and grave violations of the fundamental human rights of individuals other than its own citizens, without the permission of the state within whose territory force is applied." J. L. Holzgrefe, "The Humanitarian Intervention Debate," in *Humanitarian Intervention: Ethical, Legal and Political Dilemmas*, ed. J. L. Holzgrefe and Robert O. Keohane (Cambridge: Cambridge University Press, 2003), 18.

79. There is concern, however, that legal protection has been undermined as UNHCR has expanded its operational capacity to provide humanitarian assistance. Gil Loescher, "UNHCR and the Erosion of Refugee Protection," *Forced Migration Review* 10 (April 2001): 28–30.

80. Forsythe, *The Humanitarians*, 168.

81. Sophia Swithern, "Reclaiming Mainstreaming: Oxfam GB's Protection Approach in DRC," *Humanitarian Exchange Magazine* 39 (June 2008), http://www.odihpn.org/humanitarian -exchange-magazine/issue-39/reclaiming-mainstreaming-oxfam-gbs-protection-approach-in -drc. Or, see Bennett, who defines protection as "efforts that improve the safety of civilians exposed to widespread threats of violence, coercion or deliberate deprivation." Nicki Bennett, "International Peacekeeping Missions and Civilian Protection Mandates—Oxfam's Experience in Sudan, the Democratic Republic of Congo, Chad, and Somalia," Oxfam (September 2009): 1.

82. Oxfam International, "OI Policy Compendium Note on the Provision of Aid by Foreign Military Forces" (April 2012), http://oxfamilibrary.openrepository.com/oxfam.

83. Raymond Paternoster, "How Much Do We Really Know About Criminal Deterrence?" *Journal of Criminal Law & Criminology* 100 (2010): 765–823.

84. Author interviews.

85. Christopher Lamont, *International Criminal Justice and the Politics of Compliance* (Farnham: Ashgate, 2010).

86. By observers I mean the UN Security Council.

87. Victoria Holt and Glyn Taylor, with Max Kelly, *Protecting Civilians in the Context of UN Peacekeeping Operations: Successes, Setbacks and Remaining Challenges*, independent study jointly commissioned by UN Department of Peacekeeping Operations and Office for the Co-ordination of Humanitarian Affairs (November 2009) (New York: United Nations, 2009), 72; also available at Peacekeeping Resource Hub (http://www.unprh.unlb.org) and Reliefweb (http://www.reliefweb.int).

88. Quoted in ibid., 1.

89. Ibid., 73.

90. Bennett, "International Peacekeeping Missions and Civilian Protection Mandates," 4–5.

91. Quoted in Ferris, *The Politics of Protection*, 17.

92. "Glossary of Humanitarian Terms in Relation to the Protection of Civilians in Armed Conflict," OCHA, December 2003, 25, http://ochaonline.un.org.

93. Holt and Taylor, *Protecting Civilians in the Context of UN Peacekeeping Operations*, 192.

94. UNSC Resolution 1325 (31 October 2000); UNSC Resolution 1820 (19 June 2008).

95. UNSC Resolution 1261 (25 August 1999); UNSC Resolution 1612 (26 July 2005); UNSC Resolution 1998 (12 July 2011).

96. Sierra Leone (UNAMSIL), the Democratic Republic of the Congo (MONUC), Liberia (UNMIL), Côte d'Ivoire (UNOCI), Burundi (ONUB), Haiti (MINUSTAH), Sudan (UNMIS), Darfur, Sudan (UNAMID), Chad and the Central African Republic (MINURCAT), and Lebanon (UNIFIL).

97. The Interim Emergency Multinational Force in Bunia, Operation Artemis, in the Democratic Republic of the Congo (DRC); Operation Licorne in Côte d'Ivoire; ECOWAS in Côte d'Ivoire (ECOMICI); the African Union in Darfur, Sudan (AMIS); Eufor R.D. Congo in DRC; and the 2007 European Union operation in Chad (EUFOR).

98. See Holt and Taylor, *Protecting Civilians in the Context of UN Peacekeeping Operations*, 42–47, 371–84, for an in-depth look at the PoC mandate language.

99. Ibid., 33–34.

100. Ibid., 44.

101. Ibid., 97–101. Indeed, Holt and Taylor point out, "DPKO does not appear to have a codified understanding of what protection of civilians actually means for planning purposes" (144).

102. Author interviews.

103. Author interviews.

104. Author interviews.

105. Author interviews.

106. Dubois, "Protection: The New Humanitarian Fig-Leaf;" Ferris, *The Politics of Protection*, 79.

107. There were 122 as of 1 May 2013.

108. Eric Dachy, "Justice and Humanitarian Action: A Conflict of Interest," in *In the Shadow of "Just Wars": Violence, Politics and Humanitarian Action*, ed. Fabrice Weissman (London: Hurst, 2004), 316–17. Some will deny that they have any specific knowledge prosecutors may not already have access to. Further, there are questions about the usefulness of information provided by humanitarian organizations. The head of the DRC investigation team, Bernard Lavigne, noted that "the gap between the assessment of the humanitarian groups and the evidence was sort of a surprise," and William Pace, head of the Coalition for the International Criminal Court, observed that "human-rights and humanitarian organizations are lousy criminal investigators. They are not producing forensic evidence that can be used by a prosecutor." Quoted in Jess Bravin, "For Global Court, Ugandan Rebels Prove Tough Test," *Wall Street Journal*, 8 June 2006.

109. Some of the biggest supporters of the ICC were humanitarian organizations, such as MSF. Dachy, "Justice and Humanitarian Action," 322.

110. Ibid., 321–22.

111. Ibid., 318.

112. Gabor Rona, "The ICRC Privilege Not to Testify: Confidentiality in Action," *International Review of the Red Cross* 845 (2002).

113. Dachy, "Justice and Humanitarian Action," 322–23.

114. Such as was the case with the U.S. in Somalia, or Belgium in Rwanda.

115. Roberto Belloni, "The Tragedy of Darfur and the Limits of the 'Responsibility to Protect,'" *Ethnopolitics* 5, 4 (2006): 327–46; Alan Kuperman, "Suicidal Rebellions and the Moral Hazard of Humanitarian Intervention," *Ethnopolitics* 4, 2 (2005): 149–73.

Chapter 2. Rwanda: The Failure of "Never Again"

Epigraphs: President Bill Clinton, quoted in James Bennett, "Clinton in Africa: The Overview; Clinton Declares U.S., with World, Failed Rwandans," *New York Times*, 26 March 1998; UN Secretary-General Kofi Annan, "Secretary-General, in 'Mission of Healing' to Rwanda, Pledges Support of United Nations for Country's Search for Peace and Progress," press release, SG/SM/6552 AFR/56 (6 May 1998).

1. Michael Barnett, *Eyewitness to a Genocide* (Ithaca, N.Y.: Cornell University Press, 2002); Roméo Dallaire, *Shake Hands with the Devil: The Failure of Humanity in Rwanda* (New York: Carol & Graf, 2005); Alan J. Kuperman, *The Limits of Humanitarian Intervention: Genocide in Rwanda* (Washington, D.C.: Brookings Institution Press, 2001); Linda Melvern, *Conspiracy to Murder: The Rwandan Genocide*, rev. ed. (London: Verso, 2006); Samantha Power, *"A Problem from Hell": America and the Age of Genocide* (New York: Perennial, 2003), 329–89; Gérard Prunier, *The Rwanda Crisis* (London: Hurst, 1995).

2. Melvern, *Conspiracy to Murder*, 5–11.

3. Ibid., 13–19.

4. Dallaire had been head of the UN Observer Mission Uganda-Rwanda, which was created to support a ceasefire; ibid., 65.

5. Barnett, *Eyewitness to a Genocide*, 34–48.

6. Ibid., 71.

7. Melvern, *Conspiracy to Murder*, 73–74.

8. Indeed, plans were begun after the 1990 attack from Uganda; ibid., 20.

9. Dallaire, *Shake Hands with the Devil*, 141–46. This followed other reports of massacres at the end of 2003.

10. Ibid., 146.

11. Melvern, *Conspiracy to Murder*, 97–98.

12. Dallaire, *Shake Hands with the Devil*, 167.

13. Barnett, *Eyewitness to a Genocide*, 87–89.

14. Barrie Collins, "Shooting Down the 'Truth' About Rwanda," *Spiked*, 16 April 2012, http://www.spiked-online.com.

15. Peter Robinson and Golriz Ghahraman, "Can Rwandan President Kagame Be Held Responsible at the ICTR for the Killing of President Habyarimana?" *Journal of International Criminal Justice* 6, 5 (2008): 981–94.

16. "Rwandan Genocide: Kagame 'Cleared of Habyarimana Crash,'" *BBC News*, 10 January 2012.

17. Barnett, *Eyewitness to a Genocide*, 104.

18. Dallaire, *Shake Hands with the Devil*, 298.

19. Ibid., 289.

20. Power, *"A Problem from Hell"*, 350.

21. Scott R. Feil, "Preventing Genocide: How the Early Use of Force Might Have Succeeded in Rwanda," report to Carnegie Commission on Preventing Deadly Conflict (April 1998), http://carnegie.org/fileadmin/Media/Publications.

22. Kiran Moodley, "Bill Clinton: We Could Have Saved 300,000 Lives in Rwanda," *CNBC*, 13 March 2013.

23. Barnett, *Eyewitness to a Genocide*, 106; Dallaire, *Shake Hands with the Devil*, 298.

24. Power, *"A Problem from Hell"*, 364-70; Melvern, *Conspiracy to Murder*, 218.

25. Dallaire, *Shake Hands with the Devil*, 295.

26. Melvern, *Conspiracy to Murder*, 203.

27. Ibid., 226, 240.

28. Indeed, France had seen the 1990 invasion as an "Anglo-Saxon" plot. Prunier, *The Rwanda Crisis*, 106.

29. Power, *"A Problem from Hell"*, 352-53.

30. Melvern, *Conspiracy to Murder*, 202.

31. Power, *"A Problem from Hell"*, 357.

32. Melvern, *Conspiracy to Murder*, 202.

33. UNSC Resolution 912.

34. Barnett, *Eyewitness to a Genocide*, 127-28.

35. "The Triumph of Evil," *Frontline* (26 January 1999).

36. "Bill Clinton: We Could Have Saved 300,000 Lives in Rwanda."

37. Kuperman, *The Limits of Humanitarian Intervention*, 24.

38. Power, *"A Problem from Hell"*, 366.

39. Ibid., 358-64; Melvern, *Conspiracy to Murder*, 223-24.

40. Barnett, *Eyewitness to a Genocide*, 138; Power, *"A Problem from Hell"*, 363-64.

41. David Corn, "Lying About Rwanda's Genocide," *The Nation*, 2 April 2004.

42. Melvern, *Conspiracy to Murder*, 223.

43. Power, *"A Problem from Hell"*, 358.

44. Quoted in Melvern, *Conspiracy to Murder*, 225.

45. Power, *"A Problem from Hell"*, 357.

46. Melvern, *Conspiracy to Murder*, 223; Barnett, *Eyewitness to a Genocide*, 134.

47. Quoted in Power, *"A Problem from Hell"*, 359.

48. Ibid., 365.

49. Quoted in ibid., 364.

50. John C. Hammock and Joel R. Charny, "Emergency Response as Morality Play: The Media, the Relief Agencies, and the Need for Capacity Building," in *From Massacres to Genocide: The Media, Public Policy, and Humanitarian Crises*, ed. Robert I. Rotberg and Thomas G. Weiss (Washington, D.C.: Brookings Institution, 1996), 120-21; Noam Schimmel, "An Invisible Genocide: How the Western Media Failed to Report the 1994 Rwandan Genocide of the Tutsi and Why," *International Journal of Human Rights* 15, 7 (2011): 1125-35.

51. "Cold Choices in Rwanda," *New York Times*, 23 April 1994.

52. Melvern, *Conspiracy to Murder*, 236.

53. Ibid.

54. Edward R. Girardet, "Reporting Humanitarianism: Are the New Electronic Media Making a Difference?" in Rotberg and Weiss, eds., *From Massacres to Genocide*, 57.

55. Melvern notes that there were never more than 15 reporters in Rwanda, whereas there were 2,500 in South Africa in early May. Linda Melvern, "Missing the Story: The Media and the Rwandan Genocide," *Contemporary Security Policy* 22, 3 (2001): 98.

56. Power, *"A Problem from Hell"*, 371-72.

57. United Nations, "Rwanda—UNAMIR Background," http://www.un.org/en/peacekeeping/; Melvern, *Conspiracy to Murder*, 238.

58. Melvern, *Conspiracy to Murder*, 237.

59. Ibid., 238–39.

60. UNSC Resolution 918 (17 May 1994).

61. Melvern, *Conspiracy to Murder*, 240.

62. Dallaire, *Shake Hands with the Devil*, 432.

63. Melvern, *Conspiracy to Murder*, 243.

64. Power, *"A Problem from Hell"*, 362.

65. UNSC, "Report of the Secretary-General on the Situation in Rwanda," S/1994/640 (31 May 1994).

66. Power, *"A Problem from Hell"*, 378.

67. Melvern, *Conspiracy to Murder*, 244.

68. Dallaire, *Shake Hands with the Devil*, 425–28; Melvern, *Conspiracy to Murder*, 247–48.

69. Quoted in Prunier, *The Rwanda Crisis*, 280.

70. Quoted in ibid., 296.

71. Prunier, *The Rwanda Crisis*, 297. Barnett cites a figure of 15,000–25,000. Barnett, *Eyewitness to a Genocide*, 149. Kuperman further claims that up to 1.5 million more refugees might have fled the country, with all the attendant possibilities for dying in the camps from disease and malnutrition, if not for the presence of the French, thus saving more Hutu than Tutsi. Kuperman, *The Limits of Humanitarian Intervention*, 50.

72. Barnett, *Eyewitness to a Genocide*, 149.

73. Feil, "Preventing Genocide"; Kuperman, *The Limits of Humanitarian Intervention*, 71.

74. The White House, "President Clinton Signs New Peacekeeping Policy," press release (5 May 1994), http://www.fas.org/irp/offdocs/pdd25.htm.

75. Power, *"A Problem from Hell"*, 378–79.

76. Barnett, *Eyewitness to a Genocide*, 167.

77. Fiona Terry, *Condemned to Repeat? The Paradox of Humanitarian Action* (Ithaca, N.Y.: Cornell University Press, 2002), 171.

78. Author interviews.

79. Quoted in Terry, *Condemned to Repeat?*, 172.

80. Obviously, this was a scaling back of ambitions from the Operation Restore Hope of Somalia. Perhaps the U.S. realized it could not bring the hope themselves, but rather could only serve as a prop for hope which, as the self-help gurus will tell us, can only come from within. In this way, the refugees must support their own hope—hope that they will survive the cancer of chaos—and the U.S. would help to maintain that delusional hope—at least for a month.

81. Terry, *Condemned to Repeat?*, 172.

82. Chronology of U.S. Government Assistance to Rwanda (as of 6 April 1994), http://www.state.gov/documents/organization/165106.pdf, 7–16.

83. U.S. Committee for Refugees, *World Refugee Survey 1997* (Washington, D.C.: U.S. Committee for Refugees, 1997), 103.

84. Joel Boutroue, "Missed Opportunities: The Role of the International Community in the Return of the Rwandan Refugees from Eastern Zaire—July 1994–December 1996," Massachusetts Institute of Technology-Center for International Studies/UNHCR, February 1998, 4.

85. Michael Agier and Françoise Bouchet-Saulnier, "Humanitarian Spaces: Spaces of Exception," in *In the Shadow of "Just Wars": Violence, Politics and Humanitarian Action*, ed. Fabrice Weissman (London: Hurst, 2004), 305.

86. Author interviews.

87. Boutroue, "Missed Opportunities," 7; Howard Adelman, "The Use and Abuse of Refugees in Zaire," in *Refugee Manipulation: War, Politics and the Abuse of Human Suffering*, ed. Stephen John Stedman and Fred Tanner (Washington, D.C.: Brookings Institution Press, 2003), 100–101.

88. Boutroue, "Missed Opportunities," 9–13.

89. Tony Waters, "The Coming Rwandan Demographic Crisis, or Why Current Repatriation Policies Will Not Solve Tanzania's (or Zaire's) Refugee Problems," *Journal of Humanitarian Assistance* 4 (July 1997).

90. They could also capitalize on a speech by an official from the Ministry of Justice who said that since there were one million people killed, the government would like to have one million people in prison. Boutroue, "Missed Opportunities," 13. For more on the situation in the prisons and continued insecurity in Rwanda. see Human Rights Watch, "Rwanda: The Crisis Continues," April 1995; and Amnesty International, "Rwanda and Burundi—The Return Home: Rumours and Realities," 20 February 1996.

91. Boutroue, "Missed Opportunities," 4–8.

92. Ibid., 19.

93. Dennis McNamara, Statement Before the House Committee on International Relations, Sub-Committee on International Operations and Human Rights, Hearing on "Rwanda: Genocide and the Continuing Cycle of Violence," 5 May 1998.

94. UNHCR, "Impact of Military Personnel and the Militia Presence in Rwandese Refugee Camps and Settlements," prepared for the "Regional Conference on Assistance to Refugees, Returnees and Displaced Persons in the Great Lakes Region," Bujumbura, 12–17 February 1995, 5.

95. Boutroue, "Missed Opportunities," 20–21.

96. For a discussion of the legal status of the principle of voluntary protection, see Michael Barutciski, "Involuntary Repatriation When Refugee Protection Is No Longer Necessary: Moving Forward After the 48th Session of the Executive Committee," *International Journal of Refugee Law* 10, 1–2 (1998): 247–51.

97. Quoted in McNamara, Statement Before the House Committee on International Relations.

98. Ibid.

99. Ibid.

100. Terry, *Condemned to Repeat?*, 195.

101. Kurt Mills, "Neo-Humanitarianism: The Role of International Humanitarian Norms and Organizations in Contemporary Conflict," 173.

102. Terry, *Condemned to Repeat?*, 197.

103. Ibid., 200–205.

104. Author interviews.

105. McNamara, Statement Before the House Committee on International Relations; Boutroue, "Missed Opportunities," 41–22.

106. It is interesting to note similar situations elsewhere. For example, in Ngara, Tanzania, UNHCR also paid for the police presence, and the public face is similar. The district commissioner, for example, stated that "they [UNHCR] are our employers" and that UNHCR and the police are "sailing in one boat." At the same time, however, the police withhold information from UNHCR and do not always act in UNHCR's interest. Further, blame is always put on UNHCR for any problems because of a lack of resources that they say are needed from UNHCR. Author interviews.

107. Author interviews.

108. In fact, some familiar with the situation argue that a UN peacekeeping operation would not have been able to do any better with the same mandate—that is, without a mandate to separate intimidators, which, throughout the entire crisis, was never seriously in the offing. Author interviews.

109. Roger Winter, "Lancing the Boil: Rwanda's Agenda in Zaire," in *War and Peace in Zaire/Congo*, ed. Howard Adelman and Govind C. Rao (Trenton, N.J.: Africa World Press, 2004), 111–12.

110. Boutroue, "Missed Opportunities," 42–47. A similar agreement was also signed with the government of Tanzania. UNHCR, "Impact of Military Personnel," 9–10.

111. Stephanie T. E. Klein-Ahlbrandt, "The Kibeho Crisis: Towards a More Effective System of International Protection for IDPs," *Forced Migration Review* 2 (August 1998): 9; Adelman, "The Use and Abuse of Refugees in Zaire," 106.

112. Human Rights Watch/Arms Project, *Rwanda/Zaire: Rearming with Impunity; International Support for the Perpetrators of the Rwandan Genocide.* Washington, D.C., 1995.

113. Boutroue, "Missed Opportunities," 47–48; McNamara, Statement Before the House Committee on International Relations.

114. McNamara, Statement Before the House Committee on International Relations.

115. Boutroue, "Missed Opportunities," 48–50. The local officials had so little support from the government that at one point they requested (only partly seriously) that UNHCR loan them some trucks (which UNHCR refused to do) because they did not have enough money to rent the trucks necessary to carry out the expulsions (49).

116. Ibid., 48.

117. Ibid., 49–51.

118. Ibid., 51.

119. Ibid.

120. Ibid., 52–53.

121. Ibid., 54–55.

122. Ibid., 56–59.

123. For a brief overview of the so-called Kivu Crisis in mid- to late 1996, see Gérard Prunier, "The Geopolitical Situation in the Great Lakes Area in Light of the Kivu Crisis," WRITENET Country Papers, UNHCR, February 1997, http://www.unhcr.ch/refworld/country/writenet /wridrc.htm. On the ADFL, see William Cyrus Reed, "Guerrillas in the Midst: The Former Government of Rwanda and the Alliance of Democratic Forces for the Liberation of Congo-Zaire in Eastern Zaire," in *African Guerrillas*, ed. Christopher Clapham (Bloomington: Indiana University Press, 1998), 145–50.

124. Quoted in McNamara, Statement Before the House Committee on International Relations.

125. Ibid.

126. Boutroue, "Missed Opportunities," 24.

127. Quoted in Simon Massey, "Operation Assurance: The Greatest Intervention That Never Happened," *Journal of Humanitarian Assistance* (February 1998), http://sites.tufts.edu/jha/archives/123.

128. Massey, "Operation Assurance."

129. Ibid.

130. Ibid.

131. Quoted in ibid.

132. UNSC Resolution 1078.

133. UNSC Resolution 1080.

134. In fact, the Canadian government explicitly rejected this possibility.

135. This was a further diminution in aspiration from Operation Restore Hope and Operation Support Hope. What exactly was to be assured, except, perhaps, the resumption of humanitarian aid for a short period?

136. The UK and France also offered troops, as did some African countries. Massey, "Operation Assurance."

137. For more on Operation Assurance, see Howard Adelman and Laurence J. Baxter, "The Multi-National Force for Eastern Zaire: The Conception, Planning and Termination of OP Assurance," in Adelman and Rao, eds., *War and Peace in Zaire/Congo*.

138. Boutroue, "Missed Opportunities," McNamara, Statement Before the House Committee on International Relations; author interviews.

139. McNamara, Statement Before the House Committee on International Relations.

140. Lieutenant Colonel Thomas P. Odom, "Guerrillas from the Mist: A Defense Attaché Watches the Rwandan Patriotic Front Transform from Insurgent to Counter Insurgent," *Small Wars Journal* 5 (July 2006).

141. Linda Melvern, *A People Betrayed: The Role of the West in Rwanda's Genocide* (London: Zed Books, 2009), 253–54.

142. Victor Peskin, *International Justice in Rwanda and the Balkans* (Cambridge: Cambridge University Press, 2008), 159–160.

143. William A. Schabas, "Genocide Trials and *Gacaca* Courts," *Journal of International Criminal Justice* 3, 4 (2005): 880.

144. In November 1994 there were only twenty lawyers with formal legal education. Ibid., 883.

145. Peskin, *International Justice in Rwanda and the Balkans*, 157–58.

146. Ibid., 161–67.

147. Harmen van der Wildt, "Universal Jurisdiction Under Attack," *Journal of International Criminal Justice* 9, 5 (2011): 1061–62.

148. For an in-depth discussion of these dynamics, see Peskin, *International Justice in Rwanda and the Balkans*, 151–31.

149. Ibid., 210.

150. Charles Mironko and Peter Uvin, "Western and Local Approaches to Justice in Rwanda," *Global Governance* 9, 2 (2003): 220.

151. When Richard Goldstone, the first Prosecutor, wanted to go to Rwanda to establish a dialogue with the Rwandan government, the UN refused to pay for his flight. Switzerland, a nonmember country at the time, agreed to fund his travel. Peskin, *International Justice in Rwanda and the Balkans*, 171.

152. Melvern, *Conspiracy to Murder*, 255.

153. Mironko and Uvin, "Western and Local Approaches to Justice in Rwanda"; Schabas, "Genocide Trials and *Gacaca* Courts," 891.

154. Erin Daly, "Between Punitive and Reconstructive Justice: The Gacaca Courts in Rwanda," *New York University Journal of International Law and Politics* 34 (2002): 372.

155. Ibid., 355–96.

156. Ibid., 382.

157. Bert Ingelaere, "Does the Truth Pass Across the Fire Without Burning? Locating the Short Circuit in Rwanda's Gacaca Courts," *Journal of Modern African Studies* 47, 4 (2009): 507–28.

158. Max Rettig, "Gacaca: Truth, Justice, and Reconciliation in Postconflict Rwanda?" *African Studies Review* 51, 3 (2008): 25–50.

Chapter 3. Democratic Republic of the Congo: Protecting Civilians?

Epigraphs: Aldo Ajello, EU representative for the Great Lakes, quoted in François Ngolet, *Crisis in the Congo: The Rise and Fall of Laurent Kabila* (New York: Palgrave Macmillan, 2011), 67; UN, "Report of the Panel on United Nations Peace Operations," A/55/305-S/2000/809 (21 August 2000), 9; Michiel Hofman, Médecins sans Frontières, quoted in Nicholas Kulish and Somini Sengupta, "New U.N. Brigade's Aggressive Stance in Africa Brings Success, Risks," *New York Times*, 12 November 2013.

1. A comprehensive report published by the Office of the UNHCHR in 2010 documents in exhaustive detail this human misery. UNHCHR, *Democratic Republic of the Congo, 1993–2003:*

Report of the Mapping Exercise Documenting the Most Serious Violations of Human Rights and International Humanitarian Law Committed Within the Territory of the Democratic Republic of the Congo Between March 1993 and June 2003 (August 2010), http://www.ohchr.org/.

2. Virgil Hawkins, "Stealth Conflicts: Africa's World War in the DRC and International Consciousness," *Journal of Humanitarian Assistance* (January 2004).

3. Gerald Caplan, "Peacekeepers Gone Wild: How Much More Abuse Will the UN Ignore in Congo?" *Globe and Mail*, 3 August 2012.

4. Vava Tampa, "DR Congo: We Are All Implicated in the Carnage—We Can No Longer Ignore It," *The Guardian*, 10 October 2013.

5. Séverine Autesserre, *The Trouble with the Congo: Local Violence and the Failure of International Peacebuilding* (Cambridge: Cambridge University Press, 2010).

6. Gérard Prunier, *From Genocide to Continental War* (London: Hurst, 2009), 320.

7. Ibid., 330.

8. Filip Reyntjens, *The Great African War: Congo and Regional Geopolitics, 1996–2006* (Cambridge: Cambridge University Press, 2009), 102–7.

9. Ibid., 125.

10. Ibid., 130.

11. Ibid., 144–53.

12. Ibid., 166–69.

13. Ibid., 173–83.

14. Marc Le Pape, "Democratic Republic of Congo: Victims of No Importance," in *In the Shadow of "Just Wars": Violence, Politics and Humanitarian Action*, ed. Fabrice Weissman (London: Hurst, 2004), 211.

15. ICG, "The Kivus: The Forgotten Crucible of the Congo Conflict," (24 January 2003), 23–26; Reyntjens, *The Great African War*, 225–30.

16. For a more in-depth discussion of the various groups involved, see Prunier, *From Genocide to Continental War*, 181–203; Reyntjens, *Great African War*, 194–207, 238–44; Philip Roessler and John Prendergast, "Democratic Republic of the Congo," in *Twenty-First-Century Peace Operations*, ed. William Durch (Washington, D.C.: U.S. Institute of Peace, 2006), 236–43; Christian Scherrer, *Genocide and Crisis in Central Africa: Conflict Roots, Mass Violence, and Regional War* (Westport, Conn.: Praeger, 2002), 259–62. On the role of external actors, see John F. Clark, ed., *The African Stakes of the Congo War* (New York: Palgrave Macmillan, 2002).

17. Séverine Autesserre reminds us that the lack of authority in a Hobbesian state of nature does not necessarily lead to killing, and further that this understanding of the conflict perpetuated the belief that people in the Congo were inherently violent. This is true. However, the description still seems apt. Autesserre, *The Trouble with the Congo*, 68–72.

18. Dunn notes that this title is misleading, since it assumes a state-centric understanding of the war. Kevin C. Dunn, *Imagining the Congo: The International Relations of Identity* (New York: Palgrave Macmillan, 2003), 167–68.

19. Le Pape, "Democratic Republic of Congo," 215–18; Ngolet, *Crisis in the Congo*, 39–52.

20. Ngolet, *Crisis in the Congo*, 51.

21. Ibid., 40.

22. UNSC Resolution 1097.

23. UNSC Resolution 1161.

24. UNSC Resolutions 1170, 1196, 1197.

25. UNSC, "Report of the Secretary-General on Protection for Humanitarian Assistance to Refugees and Others in Conflict Situations," S/1998/883 (22 September 1998), 4–5.

26. For a discussion of the Lusaka peace process, see Ngolet, *Crisis in the Congo*, 68–79.

27. Roessler and Prendergast, "Democratic Republic of the Congo," 245–49.

28. Ngolet, *Crisis in the Congo*, 91.

29. This in the context of a UN report eight months earlier that to be credible and effective a peacekeeping force would require 100,000 troops. Roessler and Prendergast, "Democratic Republic of the Congo," 259.

30. Holt and Taylor, *Protecting Civilians in the Context of UN Peacekeeping Operations*, 243.

31. Ibid., 244.

32. UNSC, "Report of the Secretary-General on the United Nations Organization Mission in the Democratic Republic of the Congo," S/2000/30 (17 January 2000): 7.

33. Ibid., 13.

34. Ibid.

35. The first was the UN Mission in Sierra Leone (UNAMSIL) (1999–2005).

36. UN, "Report of the Panel on United Nations Peace Operations," 9.

37. Senator John Warner expressed concern about funds being used in Bosnia and Kosovo "being diverted to the African continent." Roessler and Prendergast, "Democratic Republic of the Congo," 251.

38. Prunier, *From Genocide to Continental War*, 247.

39. Roessler and Prendergast, "Democratic Republic of the Congo," 250–53.

40. As we shall see, this was more than three years in coming.

41. Roessler and Prendergast, "Democratic Republic of the Congo," 230. By the end of November 2000, only 245 observers were deployed. Ngolet, *Crisis in the Congo*, 97.

42. Roessler and Prendergast, "Democratic Republic of the Congo," 264–65.

43. UNSC Resolution 1332; emphasis in original.

44. Reyntjens, *The Great African War*, 252–55; ICG, "The Inter-Congolese Dialogue: Political Negotiations of Game of Bluff," (16 November 2001). See also Ngolet, *Crisis in the Congo*, 98–105.

45. Ngolet, *Crisis in the Congo*, 107–26.

46. See ibid., 139–40.

47. UNSC Resolution 1341.

48. UNSC, "Sixth Report of the Secretary-General on the United Nations Organization Mission in the Democratic Republic of the Congo," S/2001/128 (12 February 2001): 11.

49. Ibid., 8.

50. Ibid., 7.

51. By the time of Kabila's assassination there were only 500 peacekeepers deployed. Ngolet, *Crisis in the Congo*, 182.

52. Ibid., 204–214.

53. UNSC Resolution 1445. For details of some of the killing, see Ngolet, *Crisis in the Congo*, 222–23.

54. Roessler and Prendergast, "Democratic Republic of the Congo," 272.

55. Holt and Taylor, *Protecting Civilians in the Context of UN Peacekeeping Operations*, 248.

56. Roessler and Prendergast, "Democratic Republic of the Congo," 272; Holt and Taylor, *Protecting Civilians in the Context of UN Peacekeeping Operations*, 248–49.

57. Prunier, *From Genocide to Continental War*, 271.

58. UNSC, "Eleventh Report of the Secretary-General on the United Nations Organization Mission in the Democratic Republic of the Congo," S/2002/621 (5 June 2002): 11.

59. Ibid.

60. Representing 90 percent of Rwandan forces in the DRC. Le Pape, "Victims of No Importance," 214.

61. Roessler and Prendergast, "Democratic Republic of the Congo," 275–77.

62. Ibid., 278.

63. Ibid, 278–79.

64. Prunier, *From Genocide to Continental War*, 300.

65. Refugees International, "Eastern Congo: Beyond the Volcano, a Slow Motion Holocaust" (1 January 2002), http://www.kongo-kinshasa.de/dokumentef.

66. UNSC, "Twelfth Report of the Secretary-General on the United Nations Organization Mission in the Democratic Republic of Congo," S/2002/1180 (18 October 2002): 10–11.

67. Ibid., 13.

68. Ibid.

69. Ibid., 11.

70. HRW, "Ituri: 'Covered in Blood': Ethnically Targeted Violence in Northeastern DR Congo" (July 2003): 1, http://www.hrw.org/reports. Autesserre points out, however, that while Ituri became emblematic of violence in the DRC, other parts, especially the Kivus, experienced widespread violence. Autesserre, *The Trouble with the Congo*, 115.

71. ICG, "Congo Crisis: Military Intervention in Ituri" (13 June 2003): 8.

72. Ibid., 4.

73. For more on the Hema/Lendu conflict, see Ngolet, *Crisis in the Congo*, 131–34, 215–17.

74. Autesserre, *Trouble with the Congo*, 173–74.

75. ICG, "Congo Crisis: Military Intervention in Ituri," 1.

76. Ibid., 6.

77. All the major rebel groups were, at one point or another, led by a Ugandan proxy. ICG, "Congo Crisis: Military Intervention in Ituri," 3, 8–9.

78. Although Bemba was arrested for crimes committed in the Central African Republic. See Fédération International des Ligues des Droits de l'Homme, "Central African Republic: Forgotten, Stigmatized: The Double Suffering of Victims of International Crimes," 457/2 (October 2006), http://www.fidh.org; Fédération International des Ligues des Droits de l'Homme, "FIDH and the Situation in the Central African Republic Before the International Criminal Court: The Case of Jean-Pierre Bemba Gombo," 502a (July 2008), http://www.fidh.org.

79. He was promoted to colonel in the DRC armed forces.

80. These latter two groups—FRPI and FNI—were Lendu-based armed groups, while the UPC was Hema-based. Henning Tamm, "FNI and FRPI: Local Resistance and Regional Alliances in North-Eastern Congo," Rift Valley Institute, Usalama Project (2013), http://www.refworld.org; Henning Tamm, "UPC in Ituri: The External Militarization of Local Politics in North-Eastern Congo," Rift Valley Institute, Usalama Project (2013).

81. Autesserre, *The Trouble with the Congo*, 213.

82. ICG, "Congo Crisis: Military Intervention in Ituri," 12; Prunier, *From Genocide to Continental War*, 293. Although, according to the UN, a battalion of Uruguayan troops saved at least 16,000 people, and possibly many more, in May in advance of the authorization of the IEMF. It also points out, however, that the troops did not use force proactively to protect civilians, and indeed were under the impression they could not under their mandate. UN, DPKO, "Operation Artemis: The Lessons of the Interim Emergency Multinational Force," Peacekeeping Best Practices Unit (October 2004), 7–9. However, a much more damning account comes from MONUC's first force commander, who stated that MONUC forces in Bunia "carried out their mission poorly" and acted in a "totally and unacceptable" manner. Quoted in Holt and Taylor, *Protecting Civilians in the Context of UN Peacekeeping Operations*, 251–52.

83. Victoria K. Holt and Tobias C. Berkman, *The Impossible Mandate? Military Preparedness, the Responsibility to Protect, and Modern Peace Operations* (Washington, D.C.: Stimson Center, 2006), 160–61; Médecins sans Frontières, "Ituri: Unkept Promises? A Pretense of Protection and Inadequate Assistance" (25 July 2003): 3.

84. Other troop-contributing countries included Austria, Belgium, Brazil, Canada, Cyprus, Germany, Greece, Hungary, Ireland, Italy, the Netherlands, Portugal, South Africa, Spain, Sweden, and the UK. UN, "Operation Artemis: The Lessons of the Interim Emergency Multinational Force," 4.

85. Although, as the ICG pointed out at the time, "since Bunia is currently almost uninhabited, the humanitarian impact of the intervention is likely to be limited unless civilians return massively." ICG, "Congo Crisis: Military Intervention in Ituri," 14. The emptying of the city, during which more than two-thirds of the population left, appeared to have been an organized affair. MSF, "Ituri: Unkept Promises?" 9–10.

86. UNSC Resolution 1493.

87. Holt and Taylor, *Protecting Civilians in the Context of UN Peacekeeping Operations*, 254.

88. Roessler and Prendergast, "Democratic Republic of the Congo," 285.

89. Although, on at least one occasion, it did operate farther afield. Reyntjens, *The Great African War*, 220.

90. Indeed, the UPC had 15,000 militiamen just four miles out of town. Ståle Ulriksen, Catriona Gourlay, and Catriona Mace, "Operation *Artemis*: The Shape of Things to Come?" *International Peacekeeping* 11, 3 (2004): 518.

91. UN, "Operation Artemis," 13–14.

92. Ulriksen et al., "Operation *Artemis*," 518–19.

93. Holt and Berkman, *The Impossible Mandate?* 162.

94. MSF, "Ituri: Unkept Promises?" 5.

95. Ibid., 6.

96. Indeed, one source indicates 16 massacres outside Bunia during the time of Artemis's deployment. Roessler and Prendergast, "Democratic Republic of the Congo," 285.

97. Ulriksen et al., "Operation *Artemis*," 519–20.

98. Ibid., 522.

99. Holt and Taylor, *Protecting Civilians in the Context of UN Peacekeeping Operations*, 132–33.

100. Ibid., 254.

101. Autesserre, *The Trouble with the Congo*, 214.

102. Holt and Taylor, *Protecting Civilians in the Context of UN Peacekeeping Operations*, 255.

103. Quoted in Holt and Berkman, *The Impossible Mandate?* 162.

104. Roessler and Prendergast, "Democratic Republic of the Congo," 287. It was not until 2004 that the Ituri Brigade really started to show its teeth, however. Holt and Berkman, *The Impossible Mandate?* 163.

105. ICG, "The Kivus," 2.

106. Ibid., 4.

107. Ibid., 7. Interestingly, both rebel groups and Rwandan military appeared more amenable to following international humanitarian law and respecting human rights on the territory of Rwanda than across the border in the Kivus, where there is much less observation of their actions. This might provide anecdotal evidence of the effect of international norms (8).

108. IRC, "Mortality in the Democratic Republic of Congo: Results from a Nationwide Survey" (April 2003), http://www.rescue.org/.

109. IRC, "Mortality in Eastern Democratic Republic of Congo: Results from Eleven Mortality Surveys," (2001), 19, http://www.rescue.org/.

110. Le Pape, "Victims of No Importance," 224.

111. For more on Nkunda and his role as a spoiler in the peace process, see René Lemarchand, *The Dynamics of Violence in Central Africa* (Philadelphia: University of Pennsylvania Press, 2009), 17–18.

112. Prunier, *From Genocide to Continental War*, 298. The decision to stand back was reversed after six days, but the damage had been done—both to the population and to MONUC's reputation. Tasneem Mowjee, "Humanitarian Agenda 2015 Democratic Republic of Congo Case Study," Feinstein International Center, Tufts University (October 2007), 26, https://wikis.uit.tufts.edu.

113. Holt and Berkman, *The Impossible Mandate?* 163–64.

114. Roessler and Prendergast, "Democratic Republic of the Congo," 291.

115. Holt and Taylor, *Protecting Civilians in the Context of UN Peacekeeping Operations*, 258.

116. Holt and Berkman, *The Impossible Mandate?* 169–72.

117. Holt and Taylor, *Protecting Civilians in the Context of UN Peacekeeping Operations*, 97–101. Indeed, as Holt and Taylor point out, "DPKO does not appear to have a codified understanding of what protection of civilians actually means for planning purposes" (144).

118. UNSC, "Third Special Report of the Secretary-General on the United Nations Organization Mission in the Democratic Republic of the Congo," S/2004/650 (16 August 2004): 30.

119. Roessler and Prendergast, "Democratic Republic of the Congo," 297–98; Holt and Berkman, *The Impossible Mandate?* 165.

120. Reyntjens, *The Great African War*, 208.

121. A report from August 2009 noted that "One of the most vicious and salient features of this conflict is the wide-spread sexual violence being perpetrated on the women of eastern DRC." "Characterizing Sexual Violence in the Democratic Republic of the Congo: Profiles of Violence, Community Responses, and Implications for the Protection of Women," Harvard Humanitarian Initiative/Open Society Institute (August 2009), 4.

122. It singled out the "ex-FAR and Interahamwe" as groups to be targeted, perhaps reflecting the West's continuing support for Kagame.

123. Holt and Berkman, *The Impossible Mandate?* 175. Although as Prunier observes, "MONUC did not really have the stomach for a large military offensive that seemed a bit much even for their Chapter VII mandate." Prunier, *From Genocide to Continental War*, 309.

124. Reyntjens, *The Great African War*, 210–11. The Secretary-General did note, for example, the "splintering" of the FDLR hierarchy in South Kivu as a result of joint MONUC-FADRC operations. UNSC, "Twenty-First Report of the Secretary-General on the United Nations Organization Mission in the Democratic Republic of the Congo," S/2006/390 (13 June 2006), 9.

125. Holt and Taylor, *Protecting Civilians in the Context of UN Peacekeeping Operations*, 263–64.

126. Holt and Berkman, *The Impossible Mandate?* 165–66.

127. UNSC, "Eighteenth Report of the Secretary-General on the United Nations Organization Mission in the Democratic Republic of the Congo," S/2005/506 (2 August 2005), 7.

128. Reyntjens, *The Great African War*, 221. The Secretary-General gave slightly different figures: "50 recalcitrant militia leaders with some 1,200 armed elements" still at large in Ituri. UNSC, "Eighteenth Report of the Secretary-General on the United Nations Organization Mission in the Democratic Republic of the Congo," 5.

129. UNSC, "Eighteenth Report of the Secretary-General on the United Nations Organization Mission in the Democratic Republic of the Congo," 5.

130. Reyntjens, *The Great African War*, 221.

131. Médecins sans Frontières, "Nothing New in Ituri: The Violence Continues" (August 2005), 19.

132. Ibid., 19.

133. Ibid., 3.

134. UNSC Resolution 1649.

135. Holt and Taylor, *Protecting Civilians in the Context of UN Peacekeeping Operations*, 268.

136. UNSC Resolution 1671 (25 April 2006).

137. As Norheim-Martinsen observes: "the EU troops were largely based in the capital Kinshasa, which had been pacified for some time. None were deployed to the eastern parts of the DRC where trouble was more likely to occur." Martin Norheim-Martinsen, "Our Work Here Is Done: European Union Peacekeeping in Africa," *African Security Review* 20 (June 2011), 22.

138. FEWER International, "Elections, Instability and EUFOR: Recommendations for Securing the Peace in the DRC" (no date), http://www.fewer-international.org/images/lib/Elections.

139. Autesserre, *The Trouble with the Congo*, 65–66.

140. Indeed, several years later it was observed that the "'post-conflict' label remains inadequate." "Dynamics of Conflict and Forced Migration in the Democratic Republic of Congo," report of an experts workshop, Refugee Studies Centre (January 2011), 1, http://www.rsc.ox.ac.uk /pdfs/. This is reminiscent of the "postconflict label" put on Afghanistan from 2002, even though it has been obvious in the years since—and should have been obvious at the time—that it was still in the midst of conflict. Vicky Tennant, "UNHCR's Engagement with Integrated UN Missions: Report of a Lessons Learned Workshop," UNHCR Policy Development and Evaluation Service, PDES/2009/04 (August 2009), 8.

141. Autesserre, *The Trouble with the Congo*, 103.

142. Ibid., 111–13.

143. Roessler and Prendergast, "Democratic Republic of the Congo," 305.

144. Or, indeed, to enforce peace in eastern DRC. ICG, "The Kivus: The Forgotten Crucible of the Congo Conflict," 31.

145. An interesting turnabout from Afghanistan, Iraq, and elsewhere where humanitarians serve as "force multipliers" for the military.

146. MONUC officer, quoted in Holt and Berkman, *The Impossible Mandate?* 173.

147. Mowjee, "Humanitarian Agenda 2015 Democratic Republic of Congo Case Study," 17.

148. Holt and Berkman, *The Impossible Mandate?* 174.

149. UNSC, "Twentieth Report of the Secretary-General on the United Nations Organization Mission in the Democratic Republic of the Congo," S/2005/832 (28 December 2005), 7; Holt and Berkman, *The Impossible Mandate?* 175.

150. UNSC, "Twenty-First Report of the Secretary-General on the United Nations Organization Mission in the Democratic Republic of the Congo," 16.

151. Holt and Taylor, *Protecting Civilians in the Context of UN Peacekeeping Operations*, 167–68.

152. Sophia Swithern, "Reclaiming Mainstreaming: Oxfam GB's Protection Approach in DRC," *Humanitarian Exchange Magazine* 39 (June 2008).

153. Holt and Berkman, *The Impossible Mandate?* 175.

154. UNSC, "Twenty-First Report of the Secretary-General on the United Nations Organization Mission in the Democratic Republic of the Congo," 9.

155. UNSC, "Twenty-Third Report of the Secretary-General on the United Nations Organization Mission in the Democratic Republic of the Congo," S/2007/156 (20 March 2007).

156. Mowjee, "Humanitarian Agenda 2015 Democratic Republic of Congo Case Study," 22.

157. It also noted, in decidedly R2P language, although not referring to R2P, that the government of the DRC has the primary responsibility for protecting civilians.

158. UNSC Resolution 1794.

159. UNSC, "Twenty-Fifth Report of the Secretary-General on the United Nations Organization Mission in the Democratic Republic of the Congo," S/2008/218 (2 April 2008): 7.

160. Ibid., 7.

161. Ibid., 10.

162. IRC, "Mortality in the Democratic Republic of Congo: An Ongoing Crisis" (January 2008): ii–iii, http://www.rescue.org/sites/default/files/migrated/resources/2007/2006-7_congo mortalitysurvey.pdf. As the report noted, less than 10 percent of this total was the direct result of violence. Rather, most of the "excess deaths" were "attributed to easily preventable and treatable conditions such as malaria, diarrhea, pneumonia and malnutrition." The report engendered significant controversy. In particular, the Human Security Report Project questioned the IRC's methodology, asserting that the IRC had significantly overestimated the number of excess deaths. It did accept, however, that whatever the actual figure, large numbers of people had been killed as a result of the war, and that the IRC had played a significant role in bringing publicity to the

conflict. The IRC points out that the statistics were published in *The Lancet*, a highly respected medical journal. Human Security Report Project, *Human Security Report 2009/2010: The Causes of Peace and the Shrinking Costs of War* (Oxford: Oxford University Press, 2011), 123–31; "DR Congo War Deaths 'Exaggerated,'" *BBC News*, 20 January 2010; author interviews.

163. ICG, "Congo: Five Priorities for a Peacebuilding Strategy" (11 May 2009): 2–4. The Secretary-General cited 67 "security incidents" against humanitarian organizations through November 2008. UNSC, "Fourth Special Report of the Secretary-General on the United Nations Organization Mission in the Democratic Republic of the Congo," S/2008/728 (21 November 2008), 10.

164. ICG, "Congo: Four Priorities for Sustainable Peace in Ituri," (13 May 2008): i.

165. Prunier, *From Genocide to Continental War*, 322–23.

166. Holt and Taylor, *Protecting Civilians in the Context of UN Peacekeeping Operations*, 276–79. See also HRW, "Killings in Kiwanja: The UN's Inability to Protect Civilians" (12 December 2008).

167. Holt and Taylor, *Protecting Civilians in the Context of UN Peacekeeping Operations*, 281–82.

168. HRW, "Killings in Kiwanja," 28.

169. UNSC Resolution 1843.

170. HRW, "Killings in Kiwanja, 28.

171. UNSC, "Fourth Special Report of the Secretary-General on the United Nations Organization Mission in the Democratic Republic of the Congo," 19.

172. Ibid., 19.

173. ICG, "Congo: Five Priorities for a Peacebuilding Strategy," 4–5, 9.

174. ICG, "Congo: No Stability in Kivu Despite a Rapprochement with Rwanda," (16 November 2010): 3.

175. ICG, "Congo: Five Priorities for a Peacebuilding Strategy," 6.

176. UNSC, "Fourth Special Report of the Secretary-General on the United Nations Organization Mission in the Democratic Republic of the Congo," 5.

177. Holt and Taylor, *Protecting Civilians in the Context of UN Peacekeeping Operations*, 282. This had been requested by the Congolese government. UNSC, "Fourth Special Report of the Secretary-General on the United Nations Organization Mission," 11.

178. For an in-depth review of the killing by various forces during 2009 covered in the following couple of pages, see HRW, "You Will Be Punished: Attacks on Civilians in Eastern Congo" (December 2009).

179. Until this point some FARDC officers collaborated with the FDLR. ICG, "Congo: No Stability in Kivu Despite a Rapprochement with Rwanda," 4.

180. ICG, "Congo: Five Priorities for a Peacebuilding Strategy," 7–10. See also ICG, "Congo: A Comprehensive Strategy to Disarm the FDLR," (9 July 2009).

181. UNSC, "Twenty-Seventh Report of the Secretary-General on the United Nations Organization Mission in the Democratic Republic of the Congo," S/2009/160 (27 March 2009): 14.

182. "Characterizing Sexual Violence in the Democratic Republic of the Congo," 5–6.

183. Oxfam International, "Waking the Devil: The Impact of Forced Disarmament in Civilians in the Kivus" (July 2009): 2.

184. UNSC, "Report of the Secretary-General on Children and Armed Conflict in the Democratic Republic of the Congo," S/2010/369 (9 July 2010): 9–10.

185. Oxfam International, "Waking the Devil," 2–3.

186. UNSC, "Twenty-Eighth Report of the Secretary-General on the United Nations Organization Mission in the Democratic Republic of Congo," S/2009/335 (30 June 2009): 6.

187. Pierre Jacquemont, "The Dynamics of Instability in Eastern DRC," *Forced Migration Review* 36 (November 2010): 7.

188. Oxfam International, "Waking the Devil," 4–5.

189. HRW, "Eastern DR Congo: Surge in Army Atrocities" (2 November 2009), http://www.hrw.org/news/2009.

190. Xan Rice, "UN-Backed Congo Military Offensive a 'Humanitarian Disaster,'" *The Guardian*, 13 October 2009.

191. HRW, "DR Congo: Arrest Bosco Ntaganda for ICC Trial" (13 April 2012).

192. HRW, "Eastern DR Congo: Surge in Army Atrocities." Indeed, the government provided impunity for a number of CNDP leaders to induce them to integrate with the FARDC. ICG, "Congo: No Stability in Kivu Despite a Rapprochement with Rwanda," 10.

193. Although the government denied he exercised command functions during Kimia II or other FARDC operations. UNSC, "Thirtieth Report of the Secretary-General on the United Nations Organization Mission in the Democratic Republic of the Congo," S2009/623 (4 December 2009), 10.

194. HRW, "You Will Be Punished," 153–54.

195. UNSC Resolution 1896.

196. UNSC Resolution 1906.

197. UNSC, "Thirtieth Report of the Secretary-General on the United Nations Organization Mission in the Democratic Republic of the Congo," 4.

198. ICG, "Congo: No Stability in Kivu Despite a Rapprochement with Rwanda," 11.

199. UNSC, "Thirtieth Report of the Secretary-General on the United Nations Organization Mission in the Democratic Republic of the Congo," 7.

200. Ibid., 9.

201. Ibid., 12.

202. UNSC, "Thirty-First Report of the Secretary-General on the United Nations Organization Mission in the Democratic Republic of the Congo," S/2010/164 (30 March 2010): 1–2.

203. Ibid., 6–7.

204. Ibid., 14.

205. Ibid., 17.

206. "UN Official Calls DR Congo 'Rape Capital of the World,'" *BBC News*, 28 April 2010. According to the IRC, 56 percent of women who reported to the IRC had been attacked by individuals from armed groups. Sarah Mosely, Talita Cetinoglu, and Marit Glad, "Protection from Sexual Violence in DRC," *Forced Migration Review* 36 (November 2010): 15.

207. UNSC, "Thirty-First Report of the Secretary-General on the United Nations Organization Mission in the Democratic Republic of the Congo," 21–23.

208. UNSC Resolution 1925 (28 May 2010).

209. "Dynamics of Conflict and Forced Migration in the Democratic Republic of Congo," 9; Emily Paddon and Guillaume Lacaille, "Stabilising the Congo," Refugee Studies Centre (December 2011), http://www.rsc.ox.ac.uk/publications

210. Oxfam, "For Me, But Without Me, Is Against Me" (July 2012): 10, http://www.oxfamblogs.org.

211. "Dynamics of Conflict and Forced Migration in the Democratic Republic of Congo," 9.

212. UNSC, "Report of the Secretary-General on the United Nations Organization Stabilization Mission in the Democratic Republic of the Congo," S/2010/512 (8 October 2010), 17.

213. Although, as Oxfam points out, concrete data on civilian casualties in the DRC is sparse. Oxfam, "Protection of Civilians in 2010," Oxfam Briefing Paper 147 (May 2011), 13.

214. UNSC, "Report of the Secretary-General on the United Nations Organization Stabilization Mission in the Democratic Republic of the Congo," (8 October 2010): 18.

215. Ibid., 18. See also ICG, "Congo: No Stability in Kivu Despite a Rapprochement with Rwanda," 22. In January 2011 the Secretary-General noted that the loss of military helicopters

would "diminish the Mission's ability to protect civilians." UNSC, "Report of the Secretary-General on the United Nations Organization Stabilization Mission" (17 January 2011), 17.

216. ICG, "Congo: No Stability in Kivu Despite a Rapprochement with Rwanda," 6.

217. Ibid., 6–7. He was subsequently released from custody on 23 December 2011.

218. Ibid., ii.

219. ICG, "Congo: No Stability in Kivu Despite a Rapprochement with Rwanda," 9. Indeed, MONUSCO only found out about the incident a week later, even though they had a base 30 km away. Stian Kjeksrud and Jacob Aasland Ravndal, "Emerging lessons from the United Nations mission in the Congo: military contributions to the protection of civilians," *African Security Review* 20 (June 2011): 13.

220. Oxfam, "Protection of Civilians in 2010," 15.

221. ICG, "Congo: No Stability in Kivu Despite a Rapprochement with Rwanda," 7–8.

222. "Dynamics of Conflict and Forced Migration in the Democratic Republic of Congo," 5.

223. UNSC, "Report of the Secretary-General on the United Nations Organization Stabilization Mission in the Democratic Republic of the Congo," (October 2010), 7.

224. UNSC, "Report of the Secretary-General on the United Nations Organization Stabilization Mission" (12 May 2011): 9; Oxfam, "'We Are Entirely Exploitable': The Lack of Protection for Civilians in Eastern DRC" (28 July 2011): 5.

225. UNSC, "Report of the Secretary-General on the United Nations Organization Stabilization Mission in the Democratic Republic of the Congo," S/2011/656 (24 October 2011): 9.

226. Ibid., 10.

227. Ibid., 14.

228. Ibid., 6.

229. "DR Congo: Over 100,000 Flee Fresh Violence in Eastern DRC Since November," *Afrique en Ligne* (1 January 2012).

230. "Congo-Kinshasa; Violence Escalating in Eastern Country," Open Society Initiative for Southern Africa, JUSTWATCH-L listserv (26 January 2012).

231. "Bosco 'Terminator' Ntaganda Takes over DR Congo Towns," *BBC News*, 30 April 2012.

232. ICG, "Eastern Congo: Why Stabilisation Failed" (4 October 2012).

233. "DRC: Understanding Armed Group M23," *IRIN*, 22 June 2013.

234. "DRC: North Kivu in Turmoil Again," *IRIN*, 16 May 2012.

235. "DRC: Understanding Armed Group M23."

236. "DRC: Children, Young Men Flee M23 Recruitment," *IRIN*, 16 August 2012.

237. "DRC: Scores Killed as Mai-Mai Target Kinyarwanda Speakers," *IRIN*, 12 June 2012.

238. UNSC, "Addendum to the Interim Report of the Group of Experts on the Democratic Republic of Congo (S/2012/34) Concerning Violations of the Arms Embargo and Sanctions Regime by the Government of Rwanda," S/2012/348/Add.1 (27 June 2012).

239. "Joseph Kabila: 'Open Secret Rwanda Is Backing Rebel Fighters in Congo,'" *The Telegraph*, 29 July 2012; DRC_digest_ENG_11_June6_14_2012&utm_medium=email.

240. Colum Lynch, "U.N. Panel Says Rwanda Behind Congolese Mutiny," *Foreign Policy* (26 June 2012). See also HRW, "DRC: Rwanda Should Stop Aiding War Crimes Suspect" (4 June 2012).

241. UNSC, "Security Council Press Statement on the Democratic Republic of Congo," SC/10709 (16 July 2012), http://www.un.org/News/Press/docs/2012.

242. EU, "Declaration by the High Representative, Catherine Ashton, on behalf of the European Union on the Situation in the eastern Democratic Republic of Congo," 12422/1/12 REV 1 (10 July 2012), http://www.consilium.europa.eu/uedocs/.

243. "Rwanda Aid Hinges on DRC, London Says," *UPI*, 13 August 2012, posted to JUSTWATCH-L e-mail list.

244. Filip Reyntjens, "Rwanda, Ten Years On: From Genocide to Dictatorship," *African Affairs* 103 (April 2004): 177–201.

245. Chris McGreal, "U.S. Support for Rwanda Wanes amid Concern over Violence in Congo," *Guardian*, 1 August 2012, http://www.guardian.co.uk/world/2012/aug/01/us-support -rwanda-wanes-congo.

246. Louise Charbonneau, "U.N. Demands End of Foreign Support for Congo Rebels," *Reuters*, 2 August 2012.

247. ICG, "Eastern Congo: Why Stabilisation Failed," 13.

248. Drazen Jorgic, "Congo Rejects Rwandan Soldiers for Regional Anti-Rebel Force," *AlertNet*, 9 August 2012.

249. David Smith, "Rwandan Minister Is Leader of Congo Rebels, UN Says," *The Guardian*, 18 October 2012.

250. UNSC, "Letter Dated 12 November 2012 from the Chair of the Security Council Committee Established Pursuant to Resolution 1533 (2004) Concerning the Democratic Republic of the Congo to the President of Security Council," S/2012/843 (15 November 2012).

251. UNSC Resolution 2076 (20 November 2012); UNSC Resolution 2078 (28 November 2012).

252. Jessica Hatcher and Alex Perry, "Defining Peacekeeping Downward: The U.N. Debacle in Eastern Congo," *Time*, 26 November 2012.

253. Peter Jones and David Smith, "Goma Falls to Congo Rebels," *The Guardian*, 20 November 2012.

254. Jeffrey Gettleman, "'Framework' Announced for Peace in Congo,'" *New York Times*, 24 February 2013.

255. Melanie Gouby, "Congo rebel group splits over firing of president," *Associated Press*, 28 February 2013.

256. Michelle Nichols and Louise Charbonneau, "Fearing Death, Congo's 'Terminator' Fled with Help of Family," *Reuters*, 28 June 2013.

257. UNSC, "Special Report of the Secretary-General on the Democratic Republic of the Congo and the Great Lakes region," S/2013/119 (27 February 2013), 12.

258. Ibid.

259. UNSC Resolution 2098 (28 March 2013).

260. Patrick Cammaert and Fiona Blyth, "The UN Intervention Brigade in the Democratic Republic of the Congo," *International Peace Institute* (July 2013): 1.

261. Ibid., 7.

262. Ibid., 6.

263. Mark Doyle, "DR Congo Unrest: Fears over UN intervention," *BBC News*, 25 July 2013.

264. Nick Long, "UN Brigade in DRC Not Magic Solution, Says Commander," *Voice of America*, 10 July 2013.

265. Including, for example, a number of civil-military cooperation endeavors: the Protection Cluster, the Early Warning and Rapid Response Cell, the Protection Matrix, joint protection teams, community liaison interpreters, community alert networks, the Surveillance Centre, and Mobile Operating Bases. While these have had some positive effects, they are not panaceas. Kjeksrud and Ravndal, "Emerging Lessons from the United Nations Mission in the Congo," 6–9; UNSC, "Report of the Secretary-General on the United Nations Organization Stabilization Mission in the Democratic Republic of the Congo," S/2012/65 (26 January 2012): 8; Refugees International, "DR Congo: Improved Civilian Protection Activities Still Need Support" (13 November 2009), http://www.refugeesinternational.org; Mowjee, "Humanitarian Agenda 2015 Democratic Republic of Congo Case Study," 23.

266. To put it in a different context, as one MONUC staff officer put it, "There are more people at a soccer game in Chelsea on a Sunday than there are UN soldiers in the DRC."

Quoted in Kjeksrud and Ravndal, "Emerging Lessons from the United Nations Mission in the Congo," 11.

267. Author interviews.

268. Zoë Marriage, "Congo Co: Aid and Security," *Conflict, Security & Development* 10, 3 (2010): 359–60.

269. Inter-Agency Standing Committee, "Guidance Note on Using the Cluster Approach to Strengthen Humanitarian Response" (24 November 2006): 2, http://www.unhcr.org/refworld.

270. For an overview of clusters in the DRC, see Andrea Binder, Véronique de Geoffroy, and Bonaventure Sokpoh, "Democratic Republic of Congo," IASC Cluster Approach Evaluation, 2nd Phase, Global Public Policy Institute (April 2010).

271. In situations without significant displacement or in disasters, OHCHR or UNICEF might also play this role. IASC, "Guidance Note on Using the Cluster Approach to Strengthen Humanitarian Response," 3.

272. Erika Feller, "UNHCR's Role in IDP Protection: Opportunities and Challenges," *Forced Migration Review* (December 2006): 12.

273. Author interviews.

274. Feller, "UNHCR's Role in IDP Protection," 12.

275. IASC, "Guidance Note on Using the Cluster Approach to Strengthen Humanitarian Response," 14.

276. Jaya Murthy, "Mandating the Protection Cluster with the Responsibility to Protect: A Policy Recommendation Based on the Protection Cluster's Implementation in South Kivu, DRC," *Journal of Humanitarian Assistance* (5 October 2007).

277. Murthy, "Mandating the Protection Cluster with the Responsibility to Protect."

278. Mowjee, "Humanitarian Agenda 2015 Democratic Republic of Congo Case Study," 23.

279. Murthy, "Mandating the Protection Cluster with the Responsibility to Protect."

280. Ibid.

281. Mowjee, "Humanitarian Agenda 2015 Democratic Republic of Congo Case Study," 27.

282. Binder et al., "Democratic Republic of Congo," 43.

283. Vance Culbert, "Protection Cluster Co-Facilitation in the Democratic Republic of the Congo: Lessons Learned from Oxfam's Protection Cluster Support Project," Oxfam (June 2011), 5–6, http://reliefweb.int/sites/reliefweb.int/files/resources/F_R_352.pdf.

284. Tennant, "UNHCR's Engagement with Integrated UN Missions," 1.

285. UNSC, "Report of the Secretary-General on Children and Armed Conflict in the Democratic Republic of the Congo," 10.

286. Tennant, "UNHCR's Engagement with Integrated UN Missions," 7.

287. Ibid.

288. Ibid., 9.

289. Ibid., 10.

290. Author interviews.

291. Author interviews.

292. Author interviews.

293. Kurt Mills, "The Postmodern Tank of the Humanitarian International," *Peace Review* 18 (April–June 2006): 261–67.

294. Author interviews.

295. Mowjee, "Humanitarian Agenda 2015 Democratic Republic of Congo Case Study," 32.

296. Ibid., 33.

297. Binder et al., "Democratic Republic of Congo," 44.

298. Ibid., 44.

299. Mowjee, "Humanitarian Agenda 2015 Democratic Republic of Congo Case Study," 23.

300. Binder et al., "Democratic Republic of Congo," 43–44.

301. Stian Kjeksrud and Jacob Aasland Ravndal, "Protection of Civilians in Practice—Emerging Lessons from the UN Mission in the DRC," Norwegian Defence Research Establishment (15 December 2010): 14–15.

302. UN Department of Peacekeeping Operations, "United Nations Peacekeeping Operations: Principles and Guidelines" (2008): 53–54.

303. Tennant, "UNHCR's Engagement with Integrated UN Missions," 43.

304. Ibid., 42.

305. Mowjee, "Humanitarian Agenda 2015 Democratic Republic of Congo Case Study," 17.

306. Greta Zeender and Jacob Rothing, "Displacement Trends in DRC," *Forced Migration Review* 36 (November 2010): 12.

307. Binder et al., "Democratic Republic of Congo," 43.

308. Author interviews.

309. Tennant, "UNHCR's Engagement with Integrated UN Missions," 46.

310. Mowjee, "Humanitarian Agenda 2015 Democratic Republic of Congo Case Study," 33.

311. Ibid., 30.

312. HRW, "Ituri Covered in Blood," 40.

313. Mills, "Neohumanitarianism," 11.

314. HRW, "Ituri Covered in Blood," 42. Mowjee suggests the attack may have been a warning against interfering with natural resource extraction in the area, thus highlighting the problems in assigning motives, or at least the mixed motives that may be present in many situations. Mowjee, "Humanitarian Agenda 2015 Democratic Republic of Congo Case Study," 32.

315. Mills, "Neohumanitarianism," 11.

316. Indeed, MSF ran into similar problems in Ituri. It provided medical assistance to everybody, but because it was based in a mainly Hema area in Bunia, it—and other IHOs—were accused of bias. Ngolet, *Crisis in the Congo*, 133.

317. Mowjee, "Humanitarian Agenda 2015 Democratic Republic of Congo Case Study," 32.

318. Ibid., 11.

319. Ibid., 26.

320. Schabas, *Introduction to the International Criminal Court*, 44.

321. ICC, "Prosecutor Receives Referral of the Situation in the Democratic Republic of Congo," press release, ICC-OTP-20040419-50 (19 April 2004). Indeed, a state cannot refer just part of its territory to the ICC, particularly since the ICC already has jurisdiction over the entire territory of a state, regardless of whether or not a state refers itself—although, as in the case of Darfur, it appears the Security Council can engage in such a targeted referral.

322. ICC, Office of the Prosecutor, "Report on the Activities Performed During the First Three Years (June 2003–June 2006)" (12 September 2006): 10, http://www.icc-cpi.int.

323. In the early days of the ICC there were questions about whether self-referrals were even possible under the Rome Statute, although these concerns were put to rest in the *Katanga* decision in 2009. Payam Akhavan, "International Criminal Justice in the Era of Failed States: The ICC and the Self-referral Debate," in *The International Criminal Court and Complementarity: From Theory to Practice*, ed. Carsten Stahn and Mohamed M. El Zeidy (Cambridge: Cambridge University Press, 2011), 2:283–303.

324. HRW, *Courting History: The Landmark International Criminal Court's First Years* (July 2008), 40.

325. ICC, "Report on the Activities Performed During the First Three Years (June 2003–June 2006)," 2.

326. Akhavan, "International Criminal Justice in the Era of Failed States," 297.

327. HRW, *Courting History*, 41.

328. ICC, "The Office of the Prosecutor of the International Criminal Court Opens Its First Investigation," press release, ICC-OTP-20040623-59 (23 June 2004).

329. Quoted in William A. Schabas, "Prosecutorial Discretion v. Judicial Activism at the International Criminal Court," *Journal of International Criminal Justice* 6 (September 2008): 737.

330. ICC, "Situation in the Democratic Republic of Congo, in the Case of *The Prosecutor v. Thomas Lubanga Dyilo*—Warrant of Arrest," ICC-01/04-01/06 (10 February 2006).

331. The FPLC was the military wing of the UPC.

332. Schabas, *An Introduction to the International Criminal Court*, 46.

333. Ibid., 47.

334. ICC, "Decision on the Consequences of Non-Disclosure of Exculpatory Materials Covered by Article 54(3)(e) Agreements and the Application to Stay the Prosecution of the Accused, Together with Certain Other Issues Raised at the Status Conference on 10 June 2008" (13 June 2008), http://www.icc-cpi.int/iccdocs/doc/doc511249.PDF. For a broader discussion of the issue of exculpatory evidence in the Lubanga case, see Rachel Katzman, "The Non-Disclosure of Confidential Exculpatory Evidence and the Lubanga Proceedings: How the ICC Defense System Affects the Accused's Right to a Fair Trial," *Northwest University Journal of International Human Rights* 8 (Fall 2009): 77–101.

335. ICC, "Decision on the Consequences of Non-Disclosure of Exculpatory Materials," 9–13.

336. Quoted in Mona Rishmawi, "The ICC Viewed from the Office of the High Commissioner for Human Rights," in "Discussion," *Journal of International Criminal Justice* 6 (September 2008): 771.

337. Indeed, MONUC has capabilities to compile such information on a scale that NGOs and UN agencies on their own cannot. Mowjee, "Humanitarian Agenda 2015 Democratic Republic of Congo Case Study," 17; Rishmawi, "The ICC Viewed from the Office of the High Commissioner for Human Rights," 771.

338. Rishmawi, "The ICC Viewed from the Office of the High Commissioner for Human Rights," 772.

339. Schabas, *An Introduction to the International Criminal Court*, 48.

340. Schabas, "Prosecutorial Discretion v. Judicial Activism," 741.

341. Lubanga was convicted on 14 March 2012 of conscripting and enlisting children under the age of fifteen years into the FPLC and using them to participate actively in hostilities. ICC, "Situation in the Democratic Republic of Congo, in the Case of *The Prosecutor v. Thomas Lubanga Dyilo*—Judgment Pursuant to Article 74 of the Statute," ICC-01/04-01/06 (14 March 2012): 591. In July he was sentenced to fourteen years in jail. "DR Congo Warlord Thomas Lubanga Sentenced to 14 Years," *BBC News*, 10 July 2012.

342. HRW, *Selling Justice Short* (July 2009): 125–26; HRW, *Courting History*, 67–68; "Jury Still Out on ICC Trials in DRC," *IRIN* (19 January 2011). There was also anecdotal evidence that individual soldiers in Darfur were also discussing the ICC after the Security Council referral, although there is no clear evidence that this had any significant impact on their actions. Author interviews.

343. Niki Frencken, "The International Criminal Court and Deterrence—The 'Lubanga Syndrome,'" *Justice in Conflict*, 6 April 2012.

344. Including by Bosco Ntaganda, the second individual in the DRC to have an arrest warrant issued against him (see below). HRW, "DR Congo: Arrest Bosco Ntaganda for ICC Trial."

345. HRW, *Courting History*, 68–69.

346. Schabas, *An Introduction to the International Criminal Court*, 61.

347. Kate Cronin-Furman, "Managing Expectations: International Criminal Trials and the Prospects for Deterrence of Mass Atrocity," *International Journal of Transitional Justice* 7, 3 (2013): 16.

348. ICC, "Situation in the Democratic Republic of Congo, in the Case of *The Prosecutor v. Bosco Ntaganda*—Warrant of Arrest," ICC-01/04-02/06 (22 August 2006).

349. ICG, "Congo: Five Priorities for a Peacebuilding Strategy," 7–8.

350. Ibid., 8.

351. Melanie Gouby, "Congo-Kinshasa: President Kabila Hot to Nab General Ntaganda," *allAfrica.com*, 12 April 2012.

352. HRW, "DR Congo: Arrest Bosco Ntaganda for ICC Trial."

353. Perhaps it had something to do with the "'social alarm'" of using armed soldiers, as identified by the Pre-Trial Chamber—although the Prosecutor has not endorsed this criterion. Schabas, "Prosecutorial Discretion v. Judicial Activism," 742.

354. ICG, "Congo: Four Priorities for Sustainable Peace in Ituri," 20–22.

355. Schabas, "Prosecutorial Discretion v. Judicial Activism," 751.

356. Kenneth Roth, "Court from the Lobby: A NGO View," in "Discussion," *Journal of International Criminal Justice* 6 (September 2008): 764.

357. ICC, "Situation in the Democratic Republic of Congo, in the Case of *The Prosecutor v. Germain Katanga*—Warrant of Arrest," ICC-01/04-01/07 (2 July 2007).

358. ICC, "Situation in the Democratic Republic of Congo, in the Case of *The Prosecutor v. Mathieu Ngudjolo Chui*—Warrant of Arrest," ICC-01/04-02/07 (6 July 2007).

359. Ibid. (28 September 2010).

360. ICC, "Situation in the Democratic Republic of the Congo, in the case of *The Prosecutor v. Callixte Mbarushimana*—Decision on the Confirmation of Charges," ICC-01/04-10/10 (16 December 2011).

361. Phil Clark, "Chasing Cases: The ICC and the Politics of State Referral in the Democratic Republic of the Congo and Uganda," in Stahn and El Zeidy, *International Criminal Court and Complementarity*, 2: 1181–82.

362. Ibid., 1182.

363. ICC, Office of the Prosecutor, "Paper on Some Policy Issues Before the Office of the Prosecutor" (September 2003): 3.

364. See Clark, "Chasing Cases," 1185.

365. Ibid., 1188.

366. Ibid., 1190.

367. ICC, "Prosecutorial Strategy 2009–2012" (1 February 2010): 5.

368. Marlies Glasius, "A Problem, Not a Solution: Complementarity in the Central African Republic and Democratic Republic of Congo," in Stahn and El Zeidy, *International Criminal Court and Complementarity*, 1218.

369. Clark, "Chasing Cases," 1191.

370. Ibid., 1191–92.

371. Indeed, by 2004 there were forty investigations into serious human rights crimes being investigated in Bunia, and subsequently a military tribunal had handed down several judgments—for both rebels and members of FARDC—in cases involving serious crimes. Ibid., 1192–95. Human Rights Watch generally critiques the justice system as not having adequate resources and involving "political interference" and "corruption," which can affect the outcome of cases. See HRW, *Selling Justice Short*, 50; Davis and Hayner provide a similar critique of criminal justice in the DRC. Laura Davis and Priscilla Hayner, "Difficult Peace, Limited Justice: Ten Years of Peacemaking in the DRC," International Center for Transitional Justice, March 2009, 25–25, http://ictj.org/.

372. Glasius, "A Problem, Not a Solution," 1217.

373. Davis and Hayner, "Difficult Peace, Limited Justice," 26.

374. Foreign diplomat cited in Clark, "Chasing Cases," 1194.

375. Benjamin Bibas, "Kigali, Between Ntaganda and the ICC," *International Justice Tribune*, 6 June 2012.

376. Akhavan, "International Criminal Justice in the Era of Failed States," 302.

377. Ibid.

378. Ibid., 295.

379. Ibid., 303.

380. Sadiki Koko, "MONUC and the Quest for Peace in the Democratic Republic of Congo: Assessment of a Peacekeeping Mission," *African Security Review* 20 (June 2011): 36.

381. Paul D. Williams, "Enhancing Civilian Protection in Peace Operations: Insights from Africa," Africa Center for Strategic Studies, Research Paper 1 (Washington, D.C.: National Defense University Press, September 2010), 21.

382. Kjeksrud and Ravndal, "Emerging Lessons from the United Nations Mission in the Congo," 12.

383. Williams, "Enhancing Civilian Protection in Peace Operations: Insights from Africa," 21–22.

384. Author interviews.

385. Kjeksrud and Ravndal, "Emerging Lessons from the United Nations Mission in the Congo," 12.

386. Margherita Melillo, "Cooperation Between the UN Peacekeeping Operation and the ICC in the Democratic Republic of the Congo," *Journal of International Criminal Justice* 11 (2013): 766–68.

387. Ibid., 768; emphasis in original.

388. Ibid., 773.

389. Godfrey M. Musila, *Between Rhetoric and Action: The Politics, Processes and Practice of the ICC's Work in the DRC* (Pretoria: Institute for Security Studies, 2009), 30–31. Melillo notes that there are different versions of MONUC's actual role in arresting Lubanga and Katanga. Melillo, "Cooperation Between the UN Peacekeeping Operation and the ICC in the Democratic Republic of the Congo," 771–73.

390. Melillo, "Cooperation Between the UN Peacekeeping Operation and the ICC," 780–82.

391. Kjeksrud and Ravndal note the following PoC initiatives in the DRC: System-Wide Strategy; Conditionality Policy; Early Warning and Rapid Response Cell; Joint Mission Analysis Centre; Protection Cluster/Protection Matrix; Joint Protection Teams; Mobile Operating Bases; Early Warning Centres; Community Liaison Interpreters; The Handbook: Protection in Practice. Kjeksrud and Ravndal, "Emerging Lessons from the United Nations Mission in the Congo," 13–14.

392. Julie Reynaert, "MONUC/MONUSCO and Civilian Protection in the Kivus," International Peace Information Service, February 2011.

Chapter 4. Uganda (and Beyond): Testing the International Criminal Court

Epigraphs: UNHCHR, "Report of the United Nations High Commissioner for Human Rights on the Mission Undertaken by Her Office, Pursuant to Commission Resolution 2000/60, to Assess the Situation on the Ground with Regard to the Abduction of Children from Northern Uganda" (9 November 2001): 5, E/CN.4/2002/86 (hereafter referred to as UNHCHR Report on the Abduction of Children from Northern Uganda); Address by Luis Moreno-Ocampo, Prosecutor of the International Criminal Court, at the International Conference "Building a Future on Peace *and* Justice," Nuremberg (25 June 2007), http://www.peace-justice-conference.info; Agreement on Accountability and Reconciliation Between the Government of the Republic of Uganda and the Lord's Resistance Army/Movement, Juba, Sudan (29 June 2007), http://www.am icc.org/docs.

1. Adam Branch, *Displacing Human Rights: War and Intervention in Northern Uganda* (Oxford: Oxford University Press, 2011), 48.

2. See ibid., 45–53, for a more in-depth discussion.

3. HRW, *The Scars of Death: Children Abducted by the Lord's Resistance Army in Uganda* (September 1997), 72.

4. Some Rwandan officers were given significant positions in the Ugandan army. International Crisis Group, "Uganda and Rwanda: Friends or Enemies?" 4 May 2000, 2.

5. HRW, *Scars of Death*, 72.

6. Branch, *Displacing Human Rights*, 53–61.

7. They did so partly as a result of the fear engendered when the NRA instructed all Acholi former fighters to report to army headquarters. Ibid., 74.

8. Sverker Finnström, *Living with Bad Surroundings: War, History, and Everyday Moments in Northern Uganda* (Durham, N.C.: Duke University Press, 2008), 68.

9. Finnström points out that by 1988, there were twenty-seven rebel groups fighting the government in different parts of the country. There have also been attacks by Rwandan Hutu from the DRC. Ibid., 70–71.

10. Branch, *Displacing Human Rights*, 62–66.

11. Tim Allen, *Trial Justice: The International Criminal Court and the Lord's Resistance Army* (London: Zed Books, 2006), 32–35.

12. Finnström, *Living with Bad Surroundings*, 78.

13. Branch, *Displacing Human Rights*, 67.

14. Allen, *Trial Justice*, 35.

15. Finnström, *Living with Bad Surroundings*, 76.

16. HRW, *The Scars of Death*, 80.

17. Branch, *Displacing Human Rights*, 67–68.

18. Ibid., 68. Indeed, by 1989 the UPDA essentially disappeared. HRW, *The Scars of Death*, 81.

19. Allen, *Trial Justice*, 36.

20. Ibid., 37–38.

21. Ibid., 39.

22. Branch, *Displacing Human Rights*, 69.

23. Allen, *Trial Justice*, 39.

24. Branch, *Displacing Human Rights*, 68–70.

25. Ibid., 82.

26. Ibid., 71.

27. Including widespread torture, extrajudicial killings, and looting. Finnström, *Living with Bad Surroundings*, 71–72.

28. Branch, *Displacing Human Rights*, 72.

29. HRW, *The Scars of Death*, 83.

30. Mareike Schomerus, "The Lord's Resistance Army in Sudan: A History and Overview," HSBA Working Paper 8 (Geneva: Small Arms Survey, 2007): 18; Branch, *Displacing Human Rights*, 74–75.

31. The figures varied widely. UNICEF estimated 240,000 displaced in June 1997, while local officials claimed as many as two million were displaced. HRW, *The Scars of Death*, 59.

32. Finnström, *Living with Bad Surroundings*, 133.

33. Ibid., 142.

34. Indeed, at one camp in Gulu district only around 80 guards protected a camp population of 45,000. HRW, "Abducted and Abused: Renewed Conflict in Northern Uganda," July 2003, 64.

35. Ibid., 36.

36. UNHCHR Report on the Abduction of Children from Northern Uganda, 11.

37. HRW, *The Scars of Death*, 62.

38. Finnström, *Living with Bad Surroundings*, 133.

39. Branch, *Displacing Human Rights*, 92; International Crisis Group, "Building a Comprehensive Peace Strategy for Northern Uganda" (23 June 2005), 11.

40. Robert Gersony, "The Anguish of Northern Uganda: Results of a Field-Based Assessment of the Civil Conflicts in Northern Uganda," submitted to U.S. Embassy and USAID Mission, Kampala (August 1997): 59, http://pdf.usaid.gov/pdf_docs/PNACC245.pdf.

41. Branch, *Displacing Human Rights*, 93–94.

42. Ibid., 94.

43. Ibid., 95–96.

44. Quoted in ibid., 96.

45. Finnström, *Living with Bad Surroundings*, 135.

46. Ibid.

47. Ibid., 158.

48. Branch, *Displacing Human Rights*, 99.

49. HRW, "Abducted and Abused: Renewed Conflict in Northern Uganda," 64.

50. Ibid., 65.

51. Ibid.

52. Finnström, *Living with Bad Surroundings*, 136, 159. Sometimes the LRA would loot the camps of the food aid after the distribution had ended (156).

53. HRW, "Abducted and Abused: Renewed Conflict in Northern Uganda," 37.

54. Branch, *Displacing Human Rights*, 99.

55. Ibid.

56. Andrew Mwenda, "Uganda's Politics of Foreign Aid and Violent Conflict: The Political Uses of the LRA Rebellion," in *The Lord's Resistance Army: Myth and Reality*, ed. Tim Allen and Koen Vlassenroot (London: Zed, 2010), 49.

57. HRW, *The Scars of Death*, 22.

58. Ibid., 23.

59. Ibid., 69.

60. Ibid., 58.

61. Ibid., 99–100.

62. Ibid., 84–85.

63. UNHCHR Report on the Abduction of Children from Northern Uganda, 5; HRW, *The Scars of Death*, 100.

64. Branch, *Displacing Human Rights*, 134. Some parents sent released children back to the LRA. Kevin C. Dunn, "The Lord's Resistance Army and African International Relations," *African Security* 3 (2010): 55.

65. HRW, "Stolen Children: Abduction and Recruitment in Northern Uganda" (March 2003): 19.

66. HRW, "Abducted and Abused: Renewed Conflict in Northern Uganda," 56–58.

67. Ibid., 60.

68. Kenneth A. Rodman and Petie Booth, "Manipulated Commitments: The International Criminal Court in Uganda," *Human Rights Quarterly* 35, 2 (2013): 284.

69. UNGA, "Children and Armed Conflict," Report of the Secretary-General, A/61/529 (26 October 2006): 25; UNGA, "Children and Armed Conflict," Report of the Secretary-General, A/62/609 (21 December 2007), 30. The practice appeared to have stopped by 2009. UNSC, "Children and Armed Conflict," Report of the Secretary-General, S/2009/158 (26 March 2009), 28.

70. UNSC, "Report of the Secretary-General on Children and Armed Conflict in Uganda," S/2007/260 (7 May 2007).

71. UNSC, "Report of the Secretary-General on Children and Armed Conflict in Uganda," S/2008/409 (23 June 2008).

72. UNSC, "Report of the Secretary-General on Children and Armed Conflict in Uganda," S/2009/462 (15 September 2009).

73. Branch, *Displacing Human Rights*, 81.

74. Finnström, *Living with Bad Surroundings*, 99.

75. Ibid., 109; Dunn, "The Lord's Resistance Army and African International Relations," 51.

76. Although Payam Akhavan, who advised the Ugandan government on its ICC referral, maintained that "the LRA has had no coherent ideology, rational political agenda, or popular support [and is a] brutal insurgency focused on terror." Payam Akhavan, "The Lord's Resistance Army Case: Uganda's Submission of the First State Referral to the International Criminal Court," *American Journal of International Law* 99, 2 (2005): 407.

77. Finnström, *Living with Bad Surroundings*, 119–23.

78. Gersony, "The Anguish of Northern Uganda," 68.

79. Finnström, *Living with Bad Surroundings*, 242.

80. Ibid., 116.

81. "Uganda Conflict 'Worse Than Iraq,'" *BBC News* (10 November 2011).

82. Finnström, *Living with Bad Surroundings*, 112.

83. Mwenda, "Uganda's Politics of Foreign Aid and Violent Conflict," 50.

84. Finnström, *Living with Bad Surroundings*, 112.

85. There are claims that the LRA was trained by Al-Qaeda, however. Ibid., 127.

86. Branch, *Displacing Human Rights*, 86.

87. Ibid., 85.

88. Finnström, *Living with Bad Surroundings*, 113.

89. HRW, "Abducted and Abused: Renewed Conflict in Northern Uganda."

90. Ibid., 41–52.

91. Ibid., 62.

92. Mwenda, "Uganda's Politics of Foreign Aid and Violent Conflict," 52–53.

93. Carlos Rodriguez, quoted in Mareike Schomerus, "'They Forget What They Came For': Uganda's Army in Sudan,'" *Journal of Eastern African Studies* 6, 1 (2012): 7.

94. HRW, "Abducted and Abused: Renewed Conflict in Northern Uganda," 38–39.

95. Schomerus, "'They Forget What They Came For,'" 135–37, 141.

96. ICC, "President of Uganda Refers Situation Concerning the Lord's Resistance Army (LRA) to the ICC" (29 January 2004).

97. Phil Clark, "Law, Politics and Pragmatism: The ICC and Case Selection in the Democratic Republic of Congo and Uganda," in *Courting Conflict? Justice, Peace and the ICC in Africa*, ed. Nicholas Waddell and Phil Clark (London: Royal African Society, 2008), 43; HRW, *Courting History: The Landmark International Criminal Court's First Years* (July 2008), 40; author interviews; ICC, Office of the Prosecutor, "Report on the Activities Performed During the First Three Years (June 2003–June 2006)" (12 September 2006): 7.

98. Amnesty Act, 2000, http://www.ulii.org/ug/legislation/consolidated-act/294.

99. UNHCHR Report on the Abduction of Children from Northern Uganda, 2001, 14.

100. Ibid., 19.

101. Akhavan, "The Lord's Resistance Army Case," 410–11.

102. The ICC would have the authority to prosecute Kony and others regardless whether they were given amnesty.

103. Schiff, *Building the International Criminal Court*, 199.

104. In particular because of Uganda's activities in the DRC. Jess Bravin, "For Global Court, Ugandan Rebels Prove Tough Test," *Wall Street Journal*, 8 June 2006.

105. HRW, "ICC: Investigate All Sides in Uganda" (5 February 2004).

106. Branch, *Displacing Human Rights*, 187.

107. Sandrine Perrot, "Northern Uganda: A 'Forgotten Conflict,' Again? The Impact of the Internationalization of the Resolution Process," in Allen and Vlassenroot, *The Lord's Resistance Army*, 199.

108. Akhavan, "The Lord's Resistance Army Case," 409.

109. Stuart Price, "Kony Probe Begins June," *New Vision*, 30 January 2004.

110. Zachary Lomo, "The International Criminal Court Investigations: Implications for the Search for Peaceful Solutions to the Conflict in Northern Uganda," All Party Parliamentary Group on the Great Lakes Region and Genocide Prevention, Working Paper 2 (July 2004), http://appggreatlakes.org.

111. Sarah M. H. Nouwen and Wouter G. Werner, "Doing Justice to the Political: The International Criminal Court in Uganda and Sudan," *European Journal of International Law* 21, 4 (2011): 947–49.

112. Quoted in ibid., 949.

113. Ibid.

114. Price, "Kony Probe Begins June."

115. Emmy Allio, "Sudan Predicts Kony End," *New Vision*, 17 February 2004.

116. Nouwen and Werner, "Doing Justice to the Political," 953.

117. Akhavan, "The Lord's Resistance Army Case," 404.

118. ICC, "Prosecutor of the International Criminal Court Opens an Investigation into Northern Uganda" (29 July 2004).

119. ICC, "Warrant of Arrest for Joseph Kony Issued on 8 July 2005 as Amended on 27 September 2005."

120. Akhavan, "The Lord's Resistance Army Case," 411.

121. Victor Peskin, "Caution and Confrontation in the International Criminal Court's Pursuit of Accountability in Uganda and Sudan," *Human Rights Quarterly* 31, 3 (2009): 679.

122. ICG, "Shock Therapy for Northern Uganda's Peace Process" (11 April 2005), 2.

123. Allen, *Trial Justice*, 195.

124. ICG, "Shock Therapy," 2–3.

125. Ibid., 5.

126. Ibid., 2, 4.

127. Peskin, "Caution and Confrontation in the International Criminal Court's Pursuit of Accountability in Uganda and Sudan," 680. Although Atkinson argues that "there is little evidence that [the arrest warrants] played a significant role in the rebels' decision to pursue those talks." Ronald R. Atkinson, "'The Realists in Juba'? An Analysis of the Juba Peace Talks," in Allen and Vlassenroot, *The Lord's Resistance Army*, 212.

128. ICG, "Peace in Northern Uganda: Decisive Weeks Ahead," (21 February 2005): 4.

129. ICG, "Shock Therapy," 4. Although the government had twenty times more manpower in northern Uganda than the LRA, its ability to accomplish such a military victory was in question, given the army's many failings. International Crisis Group, "A Strategy for Ending Northern Uganda's Crisis" (11 January 2006).

130. ICG, "Building a Comprehensive Strategy for Northern Uganda," 7.

131. Perrot, "Northern Uganda," 189–90.

132. Peskin, "Caution and Confrontation in the International Criminal Court's Pursuit of Accountability," 681.

133. Second Report of the Prosecutor of the International Criminal Court, Mr. Luis Moreno Ocampo, to the Security Council Pursuant to UNSC 1593 (2005) (13 December 2005): 6.

134. Address by Luis Moreno-Ocampo, Prosecutor of the International Criminal Court, at the International Conference "Building a Future on Peace *and* Justice," Nuremberg (25 June 2007), http://www.peace-justice-conference.info/download/speech%20moreno.pdf.

135. Atkinson, "'The Realists in Juba'?" 213.

136. Perrot, "Northern Uganda," 199.

137. ICG, "Peace in Northern Uganda: Decisive Weeks Ahead," 8.

138. Barney Afako, "Reconciliation and Justice: 'Mato Oput' and the Amnesty Act," Conciliation Resources (2002), http://www.c-r.org.

139. Rodman and Booth, "Manipulated Commitments," 282.

140. Including, for example, Brigadier Dam Kolo, who was described as "a voice of moderation within the LRA." ICG, "Peace in Northern Uganda: Decisive Weeks Ahead," 2.

141. Lomo, "The International Criminal Court Investigations," 7.

142. Linda M. Keller, "Achieving Peace with Justice: The International Criminal Court and Ugandan Alternative Justice Mechanisms," *Connecticut Journal of International Law* 23, 2 (2008): 215. Perhaps this reduction was related to new efforts by the LRA to prevent defections, including increasing security over the children it abducted. ICG, "Building a Comprehensive Peace Strategy for Northern Uganda," 3.

143. Joanna R. Quinn, "Getting to Peace? Negotiating with the LRA in Northern Uganda," *Human Rights Review* 10, 1 (2009): 64.

144. ICG, "Building a Comprehensive Peace Strategy for Northern Uganda," 2–3.

145. ICG, "Peace in Northern Uganda?" (13 September 2006) 10–11.

146. Ibid., 13.

147. Ibid., 15.

148. ICG, "Building a Comprehensive Peace Strategy for Northern Uganda," 9.

149. Quoted in ICG, "Peace in Northern Uganda?" 16.

150. Ibid.

151. Ibid., 11.

152. ICG, "Peace in Northern Uganda: Decisive Weeks Ahead," 2.

153. Rodman and Booth, "Manipulated Commitments," 291.

154. With the significant involvement of NGOs. Simon Simonse, Willemijn Verkoren, and Gerd Junne, "NGO Involvement in the Juba Peace Talks: The Role and Dilemmas of IKV Pax Christi," in Allen and Vlassenroot, *The Lord's Resistance Army*, 223–41.

155. ICG, "Peace in Northern Uganda?" 1–2.

156. Ibid., 5–6; Schomerus, "'They Forget What They Came For,'" 8.

157. ICG, "Northern Uganda: Seizing the Opportunity for Peace" (26 April 2007), 2–4.

158. Ibid., 9.

159. Ibid., 7. The DRC government perceives this saber rattling as an attempt to divert attention from Uganda's previous and ongoing meddling in Ituri (actions that led to an International Court of Justice judgment against it in December 2005) (12).

160. Ibid., 8.

161. ICG, "Northern Uganda Peace Process: The Need to Maintain Momentum" (14 September 2007): 2–3.

162. "Agreement on Accountability and Reconciliation Between the Government of the Republic of Uganda and the Lord's Resistance Army/Movement," Juba, Sudan (29 June 2007), http://www.amicc.org/.

163. "Annexure to the Agreement on Accountability and Reconciliation," Juba, Sudan (19 February 2008), http://www.amicc.org/docs.

164. "Uganda: Government to Seek Review of ICC Indictments against LRA Leaders," *IRIN*, 21 June 2007,, http://www.irinnews.org.

165. Quoted in ICG, "Building a Comprehensive Peace Strategy for Northern Uganda," 9.

166. "Uganda Offers 'Blood Settlement' to LRA Rebels," *Reuters*, 11 March 2008.

167. As well as "plush jobs and money" for former rebel leaders. ICG, "Northern Uganda Peace Process," 8.

168. Moreno-Ocampo, "Building a Future on Peace and Justice," 4.

169. Ibid., 6.

170. Ibid., 8.

171. Ibid., 9.

172. Keller, "Achieving Peace with Justice," 222.

173. Peskin, "Caution and Confrontation in the International Criminal Court's Pursuit of Accountability," 686. For a longer discussion of Article 16 deferrals, see Keller, "Achieving Peace with Justice," 239–43.

174. Keller, "Achieving Peace with Justice," 12–47.

175. ICG, "Shock Therapy for Northern Uganda's Peace Process," 6.

176. ICC, "Policy Paper on the Interests of Justice" (September 2007): 2–3.

177. Ibid., 4–7.

178. Ibid., 1.

179. Ibid., 8.

180. Quoted in ibid.

181. ICC, "Policy Paper on the Interests of Justice," 8.

182. Ibid.

183. Peter Eichstaedt, "ICC Chief Prosecutor Talks Tough," Institute for War & Peace Reporting (7 May 2008), http://iwpr.net/report-news/icc-chief-prosecutor-talks-tough.

184. Rodman and Booth, "Manipulated Commitments," 295; "LRA Prepares for War, Not Peace," Institute for War and Peace Reporting (1 May 2008), http://iwpr.net/.

185. ICG, "Peace in Northern Uganda?" 8; ICG, "Northern Uganda Peace Process," 5.

186. Caroline Auyugi, "ICC Calls for End to LRA Aid," Institute for War & Peace Reporting (28 May 2008), http://iwpr.net/.

187. Atkinson, "'The Realists in Juba'?" 219–22.

188. ICG, "LRA: A Regional Strategy Beyond Killing Kony" (28 April 2010), 14.

189. Hillary Nsambu, "Former LRA Commander Kwoyelo Free," New Vision, 23 September 2011.

190. Ashley Benner, "Uganda Rules That Amnesty Can't Be Denied to LRA Leaders," Christian Science Monitor, 27 September 2011.

191. Small Arms Survey, "Lord's Resistance Army" (8 March 2013): 5, http://www.smallarmssurveysudan.org/.

192. "Whose Justice? Perceptions of Uganda's Amnesty Act 2000: The Potential for Conflict Resolution and Long-Term Reconciliation," Refugee Law Project, Working Paper 15, February 2005, 4, http://www.refugeelawproject.org/.

193. ICG, "Building a Comprehensive Peace Strategy for Northern Uganda," 8.

194. Ibid., 4.

195. Allen, Trial Justice, 130–31.

196. "Whose Justice?" 4–5. Allen observes that "[in] Gulu town, in particular, it is presented as a kind of 'received wisdom' the Acholi people have a special capacity to forgive, and that local understandings of justice are based on reintegration of offending people into society" (Trial Justice, 129).

197. "Whose Justice?" 3.

198. Ibid., 3, 20–22.

199. Ibid., 5.

200. Quoted in ICG, "Shock Therapy," 5.

201. Ibid., 6.

202. Allen, Trial Justice, 178–79.

203. Ibid., 83–87.

204. Save the Children in Uganda, "Child Protection Concerns Related to the ICC Investigations and Possible Prosecution of the LRA Leadership" (30 March 2005).

205. Tim Allen, "Bitter Roots: The 'Invention' of Acholi Traditional Justice," in Allen and Vlassenroot, *The Lord's Resistance Army*, 244. For an in-depth discussion of local concerns about the ICC, see Allen, *Trial Justice*, 96–127.

206. Allen, "Bitter Roots," 251; Kasaija Phillip Apuuli, "The ICC's Possible Deferral of the LRA Case to Uganda," *Journal of International Criminal Justice* 6, 4 (2008): 806.

207. Allen, "Bitter Roots," 244.

208. Ibid., 245–46.

209. Branch, *Displacing Human Rights*, 156.

210. Ibid., 158.

211. Allen, "Bitter Roots," 247–49.

212. Ibid., 249.

213. ICG, "Northern Uganda: The Road to Peace, with or Without Kony" (10 December 2008), 13.

214. Allen, "Bitter Roots," 249–51.

215. Keller, "Achieving Peace with Justice," 225–26.

216. Joyce Neu, "Briefing on the Conflict in Uganda: Hope for a Negotiated Settlement," Joan B. Kroc Institute for Peace and Justice (1 June 2005), http://www.sandiego.edu/peacestudies /documents.

217. Allen, "Bitter Roots," 252–54.

218. See Branch, *Displacing Human Rights*, 154–78, for a critique of the role of traditional justice and its instrumentalization.

219. Allen, *Trial Justice*, 147–48.

220. Ibid., 168.

221. Patrick Vinck, Phuong Pham, Eric Stover, Andrew Moss, and Marieke Wierda, "Research Note on Attitudes About Peace and Justice in Northern Uganda," International Center for Transitional Justice (January 2008): 2, http://ictj.org/.

222. Ibid., 6–7.

223. Ibid., 4.

224. ICG, "Peace in Northern Uganda?" 16.

225. ICG, "Northern Uganda Peace Process," 10.

226. Ibid., 16.

227. Allen, "Bitter Roots," 250.

228. Keller, "Achieving Peace with Justice," 235.

229. Ibid., 231.

230. ICG, "Peace in Northern Uganda?" 16.

231. Keller, "Achieving Peace with Justice," 229.

232. ICG, "Peace in Northern Uganda?" 16.

233. Keller, "Achieving Peace with Justice," 232–36.

234. "Living with Fear: A Populations-Based Survey on Attitudes About Peace, Justice, and Social Reconstruction in Eastern Democratic Republic of Congo," Human Rights Center (University of California, Berkeley), Payson Center for International Development (Tulane University), and International Center for Transitional Justice (August 2008): 2, http://www.law.berkeley .edu/files/HRC.

235. UNSC, "Report of the Secretary-General on Children and Armed Conflict in the Democratic Republic of the Congo," S/2010/369 (9 July 2010), 4.

236. HRW, "Trail of Death: LRA Atrocities in Northeastern Congo" (March 2010), 49–51.

237. Resolve, "Peace Can Be: President Obama's Chance to Help End LRA Atrocities in 2012" (February 2012): 23, http://www.scribd.com/doc/82297965/Peace-Can-Be-2012.

238. UNSC, "Report of the Secretary-General on the Activities of the United Nations Regional Office for Central Africa and on Areas Affected by the Lord's Resistance Army," S/2012/923 (13 December 2012), 13.

239. Grace Matsiko, Frank Nyakairu, and Emmanuel Gyezaho, "I Cannot Betray Kony, Museveni," *Monitor* (16 August 2006).

240. ICG, "Northern Uganda Peace Process," 9.

241. Keller, "Achieving Peace with Justice," 242.

242. I am indebted to Steve Lamony for this observation.

243. Makau Mutua, "Savages, Victims, and Saviors: The Metaphor of Human Rights," *Harvard International Law Journal* 42, 1 (2001): 201–45.

244. Branch, *Displacing Human Rights*, 182.

245. Ibid.

246. Certainly the rhetoric after 9/11 and in the context of the "War on Terror" bears this out.

247. Branch, *Displacing Human Rights*, 186.

248. Rodman and Booth, "Manipulated Commitments."

249. Branch, *Displacing Human Rights*, 191–92.

250. Ibid., 192–93.

251. Ibid., 189.

252. Olara A. Otunnu, "The Secret Genocide," *Foreign Policy*, 9 June 2006.

253. Andreas Th. Müller and Ignaz Stegmiller, "Self-Referrals on Trial: From Panacea to Patient," *Journal of International Criminal Justice* 8 (2010): 1270. Issues raised with regard to self-referrals—in particular attempts by referring states to restrict who might be investigated and to "withdraw" a referral when it is politically expedient—lead Müller and Stegmiller to conclude "that the over-extensive use of self-referrals by the OTP must come to an end," to be replaced by the use of *proprio motu* powers by the Prosecutor (1293).

254. William A. Schabas, " 'Complementarity in Practice': Some Uncomplimentary Thoughts," *Criminal Law Forum* 19, 1 (2008): 30.

255. Mamdani argues starkly: "The main external obstacle to a peace agreement between the LRA and the government of Uganda is in fact the ICC's determination to criminalize the LRA's leadership in the name of pursuing justice." Mahmood Mamdani, *Saviors and Survivors: Darfur, Politics and the War on Terror* (London: Verso, 2009), 285.

256. Priscilla Hayner, quoted in Janine Natalya Clark, "Peace, Justice and the International Criminal Court," *Journal of International Criminal Justice* 9, 3 (2011): 543.

257. Ibid., 542–43.

258. Ibid., 543.

259. Pillay argues that "The question of justice . . . is . . . the question of peace." Suren Pillay, Conclusion," in *Peace Versus Justice? The Dilemma of Transitional Justice in Africa*, ed. Chandra Lekha Sriram and Suran Pillay (Scottsville: University of KwaZulu-Natal Press, 2009), 348.

260. Branch, *Displacing Human Rights*, 212.

261. Schabas, "Complementarity in Practice," 33.

262. The Secretary-General noted that "LRA has not been present in Ugandan territory as of November 2005." UNSC, "Children and Armed Conflict" (2009): 39.

263. ICG, "Northern Uganda: The Road to Peace, with or Without Kony," 14. In June 2008, the Secretary-General noted that "the LRA elements are reported to have continued to operate relatively unfettered inside the Central African Republic, burning and vandalizing villages and stealing goods and property." UNSC, "Report of the Secretary-General on the Situation in the Central African Republic and on the Activities of the United Nations Peacebuilding Support Office in That Country," S/2008/410 (23 June 2008): 3.

264. HRW, "The Christmas Massacres: LRA Attacks on Civilians in Northern Congo" (February 2009): 13, 16, 42.

265. MONUC and UN Office of the High Commissioner for Human Rights, "Summary of Fact Finding Missions on Alleged Human Rights Violations Committed by the Lord's Resistance Army (LRA) in the Districts of Haut-Uélé and Bas-Uélé in Orientale Province of the Democratic Republic of Congo" (December 2009), 7 (hereafter MONUC-UNHCHR LRA Report).

266. Eichstaedt, "ICC Chief Prosecutor Talks Tough."

267. ICG, "Peace in Northern Uganda?" 4.

268. Ibid., 15.

269. ICG, "Northern Uganda: The Road to Peace," 16.

270. Ibid., 16; HRW, "The Christmas Massacres," 17.

271. ICG, "Northern Uganda Peace Process," 6.

272. ICG, "Peace in Northern Uganda?" 11.

273. ICG, "Northern Uganda: Seizing the Opportunity for Peace," 13.

274. HRW, "The Christmas Massacres," 6.

275. ICG, "Northern Uganda Peace Process," 6.

276. ICG, "Peace in Northern Uganda?" 11.

277. ICG, "Northern Uganda: Seizing the Opportunity for Peace," 13.

278. UNSC, "Twenty-Sixth Report of the Secretary-General on the United Nations Organization Mission in the Democratic Republic of Congo," S/2008/433 (3 July 2008): 2.

279. Ibid., 5.

280. HRW, "Christmas Massacres," 17–18, 20–27.

281. UNSC, "Report of the Secretary-General on Children and Armed Conflict in the Democratic Republic of the Congo," 3.

282. The attack involved 1,186 UPDF and 3,496 FARDC troops. UNSC, "Twenty-Seventh Report of the Secretary-General on the United Nations Organization Mission in the Democratic Republic of Congo," 4.

283. HRW, "The Christmas Massacres," 50.

284. Peter Eichstaedt, "More Robust International Action in DRC Needed," Institute for War & Peace Reporting (27 March 2009), http://iwpr.net/report-news/more-robust-international-action-drc-needed.

285. HRW, "The Christmas Massacres," 28.

286. Ibid., 29; "UN in Congo 'Gives LRA Free Rein,'" BBC News, 4 February 2009, http://news.bbc.co.uk/1/hi/world/africa/7869832.stm. The search and rescue element was prioritized as a result of pressure from the U.S. HRW, "The Christmas Massacres," 50.

287. MONUC-UNHCHR LRA Report.

288. ICG, "LRA: A Regional Strategy Beyond Killing Kony," 1.

289. UNSC, "Twenty-Seventh Report of the Secretary-General on the United Nations Organization Mission in the Democratic Republic of Congo," 5.

290. HRW, "The Christmas Massacres," 4–5, 29–41.

291. HRW, "Trail of Death: LRA Atrocities in Northeastern Congo," 16, 53, 56; ICG, "LRA," 5.

292. Peskin, "Caution and Confrontation," 688.

293. UNSC, Statement by the President of the Security Council, S/PRST/2008/48 (22 December 2008).

294. Jeffrey Gettleman and Eric Schmitt, "U.S. Aided a Failed Plan to Rout Ugandan Rebels," New York Times, 6 February 2009.

295. MONUC-UNHCHR LRA Report, 13, 18; UNSC, "Twenty-Eighth Report of the Secretary-General on the United Nations Organization Mission in the Democratic Republic of Congo," 4.

296. HRW, "Trail of Death," 58.

297. UNSC, "Twenty-Eighth Report of the Secretary-General on the United Nations Organization Mission in the Democratic Republic of Congo," 16.

298. Ibid., 6.

299. HRW, "Trail of Death," 3–4, 18–38.

300. Ibid., 16–17, 53; UNSC, "Thirtieth Report of the Secretary-General on the United Nations Organization Mission in the Democratic Republic of Congo," 20.

301. Ledio Cakaj, "The Lord's Resistance Army of Today," Enough Project, November 2010, 6, http://www.enoughproject.org/files/lra_today.pdf.

302. UNSC, "Thirty-First Report of the Secretary-General on the United Nations Organization Mission in the Democratic Republic of Congo," 1.

303. Ibid., 7.

304. ICG, "The Lord's Resistance Army: End Game?" (17 November 2011): i, 3–4, 7–8.

305. UNSC, "Report of the Secretary-General on Children and Armed Conflict in Uganda," S/2007/260 (7 May 2007).

306. UNSC, "Additional Report of the Secretary-General on Children and Armed Conflict in Uganda," S/2008/409 (23 June 2008).

307. UNSC, "Report of the Secretary-General on Children and Armed Conflict in Uganda," S/2009/462 (15 September 2009).

308. The LRA was also mentioned in a number of other reports by the Secretary-General, particularly those focused on the DRC, the CAR, and children in armed conflict more generally.

309. UNSC, "Report of the Secretary-General on the Lord's Resistance Army-Affected Areas Pursuant to Security Council Press Statement," S/2011/693 (4 November 2011): 3, 5.

310. Ibid., 9.

311. UNSC, "Report of the Secretary-General on the United Nations Organization Stabilization Mission in the Democratic Republic of Congo," S/2010/512 (8 October 2010): 5.

312. UNSC, "Report of the Secretary-General on the United Nations Organization Stabilization Mission in the Democratic Republic of Congo," S/2011/20 (17 January 2011): 4, 17.

313. UNSC, "Report of the Secretary-General on the United Nations Organization Stabilization Mission in the Democratic Republic of Congo," S/2011/298 (12 May 2011): 5.

314. UNSC, "Report of the Secretary-General on the Lord's Resistance Army-Affected Areas Pursuant to Security Council Press Statement," 8.

315. UNSC, "Letter Dated 25 June 2012 from the Secretary-General Addressed to the President of the Security Council," S/2012/481 (25 June 2012): 5.

316. UNSC, "Report of the Secretary-General on the United Nations Organization Stabilization Mission in the Democratic Republic of Congo," S/2012/65 (26 January 2012): 6, 16.

317. UNSC, "Report of the Secretary-General on the Situation of Children and Armed Conflict Affected by the Lord's Resistance Army," S/2012/365 (25 May 2012): 11–12.

318. UNSC, "Report of the Secretary-General on the United Nations Organization Stabilization Mission in the Democratic Republic of Congo," S/2012/355 (23 May 2012): 5.

319. UNSC, "Letter Dated 25 June 2012 from the Secretary-General Addressed to the President of the Security Council."

320. Enough Project, "Getting Back on Track: Implementing the UN Regional Strategy of the Lord's Resistance Army," joint NGO report (December 2012), http://www.enoughproject.org /reports.

321. OCHA, "Humanitarian Action in LRA-Affected Areas: Regional Overview of Needs and Response" (June 2012), 4, 11–12.

322. Ibid., 12.

323. African Union, "Plan of Action," Special Session of the Assembly of the Union on the Consideration and Resolution of Conflicts in Africa, SP/Assembly/PS/Plan(1) (31 August 2009), 6, http://www.peaceau.org/uploads/plan-of-action-final-eng-.pdf.

324. ICG, "The Lord's Resistance Army: End Game?" 11–12.

325. Ibid., 12.

326. Ibid., 12–13.

327. Josh Kron, "African Union to Make Push Against Rebels," *New York Times*, 23 March 2012.

328. Enough Project, "Getting Back on Track," 4; "Uganda to Withdraw Troops from Somalia Says Mukasa," *BBC News*, 2 November 2012.

329. Small Arms Survey, "Lord's Resistance Army," 4.

330. Enough Project, "Getting Back on Track," 8.

331. The government of Sudan denied the presence of any LRA in Kafia Kingi. UNSC, "Report of the Secretary-General on the Activities of the United Nations Regional Office for Central Africa and on the Lord's Resistance Army-Affected Areas," S/2013/297 (20 May 2013): 7.

332. Enough Project, "Getting Back on Track," 8–11.

333. For an overview, see Sylvester Bongani Maphosa, "Preparing for Peace: The AU Regional Cooperation Initiative for the Elimination of the LRA in Central Africa," Africa Institute of South Africa (March 2013), http://dspace.cigilibrary.org.

334. Enough Project, "Getting Back on Track," 8.

335. OCHA, "LRA Regional Update: Central African Republic, DR Congo and South Sudan (April–June 2013)" (25 July 2013), http://reliefweb.int/sites/reliefweb.int/files/.

336. HRW, "The Christmas Massacres," 49.

337. U.S. Senate, "Lord's Resistance Army Disarmament and Northern Uganda Recovery Act of 2009," S.1067, 111th Cong., 2nd sess., 5 January 2010. This act followed several other smaller initiatives in Congress to address aspects of the LRA crisis. Alexis Arieff and Lauren Ploch, "The Lord's Resistance Army: The U.S. Response," Congressional Research Service (11 April 2012): 9.

338. Barack Obama, "Statement by the President on the Signing of the Lord's Resistance Army Disarmament and Northern Uganda Recovery Act of 2009" (24 May 2010), http://www.whitehouse.gov/.

339. "Strategy to Support the Disarmament of the Lord's Resistance Army: A Strategy to Guide United States Support Across the Region for Viable Multilateral Efforts to Mitigate and Eliminate the Threat Posed to Civilians and Regional Stability Posed by the Lord's Resistance Army" (24 November 2010), http://pulitzercenter.org/sites/default/files/WhiteHouseLRAStrategy_opt.pdf (hereinafter LRA Strategy).

340. LRA Strategy, 22.

341. ICG, "The Lord's Resistance Army: End Game?" 14.

342. Adam Branch, "The Paradoxes of Protection: Aligning Against the Lord's Resistance Army," *African Security* 5, 3–4 (2012): 174.

343. Small Arms Survey, "Lord's Resistance Army," 4.

344. LRA Strategy.

345. Before the creation of AFRICOM, responsibility for U.S. military policy in Africa was shared by three commands—European Command (EUCOM), which dealt with most of the continent; Central Command (CENTCOM), dealing with East Africa; and Pacific Command (PACOM), focused on the island states off the east coast of Africa. Stefan Gänzle, "AFRICOM and U.S. Africa Policy: 'Pentagonising' Foreign Policy or Providing a Model for Joint Approaches," *African Security Review* 20, 1 (2011): 76.

346. Branch, *Displacing Human Rights*, 218–19.

347. Gänzle, "AFRICOM and U.S. Africa Policy," 76–77.

348. Branch, *Displacing Human Rights*, 225.

349. Gänzle, "AFRICOM and U.S. Africa Policy," 77.

350. Branch, *Displacing Human Rights*, 231.

351. Larry Minear, "Humanitarian Action in an Age of Terrorism," International Council on Human Rights Policy, prepared for International Expert Conference on "September 2001: Impacts on Human Rights Work" (24–25 May 2002), 9, http://www.ichrp.org/files/papers/.

352. Branch, *Displacing Human Rights*, 223.

353. Kenneth Roth, "Get Tough on Human Rights," *Foreign Policy*, November 2010.

354. Branch, *Displacing Human Rights*, 238.

355. http://invisiblechildren.com/kony/.

356. http://invisiblechildren.com/media/videos/program-media/kony-2012/.

357. Josh Kron and J. David Goodman, "Online, a Distant Conflict Soars to Topic 1," *New York Times*, 8 March 2012.

358. Including Oprah Winfrey, Justin Bieber, and Kim Kardashian. J. David Goodman and Jennifer Preston, "How the Kony Video Went Viral," *New York Times*, 9 March 2012.

359. Michael Wilkerson, "Kony 2012 Campaign: Oprah and Bracelets Won't Solve Problem," *The Guardian*, 8 March 2012; Amy C. Finnegan, "The White Girl's Burden," *Contexts* 12, 1 (2013): 30–35; http://shop.invisiblechildren.com/kony-bracelet/. By buying a bracelet—"The ultimate accessory"—you can "show your commitment to the KONY 2012 campaign."

360. Quoted in Branch, *Displacing Human Rights*, 238.

361. Quoted in Jeffrey Gettleman, "In Vast Jungle, U.S. Troops Aid in Search for Kony," *New York Times*, 29 April 2012.

362. "Reward Offered for Information on Kony," *New York Times*, 3 April 2013.

363. UNSC, "Report of the Secretary-General on the Activities of the United Nations Regional Office for Central Africa and on the Lord's Resistance Army-Affected Areas" (20 May 2013), 14.

364. "Uganda Struggles to Come to Terms with Its Disappeared," *IRIN*, 30 August 2013.

365. Ibid., 7.

366. "Joseph Kony: U.S. Doubts LRA Rebel Leader's Surrender," *BBC News*, 21 November 2103.

367. Dunn, "The Lord's Resistance Army and African International Relations," 58.

368. These included the greed of some of the negotiators, such as LRA spokesperson David Matsanga who was eventually given amnesty, who seemed more interested in enriching themselves. Stephen Oola, "Matsanga Should Not Have Been Given Amnesty," *New Vision*, 10 June 2010.

369. Bernard Momanyi, "Ugandan Leader Lashes Out at ICC," Institute for War & Peace Reporting (20 April 2013).

370. Schomerus, "They Forget What They Came For."

371. Ronald Atkinson, Phil Lancaster, Ledio Cakaj, and Guilaume Lacaille, "Do No Harm: Assessing a Military Approach to the Lord's Resistance Army," *Journal of Eastern African Studies* 6, 2 (2012): 371–82.

372. Ibid., 379.

373. Ibid., 381.

Chapter 5. Darfur: The Post-World Summit Test

Epigraphs: Robert Zoellick, U.S. deputy secretary of state, quoted in International Crisis Group, "To Save Darfur," *Africa Report* 105 (17 March 2006): 4; African diplomat, quoted in "African Union Drops Resolution Barring Arrest of Sudanese President in Continent," *Sudan Tribune* (26 July 2010); http://www.savedarfur.org.

1. As Gérard Prunier points out, this division into "African" and "Arab" is inherently contested and bears little connection to the reality of the complexity of identity construction in the

region. Gérard Prunier, *Darfur: The Ambiguous Genocide*, 2nd ed. (Ithaca, N.Y.: Cornell University Press, 2007).

2. Ibid., 92–93.

3. On the recent history of Darfur, see ibid.; Julie Flint and Alex de Waal, *Darfur: A Short History of a Long War* (London: Zed, 2005).

4. Mahmood Mamdani, *Saviors and Survivors: Darfur, Politics and the War on Terror* (London: Verso, 2009), 4.

5. Prunier, *Darfur: The Ambiguous Genocide*, 99.

6. Ibid., 102.

7. UNHCR, "Supplementary Appeal for Emergency Assistance to Sudanese in Eastern Chad," 1 September 2003.

8. Prunier, *Darfur*, 109.

9. UNHCR, "UN Refugee Agency Appeals for Emergency Funds for Sudanese Refugees" (30 January 2004), http://www.unhcr.org/. "Race against time" became a favorite phrase to describe the situation in Darfur, as the UN, governmental officials, and NGOs also used it throughout 2004 and beyond. Focusing on the immediate need to feed people contributed to the depoliticization of the situation. "Sudanese Children Dying of Hunger," *BBC News*, 9 June 2004; "Sudan Aid Arrives, 'More Needed,'" *BBC News*, 29 July 2004; World Food Program, "New Donations Boost Rations But More Contributions Needed for Sudan," 29 May 2006.

10. Prunier, *Darfur*, 89–90; Samantha Power, "Dying in Darfur," *New Yorker*, 30 August 2004.

11. Prunier, *Darfur*, 112–14.

12. Nicholas D. Kristof, "Will We Say 'Never Again' Yet Again?" *New York Times*, 27 March 2004.

13. Prunier, *Darfur*, 114; Power, "Dying in Darfur."

14. Power, "Dying in Darfur."

15. ICG, "To Save Darfur," 14–15, http://www.crisisgroup.org/library/documents/africa/horn_of_africa/105_to_save_darfur.pdf.

16. African Union Peace and Security Council, Communiqué of the Seventeenth Meeting of the Peace and Security Council, PSC/PR/Comm.(XVII) (20 October 2004), http://www.africa-union.org/news_events/Communiqués/Communiqué%20_Eng%2020%20oct%202004.pdf.

17. Linnea Bergholm, "The African Union, the United Nations and Civilian Protection Challenges in Darfur," Refugee Studies Centre, Oxford University, Working Paper 63 (May 2010), 22.

18. Ibid., 24.

19. "US House Calls Darfur 'Genocide,'" *BBC News*, 23 July 2004.

20. Although, certainly not for Sudan. It had signed the Genocide Convention only ten months before Powell's statement, and, as Flint and de Waal observe, "now saw this legalistic quibbling as proof that even an international covenant like the Genocide Convention was just a piece of paper," Flint and de Waal, *Darfur*, 131–32.

21. Eric Reeves, "Europe's Indifference to Darfur," *New Republic*, 27 October 2006, posted on JUSTWATCH-L e-mail list.

22. Power, "Dying in Darfur."

23. Prunier, *Darfur*, 145.

24. "Report of the International Commission of Inquiry on Darfur to the United Nations Secretary-General" (25 January 2005), http://www.un.org/news/dh/sudan/com_inq_darfur.pdf; William A. Schabas, "Darfur and the 'Odious Scourge': The Commission of Inquiry's Findings on Genocide," *Leiden Journal of International Law* 18, 4 (2005): 871–85; Dawn L. Rothe and Christopher W. Mullins, "Darfur and the Politicization of International Law," *Humanity & Society* 31, 1 (2007): 83–107.

25. Mamdani, *Saviors and Survivors*, 7.

26. Warren Hoge, "U.N. Votes to Send Any Sudan War Crime Suspects to World Court," *New York Times*, 1 April 2005.

27. "Court Probes Sudan 'War Crimes,'" *BBC News*, 5 June 2005.

28. Author interviews.

29. ICG, "To Save Darfur," 2.

30. Quoted in ibid., 4.

31. Ibid., 5, 7–13.

32. An indicator of its weakness vis-à-vis Khartoum is that its 25 helicopters were based at government airfields, which closed at dark. Ibid., 16. For a further critique of AMIS, see Eric Reeves, "Genocide Without End? The Destruction of Darfur," *Dissent* (Summer 2007).

33. UNSC, "Report of the Secretary-General on Darfur," S/20006/591 (28 July 2006).

34. UNSC, "Letter Dated 17 August from the Secretary-General Addressed to the President of the Security Council," S/2006/665 (17 August 2006).

35. Kofi Annan stated that "the document does not indicate a willingness on the part of the Government of Sudan to agree to a transition to a United Nations operation in Darfur." UNSC, "Letter Dated 10 August from the Secretary-General Addressed to the President of the Security Council," S/2006/645 (14 August 2006).

36. U.S. White House, "President Bush Addresses United Nations General Assembly" (19 September 2006), http://www.whitehouse.gov.

37. Robert F. Worth, "Sudan Says It Will Accept U.N.-African Peace Force in Darfur," *New York Times*, 17 November 2006.

38. Victoria Holt and Glyn Taylor, with Max Kelly, *Protecting Civilians in the Context of UN Peacekeeping Operations: Successes, Setbacks and Remaining Challenges*, Independent study jointly commissioned by the Department of Peacekeeping Operations and Office for the Coordination of Humanitarian Affairs, United Nations, November 2009. http://reliefweb.int/, 342–43.

39. Ibid., 350; UNSC, "Report of the Secretary-General and the Chairperson of the African Union Commission on the Hybrid Operation in Darfur," S/2007/307/Rev.1 (5 June 2007): 19.

40. Jeffrey Gettleman, "Chaos in Darfur on Rise as Arabs Fight with Arabs," *New York Times*, 3 September 2007; HRW, "Darfur 2007: Chaos by Design" (September 2007).

41. Jeffrey Gettleman, "Darfur Rebels Kill 10 in Peace Force," *New York Times*, 1 October 2007.

42. Holt and Taylor, *Protecting Civilians in the Context of UN Peacekeeping Operations*, 359.

43. Ibid., 346.

44. Ibid., 347.

45. Ibid., 348.

46. Evelyn Leopold, "UN, AU Differ on Composition of Darfur Peace Force," *Reuters*, 21 September 2007.

47. "UNAMID Deployment on the Brink: The Road to Security in Darfur Blocked by Government Obstruction," Joint NGO Report, December 2007, http://www.humanrightsfirst.info/pdf/071221-ij-UNAMID-joint-report.pdf.

48. Claudia Parsons, "U.N. Urgently Seeking Helicopters for Darfur Force," *Reuters*, 21 October 2007, posted on JUSTWATCH-L e-mail list. At the same time, China and Russia were supplying Sudan with attack helicopters that were used in Darfur, in defiance of a UN arms embargo. Ian Taylor, "The People's Republic of China," in *The International Politics of Mass Atrocities: The Case of Darfur*, ed. David R. Black and Paul D. Williams (New York: Routledge, 2010), 182. This contributed to the rhetoric of the "Genocide Olympics" in which activists attempted to connect China's role in Darfur to the 2008 Beijing Olympics (182–86).

49. Gareth Evans, *The Responsibility to Protect: Ending Mass Atrocity Crimes Once and For All* (Washington, D.C.: Brookings Institution Press, 2008): 178.

50. "U.N. Force Takes Control in Darfur," *New York Times* (AP), 31 December 2007.

51. "UN Chief Sees Obstacles to Helping Darfur, Somalia," *Associated Press*, 7 October 2008, posted on JUSTWATCH e-mail list. As of July 2009, eighteen months after UNAMID began deployment, the helicopters still had not arrived, nor had the required troops. Andrew Heavens, "Darfur Peacekeepers Still Waiting for Helicopters: UN," *Reuters*, 12 July 2009.

52. UNSC, "Report of the Secretary-General on the Deployment of the African Union-United Nations Hybrid Operation in Darfur," S/2008/659 (17 October 2008), 5–12.

53. Ibid., 9.

54. ICG, "Sudan: Justice, Peace and the ICC" (17 July 2009), i.

55. UNSC, "Report of the Secretary-General on the Deployment of the African-Union-United Nations Hybrid Operation in Darfur," S/2009/83 (10 February 2009), 1, 4–9, 11.

56. UNSC, "Report of the Secretary-General on the Deployment of the African-Union-United Nations Hybrid Operation in Darfur," S/2009/201 (14 April 2009): 1.

57. ICC, "Seventh Report of the Prosecutor of the International Criminal Court to the UN Security Council Pursuant to UNSCR 1593 (2005)," http://www.iccnow.org/documents/7thUNSCversionsenttoUN29may.pdf.

58. ICG, "Sudan: Justice, Peace and the ICC," 11.

59. Alaa Shahine, "Sudan Says No Evidence Against ICC Darfur Suspect," *Reuters*, 3 May 2007, posted on JUSTWATCH-L e-mail list.

60. ICG, "Sudan: Justice, Peace and the ICC," 6.

61. Colum Lynch and Nora Boustany, "Sudan Leader to be Charged with Genocide," *Washington Post*, 11 July 2008; ICC, "ICC Prosecutor Presents Case Against Sudanese President, Hassan Ahmad AL BASHIR, for Genocide, Crimes Against Humanity and War," press release (14 July 2008), ICC-OTP-20080714-PR341, http://www.icc-cpi.int/menus/icc.

62. Julie Flint and Alex de Waal, "This Prosecution Will Endanger the People We Wish to Defend in Sudan," *The Observer*, 13 July 2008.

63. Marlise Simons, Lydia Polgreen, and Jeffrey Gettleman, "Arrest Is Sought of Sudan Leader in Genocide Case," *New York Times*, 15 July 2008. Roberto Belloni makes a similar argument with respect to expectations by rebel groups for intervention on their behalf. Belloni, "The Tragedy of Darfur and the Limits of the 'Responsibility to Protect,'" 327–46.

64. Colum Lynch, "Indictment of Sudanese Leader Seen as Threat to Peacekeepers," *Washington Post*, 20 July 2008.

65. Steve Bloomfield, "African Union: Suspend Sudan Genocide Charge," *The Independent*, 15 July 2008; John Norris, David Sullivan, and John Prendergast, "The Merits of Justice," Enough Project, July 2008, http://www.enoughproject.org/files/reports/ICC_report_071408.pdf.

66. Thijs Bouwknegt, "Sudan to Revive Darfur Court," *Radio Netherlands Worldwide*, 25 July 2008.

67. Charbonneau, "UN May Want to Suspend ICC Action on Bashir—Russia."

68. Neil MacFarquhar and Marlise Simons, "UN Panel Says Sudan Expulsion of Aid Groups Is 'Deplorable,'" *New York Times*, 6 March 2009.

69. "U.N. Council Set to Renew Darfur Peacekeeping Mandate," *Reuters*, 31 July 2008, posted on JUSTWATCH-L e-mail list.

70. "Charging Sudan's Beshir Would Wreck Darfur Peace: Mbeki," *Agence France-Presse*, 26 July 2008, posted on JUSTWATCH-L e-mail list.

71. "UN Split over Darfur Peace Force," *BBC News*, 29 July 2008.

72. ICG, "Sudan: Justice, Peace and the ICC," 15–16.

73. France declared it would veto any Security Council resolution that suspended ICC actions against Bashir, and the United Kingdom said that it would not support such a suspension. Both countries left open the possibility of suspending the investigation, but provided unclear conditions for this to happen. "France Will Veto Any Resolution Deferring Sudan President Indict-

ment: Official," *Sudan Tribune*, 19 September 2008, posted on JUSTWATCH-L e-mail list; "British Official Denies Plans to Freeze ICC Indictment of Sudan's Bashir," *Sudan Tribune*, 19 September 2008, posted on JUSTWATCH-L e-mail list; Julian Borger, "Khartoum Conundrum," *The Guardian*, 16 October 2008.

74. "U.N. Votes to Extend Mission in Darfur," *CNN*, 1 August 2008.

75. ICG, "Sudan: Justice, Peace and the ICC," 17.

76. African Union, Peace and Security Council, 142nd Meeting (21 July 2008), http://www.sudantribune.com/spip.php?article27982.

77. UNSC Resolution 1828 (31 July 2008).

78. African Union Assembly, "Decision on the Report of the Commission on the Abuse of the Principle of Universal Jurisdiction" (1 July 2008), 11th Ord. Sess., A.U. Doc. Assembly /AU/14(XI).

79. Geneuss, "Fostering a Better Understanding of Universal Jurisdiction," 946; African Union, Peace and Security Council, Press Statement (11 July 2008), 141st Meeting, A.U. Doc. PSC/PR/BR(CXLI).

80. Jalloh, "Universal Jurisdiction, Universal Prescription?," 20–21, 29; Geneuss, "Fostering a Better Understanding of Universal Jurisdiction," 946.

81. Geneuss, "Fostering a Better Understanding of Universal Jurisdiction," 946.

82. See also "AU-EU Technical Ad Hoc Expert Group on the Principle of Universal Jurisdiction Report" (15 April 2009) (hereafter AU-EU Report), http://www.africa-union.org.

83. African Union, Peace and Security Council, "Communiqué of the 142nd Meeting of the Peace and Security Council" (21 July 2008), 142d mtg., A.U. Doc. PSC/MIN/Comm(CXLII)Rev.1 (hereinafter 142d Meeting Communiqué).

84. "Tenth Report of the Prosecutor of the International Criminal Court to the UN Security Council Pursuant to UNSCR 1593 (2005)" (4 December 2009); African Union, Peace and Security Council, "Report of the African Union High-Level Panel on Darfur, Darfur: The Quest for Peace, Justice, and Reconciliation" (29 October 2009): 56, 207th mtg., A.U. Doc. PSC/AHG/2(CCVII), http://www.darfurpanel.org/2.html.

85. "Darfur Militia Leader in Custody," *BBC News*, 13 October 2008; Jeffrey Gettleman, "Sudan Arrests Militia Chief Facing Trial," *New York Times*, 14 October 2008.

86. African Union Assembly, "Decision on the Application by the International Criminal Court (ICC) Prosecutor for the Indictment of the President of the Republic of Sudan" (3 February 2009), 12th Ord. Sess., A.U. Doc. Assembly/AU/Dec.221(XII).

87. Marlise Simons and Neil MacFarquhar, "Court Issues Arrest Warrant for Sudan's Leader," *New York Times* (5 March 2009). ICC, "Situation in Darfur, Sudan, in the Case of *The Prosecutor v. Omar Hassan Ahmad Al Bashir*: Warrant of Arrest for Omar Hassan Ahmad Al Bashir," Case No. ICC-02/05-01/09 (4 March 2009), http://www.icc-cpi.int/iccdocs/doc/doc639078.pdf.

88. African Union Peace and Security Council, "Communiqué of the 175th Meeting of the Peace and Security Council" (5 March 2009), 175th mtg., A.U. Doc. PSC/PR/Comm(CLXXV).

89. Author interviews.

90. Coalition for the International Criminal Court, press release, "Global Coalition Says AU States Parties to International Criminal Court Have Legal Obligation to Cooperate with ICC" (7 July 2009), http://www.iccnow.org/documents/AU_Summit_PR_CICC_7July_09_Eng.pdf.

91. "African Countries Back Away from ICC Withdrawal Demand," *Sudan Tribune*, 8 June 2009.

92. "Joint Darfur Aid Warning Issued," *BBC News*, 24 March 2009; Christopher Fournier, "Punishment or Aid," *New York Times*, 28 March 2009. One of those organizations identified as providing information to the ICC was the International Rescue Committee. However, rather than providing information, there was an attempt to have a discussion within the organization about

how to deal with the ICC. This was put into an internal document, which was used as an excuse to accuse the IRC—and others—of collaborating with the ICC. Author interviews.

93. Neil MacFarquhar and Marlise Simons, "UN Panel Says Sudan Expulsion of Aid Groups Is 'Deplorable.'"

94. Julie Flint and Alex de Waal, "To Put Justice Before Peace Spells Disaster for Sudan," *The Guardian*, 6 March 2009.

95. Neil MacFarquhar, "U.N. Official Says Darfur Continues to Crumble," *New York Times*, 20 March 2009.

96. Flint and de Waal, "To Put Justice Before Peace Spells Disaster for Sudan."

97. Author interviews.

98. "Expelled U.S. Aid Groups Deny Return to Sudan," *Sudan Tribune*, 12 June 2009.

99. Author interviews.

100. UNSC, "Report of the Secretary-General on the Deployment of the African-Union–United Nations Hybrid Operation in Darfur," S/2009/297 (9 June 2009): 5.

101. "Darfur Rebel Group Pulls Out of Peace Talks," *Radio France Internationale* (21 March 2009).

102. UNSC, "Report of the Secretary-General on the Deployment of the African-Union–United Nations Hybrid Operation in Darfur," S/2009/201 (14 April 2009): 2.

103. UNSC, "Report of the Secretary-General on the Deployment of the African-Union–United Nations Hybrid Operation in Darfur," S/2009/352 (13 July 2009): 1.

104. ICG, "Sudan: Preventing Implosion" (17 December 2009), 9.

105. ICG, "Sudan: Justice, Peace and the ICC," 19–20.

106. Ibid., 21.

107. Ibid., 22.

108. UNSC, "Report of the Secretary-General on the Deployment of the African-Union–United Nations Hybrid Operation in Darfur" (14 April 2009), 11.

109. Ibid.

110. Ibid.

111. Ibid., 12.

112. African Union Assembly, "Decision on the Abuse of the Principle of Universal Jurisdiction" (3 July 2009), 13th Ord. Sess., A.U. Doc. Assembly/AU/11(XIII).

113. Mills, "'Bashir Is Dividing Us,'" 424–25.

114. Colum Lynch, "International Court Under Unusual Fire," *Washington Post*, 30 June 2009; CICC, "Global Coalition Says AU States Parties to International Criminal Court Have Legal Obligation to Cooperate with ICC"; author interviews.

115. Author interviews.

116. "Botswana Rebels Against AU over Bashir," *ABC News*, 5 July 2009.

117. "African Union Defies ICC over Bashir Extradition," *ABC News*, 5 July 2009.

118. African Union Assembly, "Decision on the Meeting of African States Parties to the Rome Statue of the International Criminal Court (ICC)" (3 July 2009), 13th Ord. Sess., A.U. Doc. Assembly/AU/13(XIII).

119. "Sudan Reverses Course on ICC Arrest Warrant for Bashir," *Sudan Tribune*, 30 July 2009.

120. "Uganda Pledges to Arrest Sudanese President," *Toronto Star*, 13 July 2009.

121. African Union, Peace and Security Council, "Darfur: The Quest for Peace," Report of the African Union High-Level Panel on Darfur (29 October 2009).

122. Ibid., 9.

123. Ibid., 3.

124. Ibid., xix.

125. Ibid., xvi.

126. Ibid., 65.

127. Author interviews.

128. African Union Executive Council, "Report of the Commission on the Outcome and Deliberations of the 8th Session of the Assembly of States Parties to the Rome Statute of the ICC Held at The Hague, Netherlands from 16 to 26 November 2009," 16th Ord. Sess., 29 January 2010, Annex 2, A.U. Doc. EX.CL/568(XVI).

129. Ibid.

130. Wafula Okumu, "Africa and the UN Security Council Permanent Seats," *Pambazuka News*, 28 April 2005.

131. African Union Executive Council, "The Common African Position on the Proposed Reform of the United Nations: '*The Ezulwini Consensus*'" (8 March 2005), 7th Extraord. Sess., A.U. Doc. Ext/EX.CL/2(VII).

132. AU Executive Council, "Report of the Commission on the Outcome and Deliberations of the 8th Session." See also AU, "Report of the 2nd Ministerial Meeting on the Rome Statute of the International Criminal Court (ICC)" (6 November 2009), Min/ICC/Legal/Rpt. III.

133. Max du Plessis, "The International Criminal Court That Africa Wants," Institute for Security Studies (August 2010): 78–79, http://www.issafrica.org/uploads/Mono172.pdf.

134. African Union Assembly, "Decision on the Hissene Habre Case" (2 February 2010), 14th Ord. Sess., A.U. Doc Assembly/AU/Dec.272(XIV).

135. Although, as the situation in Syria illustrates, if you are a key ally of a member with the veto, you may have less to worry about.

136. ICC Assembly of States Parties, "Strengthening the International Criminal Court and the Assembly of States Parties" (26 November 2009), I.C.C. Doc. ICC-ASP/8/Res.3 (2009).

137. Author interviews.

138. Author interviews.

139. "Darfur: Bashir Genocide Charges to Be Reconsidered," *BBC News*, 3 February 2010.

140. AU, "Communiqué on the 3 February 2010 Judgment of the International Criminal Court Appeals Chamber on Darfur" (4 February 2010), http://www.africa-union.org/root/ar/index/Communique%20Feb%204%202010%20eng.pdf.

141. Author interviews.

142. "ICC Prosecutor: Sudan Poll Like Vote Under Hitler," *Reuters*, 23 March 2010.

143. African Union, "Statement by Mr. Ben Kioko, Legal Counsel of the African Union Commission on Behalf of the AU Commission, at the Review Conference of the Rome Statute of the International Criminal Court (ICC), Kampala, Uganda, 31 May–11 June 2010."

144. ICC, "Situation in Darfur, Sudan, in the *Case of Prosecutor v. Omar Hassan Ahmad Al Bashir*, Second Warrant of Arrest for Omar Hassan Ahmad Al Bashir, Case No. ICC-02/05-01/09" (12 July 2010), http://www.icc-cpi.int/iccdocs/doc/doc907140.pdf.

145. "African Union Moves Aggressively to Shield Bashir from Prosecution," *Sudan Tribune*, 29 July 2010.

146. Savious Kwinika, "Sudan President Bashir, Accused of War Crimes, Would Be Arrested in South Africa, Says ANC," *Christian Science Monitor*, 28 July 2010.

147. "African Union Drops Resolution Barring Arrest of Sudanese President in Continent."

148. Ibid.

149. "Bashir Defies Warrant on Chad Trip," *Al Jazeera*, 22 July 2010.

150. "ICC Urges U.N. Action on Bashir Visit to Djibouti," *Reuters*, 12 May 2011.

151. "Sudan's Omar al-Bashir in Malawi: ICC Wants Answers," *BBC News*, 20 October 2011.

152. Alan Cowell, "Sudan Leader Travels Despite Warrant," *New York Times*, 27 August 2010.

153. In July 2013 Bashir left Nigeria, where he was attending an AU summit, after the ICC demanded that Nigeria arrest him, although Nigerian officials had also declared that they would not arrest Bashir as a result of the AU decision not to cooperate with the ICC on Bashir. "Diplomat: Sudan Leader Has Fled Nigeria," *Associated Press*, 16 July 2013, posted on JUSTWATCH

e-mail list; "Nigeria Would Have Blocked Visit by Sudan's Bashir if It Knew Ahead of Time: Report," *Sudan Tribune*, 21 July 2013.

154. "Kenyan PM Says Bashir Must Stand Before ICC, Wants Apology Made to Int'l Community," *Sudan Tribune*, 30 August 2010.

155. "East Africa Meeting Change Helps Sudan's Bashir," *Associated Press*, 27 October 2010.

156. "Kenya Parliament Holds Emergency Debate on ICC Pull-out," *BBC News*, 5 September 2013.

157. "African Union Summit on ICC Pullout over Ruto Trial," *BBC News*, 20 September 2013.

158. Coalition for the International Criminal Court, "AU Pits Presidential Immunity Against Human Security," press release (15 October 2013), http://www.coalitionfortheicc.org/documents /CICC_PR_AU_summit_conclusion_OCT_2013_ENG.pdf.

159. Colum Lynch, "Sudan's Omar al-Bashir Cancels U.N. Trip," *Foreign Policy*, 25 September 2013.

160. Quoted in Holt and Taylor, *Protecting Civilians in the Context of UN Peacekeeping Operations*, 353.

161. Ibid.

162. Ibid., 354.

163. Julian Borger, "Darfur Peacekeepers Struggling to Cope," *The Guardian*, 12 September 2008.

164. "UNAMID Celebrates Deployment of Tactical Helicopters," press release, African Union—United Nations Mission in Darfur (27 February 2010), http://unamid.unmissions.org /Default.aspx?tabid=899&ctl=Details&mid=1072&ItemID=7898.

165. "Sudan Lifts Flight Ban on UNAMID Helicopters," *Sudan Tribune*, 18 June 2010.

166. "UNAMID Deployment on the Brink."

167. Bergholm, "The African Union, the United Nations and Civilian Protection Challenges in Darfur," 24.

168. Holt and Taylor, *Protecting Civilians in the Context of UN Peacekeeping Operations*, 354; as of the end of October 2013, UNAMID had lost 168 personnel.

169. Ibid., 358.

170. http://http://www.americanprogress.org.

171. Lucy Fleming, "Darfur: Where Celebrities Love to Tread," *BBC News* (9 February 2010); Mamdani, *Saviors and Survivors*, 53–55.

172. David Lanz, "Save Darfur: A Movement and Its Discontents," *African Affairs* 108, 4 (2009): 670.

173. Rob Crilly, "The Killing Continues in Darfur's Forgotten War," *The Telegraph* (31 July 2013).

174. Fleming, "Darfur: Where Celebrities Love to Tread." As Lanz observes, "Save Darfur's insistence on humanitarian intervention has distorted the expectations of Darfur rebel movements." Lanz, "Save Darfur," 676.

175. Certainly this has been the case in Syria as the international community vacillated over how to respond.

176. Alex de Waal, "Why Darfur Intervention Is a Mistake," *BBC News* (21 May 2008); Gareth Evans, "The Responsibility to Protect and the Use of Force," presentation by Gareth Evans, president, International Crisis Group, to Seminar on International Use of Force, World Legal Forum, The Hague (11 December 2007), http://www.worldlegalforum.org/Docs/Speech%20Gareth %20Evans.pdf. In May 2007, Action Against Hunger, one of the few NGOs on the ground, argued that "An intervention would most likely make an already bad situation even worse by triggering yet more violence." Quoted in Foley, *The Thin Blue Line*, 11. Lanz notes that Save Darfur's focus changed from calling for a major military action of the scale and type of Kosovo to sup-

porting the deployment of a robust UN peacekeeping mission. Lanz, "Save Darfur," 672–73. Mamdani, *Saviors and Survivors*, 50.

177. Mamdani, *Saviors and Survivors*, 48–71.

178. Ibid., 6.

179. Ibid., 271–73.

180. UNSC, "Report of the Secretary-General on the African Union–United Nations Hybrid Operation in Darfur," S/2010/50 (29 January 2010): 11.

181. UNSC Resolution 1935 (30 July 2010).

182. UNSC, "Report of the Secretary-General on the African Union–United Nations Hybrid Operation in Darfur" (29 January 2010), 7–8.

183. Ibid., 9.

184. UNSC, "Report of the Secretary-General on the African Union-United Nations Hybrid Operation in Darfur," S/2010/382 (14 July 2010): 8.

185. Ibid., 13.

186. UNSC, "Report of the Secretary-General on the African Union-United Nations Hybrid Operation in Darfur," S/2011/22 (18 January 2011), 7.

187. UNSC, "Report of the Secretary-General on the African Union-United Nations Hybrid Operation in Darfur," S/2011/643 (12 October 2011), 1.

188. Small Arms Survey, "Liberation and Justice Movement," Human Security Baseline Assessment (HSBA) for Sudan and South Sudan (8 October 2012), http://www.smallarmssurvey sudan.org/fileadmin/docs.

189. "Darfur Rebel Alliance Makes Peace with Sudan," *BBC News* (18 March 2010).

190. UNSC, 6589th meeting, S/PV.6589 (22 July 2011).

191. UNSC, "Report of the Secretary-General on the African Union-United Nations Hybrid Operation in Darfur," S/2012/231 (17 April 2012).

192. UNSC, "Report of the Secretary-General on the African Union-United Nations Hybrid Operation in Darfur," S/2012/548 (16 July 2012): 8–9.

193. UNSC, "Report of the Secretary-General on the African Union-United Nations Hybrid Operation in Darfur," S/2012/771 (16 October 2012): 17.

194. UNSC, Resolution 2063 (31 July 2012).

195. Isma'il Kushkush, "New Strife in Darfur Leaves Many Seeking Refuge," *New York Times*, 23 May 2013.

196. UNSC, "Report of the Secretary-General on the African Union-United Nations Hybrid Operation in Darfur," S/2013/420 (12 July 2013), 4.

197. Eric Reeves, "Humanitarian Conditions in Darfur: Relief Efforts Perilously Close to Collapse (Two Parts)" (15 August 2013), http://www.sudanreeves.org. Reeves notes that the figure of 300,000 dead used by the UN is, as John Holmes, undersecretary-general for humanitarian affairs, admitted, "not a very scientifically based figure." The 300,000 figure corresponds to the results of a study published in *The Lancet* in 2010, although Reeves argues that the figure for all war-related deaths is higher—as much as 500,000. Olivier Degomme and Debarati Guha-Sapir, "Patterns of Mortality Rates in Darfur Conflict," *The Lancet* 375 (2010): 294–300. The Save Darfur movement claimed that 400,000 had been killed in the first three years of the war, though there was little to back this figure up. Medina Haeri, "Saving Darfur: Does Advocacy Help or Hinder Conflict Resolution?" *Praxis* 23 (2008): 41. Mamdani critiques all the estimates, noting that the U.S. Department of State issued a much lower estimate in 2005, on the order of 60,000–160,000. He also notes that Reeves lowered his figures in 2005 and 2006. Mamdani, *Saviors and Survivors*, 26–33.

198. "The Humanitarian Situation in Darfur," *IRIN*, 15 August 2013.

199. UNSC, "Report of the Secretary-General on the African Union-United Nations Hybrid Operation in Darfur" (12 July 2013), 1.

200. Ibid., 2.

201. Ibid., 8.

202. Ibid., 10.

203. Ibid., 15.

204. UNSC Resolution 2113 (30 July 2013).

205. Quoted in Eric Reeves, "Humanitarian Conditions in Darfur: A Climate of Violence and Extreme Insecurity," *Sudan Tribune*, 4 August 2013.

206. Philip Kastner, "The ICC in Darfur—Savior or Spoiler?" *Journal of International and Comparative Law* 14, 1 (2007): 145–88.

207. ICC, "*The Prosecutor v. Bahar Idriss Abu Garda.*"

208. American Non-Governmental Organizations Coalition for the International Criminal Court, "Case: Abdallah Banda Abakaer Nourain and Saleh Mohammed Jerbo Jamus," http://www.amicc.org/icc/banda.

209. "Former UN Rights Chief Says UNSC Referral of Darfur to ICC a 'Very Bad Idea,'" *Sudan Tribune*, 22 July 2013.

210. Don Hubert and Cynthia Brassard-Boudreau, 'Shrinking Humanitarian Access? Trends and Prospects,' *Journal of Humanitarian Assistance* (November 2010).

211. Fabrice Weissman, "Humanitarian Dilemmas in Darfur," Médecins sans Frontières (July 2008): 1, http://www.msf.fr/sites/www.msf.fr/files/214a9aa0483c6e560e05cdafb00beb11.pdf. Two years earlier, UNICEF had identified the DRC as "'world's deadliest humanitarian crisis since World War II.'" Quoted in Mamdani, *Saviors and Survivors*, 21. So, one may question why it was not the deadliest situation that warranted the greatest response?

212. Kurt Mills, "Constructing Humanitarian Space in Darfur," *International Journal of Human Rights* 17, 5–6 (2013): 605–18.

213. However, Weissman notes that humanitarians themselves have been worried about diversions of aid and the perverse effects of aid, such as creating a pull factor to IDP camps. He downplays both concerns. He does note, however, that "Humanitarian organizations have many fewer qualms about working in rebel-held areas," which raises interesting questions about political neutrality. Weissman, "Humanitarian Dilemmas in Darfur," 3–5, 11.

214. Reeves, "Humanitarian Conditions in Darfur."

Chapter 6. Realizing R2P^3: Labeling, Institutions, and Authority

Epigraphs: *The National Security Strategy of the United States of America* (March 2006), 17; former president Bill Clinton, quoted in Kirin Moodley, "Bill Clinton: We Could Have Saved 300,000 Lives in Rwanda," *CNBC* (13 March 2013).

1. Michael Walzer, "The Politics of Rescue," *Dissent* (Winter 1995): 35–41.

2. As Dunn puts it, Africa is perceived as "a land of AIDS, the Ebola virus, inherent savagery, and barbarism, an apolitical chaos beyond the rational comprehension of the 'civilized' West." Kevin C. Dunn, *Imagining the Congo: The International Relations of Identity* (New York: Palgrave Macmillan, 2003), 165.

3. Somini Sengupta, "Stopping Bloodshed in the Central African Republic amid Ghosts of Genocide," *New York Times*, 9 December 2013.

4. Ibid.

5. Alissa J. Rubin, "African Crisis Is Tougher Than France Expected," *New York Times*, 13 December 2013.

6. Sengupta, "Stopping Bloodshed in the Central African Republic amid Ghosts of Genocide."

7. Ibid.

8. Ellen Lutz, "Transitional Justice: Lessons Learned and the Road Ahead," in *Transitional Justice in the Twenty-First Century: Beyond Truth Versus Justice*, ed. Naomi Roht-Arriaza and Javier Mariezcurrena (Cambridge: Cambridge University Press, 2006), 327.

9. Leslie Vinjamuri, "Deterrence, Democracy, and the Pursuit of International Justice," *Ethics & International Affairs* 24, 2 (2010): 191–211.

10. Melissa Labonte, *Human Rights and Humanitarian Norms, Strategic Framing, and Intervention: Lessons for the Responsibility to Protect* (New York: Routledge, 2013).

11. Jean-Hervé Bradol, Introduction to *In the Shadow of "Just Wars": Violence, Politics and Humanitarian Action*, ed. Fabrice Wsissman (London: Hurst, 2004), 6.

12. And political issues. There is a difference of opinion in Western capitals regarding whether this would be a good idea. France is particularly worried about the AU acting independently of the Security Council, whereas the UK is more relaxed about this possibility. Author interviews.

13. Linnéa Gelot, *Legitimacy, Peace Operations and Global-Regional Security: The African Union-United Nations Partnership in Darfur* (London: Routledge, 2012), 136–37.

14. A parallel can be made with current efforts by the UK government to push back against the authority of the European Court of Human Rights—as well as other European institutions. This highlights the tensions between long-term normative development and short-term political interests. It also illustrates that a certain level of reluctance to fully embrace human rights norms and institutions is not limited to one part of the world.

15. HRW, "African States: Reject Immunity for Leaders" (25 August 2014), http://www.hrw .org/news/2014/08/24/african-states-reject-immunity-leaders.

16. Alex Vines, "A Decade of African Peace and Security Architecture," *International Affairs* 89, 1 (2013): 89–109, 89. See also Ulf Engel and João Gomes Porto, *Africa's New Peace and Security Architecture: Promoting Norms, Institutionalizing Solutions* (Farnham: Ashgate, 2010).

17. See the Humanitarian Accountability Partnership, http://www.hapinternational.org, and the Sphere Project, http://www.sphereproject.org.

18. Author interviews.

BIBLIOGRAPHY

"Address by Luis Moreno-Ocampo, Prosecutor of the International Criminal Court, at the International Conference 'Building a Future on Peace *and* Justice.'" Nuremberg, 25 June 2007. http://www.peace-justice-conference.info/download/speech%20moreno.pdf.

Adelman, Howard. "The Use and Abuse of Refugees in Zaire." In *Refugee Manipulation: War, Politics, and the Abuse of Human Suffering*, ed. Stephen John Stedman and Fred Tanner. Washington, D.C.: Brookings Institution Press, 2003.

Adleman, Howard, and Laurence J. Baxter. "The Multi-National Force for Eastern Zaire: The Conception, Planning and Termination of OP Assurance." In *War and Peace in Zaire/Congo*, ed. Howard Adelman and Govind C. Rao. Trenton, N.J.: Africa World Press, 2004.

Afako, Barney. "Reconciliation and Justice: 'Mato Oput' and the Amnesty Act." Conciliation Resources, 2002. http://www.c-r.org/accord-article/reconciliation-and-justice-'mato-oput'-and-amnesty-act-2002.

"African Countries Back Away from ICC Withdrawal Demand." *Sudan Tribune*, 8 June 2009.

African Union. "Communique on the 3 February 2010 Judgment of the International Criminal Court Appeals Chamber on Darfur." 4 February 2010. http://www.africa-union.org.

———. "Plan of Action." Special Session of the Assembly of the Union on the Consideration and Resolution of Conflicts in Africa, SP/Assembly/PS/Plan(1), 31 August 2009. http://www.peaceau.org/uploads/plan-of-action-final-eng-.pdf.

———. "Report of the 2nd Ministerial Meeting on the Rome Statute of the International Criminal Court (ICC)." Min/ICC/Legal/Rpt. III, 6 November 2009.

———. "Statement by Mr. Ben Kioko, Legal Counsel of the African Union Commission on Behalf of the AU Commission, at the Review Conference of the Rome Statute of the International Criminal Court (ICC), Kampala, Uganda, 31 May–11 June 2010."

African Union Assembly. "Decision on the Abuse of the Principle of Universal Jurisdiction." 13th Ord. Sess., A.U. Doc. Assembly/AU/11(XIII). 3 July 2009.

———. "Decision on the Application by the International Criminal Court (ICC) Prosecutor for the Indictment of the President of the Republic of Sudan." 12th Ord. Sess., A.U. Doc. Assembly/AU/Dec.221(XII). 3 February 2009.

———. "Decision on the Hissene Habre Case." 14th Ord. Sess., A.U. Doc Assembly/AU/Dec.272(XIV). 2 February 2010.

———. "Decision on the Meeting of African States Parties to the Rome Statue of the International Criminal Court (ICC)." 13th Ord. Sess., A.U. Doc. Assembly/AU/13(XIII). 3 July 2009.

———. "Decision on the Report of the Commission on the Abuse of the Principle of Universal Jurisdiction." 11th Ord. Sess., A.U. Doc. Assembly/AU/14(XI). 1 July 2008.

African Union, Executive Council. "The Common African Position on the Proposed Reform of the United Nations: 'The Ezulwini Consensus.'" 7th Extraord. Sess., A.U. Doc. Ext/EX. CL/2(VII). 8 March 2005.

——. "Report of the Commission on the Outcome and Deliberations of the 8th Session of the Assembly of States Parties to the Rome Statute of the ICC Held at The Hague, Netherlands from 16 to 26 November 2009." 16th Ord. Sess., Annex 2, A.U. Doc. EX.CL/568(XVI). 29 January 2010.

African Union, Peace and Security Council. 142nd Meeting. 21 July 2008. http://www.sudantri bune.com/spip.php?article27982.

——. "Communiqué of the Seventeenth Meeting of the Peace and Security Council." PSC/PR/ Comm.(XVII). 20 October 2004.

——. "Communique of the 142nd Meeting of the Peace and Security Council." 142d mtg., A.U. Doc. PSC/MIN/Comm(CXLII)Rev.1. 21 July 2008.

——. "Communique of the 175th Meeting of the Peace and Security Council." 175th mtg., A.U. Doc. PSC/PR/Comm(CLXXV). 5 March 2009.

——. Press Statement. 141st Meeting, A.U. Doc. PSC/PR/BR(CXLI). 11 July 2008.

——. "Darfur: The Quest for Peace." Report of the African Union High-Level Panel on Darfur. 29 October 2009.

"African Union Defies ICC over Bashir Extradition." *ABC News*, 5 July 2009.

"African Union Drops Resolution Barring Arrest of Sudanese President in Continent." *Sudan Tribune*, 26 July 2010.

"African Union Moves Aggressively to Shield Bashir from Prosecution." *Sudan Tribune*, 29 July 2010.

"African Union Summit on ICC Pullout over Ruto Trial." *BBC News*, 20 September 2013.

Agier, Michael, and Françoise Bouchet-Saulnier. "Humanitarian Spaces: Spaces of Exception." In *In the Shadow of "Just Wars": Violence, Politics and Humanitarian Action*, ed. Fabrice Weissman. London: Hurst, 2004.

"Agreement on Accountability and Reconciliation Between the Government of the Republic of Uganda and the Lord's Resistance Army/Movement." Juba, Sudan, 29 June 2007. http://www .amicc.org/docs/Agreement_on_Accountability_and_Reconciliation.pdf.

Akhavan, Payam. "International Criminal Justice in the Era of Failed States: The ICC and the Self-Referral Debate." In *The International Criminal Court and Complementarity: From Theory to Practice*, vol. 2, ed. Carsten Stahn and Mohamed M. El Zeidy. Cambridge: Cambridge University Press, 2011.

——. "The Lord's Resistance Army Case: Uganda's Submission of the First State Referral to the International Criminal Court." *American Journal of International Law* 99, 2 (2005): 403–21.

Allen, Tim. "Bitter Roots: The 'Invention' of Acholi Traditional Justice." In *The Lord's Resistance Army: Myth and Reality*, ed. Tim Allen and Koen Vlassenroot. London: Zed, 2010.

——. *Trial Justice: The International Criminal Court and the Lord's Resistance Army*. London: Zed, 2006.

Allen, Tim, and Koen Vlassenroot, eds. *The Lord's Resistance Army: Myth and Reality*. London: Zed, 2010.

Allio, Emmy. "Sudan Predicts Kony End." *New Vision*, 17 February 2004.

American Non-Governmental Organizations Coalition for the International Criminal Court. "Case: Abdallah Banda Abakaer Nourain and Saleh Mohammed Jerbo Jamus." http://www .amicc.org/icc/banda.

Amnesty Act. 2000. http://www.ulii.org/ug/legislation/consolidated-act/294.

Amnesty International. *Annual Report 2013*. http://amnesty.org/en/region/rwanda/report-2013.

——. "Rwanda and Burundi—The Return Home: Rumours and Realities." 20 February 1996.

Anderson, Mary B. *Do No Harm: How Aid Can Support Peace or War*. Boulder, Colo.: Lynne Rienner, 1999.

Annan, Kofi. *In Larger Freedom: Towards Development, Security and Human Rights for All*. Report of the Secretary-General, United Nations. A/59/2005. http://www.un.org.

——. "Two Concepts of Sovereignty." *Economist* 352 (18 September 1999).

"Annexure to the Agreement on Accountability and Reconciliation." Juba, Sudan: 19 February 2008. http://www.amicc.org/.

Apuuli, Kasaija Phillip. "The ICC's Possible Deferral of the LRA Case to Uganda." *Journal of International Criminal Justice* 6, 4 (2008): 801–13.

Arieff, Alexis, and Lauren Ploch. "The Lord's Resistance Army: The U.S. Response." Congressional Research Service, 11 April 2012.

Atkinson, Ronald R. "'The Realists in Juba'? An Analysis of the Juba Peace Talks." In *The Lord's Resistance Army: Myth and Reality*, ed. Tim Allen and Koen Vlassenroot. London: Zed, 2010.

Atkinson, Ronald, Phil Lancaster, Ledio Cakaj, and Guilaume Lacaille. "Do No Harm: Assessing a Military Approach to the Lord's Resistance Army." *Journal of Eastern African Studies* 6, 2 (2012): 371–82.

AU-EU Technical Ad Hoc Expert Group on the Principle of Universal Jurisdiction Report. 15 April 2009. http://www.africa-union.org.

Autesserre, Séverine. *The Trouble with the Congo: Local Violence and the Failure of International Peacebuilding.* Cambridge: Cambridge University Press, 2010.

Auyugi, Caroline. "ICC Calls for End to LRA Aid." Institute for War & Peace Reporting, 28 May 2008. http://iwpr.net.

Barnett, Michael. *Empire of Humanity: A History of Humanitarianism.* Ithaca, N.Y.: Cornell University Press, 2011.

——. *Eyewitness to a Genocide.* Ithaca, N.Y.: Cornell University Press, 2002.

Barnett, Michael, and Jack Snyder. "The Grand Strategies of Humanitarianism." In *Humanitarianism in Question: Politics, Power, Ethics*, ed. Michael Barnett and Thomas G. Weiss. Ithaca, N.Y.: Cornell University Press, 2008.

Barnett, Michael, and Thomas G. Weiss. "Humanitarianism: A Brief History to the Present." In *Humanitarianism in Question: Politics, Power, Ethics*, ed. Michael Barnett and Thomas G. Weiss. Ithaca, N.Y.: Cornell University Press, 2008.

——, eds. *Humanitarianism in Question: Politics, Power, Ethics.* Ithaca, N.Y.: Cornell University Press, 2008.

Barutciski, Michael. "Involuntary Repatriation When Refugee Protection Is No Longer Necessary: Moving Forward after the 48th Session of the Executive Committee." *International Journal of Refugee Law* 10, 1–2 (1998): 247–51.

——. "Tensions Between the Refugee Concept and the IDP Debate." *Forced Migration Review* 3 (December 1998): 11–14.

"Bashir Defies Warrant on Chad Trip." *Al Jazeera*, 22 July 2010.

Bass, Gary J. *Freedom's Battle: The Origins of Humanitarian Intervention.* New York: Knopf, 2008.

Bellamy, Alex J. *Responsibility to Protect.* Cambridge: Polity, 2009.

Belloni, Roberto. "The Tragedy of Darfur and the Limits of the 'Responsibility to Protect.'" *Ethnopolitics* 5, 4 (2006): 327–46.

Benner, Ashley. "Uganda Rules That Amnesty Can't Be Denied to LRA Leaders." *Christian Science Monitor*, 27 September 2011.

Bennett, James. "Clinton in Africa: The Overview; Clinton Declares U.S., with World, Failed Rwandans." *New York Times*, 26 March 1998.

Bennett, Nicki. "International Peacekeeping Missions and Civilian Protection Mandates—Oxfam's Experience in Sudan, the Democratic Republic of Congo, Chad, and Somalia." Oxfam. September 2009.

Bergholm, Linnea. "The African Union, the United Nations and Civilian Protection Challenges in Darfur." Refugee Studies Centre, Oxford University, Working Paper Series 63. May 2010.

Berry, Nicholas O. *War and the Red Cross: The Unspoken Mission.* New York: St. Martin's, 1997.

Bibas, Benjamin. "Kigali, Between Ntaganda and the ICC." *International Justice Tribune*, 6 June 2012.

Binder, Andrea, Véronique de Geoffroy, and Bonaventure Sokpoh. "Democratic Republic of Congo." IASC Cluster Approach Evaluation, 2nd Phase. Global Public Policy Institute. April 2010.

Bloomfield, Steve. "African Union: Suspend Sudan Genocide Charge." *Independent*, 15 July 2008.

Borger, Julian. "Darfur Peacekeepers Struggling to Cope." *The Guardian*, 12 September 2008.

———. "Khartoum Conundrum." *The Guardian*, 16 October 2008.

"Bosco 'Terminator' Ntaganda Takes over DR Congo Towns." *BBC News*, 30 April 2012.

"Botswana Rebels Against AU over Bashir." *ABC News*, 5 July 2009.

Boutroue, Joel. "Missed Opportunities: The Role of the International Community in the Return of the Rwandan Refugees from Eastern Zaire—July 1994–December 1996." Massachusetts Institute of Technology Center for International Studies/UNHCR. February 1998.

Bouwknegt, Thijs. "Sudan to Revive Darfur Court." *Radio Netherlands Worldwide*, 25 July 2008.

Bradol, Jean-Hervé. Introduction to *In the Shadow of "Just Wars": Violence, Politics and Humanitarian Action*, ed. Fabrice Weissman. London: Hurst, 2004.

Branch, Adam. *Displacing Human Rights: War and Intervention in Northern Uganda*. Oxford: Oxford University Press, 2011.

———. "The Paradoxes of Protection: Aligning Against the Lord's Resistance Army." *African Security* 5, 3–4 (2012): 160–78.

Bravin, Jess. "For Global Court, Ugandan Rebels Prove Tough Test." *Wall Street Journal*, 8 June 2006.

"British Official Denies Plans to Freeze ICC indictment of Sudan's Bashir." *Sudan Tribune*, 19 September 2008. Posted on JUSTWATCH-L e-mail list.

Cakaj, Ledio. "The Lord's Resistance Army of Today." Enough Project. November 2010. http://www.enoughproject.org/files/lra_today.pdf.

Cammaert, Patrick, and Fiona Blyth. "The UN Intervention Brigade in the Democratic Republic of the Congo." International Peace Institute, July 2013. http://mercury.ethz.ch/serviceengine/Files/ISN/166530/ipublicationdocument_singledocument/ef4e0719-0fc6-4d16-8ccd-8016679eb6b0/en/ipi_e_pub_un_intervention_brigade.pdf.

Caplan, Gerald. "Peacekeepers Gone Wild: How Much More Abuse Will the UN Ignore in Congo?" *Globe and Mail*, 3 August 2012.

Chandler, David. "The Road to Military Humanitarianism: How the Human Rights NGOs Shaped a New Humanitarian Agenda." *Human Rights Quarterly* 23 (August 2001): 678–700.

"Characterizing Sexual Violence in the Democratic Republic of the Congo: Profiles of Violence, Community Responses, and Implications for the Protection of Women." Harvard Humanitarian Initiative/Open Society Institute. August 2009.

Charbonneau, Louise. "U.N. Demands End of Foreign Support for Congo Rebels." *Reuters*, 2 August 2012.

———. "UN May Want to Suspend ICC Action on Bashir—Russia." *Reuters*, 22 July 2008. Posted on JUSTWATCH-L e-mail list.

"Charging Sudan's Beshir Would Wreck Darfur Peace: Mbeki." *Agence France-Presse*, 26 July 2008. Posted on JUSTWATCH-L e-mail list.

"Chronology of U.S. Government Assistance to Rwanda (as of April 6, 1994)." http://www.state.gov/documents/organization/165106.pdf.

Clark, Janine Natalya. "Peace, Justice and the International Criminal Court." *Journal of International Criminal Justice* 9, 3 (2011): 521–45.

Clark, John F., ed. *The African Stakes of the Congo War*. New York: Palgrave Macmillan, 2002.

Clark, Phil. "Chasing Cases: The ICC and the Politics of State Referral in the Democratic Republic of the Congo and Uganda." In *The International Criminal Court and Complementarity:*

From Theory to Practice, vol. 2, ed. Carsten Stahn and Mohamed M. El Zeidy. Cambridge: Cambridge University Press, 2011.

———. "Law, Politics and Pragmatism: The ICC and Case Selection in the Democratic Republic of Congo and Uganda." In *Courting Conflict? Justice, Peace and the ICC in Africa*, ed. Nicholas Waddell and Phil Clark. London: Royal African Society, 2008.

Coalition for the International Criminal Court. "AU Pits Presidential Immunity Against Human Security." Press release. 15 October 2013. http://www.coalitionfortheicc.org.

———. "Global Coalition Says AU States Parties to International Criminal Court Have Legal Obligation to Cooperate with ICC." Press release. 7 July 2009. http://www.iccnow.org.

"Cold Choices in Rwanda." *New York Times*, 23 April 1994.

Collins, Barrie. "Shooting Down the 'Truth' About Rwanda." *Spiked*, 16 April 2012.

"Congo-Kinshasa; Violence Escalating in Eastern Country." Open Society Initiative for Southern Africa. 26 January 2012. Posted on JUSTWATCH-L e-mail list.

Corn, David. "Lying About Rwanda's Genocide." *The Nation*, 2 April 2004.

"Court Probes Sudan 'War Crimes.' " *BBC News*, 5 June 2005.

Cowell, Alan. "Sudan Leader Travels despite Warrant." *New York Times*, 27 August 2010.

Crilly, Rob. "The Killing Continues in Darfur's Forgotten War." *The Telegraph*, 31 July 2031.

Cronin-Furman, Kate. "Managing Expectations: International Criminal Trials and the Prospects for Deterrence of Mass Atrocity." *International Journal of Transitional Justice* 7, 3 (2013): 434–54.

Culbert, Vance. "Protection Cluster Co-Facilitation in the Democratic Republic of Congo: Lessons Learned from Oxfam's Protection Cluster Support Project." Oxfam. June 2011. http://reliefweb.int.

Dachy, Eric. "Justice and Humanitarian Action: A Conflict of Interest." In *In the Shadow of "Just Wars": Violence, Politics and Humanitarian Action*, ed. Fabrice Weissman. London: Hurst, 2004.

Dallaire, Roméo. *Shake Hands with the Devil: The Failure of Humanity in Rwanda*. New York: Carroll & Graf, 2005.

Daly, Erin. "Between Punitive and Reconstructive Justice: The Gacaca Courts in Rwanda." *New York University Journal of International Law and Politics* 34 (2002): 355–96.

"Darfur: Bashir Genocide Charges to Be Reconsidered." *BBC News*, 3 February 2010.

"Darfur Militia Leader in Custody." *BBC News*, 13 October 2008.

"Darfur Rebel Alliance Makes Peace with Sudan." *BBC News*, 18 March 2010.

"Darfur Rebel Group Pulls Out of Peace Talks." *Radio France Internationale*, 21 March 2009.

Davis, Laura, and Priscilla Hayner "Difficult Peace, Limited Justice: Ten Years of Peacemaking in the DRC." International Center for Transitional Justice, March 2009. http://ictj.org/sites/default/files/ICTJ-DRC-Difficult-Peace-2009-English.pdf.

Deng, Francis. *Sovereignty as Responsibility: Crisis Management in Africa*. Washington, D.C.: Brookings Institution, 1996.

de Waal, Alex. *Famine Crimes: Politics and the Disaster Relief Industry in Africa*. Woodbridge: James Currey, 1997.

———. "Why Darfur Intervention Is a Mistake." *BBC News*, 21 May 2008.

Degomme, Olivier, and Debarati Guha-Sapir. "Patterns of Mortality Rates in Darfur Conflict." *Lancet* 375 (2010): 294–300.

"Diplomat: Sudan Leader Has Fled Nigeria." Associated Press, 16 July 2013. Posted on JUSTWATCH e-mail list.

Doyle, Mark. "DR Congo Unrest: Fears over UN Intervention." *BBC News*, 25 July 2013.

"DR Congo: Over 100,000 Flee Fresh Violence in Eastern DRC Since November." *Afrique en ligne*, 1 January 2012.

"DR Congo War Deaths 'Exaggerated.' " *BBC News*, 20 January 2010.

"DR Congo Warlord Thomas Lubanga Sentenced to 14 Years." *BBC News*, 10 July 2012.

"DRC: Children, Young Men Flee M23 Recruitment." *IRIN*, 16 August 2012.

"DRC: North Kivu in Turmoil Again." *IRIN*, 16 May 2012.

"DRC: Scores Killed as Mai-Mai Target Kinyarwanda Speakers." *IRIN*, 12 June 2012.

"DRC: Understanding Armed Group M23." *IRIN*, 22 June 2013.

Dubois, Marc. "Protection: The New Humanitarian Fig-Leaf." Presented to conference Protecting People in Conflict and Crisis, Refugee Studies Centre, Oxford University. 22–24 September 2009. http://www.rsc.ox.ac.uk/pdfs/endnotemarkdubois.pdf.

Dukalskis, Alexander, and Robert C. Johansen. "Measuring Acceptance of International Enforcement of Human Rights: The United States, Asia, and the International Criminal Court." *Human Rights Quarterly* 35, 3 (2013): 569–97.

Dunn, Kevin C. *Imagining the Congo: The International Relations of Identity*. New York: Palgrave Macmillan, 2003.

———. "The Lord's Resistance Army and African International Relations." *African Security* 3 (1 2010): 46–63.

du Plessis, Max. "The International Criminal Court That Africa Wants." Institute for Security Studies. August 2010. http://www.issafrica.org/uploads/Mono172.pdf.

"Dynamics of Conflict and Forced Migration in the Democratic Republic of Congo." Report of an Experts' Workshop, Refugee Studies Centre. January 2011. http://www.rsc.ox.ac.uk/. "East Africa Meeting Change Helps Sudan's Bashir." *Associated Press*, 27 October 2010.

Eichstaedt, Peter. "ICC Chief Prosecutor Talks Tough." Institute for War & Peace Reporting. 7 May 2008. http://iwpr.net/.

———. "More Robust International Action in DRC Needed." Institute for War & Peace Reporting. 27 March 2009. http://iwpr.net/.

Engel, Ulf, and João Gomes Porto, eds. *Africa's New Peace and Security Architecture: Promoting Norms, Institutionalizing Solutions*. Farnham: Ashgate, 2010.

Enough Project. "The Democratic Republic of Congo: Taking a Stand on Security Sector Reform." 16 April 2012. http://www.enoughproject.org.

———. "Getting Back on Track: Implementing the UN Regional Strategy of the Lord's Resistance Army." Joint NGO report. December 2012. http://www.enoughproject.org.

Erskine, Toni, ed. *Can Institutions Have Responsibilities? Collective Moral Agency and International Relations*. Basingstoke: Palgrave, 2003.

European Union. "Declaration by the High Representative, Catherine Ashton, on Behalf of the European Union on the Situation in the Eastern Democratic Republic of Congo." 12422/1/12 REV 1. 10 July 2012.

Evans, Gareth. "The Responsibility to Protect and the Use of Force." Presentation by Gareth Evans, president, International Crisis Group, to Seminar on International Use of Force, World Legal Forum, The Hague. 11 December 2007. http://www.worldlegalforum.org/.

———. *The Responsibility to Protect: Ending Mass Atrocity Crimes Once and for All*. Washington, D.C.: Brookings Institution Press, 2008.

"Expelled US Aid Groups Deny Return to Sudan." *Sudan Tribune*, 12 June 2009.

Fédération internationale des ligues des droits de l'Homme. "Central African Republic: Forgotten, Stigmatized: The Double Suffering of Victims of International Crimes." 457/2. October 2006. http://www.fidh.org/.

———. "FIDH and the Situation in the Central African Republic Before the International Criminal Court: The Case of Jean-Pierre Bemba Gombo." 502a. July 2008. http://www.fidh.org/.

Feil, Scott R. "Preventing Genocide: How the Early Use of Force Might Have Succeeded in Rwanda." A Report to the Carnegie Commission on Preventing Deadly Conflict. April 1998. http://carnegie.org.

Feller, Erika. "UNHCR's Role in IDP Protection: Opportunities and Challenges." *Forced Migration Review* (December 2006): 11–13.

Ferris, Elizabeth G. *The Politics of Protection: The Limits of Humanitarian Action.* Washington, D.C.: Brookings Institution Press, 2011.

FEWER International. "Elections, Instability, and EUFOR: Recommendations for Securing the Peace in the DRC." No date. http://www.fewer-international.org/.

Finnegan, Amy C. "The White Girl's Burden." *Contexts* 12, 1 (2013): 30–35.

Finnström, Sverker. *Living with Bad Surroundings: War, History, and Everyday Moments in Northern Uganda.* Durham, N.C.: Duke University Press, 2008.

Fleming, Lucy. "Darfur: Where Celebrities Love to Tread." *BBC News*, 9 February 2010.

Flint, Julie, and Alex de Waal. *Darfur: A Short History of a Long War.* London: Zed, 2005.

———. "This Prosecution Will Endanger the People We Wish to Defend in Sudan." *Observer*, 13 July 2008.

———. "To Put Justice Before Peace Spells Disaster for Sudan." *The Guardian*, 6 March 2009.

Foley, Conor. *The Thin Blue Line: How Humanitarianism Went to War.* London: Verso, 2008.

"Former UN Rights Chief Says UNSC Referral of Darfur to ICC a 'Very Bad Idea.'" *Sudan Tribune*, 22 July 2013.

Forsythe, David P. *The Humanitarians: The International Committee of the Red Cross.* Cambridge: Cambridge University Press, 2005.

———. "US Foreign Policy and Human Rights: Situating Obama." *Human Rights Quarterly* 33, 3 (2011): 767–89.

Fournier, Christopher. "Punishment or Aid." *New York Times*, 28 March 2009.

"France Will Veto Any Resolution Deferring Sudan President Indictment: Official." *Sudan Tribune*, 19 September 2008. Posted on JUSTWATCH-L e-mail list.

Frelick, Bill. "'Preventive Protection' and the Right to Seek Asylum: A Preliminary Look at Bosnia and Croatia." *International Journal of Refugee Law* 4, 4 (1992): 439–54.

Frencken, Niki. "The International Criminal Court and Deterrence—The 'Lubanga Syndrome.'" *Justice in Conflict*, 6 April 2012.

Gänzle, Stefan. "AFRICOM and US Africa Policy: 'Pentagonising' Foreign Policy or Providing a Model for Joint Approaches." *African Security Review* 20, 1 (2011): 70–82.

Gelot, Linnéa. *Legitimacy, Peace Operations and Global-Regional Security: The African Union-United Nations Partnership in Darfur.* London: Routledge, 2012.

Geneuss, Julia. "Fostering a Better Understanding of Universal Jurisdiction: A Comment on the AU-EU Expert Report on the Principle of Universal Jurisdiction." *Journal of International Criminal Justice* 7, 5 (2009): 945–62.

Gersony, Robert. "The Anguish of Northern Uganda: Results of a Field-Based Assessment of the Civil Conflicts in Northern Uganda." Submitted to United States Embassy and USAID Mission, Kampala. August 1997. http://pdf.usaid.gov/pdf_docs/PNACC245.pdf.

Gettleman, Jeffrey. "Chaos in Darfur on Rise as Arabs Fight with Arabs." *New York Times*, 3 September 2007.

———. "Darfur Rebels Kill 10 in Peace Force." *New York Times*, 1 October 2007.

———. "'Framework' Announced for Peace in Congo." *New York Times*, 24 February 2013.

———. "In Vast Jungle, U.S. Troops Aid in Search for Kony." *New York Times*, 29 April 2012.

———. "Sudan Arrests Militia Chief Facing Trial." *New York Times*, 14 October 2008.

Gettleman, Jeffrey, and Eric Schmitt. "U.S. Aided a Failed Plan to Rout Ugandan Rebels." *New York Times*, 6 February 2009.

Girardet, Edward R. "Reporting Humanitarianism: Are the New Electronic Media Making a Difference?" In *From Massacres to Genocide: The Media, Public Policy, and Humanitarian Crises*, ed. Robert I. Rotberg and Thomas G. Weiss. Washington, D.C.: Brookings Institution, 1996.

Glasius, Marlies. "A Problem, Not a Solution: Complementarity in the Central African Republic and Democratic Republic of Congo." In *The International Criminal Court and Complementarity: From Theory to Practice*, vol. 2, ed. Carsten Stahn and Mohamed M. El Zeidy. Cambridge: Cambridge University Press, 2011.

Goodman, J. David, and Jennifer Preston. "How the Kony Video Went Viral." *New York Times*, 9 March 2012.

Gouby, Melanie. "Congo-Kinshasa: President Kabila Hot to Nab General Ntaganda." allAfrica. com, 12 April 2012.

———. "Congo Rebel Group Splits over Firing of President." *Associated Press*, 28 February 2013. Posted to JUSTWATCH-L e-mail list.

Haeri, Medina. "Saving Darfur: Does Advocacy Help or Hinder Conflict Resolution?" *Praxis* 23 (2008): 33–46.

Hammock, John C., and Joel R. Charny. "Emergency Response as Morality Play: The Media, the Relief Agencies, and the Need for Capacity Building." In *From Massacres to Genocide: The Media, Public Policy, and Humanitarian Crises*, ed. Robert I. Rotberg and Thomas G. Weiss. Washington, D.C.: Brookings Institution, 1996.

Hardt, Michael, and Antonio Negri. *Empire*. Cambridge, Mass.: Harvard University Press, 2000.

Hatcher, Jessica, and Alex Perry. "Defining Peacekeeping Downward: The U.N. Debacle in Eastern Congo." *Time*, 26 November 2012.

Hathaway, James C. "New Directions to Avoid Hard Problems: The Distortion of the Palliative Role of Refugee Protection." *Journal of Refugee Studies* 8, 3 (1995): 288–94.

Hawkins, Virgil. "Stealth Conflicts: Africa's World War in the DRC and International Consciousness." *Journal of Humanitarian Assistance* (January 2004).

Heavens, Andrew. "Darfur Peacekeepers Still Waiting for Helicopters: UN." *Reuters*, 12 July.

High-Level Panel on Threats, Challenges and Change. *A More Secure World: Our Shared Responsibility*. United Nations. 2004. http://www.un.org/secureworld/.

Hoge, Warren. "U.N. Votes to Send Any Sudan War Crime Suspects to World Court." *New York Times*, 1 April 2005.

Holt, Victoria K., and Tobias C. Berkman. *The Impossible Mandate? Military Preparedness, the Responsibility to Protect, and Modern Peace Operations*. Washington, D.C.: Henry L. Stimson Center, 2006.

Holt, Victoria, and Glyn Taylor, with Max Kelly. *Protecting Civilians in the Context of UN Peacekeeping Operations: Successes, Setbacks and Remaining Challenges*. Independent study jointly commissioned by the Department of Peacekeeping Operations and the Office for the Coordination of Humanitarian Affairs, United Nations. November 2009. http://reliefweb.int/.

Holzgrefe, J. L. "The Humanitarian Intervention Debate." In *Humanitarian Intervention: Ethical, Legal and Political Dilemmas*, ed. J. L. Holzgrefe and Robert O. Keohane. Cambridge: Cambridge University Press, 2003.

Hubert, Don, and Cynthia Brassard-Boudreau. "Shrinking Humanitarian Access? Trends and Prospects." *Journal of Humanitarian Assistance* (November 2010).

"The Humanitarian Situation in Darfur." *IRIN News*, 15 August 2013.

Human Rights Watch. "Abducted and Abused: Renewed Conflict in Northern Uganda." July 2003.

———. "African States: Reject Immunity for Leaders." 25 August 2014.

———. "The Christmas Massacres: LRA Attacks on Civilians in Northern Congo." February 2009.

———. *Courting History: The Landmark International Criminal Court's First Years*. July 2008.

———. "Darfur 2007: Chaos by Design." September 2007.

———. "DR Congo: Arrest Bosco Ntaganda for ICC Trial." 13 April 2012.

———. "DRC: Rwanda Should Stop Aiding War Crimes Suspect." 4 June 2012.

———. "Eastern DR Congo: Surge in Army Atrocities." 2 November 2009.

———. "ICC: Investigate All Sides in Uganda." 5 February 2004.

———. "Ituri: 'Covered in Blood': Ethnically Targeted Violence in Northeastern DR Congo." July 2003.

———. "Killings in Kiwanja: The UN's Inability to Protect Civilians." 12 December 2008.

———. "Rwanda: The Crisis Continues." April 1995.

———. "The Scars of Death: Children Abducted by the Lord's Resistance Army in Uganda." September 1997.

———. Selling Justice Short. July 2009.

———. "Stolen Children: Abduction and Recruitment in Northern Uganda." March 2003.

———. "Trail of Death: LRA Atrocities in Northeastern Congo." March 2010.

———. "You Will Be Punished: Attacks on Civilians in Eastern Congo." December 2009.

Human Rights Watch/Arms Project. Rwanda/Zaire: Rearming with Impunity; International Support for the Perpetrators of the Rwandan Genocide. Washington, D.C.: Human Rights Watch, 1995.

Human Security Report Project. Human Security Report 2009/2010: The Causes of Peace and the Shrinking Costs of War. Oxford: Oxford University Press, 2011.

Hyndman, Jennifer. "Preventive, Palliative, or Punitive? Safe Spaces in Bosnia-Herzegovina, Somalia, and Sri Lanka." Journal of Refugee Studies 16, 2 (2003): 167–85.

"ICC Prosecutor: Sudan Poll Like Vote Under Hitler." Reuters, 23 March 2010.

"ICC Urges U.N. Action on Bashir Visit to Djibouti." Reuters, 12 May 2011.

Ingelaere, Bert. "Does the Truth Pass Across the Fire Without Burning? Locating the Short Circuit in Rwanda's Gacaca Courts." Journal of Modern African Studies 47, 4 (2009): 507–28.

Inter-Agency Standing Committee. "Guidance Note on Using the Cluster Approach to Strengthen Humanitarian Response." 24 November 2006. http://www.unhcr.org/refworld.

International Commission on Intervention and State Sovereignty. The Responsibility to Protect. Ottawa: International Development Research Centre, 2001.

International Criminal Court. "Decision on the Consequences of Non-disclosure of Exculpatory Materials Covered by Article 54(3)(e) Agreements and the Application to Stay the Prosecution of the Accused, Together with Certain Other Issues Raised at the Status Conference on 10 June 2008." 13 June 2008. http://www.icc-cpi.int/.

———. Decision on the "Prosecutor's Application Pursuant to Article 58 as to Muammar Mohammed Abu Minyar Gaddafi, Saif Al-Islam Gaddafi and Abdullah Al-Senussi." 27 June 2011. http://www.icc-cpi.int.

———. "ICC Arrest Jean-Pierre Bemba—Massive Sexual Crimes in Central African Republic Will Not Go Unpunished." 24 May 2008. http://www.icc-cpi.int.

———. "ICC Prosecutor Presents Case Against Sudanese President, Hassan Ahmad AL BASHIR, for Genocide, Crimes Against Humanity and War." Press release. ICC-OTP-20080714-PR341. 14 July 2008. http://www.icc-cpi.int.

———. "The Office of the Prosecutor of the International Criminal Court Opens Its First Investigation." Press release. ICC-OTP-20040623-59. 23 June 2004. http://www.icc-cpi.int.

———. "Policy Paper on the Interests of Justice." September 2007.

———. "President of Uganda Refers Situation Concerning the Lord's Resistance Army (LRA) to the ICC." 29 January 2004.

———."Prosecutor of the International Criminal Court Opens an Investigation into Northern Uganda." 29 July 2004.

———. "Prosecutor Receives Referral of the Situation in the Democratic Republic of Congo." Press release. ICC-OTP-20040419-50. 19 April 2004. http://www.icc-cpi.int.

———. "The Prosecutor v. Bahar Idriss Abu Garda." http://www.icc-cpi.int.

———. "Prosecutorial Strategy 2009–2012." 1 February 2010. http://www.icc-cpi.int.

————. Review Conference of the Rome Statute Concludes in Kampala. ICC-ASP-20100612-PR546. 12 June 2010. http://reliefweb.int/node/357833.

————. "Seventh Report of the Prosecutor of the International Criminal Court to the UN Security Council Pursuant to UNSCR 1593 (2005)." http://www.iccnow.org/.

————. "Situation in Darfur, Sudan, in the Case of *The Prosecutor v. Omar Hassan Ahmad Al Bashir*, Second Warrant of Arrest for Omar Hassan Ahmad Al Bashir." Case ICC-02/05-01/09. 12 July 2010. http://www.icc-cpi.int/iccdocs/doc/doc907140.pdf.

————. "Situation in Darfur, Sudan, in the Case of *The Prosecutor v. Omar Hassan Ahmad Al Bashir*: Warrant of Arrest for Omar Hassan Ahmad Al Bashir." Case ICC-02/05-01/09. 4 March 2009. http://www.icc-cpi.int.

————. "Situation in the Democratic Republic of Congo, in the Case of *The Prosecutor v. Bosco Ntaganda*: Warrant of Arrest." ICC-01/04-02/06. 22 August 2006.

————. "Situation in the Democratic Republic of the Congo, in the Case of *The Prosecutor v. Callixte Mbarushimana*: Decision on the Confirmation of Charges." ICC-01/04-10/10. 16 December 2011.

————. "Situation in the Democratic Republic of Congo, in the Case of *The Prosecutor v. Callixte Mbarushimana*: Warrant of Arrest." ICC-01/04-1/10. 28 September 2010.

————. "Situation in the Democratic Republic of Congo, in the Case of *The Prosecutor v. Germain Katanga*: Warrant of Arrest." ICC-01/04-01/0. 2 July 2007.

————. "Situation in the Democratic Republic of Congo, in the Case of *The Prosecutor v. Mathieu Ngudjolo Chui*: Warrant of Arrest." ICC-01/04-02/07. 6 July 2007.

————. "Situation in the Democratic Republic of Congo, in the Case of *The Prosecutor v. Thomas Lubanga Dyilo*: Judgment Pursuant to Article 74 of the Statute." ICC-01/04-01/06. 14 March 2012.

————. "Situation in the Democratic Republic of Congo, in the Case of *The Prosecutor v. Thomas Lubanga Dyilo*: Warrant of Arrest." ICC-01/04-01/06. 10 February 2006.

————. "Situations and Cases. http://www.icc-cpi.int.

————. "Warrant of Arrest for Joseph Kony Issued on 8 July 2005 as Amended on 27 September 2005." http://www.icc-cpi.int.

————. "Warrant of Arrest for Laurent Gbagbo." 23 November 2011. http://www.icc-cpi.int.

————. "Warrant of Arrest for Omar Hassan Ahmed Al Bashir." 4 March 2009. http://www.icc-cpi.int/.

International Criminal Court, Assembly of States Parties. "Strengthening the International Criminal Court and the Assembly of States Parties." I.C.C. Doc. ICC-ASP/8/Res.3. 26 November 2009.

International Criminal Court, Office of the Prosecutor. "Paper on Some Policy Issues Before the Office of the Prosecutor." September 2003. http://www.icc-cpi.int.

————. "Report on Preliminary Examination Activities 2012." November 2012. http://www.icc-cpi.int.

————. "Report on the Activities Performed During the First Three Years (June 2003–June 2006)." 12 September 2006. http://www.icc-cpi.int.

International Crisis Group. "Building a Comprehensive Peace Strategy for Northern Uganda." 23 June 2005.

————. "Congo: A Comprehensive Strategy to Disarm the FDLR." 9 July 2009.

————. "Congo Crisis: Military Intervention in Ituri." 13 June 2003.

————. "Congo: Five Priorities for a Peacebuilding Strategy." 11 May 2009.

————. "Congo: Four Priorities for Sustainable Peace in Ituri." 13 May 2008.

————. "Congo: No Stability in Kivu Despite a Rapprochement with Rwanda." 16 November 2010.

————. "Eastern Congo: The ADF-NALU's Lost Rebellion." 19 December 2012.

————. "Eastern Congo: Why Stabilisation Failed." 4 October 2012.
————. "The Inter-Congolese Dialogue: Political Negotiations of Game of Bluff." 16 November 2001.
————. "The Kivus: The Forgotten Crucible of the Congo Conflict." 24 January 2003.
————. "The Lord's Resistance Army: End Game?" 17 November 2011.
————. "LRA: A Regional Strategy Beyond Killing Kony." 28 April 2010.
————. "Northern Uganda Peace Process: The Need to Maintain Momentum." 14 September 2007.
————. "Northern Uganda: The Road to Peace, with or Without Kony." 10 December 2008.
————. "Northern Uganda: Seizing the Opportunity for Peace." 26 April 2007.
————. "Peace in Northern Uganda: Decisive Weeks Ahead." 21 February 2005.
————. Peace in Northern Uganda? 13 September 2006.
————. "Shock Therapy for Northern Uganda's Peace Process." 11 April 2005.
————. "A Strategy for Ending Northern Uganda's Crisis." 11 January 2006.
————. "Sudan: Justice, Peace and the ICC." 17 July 2009.
————. "Sudan: Preventing Implosion." 17 December 2009.
————. "To Save Darfur." 17 March 2006.
————. "Uganda and Rwanda: Friends or Enemies?" 4 May 2000.
International Rescue Committee. "Mortality in the Democratic Republic of Congo: An Ongoing Crisis." January 2008. http://www.rescue.org.
————. "Mortality in the Democratic Republic of Congo: Results from a Nationwide Survey." April 2003. http://www.rescue.org.
————. "Mortality in Eastern Democratic Republic of Congo: Results from Eleven Mortality Surveys." 2001. http://www.rescue.org/.
Jacquemont, Pierre. "The Dynamics of Instability in Eastern DRC." *Forced Migration Review* 36 (November 2010): 6–7.
Jalloh, Christopher C. "Universal Jurisdiction, Universal Prescription? A Preliminary Assessment of the African Union Perspective on Universal Jurisdiction." *Criminal Law Forum* 21 (2010): 1–65.
"Joint Darfur Aid Warning Issued." *BBC News*, 24 March 2009.
Jones, Peter, and David Smith. "Goma Falls to Congo Rebels." *The Guardian*, 20 November 2012.
Jorgic, Drazen. "Congo Rejects Rwandan Soldiers for Regional Anti-Rebel Force." *AlertNet*, 9 August 2012.
"Joseph Kabila: 'OpenSecret Rwanda Is Backing Rebel Fighters in Congo'." *The Telegraph*, 29 July 2012.
"Joseph Kony: US Doubts LRA Rebel Leader's Surrender." *BBC News*, 21 November 2103.
"Jury Still out on ICC Trials in DRC." *IRIN*, 19 January 2011.
Kaldor, Mary. *New and Old Wars: Organized Violence in a Global Era*. 2nd ed. Stanford, Calif.: Stanford University Press, 2007.
Kastner, Philip. "The ICC in Darfur: Savior or Spoiler?" *Journal of International and Comparative Law* 14, 1 (2007): 145–88.
Katzman, Rachel. "The Non-Disclosure of Confidential Exculpatory Evidence and the Lubanga Proceedings: How the ICC Defense System Affects the Accused's Right to a Fair Trial." *Northwest University Journal of International Human Rights* 8 (Fall 2009): 77–101.
Keller, Linda M. "Achieving Peace with Justice: The International Criminal Court and Ugandan Alternative Justice Mechanisms." *Connecticut Journal of International Law* 23, 2 (2008): 209–79.
Kennedy, David. *The Dark Sides of Virtue: Reassessing International Humanitarianism*. Princeton, N.J.: Princeton University Press, 2004.
"Kenya Parliament Holds Emergency Debate on ICC Pull-out." *BBC News*, 5 September 2013.

"Kenyan PM Says Bashir Must Stand Before ICC, Wants Apology Made to Int'l Community." *Sudan Tribune*, 30 August 2010.

Kjeksrud, Stian, and Jacob Aasland Ravndal. "Emerging Lessons from the United Nations Mission in the Congo: Military Contributions to the Protection of Civilians." *African Security Review* 20 (June 2011): 3–16.

———. "Protection of Civilians in Practice—Emerging Lessons from the UN Mission in the DRC." Norwegian Defence Research Establishment. 15 December 2010.

Klein-Ahlbrandt, Stephanie T. E. "The Kibeho Crisis: Towards a More Effective System of International Protection for IDPs." *Forced Migration Review* 2 (August 1998): 8–11.

Koko, Sadiki. "MONUC and the Quest for Peace in the Democratic Republic of Congo: Assessment of a Peacekeeping Mission." *African Security Review* 20 (June 2011): 29–41.

Kristof, Nicholas D. "Will We Say 'Never Again' Yet Again?" *New York Times*, 27 March 2004.

Kron, Josh. "African Union to Make Push Against Rebels." *New York Times*, 23 March 2012.

Kron, Josh, and J. David Goodman. "Online, a Distant Conflict Soars to Topic 1." *New York Times*, 8 March 2012.

Kulish, Nicholas, and Somini Sengupta. "New U.N. Brigade's Aggressive Stance in Africa Brings Success, Risks." *New York Times*, 12 November 2013.

Kuperman, Alan J. *The Limits of Humanitarian Intervention: Genocide in Rwanda*. Washington, D.C.: Brookings Institution Press, 2001.

———. "Suicidal Rebellions and the Moral Hazard of Humanitarian Intervention." *Ethnopolitics* 4, 2 (2005): 149–73.

Kushkush, Isma'il. "New Strife in Darfur Leaves Many Seeking Refuge." *New York Times*, 23 May 2013.

Kwinika, Savious. "Sudan President Bashir, Accused of War Crimes, Would Be Arrested in South Africa, Says ANC." *Christian Science Monitor*, 28 July 2010.

Labonte, Melissa. *Human Rights and Humanitarian Norms, Strategic Framing, and Intervention: Lessons for the Responsibility to Protect*. New York: Routledge, 2013.

Lamont, Christopher. *International Criminal Justice and the Politics of Compliance*. Farnham: Ashgate, 2010.

Lanz, David. "Save Darfur: A Movement and Its Discontents." *African Affairs* 108, 4 (2009): 669–77.

Lemarchand, René. *The Dynamics of Violence in Central Africa*. Philadelphia: University of Pennsylvania Press, 2009.

Lemkin, Raphael. *Axis Rule in Occupied Europe: Laws of Occupation, Analysis of Government, Proposals for Redress*. Washington, D.C.: Carnegie Endowment for World Peace, 1944.

Leonard, Eric K. *The Onset of Global Governance: International Relations Theory and the International Criminal Court*. Aldershot: Ashgate, 2005.

Leonard, Eric K., and Steven C. Roach. "From Realism to Legalization: A Rationalist Assessment of the International Criminal Court in the Democratic Republic of Congo." In *Governance, Order and the International Criminal Court: Between Realpolitik and a Cosmopolitan Court*, ed. Steven C. Roach. Oxford: Oxford University Press, 2009.

Leopold, Evelyn. "Military Intervention and the Humanitarian 'Force Multiplier.'" *Global Governance* 13, 1 (2007): 99–118.

———. "UN, AU Differ on Composition of Darfur Peace Force." *Reuters*, 21 September 2007.

Le Pape, Marc. "Democratic Republic of Congo: Victims of No Importance." In *In the Shadow of "Just Wars": Violence, Politics and Humanitarian Action*, ed. Fabrice Weissman. London: Hurst, 2004.

"Living with Fear: A Populations-Based Survey on Attitudes About Peace, Justice, and Social Reconstruction in Eastern Democratic Republic of Congo." Human Rights Center (University of California, Berkeley), Payson Center for International Development (Tulane University), and International Center for Transitional Justice. August 2008.

Loescher, Gil. "UNHCR and the Erosion of Refugee Protection." *Forced Migration Review* 10 (April 2001): 28–30.

———. *The UNHCR and World Politics: A Perilous Path*. Oxford: Oxford University Press, 2001.

Lomo, Zachary. "The International Criminal Court Investigations: Implications for the Search for Peaceful Solutions to the Conflict in Northern Uganda." All Party Parliamentary Group on the Great Lakes Region and Genocide Prevention, Working Paper 2. July 2004. http://appggreatlakes.org/document-library/document-library/finish/4-appg-reports/42-lomo-august-2004-final/0.html.

Long, Nick. "UN Brigade in DRC Not Magic Solution, Says Commander." *Voice of America*, 10 July 2013.

"LRA Prepares for War, Not Peace." Institute for War & Peace Reporting. 1 May 2008. http://iwpr.net/report-news/lra-prepares-war-not-peace.

Lutz, Ellen. "Transitional Justice: Lessons Learned and the Road Ahead." In *Transition Justice in the Twenty-First Century: Beyond Truth Versus Justice*, ed. Naomi Roht-Arriaza and Javier Mariezcurrena. Cambridge: Cambridge University Press, 2006.

Lynch, Colum. "Indictment of Sudanese Leader Seen as Threat to Peacekeepers." *Washington Post*, 20 July 2008.

———. "International Court Under Unusual Fire." *Washington Post*, 30 June 2009.

———. "Sudan's Omar al-Bashir Cancels U.N. Trip." *Foreign Policy*, 25 September 2013.

———. "U.N. Panel Says Rwanda Behind Congolese Mutiny." *Foreign Policy*, 26 June 2012.

Lynch, Colum, and Nora Boustany. "Sudan Leader to Be Charged with Genocide." *Washington Post*, 11 July 2008.

MacFarquhar, Neil. "U.N. Official Says Darfur Continues to Crumble." *New York Times*, 20 March 2009.

MacFarquhar, Neil, and Marlise Simons. "UN Panels Says Sudan Expulsion of Aid Groups Is 'Deplorable.'" *New York Times*, 6 March 2009.

Mamdani, Mahmood. *Saviors and Survivors: Darfur, Politics and the War on Terror*. London: Verso, 2009.

Maphosa, Sylvester Bongani. "Preparing for Peace: The AU Regional Cooperation Initiative for the Elimination of the LRA in Central Africa." Africa Institute of South Africa. March 2013. http://dspace.cigilibrary.org/jspui/bitstream/123456789/33792/3/Preparing-for-peace.-The-AU-regional-cooperation-.pdf.

Marriage, Zoë. "Congo Co: Aid and Security." *Conflict, Security & Development* 10 3 (2010): 353–77.

Massey, Simon. "Operation Assurance: The Greatest Intervention That Never Happened." *Journal of Humanitarian Assistance* (February 1998).

Matsiko, Grace, Frank Nyakairu, and Emmanuel Gyezaho. "I Cannot Betray Kony, Museveni." *Monitor*, 16 August 2006.

McGreal, Chris. "US Support for Rwanda Wanes amid Concern over Violence in Congo." *The Guardian*, 1 August 2012.

McNamara, Dennis. Statement Before the House Committee on International Relations, Sub-Committee on International Operations and Human Rights, Hearing on "Rwanda: Genocide and the Continuing Cycle of Violence." 5 May 1998.

Médecins Sans Frontières. "Ituri: Unkept Promises? A Pretense of Protection and Inadequate Assistance." 25 July 2003.

———. "Nothing New in Ituri: The Violence Continues." August 2005.

Melillo, Margherita. "Cooperation Between the UN Peacekeeping Operation and the ICC in the Democratic Republic of the Congo." *Journal of International Criminal Justice* 11, 4 (2013): 766–68.

Melvern, Linda. *Conspiracy to Murder: The Rwandan Genocide.* Rev. ed. London: Verso, 2006.

———. "Missing the Story: The Media and the Rwandan Genocide." *Contemporary Security Policy* 22, 3 (2001): 91–106.

———. *A People Betrayed: The Role of the West in Rwanda's Genocide.* Rev. ed. London: Zed Books, 2009.

Mennecke, Martin. "What's in a Name? Reflections on Using, Not Using, and Overusing the 'G-Word.'" *Genocide Studies and Prevention* 2, 1 (2007): 57–72.

Mills, Kurt. "'Bashir Is Dividing Us': Africa and the International Criminal Court." *Human Rights Quarterly* 34, 3 (2012): 404–47.

———. "Constructing Humanitarian Space in Darfur." *International Journal of Human Rights* 17, 5–6 (2013): 605–18.

———. *Human Rights in the Emerging Global Order: A New Sovereignty?* Basingstoke: Macmillan, 1998.

———. "Neo-Humanitarianism: The Role of International Humanitarian Norms and Organizations in Contemporary Conflict." *Global Governance* 11 (2005): 161–83.

———. "The Postmodern Tank of the Humanitarian International." *Peace Review* 18 (April–June 2006): 261–67.

———. "United Nations Intervention in Refugee Crises After the Cold War." *International Politics* 35 (December 1998): 391–424.

Mills, Kurt, and David Karp, eds. *Human Rights Protection in Global Politics: Responsibilities of States and Non-State Actors.* Basingstoke: Palgrave Macmillan, 2015.

Mills, Kurt, and Anthony Lott. "From Rome to Darfur: Norms and Interests in US Policy Toward the International Criminal Court." *Journal of Human Rights* 6, 4 (2007): 497–521.

Mills, Kurt, and Cian O'Driscoll. "From Humanitarian Intervention to the Responsibility to Protect." In *The International Studies Encyclopedia*, ed. Robert Denemark. London: Wiley-Blackwell, 2010.

Minear, Larry. "Humanitarian Action in an Age of Terrorism." International Council on Human Rights Policy. Prepared for the International Expert Conference on September 2001: Impacts on Human Rights Work. 24–25 May 2002. http://www.ichrp.org/files/papers/70/118_Humanitarian_Action_in_an_Age_of_Terrorism_Larry_Minear_May_2002_background_paper.pdf.

Minear, Larry, Ted van Baarda, and Marc Sommers. "NATO and Humanitarian Action in the Kosovo Crisis." Thomas J. Watson Jr. Institute for International Studies, Brown University, Occasional Paper 36. 2000. http://www.watsoninstitute.org/pub/OP36.pdf.

Minnow, Martha. "Naming Horror: Legal and Political Words for Mass Atrocities." *Genocide Studies and Prevention* 2, 1 (2007): 37–41.

Mironko, Charles, and Peter Uvin. "Western and Local Approaches to Justice in Rwanda." *Global Governance* 9, 2 (2003): 219–31.

Momanyi, Bernard. "Ugandan Leader Lashes Out at ICC." Institute for War & Peace Reporting. 20 April 2013. http://iwpr.net/report-news/ugandan-leader-lashes-out-icc.

MONUC and UN Office of the High Commissioner for Human Rights. "Summary of Fact-Finding Missions on Alleged Human Rights Violations Committed by the Lord's Resistance Army (LRA) in the Districts of Haut-Uélé and Bas-Uélé in Orientale Province of the Democratic Republic of Congo." December 2009.

Moodley, Kiran. "Bill Clinton: We Could Have Saved 300,000 Lives in Rwanda." *CNBC*, 13 March 2013.

Mooney, Erin D. "Presence, Ergo Protection? UNPROFOR, UNHCR and the ICRC in Croatia and Bosnia and Herzegovina." *International Journal of Refugee Law* 7, 3 (1995): 407–35.

Moreno-Ocampo, Luis, Prosecutor of the International Criminal Court. "Building a Future on Peace and Justice." Nuremberg, 24–25 June 2007.

Mosely, Sarah, Talita Cetinoglu, and Marit Glad. "Protection from Sexual Violence in DRC." *Forced Migration Review* 36 (November 2010): 14–15.

Mowjee, Tasneem. "Humanitarian Agenda 2015 Democratic Republic of Congo Case Study." Feinstein International Center, Tufts University, October 2007.

Müller, Andreas Th., and Ignaz Stegmiller. "Self-Referrals on Trial: From Panacea to Patient." *Journal of International Criminal Justice* 8, 5 (2010): 1267–94.

Murthy, Jaya. "Mandating the Protection Cluster with the Responsibility to Protect: A Policy Recommendation Based on the Protection Cluster's Implementation in South Kivu, DRC." *Journal of Humanitarian Assistance* (5 October 2007).

Musila, Godfrey M. *Between Rhetoric and Action: The Politics, Processes and Practice of the ICC's Work in the DRC.* Pretoria: Institute for Security Studies, 2009.

Mutua, Makau. "Savages, Victims, and Saviors: The Metaphor of Human Rights." *Harvard International Law Journal* 42, 1 (2001): 201–45.

Mwenda, Andrew. "Uganda's Politics of Foreign Aid and Violent Conflict: The Political Uses of the LRA Rebellion." In *The Lord's Resistance Army: Myth and Reality*, ed. Tim Allen and Koen Vlassenroot. London: Zed Books, 2010.

The National Security Strategy of the United States of America. September 2006.

Neu, Joyce. "Briefing on the Conflict in Uganda: Hope for a Negotiated Settlement." Joan B. Kroc Institute for Peace and Justice. 1 June 2005. http://www.sandiego.edu/peacestudies/documents /ipj/reports/ipjarticles/JNremarks5-30-05 (2)[1].pdf.

Ngolet, François. *Crisis in the Congo: The Rise and Fall of Laurent Kabila.* New York: Palgrave Macmillan, 2011.

Nichols, Michelle and Louise Charbonneau. "Fearing Death, Congo's 'Terminator' Fled with Help of Family." *Reuters*, 28 June 2013.

"Nigeria Would Have Blocked Visit by Sudan's Bashir if It Knew Ahead of Time: Report." *Sudan Tribune*, 21 July 2013.

Norheim-Martinsen, Per Martin. "Our Work Here Is Done: European Union Peacekeeping in Africa." *African Security Review* 20 (June 2011): 17–28.

Norris, John, David Sullivan, and John Prendergast. "The Merits of Justice." Enough Project. July 2008. http://www.enoughproject.org/files/reports/ICC_report_071408.pdf.

Nouwen, Sarah M. H., and Wouter G. Werner. "Doing Justice to the Political: The International Criminal Court in Uganda and Sudan." *European Journal of International Law* 21, 4 (2011): 941–65.

Nsambu, Hillary. "Former LRA Commander Kwoyelo Free." *New Vision*, 23 September 2011.

Obama, Barack. "Statement by the President on the Signing of the Lord's Resistance Army Disarmament and Northern Uganda Recovery Act of 2009." 24 May 2010. http://www.whitehouse .gov/the-press-office/statement-president-signing-lords-resistance-army-disarmament-and -northern-uganda-r.

Odom, Lieutenant Colonel Thomas P. "Guerrillas from the Mist: A Defense Attaché Watches the Rwandan Patriotic Front Transform from Insurgent to Counter Insurgent." *Small Wars Journal* 5 (July 2006): 1–14.

Office for the Coordination of Humanitarian Assistance. "Humanitarian Action in LRA-Affected Areas: Regional Overview of Needs and Response." June 2012. http://reliefweb.int/report /democratic-republic-congo/humanitarian-action-lra-affected-areas-regional-overview -needs-and.

———. "LRA Regional Update: Central African Republic, DR Congo and South Sudan (April–June 2013)." 25 July 2013. http://reliefweb.int/sites/reliefweb.int/files/resources/LRA%20Regional%20Update%20%28April%20-%20June%202013%29.pdf.

———. OCHA Financial Tracking Service. http://fts.unocha.org/.

Okumu, Wafula. "Africa and the UN Security Council Permanent Seats." *Pambazuka News*, 28 April 2005.

Oola, Stephen. "Matsanga Should Not Have Been Given Amnesty." *New Vision*, 10 June 2010.

Otunnu, Olara A. "The Secret Genocide." *Foreign Policy*, 9 June 2006.

Oxfam. "For Me, But Without Me, Is Against Me." July 2012. http://www.oxfamblogs.org.

———. "Protection of Civilians in 2010." Oxfam Briefing Paper 147. May 2011.

———. "'We Are Entirely Exploitable': The Lack of Protection for Civilians in Eastern DRC." 28 July 2011.

Oxfam International. "OI Policy Compendium Note on the Provision of Aid by Foreign Military Forces." April 2012. policy-practice.oxfam.org.uk.

———. "Waking the Devil: The Impact of Forced Disarmament in Civilians in the Kivus." July 2009.

Paddon, Emily, and Guillaume Lacaille. "Stabilising the Congo." Refugee Studies Centre. December 2011. http://www.rsc.ox.ac.uk/publications/policy-briefings/RSCPB8-StabilisingCongo.pdf.

Parsons, Claudia. "U.N. Urgently Seeking Helicopters for Darfur Force." Reuters, 21 October 2007. Posted on JUSTWATCH-L e-mail list.

Paternoster, Raymond. "How Much Do We Really Know About Criminal Deterrence?" *Journal of Criminal Law & Criminology* 100, . 3 (2010): 765–823.

Perrot, Sandrine. "Northern Uganda: A 'Forgotten Conflict,' Again? The Impact of the Internationalization of the Resolution Process." In *The Lord's Resistance Army: Myth and Reality*, ed. Tim Allen and Koen Vlassenroot. London: Zed, 2010.

Peskin, Victor. "Caution and Confrontation in the International Criminal Court's Pursuit of Accountability in Uganda and Sudan." *Human Rights Quarterly* 31, 3 (2009): 655–91.

———. *International Justice in Rwanda and the Balkans*. Cambridge: Cambridge University Press, 2008.

Pillay, Suren. "Conclusion." In *Peace Versus Justice? The Dilemma of Transitional Justice in Africa*, ed. Chandra Lekha Sriram and Suren Pillay. Scottsville: University of KwaZulu-Natal Press, 2009.

Power, Samantha. "Dying in Darfur." *New Yorker*, 30 August 2004.

———."A Problem from Hell": America and the Age of Genocide. New York: Perennial, 2002.

Price, Stuart. "Kony Probe Begins June." *New Vision*, 30 January 2004.

The Princeton Principles on Universal Jurisdiction. Princeton Project on Universal Jurisdiction, 2001. http://lapa.princeton.edu/hosteddocs/unive_jur.pdf.

Prunier, Gérard. *Darfur: The Ambiguous Genocide*. 2nd ed. Ithaca, N.Y.: Cornell University Press, 2007.

———. *From Genocide to Continental War*. London: Hurst, 2009.

———. "The Geopolitical Situation in the Great Lakes Area in Light of the Kivu Crisis." WRITENET Country Papers. UNHCR. February 1997. http://www.unhcr.ch/refworld/country/writenet/wridrc.htm.

———. *The Rwanda Crisis*. London: Hurst, 1995.

Quinn, Joanna R. "Getting to Peace? Negotiating with the LRA in Northern Uganda." *Human Rights Review* 10, 1 (2009): 55–71.

Ratner, Steven R., Jason S. Abrams, and James L. Bischoff. *Accountability for Human Rights Atrocities in International Law*. Oxford: Oxford University Press.

Reed, William Cyrus. "Guerrillas in the Midst: The Former Government of Rwanda and the Alliance of Democratic Forces for the Liberation of Congo-Zaire in Eastern Zaire." In *African Guerrillas,* ed. Christopher Clapham. Bloomington: Indiana University Press, 1998.

Reeves, Eric. "Europe's Indifference to Darfur." *New Republic,* 27 October 2006. Posted on JUST-WATCH e-mail list.

———. "Genocide Without End? The Destruction of Darfur." *Dissent* (Summer 2007).

———. "Humanitarian Conditions in Darfur: A Climate of Violence and Extreme Insecurity." *Sudan Tribune,* 4 August 2013.

———. "Humanitarian Conditions in Darfur: Relief Efforts Perilously Close to Collapse (Two Parts)." 15 August 2013. http://www.sudanreeves.org.

Refugees International. "DR Congo: Improved Civilian Protection Activities Still Need Support." 13 November 2009. http://www.refugeesinternational.org.

———. "Eastern Congo: Beyond the Volcano, a Slow Motion Holocaust." 1 January 2002. http://www.kongo-kinshasa.de/dokumente/ngo/refint_0102.pdf.

"Report of the International Commission of Inquiry on Darfur to the United Nations Secretary-General." 25 January 2005. http://www.un.org/news/dh/sudan/com_inq_darfur.pdf.

Resolve. "Peace Can Be: President Obama's Chance to Help End LRA Atrocities in 2012." February 2012. http://www.scribd.com/doc.

Rettig, Max. "Gacaca: Truth, Justice, and Reconciliation in Postconflict Rwanda?" *African Studies Review* 51, 3 (2008): 25–50.

"Reward Offered for Information on Kony." *New York Times,* 3 April 2013.

Reynaert, Julie. "MONUC/MONUSCO and Civilian Protection in the Kivus." International Peace Information Service. February 2011. http://www.ipisresearch.

Reyntjens, Filip. *The Great African War: Congo and Regional Geopolitics, 1996–2006.* Cambridge: Cambridge University Press, 2009.

———. "Rwanda, Ten Years On: From Genocide to Dictatorship." *African Affairs* 103 (April 2004): 177–201.

Rice, Xan. "UN-Backed Congo Military Offensive a 'Humanitarian Disaster.'" *The Guardian,* 13 October 2009.

Rieff, David. *A Bed for the Night: Humanitarianism in Crisis.* New York: Simon & Schuster, 2002.

Rishmawi, Mona. "The ICC Viewed from the Office of the High Commissioner for Human Rights." In "Discussion." *Journal of International Criminal Justice* 6 (September 2008): 763–81.

Roach, Steven C., ed. *Governance, Order and the International Criminal Court: Between Realpolitik and a Cosmopolitan Court.* Oxford: Oxford University Press, 2009.

Roberts, Adam. "NATO's 'Humanitarian War' over Kosovo." *Survival* 41, 3 (1999): 102–23.

Robinson, Peter, and Golriz Ghahraman. "Can Rwandan President Kagame Be Held Responsible at the ICTR for the Killing of President Habyarimana?" *Journal of International Criminal Justice* 6, 5 (2008): 981–94.

Rodman, Kenneth A., and Petie Booth. "Manipulated Commitments: The International Criminal Court in Uganda." *Human Rights Quarterly* 35, 2 (2013): 271–303.

Roessler, Philip, and John Prendergast. "Democratic Republic of the Congo." In *Twenty-First-Century Peace Operations,* ed. William Durch. Washington, D.C.: U.S. Institute of Peace, 2006.

Roht-Arriaza, Naomi. *The Pinochet Effect: Transnational Justice.* Philadelphia: University of Pennsylvania Press, 2006.

Rona, Gabor. "The ICRC Privilege Not to Testify: Confidentiality in Action." *International Review of the Red Cross* 845 (2002).

Rotberg, Robert I., and Thomas G. Weiss, eds. *From Massacres to Genocide: The Media, Public Policy, and Humanitarian Crises.* Washington, D.C.: Brookings Institution, 1996.

Roth, Kenneth. "Court from the Lobby: A NGO View." In "Discussion." *Journal of International Criminal Justice* 6 (September 2008): 763–81.

———. "Get Tough on Human Rights." *Foreign Policy*, November 2010.

Rothe, Dawn L., and Christopher W. Mullins. "Darfur and the Politicization of International Law." *Humanity & Society* 31, 1 (2007): 83–107.

Rubin, Alissa J. "African Crisis Is Tougher Than France Expected." *New York Times*, 13 December 2013.

"Rwanda Aid Hinges on DRC, London Says." UPI, 13 August 2012. Posted to JUSTWATCH-L e-mail list.

"Rwandan Genocide: Kagame 'Cleared of Habyarimana Crash.'" *BBC News*, 10 January 2012.

Save the Children in Uganda. "Child Protection Concerns Related to the ICC Investigations and Possible Prosecution of the LRA Leadership." 30 March 2005.

Schabas, William A. "'Complementarity in Practice': Some Uncomplimentary Thoughts." *Criminal Law Forum* 19, 1 (2008): 5–33.

———. "Darfur and the 'Odious Scourge': The Commission of Inquiry's Findings on Genocide." *Leiden Journal of International Law* 18, 4 (2005): 871–85.

———. "Genocide Trials and *Gacaca* Courts." *Journal of International Criminal Justice* 3, 4 (2005): 879–95.

———. *An Introduction to the International Criminal Court*. 4th ed. Cambridge: Cambridge University Press, 2011.

———. "Prosecutorial Discretion *v.* Judicial Activism at the International Criminal Court." *Journal of International Criminal Justice* 6 (September 2008): 731–61.

———. "Semantics or Substance? David Scheffer's Welcome Proposal to Strengthen Criminal Accountability for Atrocities." *Genocide Studies and Prevention* 2. 1 (2007): 31–36.

Scheffer, David. "Genocide and Atrocity Crimes." *Genocide Studies and Prevention* 1 3 (2006): 229–50.

Scherrer, Christian P. *Genocide and Crisis in Central Africa: Conflict Roots, Mass Violence, and Regional War*. Westport, Conn.: Praeger, 2002.

Schiff, Benjamin N. *Building the International Criminal Court*. Cambridge: Cambridge University Press, 2008.

Schimmel, Noam. "An Invisible Genocide: How the Western Media Failed to Report the 1994 Rwandan Genocide of the Tutsi and Why." *International Journal of Human Rights* 15, 7 (2011): 1125–35.

Schomerus, Mareike. "The Lord's Resistance Army in Sudan: A History and Overview." Human Security Baseline Assessment Working Paper 8. Geneva: Small Arms Survey, 2007.

———. "'They Forget What They Came For': Uganda's Army in Sudan." *Journal of Eastern African Studies* 6, 1 (2012): 124–53.

"Second Report of the Prosecutor of the International Criminal Court, Mr. Luis Moreno Ocampo, to the Security Council Pursuant to UNSC 1593 (2005)." 13 December 2005.

Sengupta, Somini. "Stopping Bloodshed in the Central African Republic amid Ghosts of Genocide." *New York Times*, 9 December 2013.

Sewall, Sarah, Dwight Raymond, and Sally Chin. *MARO—Mass Atrocity Response Operations: A Military Planning Handbook*. Carr Center for Human Rights Policy, Harvard Kennedy School, and U.S. Army Peacekeeping and Stability Operations Institute. May 2010. http://www.hks.harvard.edu/cchrp/maro/pdf/MARO_Handbook_v9.pdf.

Shahine, Alaa. "Sudan Says No Evidence Against ICC Darfur Suspect." *Reuters*, 3 May 2007. Posted on JUSTWATCH-L e-mail list.

Simons, Marlise. "Karadzic Accuses His Accusers." *New York Times*, 2 August 2008.

Simons, Marlise, and Neil MacFarquhar. "Court Issues Arrest Warrant for Sudan's Leader." *New York Times*, 5 March 2009.

Simons, Marlise, Lydia Polgreen, and Jeffrey Gettleman. "Arrest Is Sought of Sudan Leader in Genocide Case." *New York Times*, 15 July 2008.

Simonse, Simon, Willemijn Verkoren, and Gerd Junne. "NGO Involvement in the Juba Peace Talks: The Role and Dilemmas of IKV Pax Christi." In *The Lord's Resistance Army: Myth and Reality*, ed. Tim Allen and Koen Vlassenroot. London: Zed, 2010.

Slim, Hugo. "International Humanitarianism's Engagement with Civil War in the 1990s." *Journal of Humanitarian Assistance* (June 2002).

Small Arms Survey. "Liberation and Justice Movement." Human Security Baseline Assessment (HSBA) for Sudan and South Sudan. 8 October 2012. http://www.smallarmssurveysudan.org/fileadmin/docs/facts-figures/sudan/darfur/armed-groups/opposition/HSBA-Armed-Groups-LJM.pdf.

———. "Lord's Resistance Army." 8 March 2013. http://www.smallarmssurveysudan.org/filead min/docs/facts-figures/south-sudan/armed-groups/lra/LRA_8_March.pdf.

Smith, David. "Rwandan Minister Is Leader of Congo Rebels, UN Says." *The Guardian*, 18 October 2012.

"Strategy to Support the Disarmament of the Lord's Resistance Army: A Strategy to Guide United States Support Across the Region for Viable Multilateral Efforts to Mitigate and Eliminate the Threat Posed to Civilians and Regional Stability Posed by the Lord's Resistance Army." 24 November 2010. http://pulitzercenter.org/sites/default/files/WhiteHouseLRAStrategy_opt.pdf

"Sudan Aid Arrives, 'More Needed.'" *BBC News*, 29 July 2004.

"Sudan Lifts Flight Ban on UNAMID Helicopters." *Sudan Tribune*, 18 June 2010.

"Sudan Reverses Course on ICC Arrest Warrant for Bashir." *Sudan Tribune*, 30 July 2009.

"Sudanese Children Dying of Hunger." *BBC News*, 9 June 2004.

"Sudan's Omar al-Bashir in Malawi: ICC Wants Answers." *BBC News*, 20 October 2011.

Swithern, Sophia. "Reclaiming Mainstreaming: Oxfam GB's Protection Approach in DRC." *Humanitarian Exchange Magazine* 39 (June 2008): 7–11.

Tamm, Henning. "FNI and FRPI: Local Resistance and Regional Alliances in North-eastern Congo." Rift Valley Institute, Usalama Project, 2013. http://www.refworld.org/docid/51d3d3be4.html.

———. "UPC in Ituri: The External Militarization of Local Politics in North-eastern Congo." Rift Valley Institute, Usalama Project, 2013. http://www.refworld.org/docid/51d2c07e4.html.

Tampa, Vava. "DR Congo: We Are All Implicated in the Carnage–We Can No Longer Ignore It." *The Guardian*, 10 October 2013.

Taylor, Ian. "The People's Republic of China." In *The International Politics of Mass Atrocities: The Case of Darfur*, ed. David R. Black and Paul D. Williams. New York: Routledge, 2010.

Tennant, Vicky. "UNHCR's Engagement with Integrated UN Missions: Report of a Lessons Learned Workshop." UNHCR Policy Development and Evaluation Service. PDES/2009/04. August 2009.

"Tenth Report of the Prosecutor of the International Criminal Court to the UN Security Council Pursuant to UNSCR 1593 (2005)." 4 December 2009.

Terry, Fiona. *Condemned to Repeat? The Paradox of Humanitarian Action*. Ithaca, N.Y.: Cornell University Press, 2002.

"The Triumph of Evil." *Frontline*, 26 January 1999.

"Uganda Conflict 'Worse Than Iraq.'" *BBC News*, 10 November 2011.

"Uganda: Government to Seek Review of ICC Indictments Against LRA Leaders." *IRIN*, 21 June 2007.

"Uganda Offers 'Blood Settlement' to LRA Rebels." *Reuters*, 11 March 2008.

"Uganda Pledges to Arrest Sudanese President." *Toronto Star*, 13 July 2009.

"Uganda Struggles to Come to Terms with Its Disappeared." *IRIN*, 30 August 2013.

"Uganda to Withdraw Troops from Somalia Says Mukasa." *BBC News*, 2 November 2012.

Ulriksen, Ståle, Catriona Gourlay, and Catriona Mace. "Operation *Artemis*: The Shape of Things to Come?" *International Peacekeeping* 11, 3 (2004): 508–25.

"UNAMID Celebrates Deployment of Tactical Helicopters." Press release, African Union—United Nations Mission in Darfur. 27 February 2010. http://unamid.unmissions.org.

"UNAMID Deployment on the Brink: The Road to Security in Darfur Blocked by Government Obstruction." Joint NGO report. December 2007. http://www.humanrightsfirst.info.

"UN Chief Sees Obstacles to Helping Darfur, Somalia." Associated Press, 7 October 2008. Posted on JUSTWATCH e-mail list.

"U.N. Council Set to Renew Darfur Peacekeeping Mandate." Reuters, 31 July 2008. Posted on JUSTWATCH-L e-mail list.

"U.N. Force Takes Control in Darfur." *New York Times* (AP), 31 December 2007.

"UN in Congo 'Gives LRA Free Rein.'" *BBC News*, 4 February 2009.

UN, Department of Peacekeeping Operations. "Operation Artemis: The Lessons of the Interim Emergency Multinational Force." Peacekeeping Best Practices Unit. October 2004.

———. "United Nations Peacekeeping Operations: Principles and Guidelines." 2008.

UN General Assembly. 2005 World Summit Outcome. A/Res/60/1. 15 September 2005.

———. "Children and Armed Conflict." Report of the Secretary-General. A/61/529. 26 October 2006.

———. "Children and Armed Conflict." Report of the Secretary-General. A/62/609. 21 December 2007.

———. "Financing of the United Nations Organization Stabilization Mission in the Democratic Republic of the Congo." A/66/584/Add.1. 14 June 2012.

UN High Commissioner for Human Rights. *Democratic Republic of the Congo, 1993–2003: Report of the Mapping Exercise Documenting the Most Serious Violations of Human Rights and International Humanitarian Law Committed Within the Territory of the Democratic Republic of the Congo Between March 1993 and June 2003*. August 2010. http://www.ohchr.org.

———. "Report of the United Nations High Commissioner for Human Rights on the Mission Undertaken by Her Office, Pursuant to Commission Resolution 2000/60, to Assess the Situation on the Ground with Regard to the Abduction of Children from Northern Uganda." 9 November 2001. E/CN.4/2002/86.

UN High Commissioner for Refugees. "Impact of Military Personnel and the Militia Presence in Rwandese Refugee Camps and Settlements." Prepared for the "Regional Conference on Assistance to Refugees, Returnees and Displaced Persons in the Great Lakes Region." Bujumbura, Burundi, February 12–17, 1995.

———. *State of the World's Refugees 2006: Human Displacement in the New Millennium*. Oxford: Oxford University Press, 2006.

———. "Supplementary Appeal for Emergency Assistance to Sudanese in Eastern Chad." 1 September 2003.

———. "UN Refugee Agency Appeals for Emergency Funds for Sudanese Refugees." 30 January 2004. http://www.unhcr.org/news/NEWS/401a74fb2.html.

United Nations. "Report of the Panel on United Nations Peace Operations." A/55/305-S/2000/809. 21 August 2000.

———. "Rwanda—UNAMIR Background." http://www.un.org.

UN Office for the Coordination of Humanitarian Affairs. "Glossary of Humanitarian Terms in Relation to the Protection of Civilians in Armed Conflict." December 2003. http://ochaonline.un.org.

"UN Official Calls DR Congo 'Rape Capital of the World." *BBC News*, 28 April 2010.

UN Secretary-General Kofi Annan. "Secretary-General, in 'Mission of Healing' to Rwanda, Pledges Support of United Nations for Country's Search for Peace and Progress." Press release. SG/SM/6552 AFR/56. 6 May 1998. http://www.un.org/News/Press/docs/1998/19980506 .SGSM6552.html.

UN Security Council. "Addendum to the Interim Report of the Group of Experts on the Democratic Republic of Congo (S/2012/34) Concerning Violations of the Arms Embargo and Sanctions Regime by the Government of Rwanda." S/2012/348/Add.1. 27 June 2012.

———. "Additional Report of the Secretary-General on Children and Armed Conflict in Uganda." S/2008/409. 23 June 2008.

———. "Children and Armed Conflict." Report of the Secretary-General. S/2009/158. 26 March 2009.

———. "Eighteenth Report of the Secretary-General on the United Nations Organization Mission in the Democratic Republic of the Congo." S/2005/506. 2 August 2005.

———. "Eleventh Report of the Secretary-General on the United Nations Organization Mission in the Democratic Republic of the Congo." S/2002/621. 5 June 2002.

———. "Final Report of the Commission of Experts Established Pursuant to Security Council Resolution 780 (1992)." S/1994/674. 27 May 1994.

———. "Fourth Special Report of the Secretary-General on the United Nations Organization Mission in the Democratic Republic of the Congo." S/2008/728. 21 November 2008.

———. "Letter Dated 10 August from the Secretary-General Addressed to the President of the Security Council." S/2006/645. 14 August 2006.

———. "Letter Dated 12 November 2012 from the Chair of the Security Council Committee Established Pursuant to Resolution 1533 (2004) Concerning the Democratic Republic of the Congo to the President of Security Council." S/2012/843. 15 November 2012.

———. "Letter Dated 17 August from the Secretary-General Addressed to the President of the Security Council." S/2006/665. 17 August 2006.

———. "Letter Dated 25 June 2012 from the Secretary-General Addressed to the President of the Security Council." S/2012/481. 25 June 2012.

———. "Report of the Secretary-General and the Chairperson of the African Union Commission on the Hybrid Operation in Darfur." S/2007/307/Rev.1. 5 June 2007.

———. "Report of the Secretary-General on Children and Armed Conflict in the Democratic Republic of the Congo." S/2010/369. 9 July 2010.

———. "Report of the Secretary-General on Children and Armed Conflict in Uganda." S/2007/260. 7 May 2007.

———. "Report of the Secretary-General on Children and Armed Conflict in Uganda." S/2008/409. 23 June 2008.

———. "Report of the Secretary-General on Children and Armed Conflict in Uganda." S/2009/462. 15 September 2009.

———. "Report of the Secretary-General on Children and Armed Conflict in the Democratic Republic of the Congo." S/2008/693. 10 November 2008.

———. "Report of the Secretary-General on Children and Armed Conflict in the Democratic Republic of the Congo." S/2010/369. 9 July 2010.

———. "Report of the Secretary-General on Darfur." S/20006/591. 28 July 2006.

———. "Report of the Secretary-General on Protection for Humanitarian Assistance to Refugees and Others in Conflict Situations." S/1998/883. 22 September 1998.

———. "Report of the Secretary-General on the Activities of the United Nations Regional Office for Central Africa and on Areas Affected by the Lord's Resistance Army." S/2012/923. 13 December 2012.

———. "Report of the Secretary-General on the Activities of the United Nations Regional Office for Central Africa and on the Lord's Resistance Army-Affected Areas." S/2013/297. 20 May 2013.

———. "Report of the Secretary-General on the African Union-United Nations Hybrid Operation in Darfur." S/2010/50. 29 January 2010.

——. "Report of the Secretary-General on the African Union-United Nations Hybrid Operation in Darfur." S/2010/213. 28 April 2010.

——. "Report of the Secretary-General on the African Union-United Nations Hybrid Operation in Darfur." S/2010/382. 14 July 2010.

——. "Report of the Secretary-General on the African Union-United Nations Hybrid Operation in Darfur." S/2011/22. 18 January 2011.

——. "Report of the Secretary-General on the African Union-United Nations Hybrid Operation in Darfur." S/2011/643. 12 October 2011.

——. "Report of the Secretary-General on the African Union-United Nations Hybrid Operation in Darfur." S/2012/231. 17 April 2012.

——. "Report of the Secretary-General on the African Union-United Nations Hybrid Operation in Darfur." S/2012/548. 16 July 2012.

——. "Report of the Secretary-General on the African Union-United Nations Hybrid Operation in Darfur." S/2012/771. 16 October 2012.

——. "Report of the Secretary-General on the African Union-United Nations Hybrid Operation in Darfur." S/2013/420. 12 July 2013.

——. "Report of the Secretary-General on the Deployment of the African-Union-United Nations Hybrid Operation in Darfur." S/2008/659. 17 October 2008.

——. "Report of the Secretary-General on the Deployment of the African-Union-United Nations Hybrid Operation in Darfur." S/2009/83. 10 February 2009.

——."Report of the Secretary-General on the Deployment of the African-Union-United Nations Hybrid Operation in Darfur." S/2009/201. 14 April 2009.

——. "Report of the Secretary-General on the Deployment of the African-Union-United Nations Hybrid Operation in Darfur." S/2009/297. 9 June 2009.

——. "Report of the Secretary-General on the Deployment of the African-Union-United Nations Hybrid Operation in Darfur." S/2009/352. 13 July 2009.

——. "Report of the Secretary-General on the Lord's Resistance Army-Affected Areas Pursuant to Security Council Press Statement." S/2011/693. 4 November 2011.

——."Report of the Secretary-General on the Situation in Rwanda." S/1994/640. 31 May 1994.

——. "Report of the Secretary-General on the Situation in the Central African Republic and on the Activities of the United Nations Peacebuilding Support Office in That Country." S/2008/410. 23 June 2008.

——. "Report of the Secretary-General on the Situation of Children and Armed Conflict Affected by the Lord's Resistance Army." S/2012/365. 25 May 2012.

——. "Report of the Secretary-General on the United Nations Organization Mission in the Democratic Republic of the Congo." S/2000/30. 17 January 2000.

——. "Report of the Secretary-General on the United Nations Organization Stabilization Mission in the Democratic Republic of the Congo." S/2010/512. 8 October 2010.

——. "Report of the Secretary-General on the United Nations Organization Stabilization Mission in the Democratic Republic of the Congo." S/2011/20. 17 January 2011.

——. "Report of the Secretary-General on the United Nations Organization Stabilization Mission in the Democratic Republic of the Congo." S/2011/298. 12 May 2011.

——. "Report of the Secretary-General on the United Nations Organization Stabilization Mission in the Democratic Republic of the Congo." S/2011/656. 24 October 2011.

——. "Report of the Secretary-General on the United Nations Organization Stabilization Mission in the Democratic Republic of the Congo." S/2012/65. 26 January 2012.

——. "Security Council Press Statement on the Democratic Republic of Congo." SC/10709. 16 July 2012.

———. "Sixth Report of the Secretary-General on the United Nations Organization Mission in the Democratic Republic of the Congo." S/2001/128. 12 February 2001.

———. "Special Report of the Secretary-General on the Democratic Republic of the Congo and the Great Lakes Region." S/2013/119. 27 February 2013.

———. "Statement by the President of the Security Council." S/PRST/2006/28. 22 June 2006.

———. "Statement by the President of the Security Council." S/PRST/2008/48. 22 December 2008.

———. "Third Special Report of the Secretary-General on the United Nations Organization Mission in the Democratic Republic of the Congo." S/2004/650. 16 August 2004.

———. "Thirtieth Report of the Secretary-General on the United Nations Organization Mission in the Democratic Republic of the Congo." S2009/623. 4 December 2009.

———. "Thirty-First Report of the Secretary-General on the United Nations Organization Mission in the Democratic Republic of the Congo." S/2010/164. 30 March 2010.

———. "Twelfth Report of the Secretary-General on the United Nations Organization Mission in the Democratic Republic of the Congo." S/2002/1180. 18 October 2002.

———. "Twentieth Report of the Secretary-General on the United Nations Organization Mission in the Democratic Republic of the Congo." S/2005/832. 28 December 2005.

———. "Twenty-Eighth Report of the Secretary-General on the United Nations Organization Mission in the Democratic Republic of Congo." S/2009/335. 30 June 2009.

———. "Twenty-Fifth Report of the Secretary-General on the United Nations Organization Mission in the Democratic Republic of the Congo." S/2008/218. 2 April 2008.

———. "Twenty-First Report of the Secretary-General on the United Nations Organization Mission in the Democratic Republic of the Congo." S/2006/390. 13 June 2006.

———. "Twenty-Ninth Report of the Secretary-General on the United Nations Organization Mission in the Democratic Republic of the Congo." S/2009/472. 18 September 2009.

———. "Twenty-Seventh Report of the Secretary-General on the United Nations Organization Mission in the Democratic Republic of the Congo." S/2009/160. 27 March 2009.

———. "Twenty-Sixth Report of the Secretary-General on the United Nations Organization Mission in the Democratic Republic of the Congo." S/2008/433. 3 July 2008.

———. "Twenty-Third Report of the Secretary-General on the United Nations Organization Mission in the Democratic Republic of the Congo." S/2007/156. 20 March 2007.

"UN Split over Darfur Peace Force." *BBC News*, 29 July 2008.

United States Senate. "Lord's Resistance Army Disarmament and Northern Uganda Recovery Act of 2009." S.1067. 111th Cong., 2nd sess.

United States, White House. "President Bush Addresses United Nations General Assembly." 19 September 2006. http://www.whitehouse.gov/news/releases/2006/09/20060919-4.html.

———. *World Refugee Survey 1997*. Washington, D.C.: U.S. Committee for Refugees, 1997.

"U.N. Votes to Extend Mission in Darfur." *CNN*, 1 August 2008.

"U.S. House Calls Darfur 'Genocide.'" *BBC News*, 23 July 2004.

van der Wildt, Harmen. "Universal Jurisdiction Under Attack." *Journal of International Criminal Justice* 9, 5 (2011): 1043–66.

Vinck, Patrick, Phuong Pham, Eric Stover, Andrew Moss, and Marieke Wierda. "Research Note on Attitudes About Peace and Justice in Northern Uganda." International Center for Transitional Justice, January 2008. http://ictj.org/sites/default/files/ICTJ-Uganda-Survey-Research-2008-English.pdf.

Vines, Alex. "A Decade of African Peace and Security Architecture." *International Affairs* 89, 1 (2013): 89–109.

Vinjamuri, Leslie. "Deterrence, Democracy, and the Pursuit of International Justice." *Ethics & International Affairs* 24, 2 (2010): 191–211.

Walzer, Michael. "The Politics of Rescue." *Dissent* (Winter 1995): 35–41.

Waters, Tony. "The Coming Rwandan Demographic Crisis, or Why Current Repatriation Poli-cies Will Not Solve Tanzania's (or Zaire's) Refugee Problems." *Journal of Humanitarian Assistance* (4 July 1997).

Weiss, Thomas G., and Jarat Chopra. "Sovereignty Is No Longer Sacrosanct: Codifying Human-itarian Intervention." *Ethics & International Affairs* 6 (1992): 95–117.

Weiss, Thomas G., and Amir Pasic. "Reinventing UNHCR: Enterprising Humanitarians in the Former Yugoslavia." *Global Governance* 3, 1 (1997): 41–57.

Weissman, Fabrice. "Humanitarian Dilemmas in Darfur." Médecins Sans Frontières. July 2008. http://www.msf.fr/sites/www.msf.fr/files/214a9aa0483c6e560e05cdafb00beb11.pdf.

————, ed. *In the Shadow of "Just Wars": Violence, Politics and Humanitarian Action*. London: Hurst, 2004.

West, Katrina. *Agents of Altruism: The Expansion of Humanitarian NGOs in Rwanda and Afghan-istan*. Aldershot: Ashgate, 2001.

Wheeler, Nicholas J. *Saving Strangers: Humanitarian Intervention in International Society*. Ox-ford: Oxford University Press, 2000.

White House. "President Clinton Signs New Peacekeeping Policy." Press release. 5 May 1994. http://www.fas.org/irp/offdocs/pdd25.htm.

"Whose Justice? Perceptions of Uganda's Amnesty Act 2000: The Potential for Conflict Resolu-tion and Long-Term Reconciliation." Refugee Law Project, Working Paper 15, February 2005, 4. http://www.refugeelawproject.org/working_papers/RLP.WP15.pdf.

Wilkerson, Michael. "Kony 2012 Campaign: Oprah and Bracelets Won't Solve Problem." *The Guardian*, 8 March 2012.

Williams, Paul D. "Enhancing Civilian Protection in Peace Operations: Insights from Africa." Africa Center for Strategic Studies, Research Paper 1. Washington, D.C.: National Defense University Press, September 2010.

Winter, Roger. "Lancing the Boil: Rwanda's Agenda in Zaire." In *War and Peace in Zaire/Congo*, ed. Howard Adelman and Govind C. Rao. Trenton, N.J.: Africa World Press, 2004.

World Food Program. "New Donations Boost Rations But More Contributions Needed for Sudan." 29 May 2006. http://www.wfp.org.

World Health Organization. "WHO Definition of Palliative Care." http://www.who.int/cancer /palliative/definition/en/.

Worth, Robert F. "Sudan Says It Will Accept U.N.-African Peace Force in Darfur." *New York Times*, 17 November 2006.

Zeender, Greta, and Jacob Rothing. "Displacement Trends in DRC." *Forced Migration Review* 36 (November 2010): 10–12.

INDEX

ACKNOWLEDGMENTS

Getting a handle on three sets of interrelated norms and practices, and then trying to understand four interrelated conflicts and how those norms and practices played out in these cases took rather longer than I had planned. And it entailed a very broad range of research activities. I had to immerse myself not only in the histories of these conflicts, but also how the international community interacted with them. This required relying significantly on a vast array of reports and other documents from the UN international security, human rights and humanitarian realms, as well as the AU, ICC, and NGO sources. It also entailed interviewing diplomats, policymakers and practitioners from many of the different organizations involved in these crises. I interviewed individuals at UN headquarters in New York and Geneva, AU headquarters in Addis Ababa, and the ICC in The Hague, as well as policymakers in London. In all these places I also interviewed humanitarian practitioners who, while frequently on the political sidelines of these conflicts, have extraordinary insight and play very significant roles—whether they intend to or not. I was particularly fortunate to be able to attend an Assembly of States Parties of the ICC in The Hague with NGO accreditation, enabling me to sit in on extraordinary meetings and gain significant insight into the workings of, and politics surrounding, the ICC. This book also draws on earlier research I did in Rwanda and Tanzania a few years after the genocide. Given the sensitive nature of the issues discussed and the positions of the people I interviewed, they are not named in the book. But I owe them a very significant note of gratitude—to a person they were open and forthcoming and generous with their time.

A number of other people and organizations also deserve a note of thanks. My editor at the University of Pennsylvania Press, Peter Agree, has been extremely patient as this book has taken shape. Two of my postgraduate students—Christopher Lamont and Beth Pearson—provided significant research help at various stages of the project. Most of the interviews were carried out while I was on study leave from the University of Glasgow in the autumn of 2009. This research was funded by the British Academy and the Carnegie Trust for the Universities of Scotland. The Coalition for the International Criminal Court facilitated my accreditation to the Assembly of States Parties meeting in November 2009. In the spring of 2012 I was fortunate to have been given a fellowship by the Human Rights Consortium, School of Advanced Study, University of London, which allowed me to spend a very fruitful couple of months in London working on the book. Various parts of the book benefited from feedback from the Global and Regional Governance Group at the University of Glasgow and from presentations at the annual meetings of the International Studies Association, as well as at the Universities of Aberdeen, Addis Ababa, Birmingham, New South Wales, Queensland, Sydney, and St. Andrews, the School of Oriental and African Studies, School of Advanced Study, and University College London, University of London, and Connecticut College.

Parts of the manuscript were read and commented on by Tristan Anne Borer, Melissa Labonte, Steve Lamony, and Sheila Mills. Tristan and Melissa provided incomparable friendship and encouragement, and Steve provided a welcome perspective from the NGO world. But of course my most humble gratitude must go to my wife Sheila, whose love and support made this book possible.

I gratefully thank Africa World Press, *Global Responsibility to Protect*, and *Journal of Human Rights* for providing permission to include elements of previously published work:

"Refugee Return from Zaire to Rwanda: The Role of UNHCR," in *War and Peace in Zaire/Congo: Analyzing and Evaluating Intervention, 1996–97*, ed. Howard Adelman and Govind C. Rau (Trenton, N.J.: Africa World Press, 2004), 163–85
"Vacillating on Darfur: Responsibility to Protect, to Prosecute, or to Feed?" *Global Responsibility to Protect* 1, 4 (2009): 532–59
"R2P³: Protecting, Prosecuting or Palliating in Mass Atrocity Situations?" *Journal of Human Rights* 12, 3 (2013): 333–56.
I also thank the United Nations for allowing me to reproduce the maps found in the book.